Wonderland

STORY & ART BY
Yugo Ishikawa

2

She woke up to find the world completely changed.

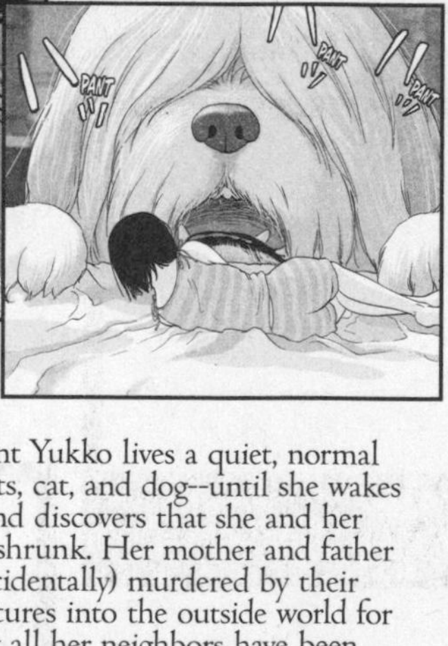
PANT
PANT
PANT

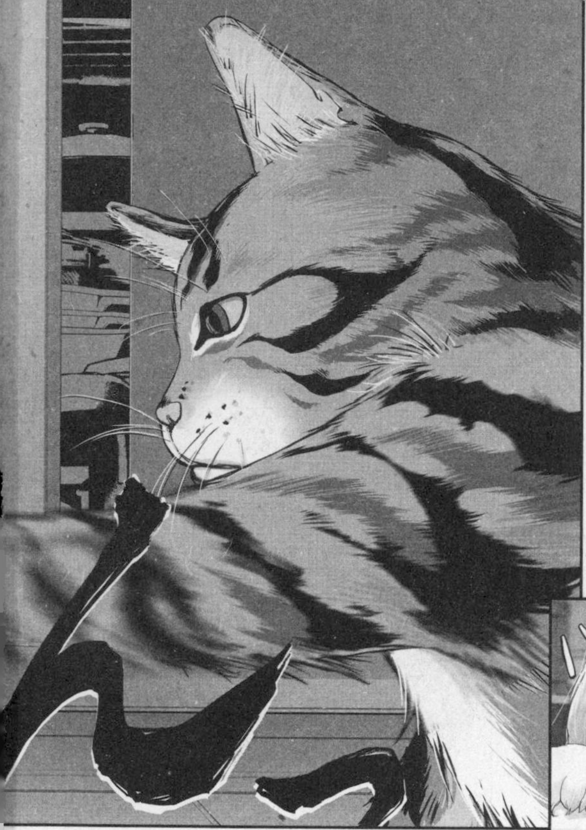

High school student Yukko lives a quiet, normal life with her parents, cat, and dog--until she wakes up one morning and discovers that she and her parents have been shrunk. Her mother and father are cruelly (and accidentally) murdered by their cat. When she ventures into the outside world for help, she finds that all her neighbors have been shrunk, too--and that they're being chased by feral cats and crows.

Is it all just a dream? Just what in the world is going on?

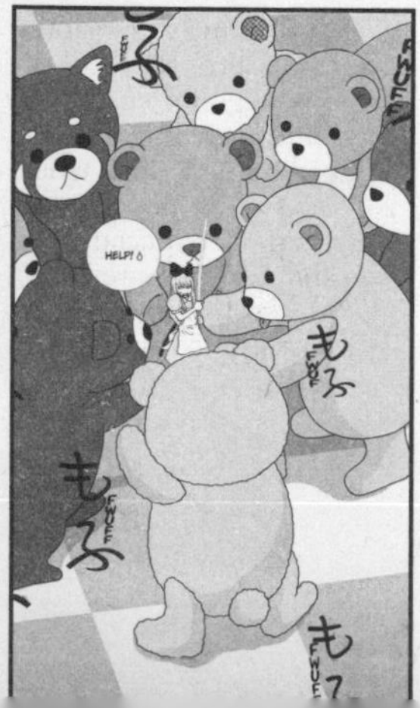
HELP!
もふ
FWUF
もふ
FWUF

Story

Characters

Yukko
Wakes up to find that she shrank while she was asleep

ALICE.

Alice
A mysterious girl who joins up with Yukko.

POCO!

PANT
PANT
PANT
PANT
WILD
WOOF

Poco
Yukko's dog.

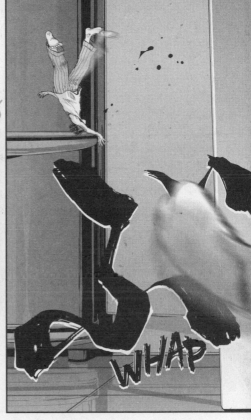

WHAP

Yukko and her beloved pup, Poco, head off to get help and end up running into a strange girl named Alice who doesn't speak Japanese. Using her special abilities, she saves Yukko from serious harm...but what is she, really?

Contents

Chapter 10: Friends

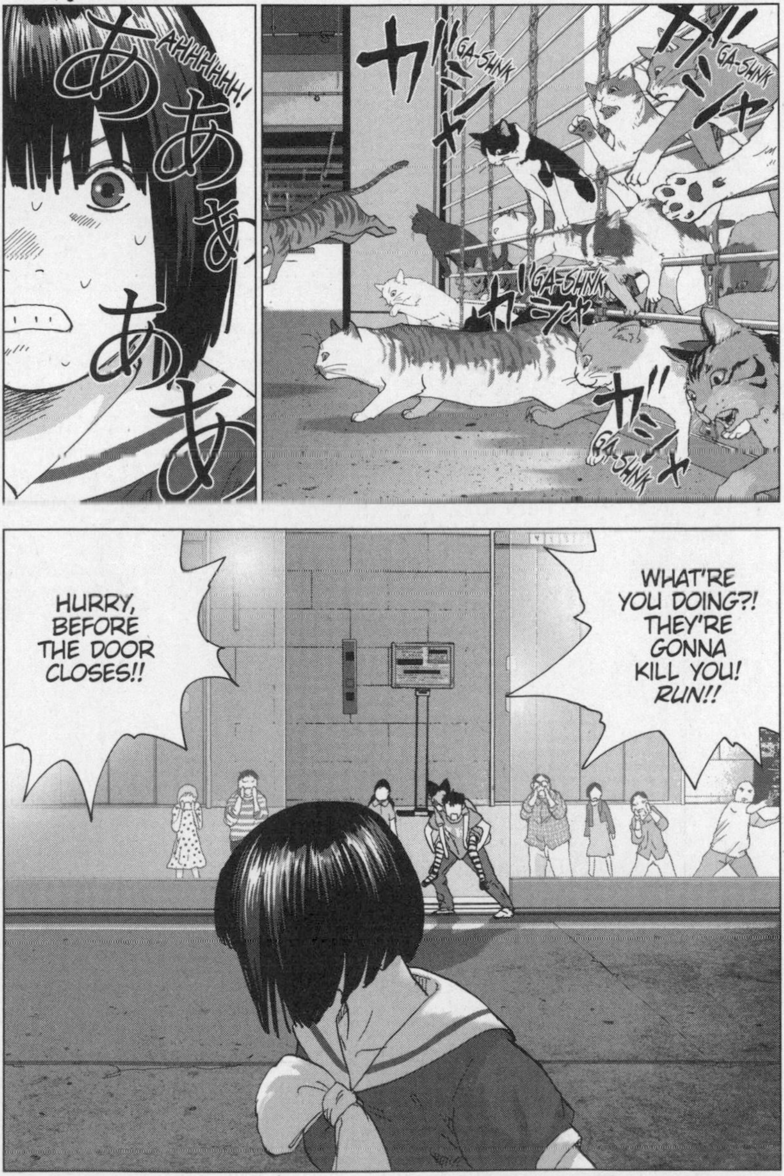
GA-SHNK
GA-SHNK
GA-SHNK
GA-SHNK
ああああああ
AHHHHHH!
WHAT'RE YOU DOING?! THEY'RE GONNA KILL YOU! RUN!!
HURRY, BEFORE THE DOOR CLOSES!!

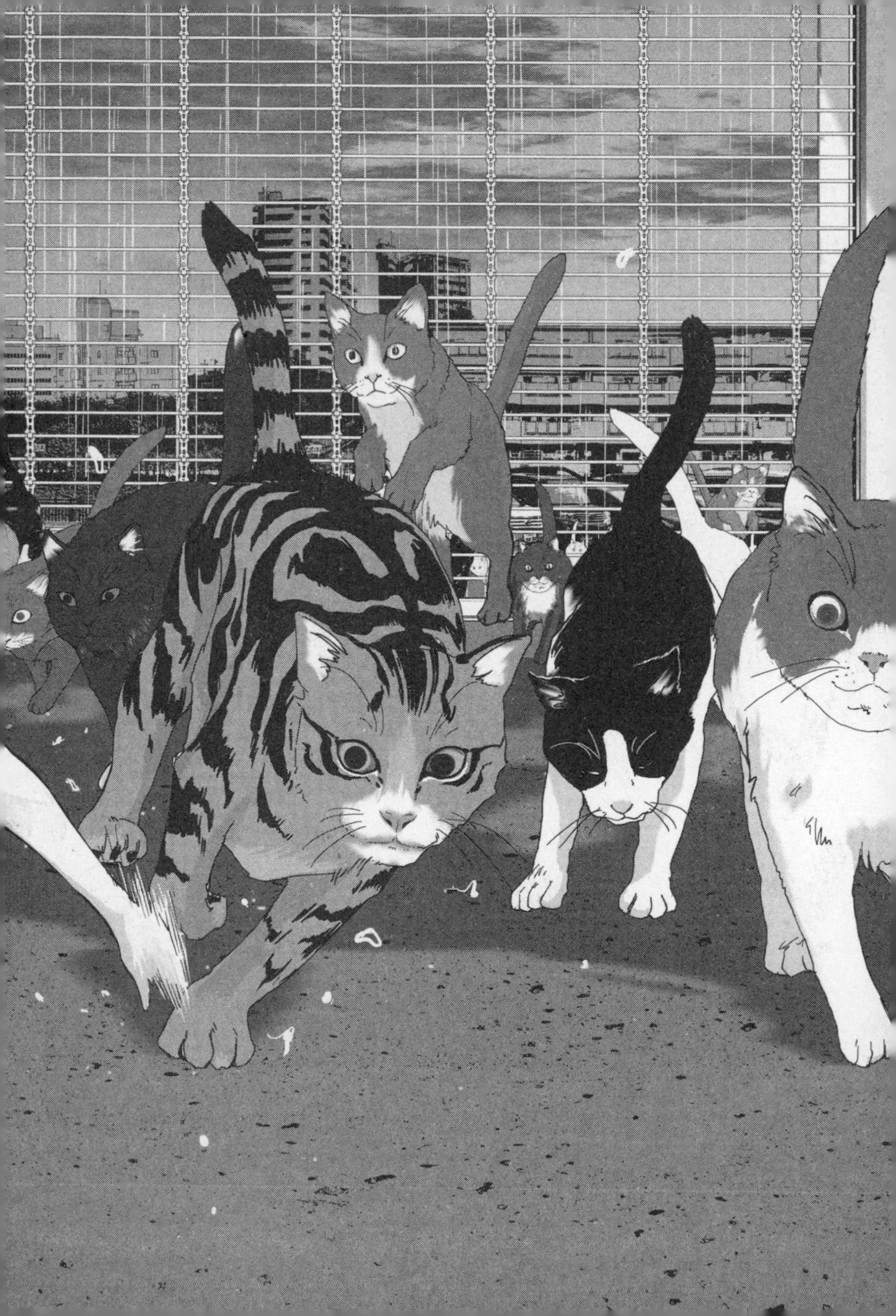

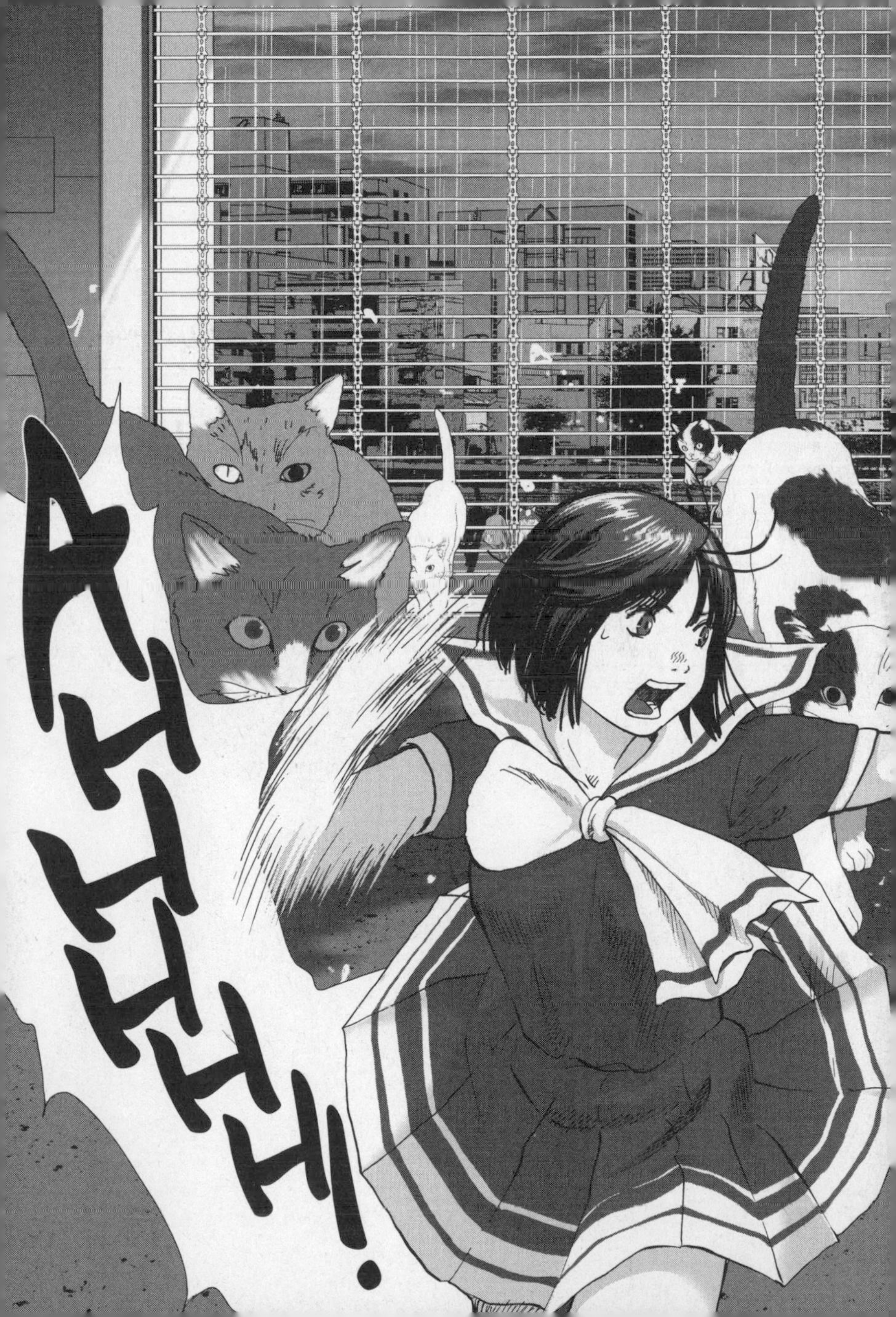
AIIIII!

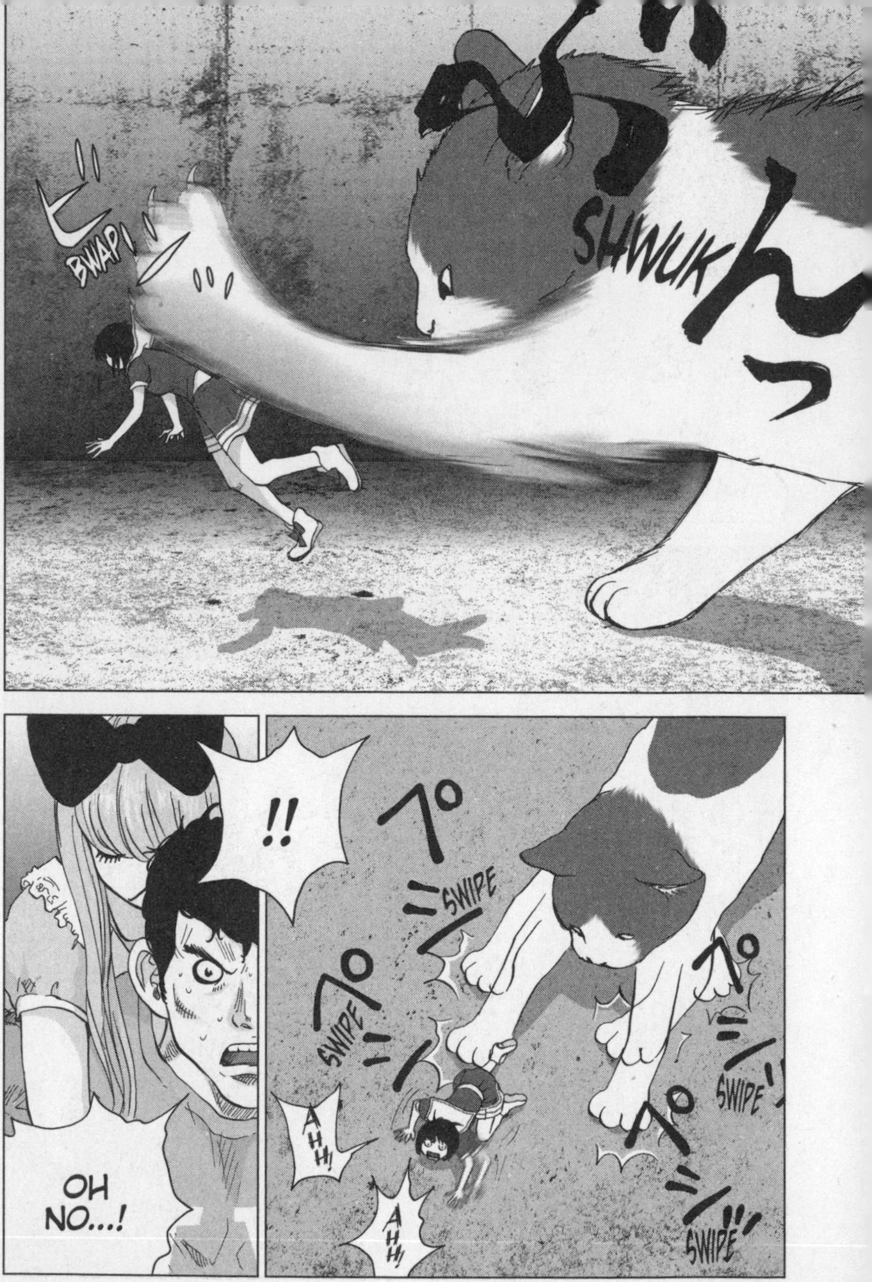
BWAP!
SHWUK
SWIPE
SWIPE
SWIPE
SWIPE
AHH!
AHH!
!!
OH NO...!

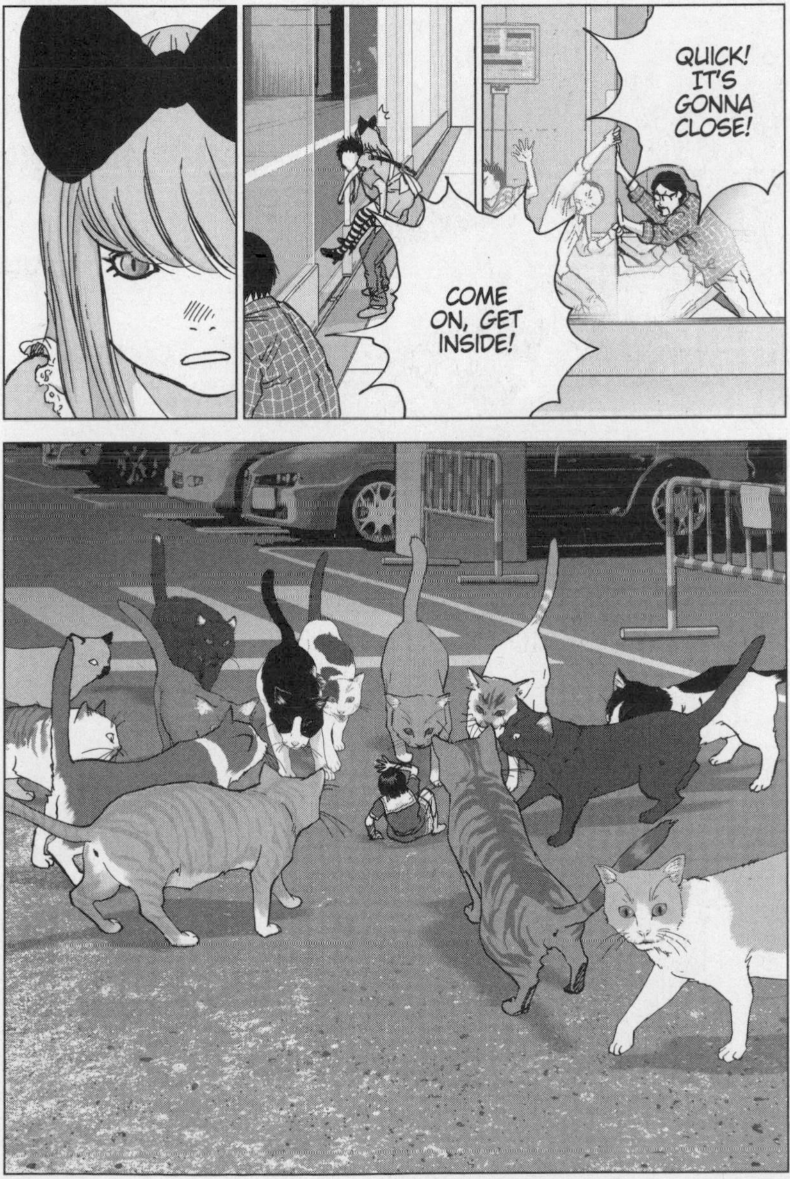
QUICK! IT'S GONNA CLOSE!
COME ON, GET INSIDE!

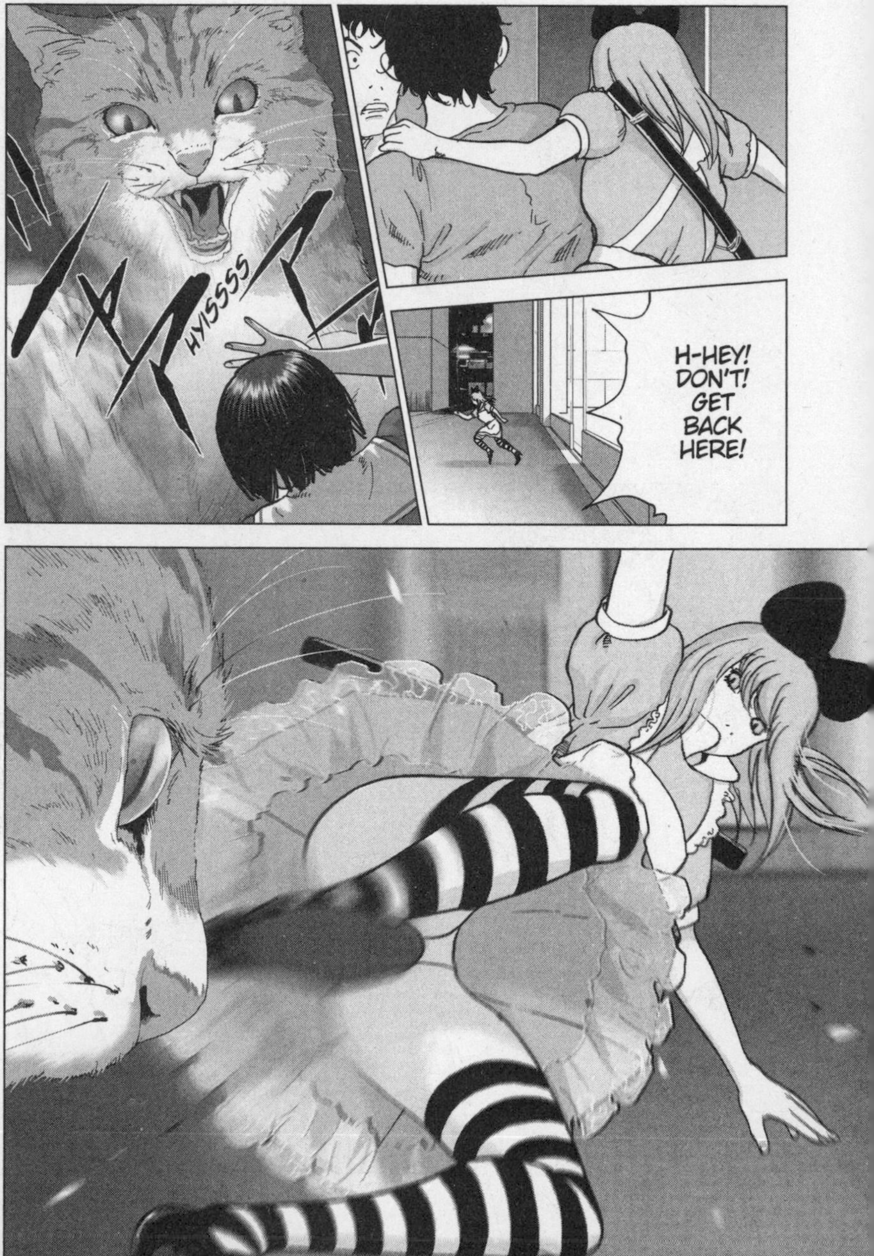
H-HEY! DON'T! GET BACK HERE!
HYISSSS

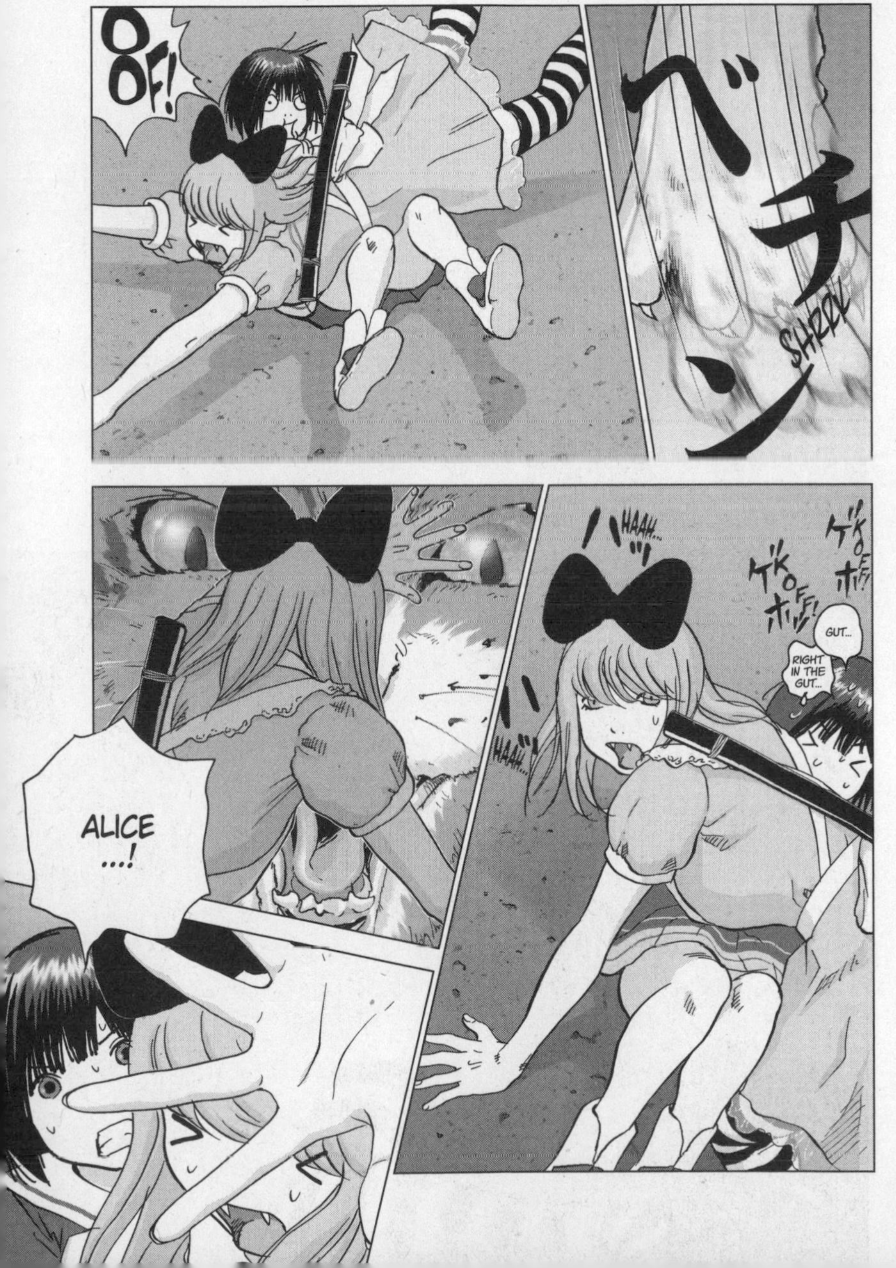

ベチン
SHRRK
OOF!
HAAH...
HAAH...
KOFF!
KOFF!
GUT...
RIGHT IN THE GUT...
ALICE ...!

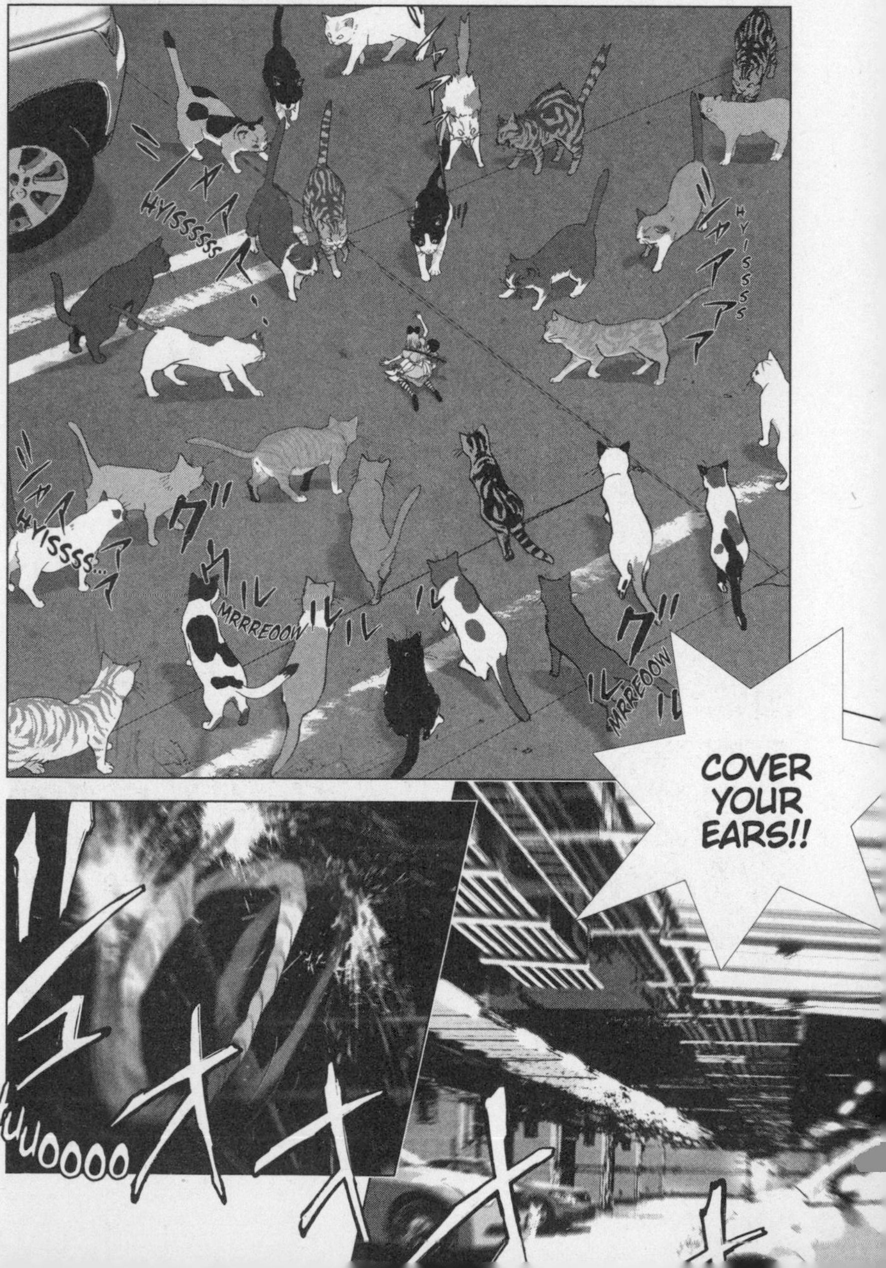
HYISSSS
HYISSSSSS
HYISSSS...
MRRREOOW
MRRREOOW
COVER YOUR EARS!!
SHUUOOOO

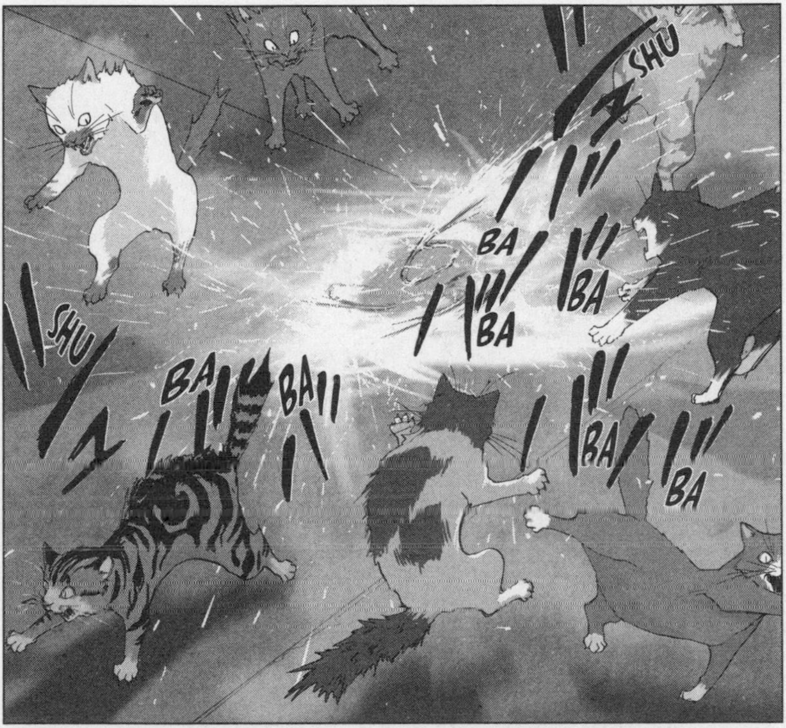
SHU
BA
BA
BA
BA
BA
BA!!
BA
SHU

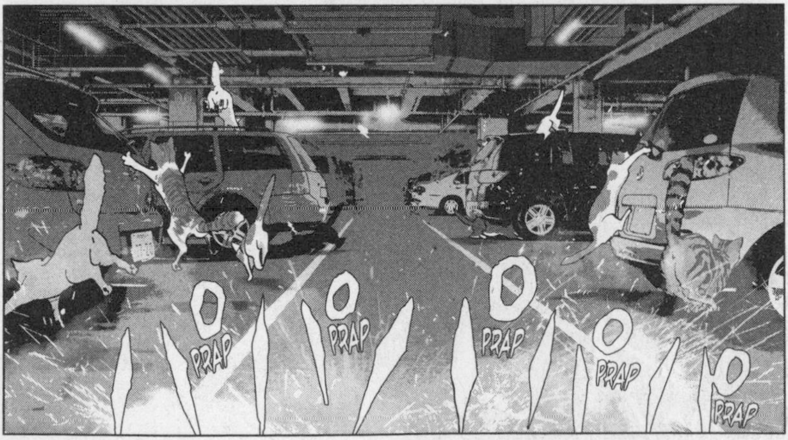
PRAP
PRAP
PRAP
PRAP
PRAP

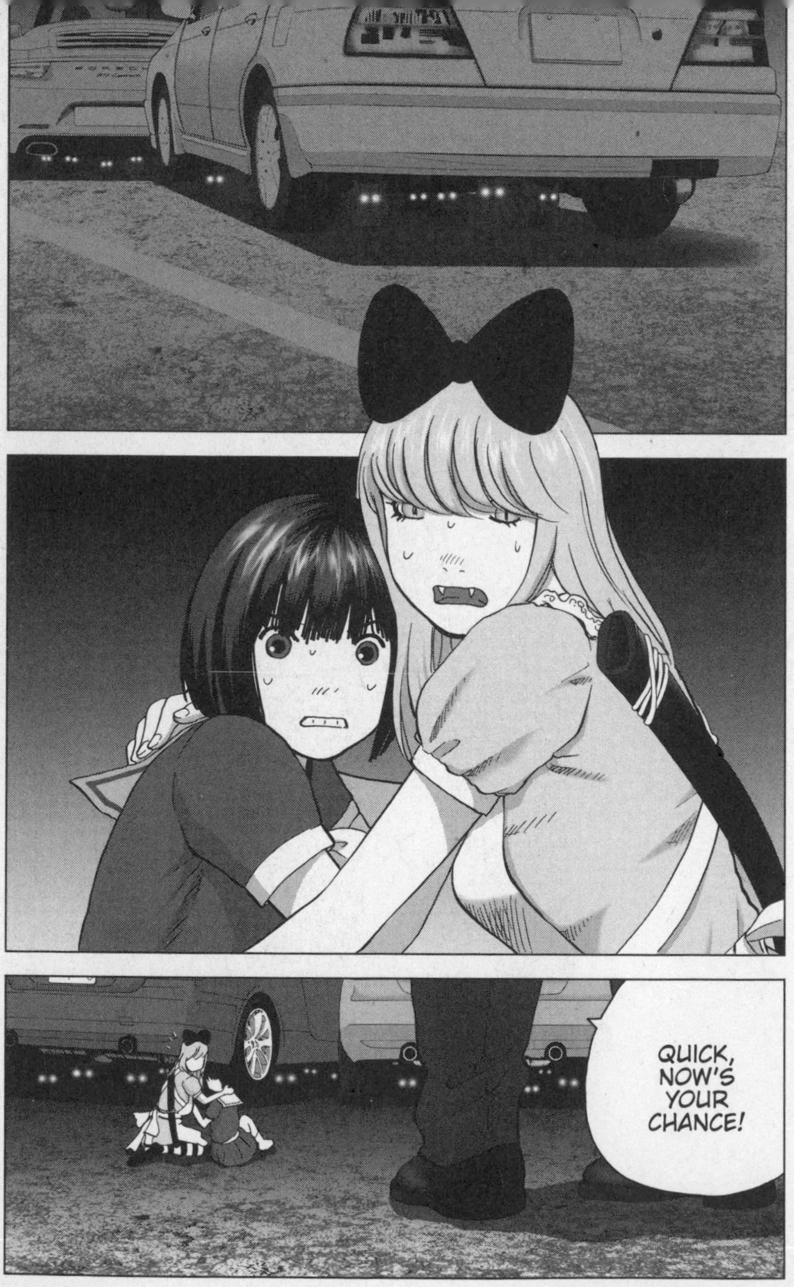
QUICK, NOW'S YOUR CHANCE!

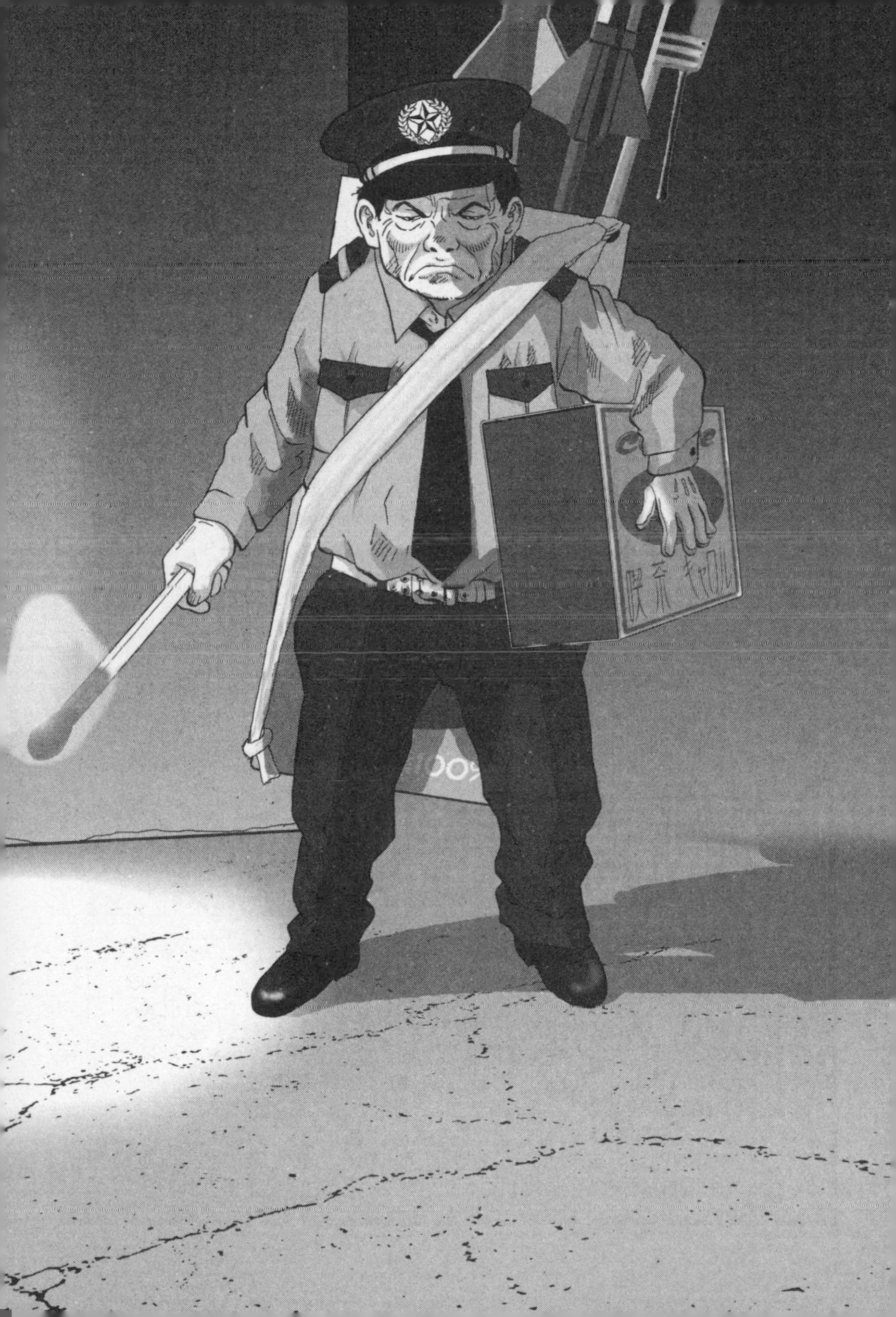
喫茶 キャロル

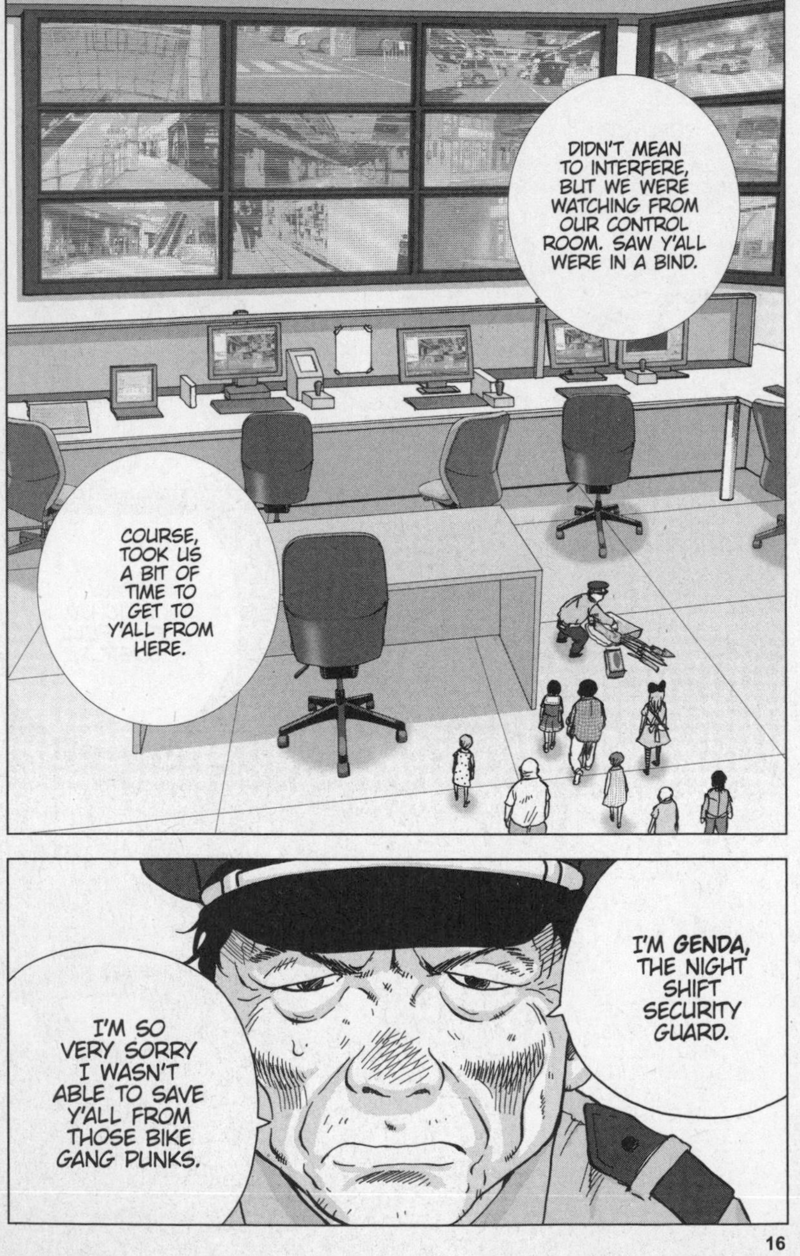

DIDN'T MEAN TO INTERFERE, BUT WE WERE WATCHING FROM OUR CONTROL ROOM. SAW Y'ALL WERE IN A BIND.
COURSE, TOOK US A BIT OF TIME TO GET TO Y'ALL FROM HERE.
I'M GENDA, THE NIGHT SHIFT SECURITY GUARD.
I'M SO VERY SORRY I WASN'T ABLE TO SAVE Y'ALL FROM THOSE BIKE GANG PUNKS.

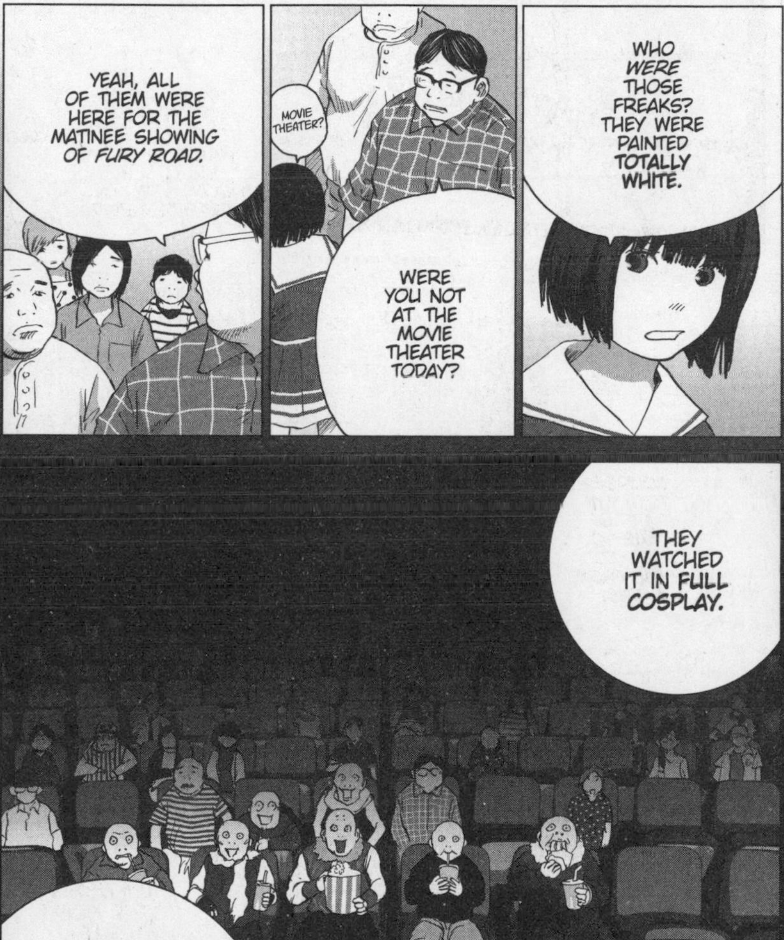
WHO WERE THOSE FREAKS? THEY WERE PAINTED TOTALLY WHITE.
WERE YOU NOT AT THE MOVIE THEATER TODAY?
MOVIE THEATER?
YEAH, ALL OF THEM WERE HERE FOR THE MATINEE SHOWING OF *FURY ROAD.*
THEY WATCHED IT IN FULL COSPLAY.
THEY WERE PRETTY QUIET AND WELL-BEHAVED DURING THE FILM. BUT AFTER THAT... WELL, IT WAS A DIFFERENT STORY...

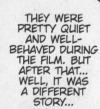

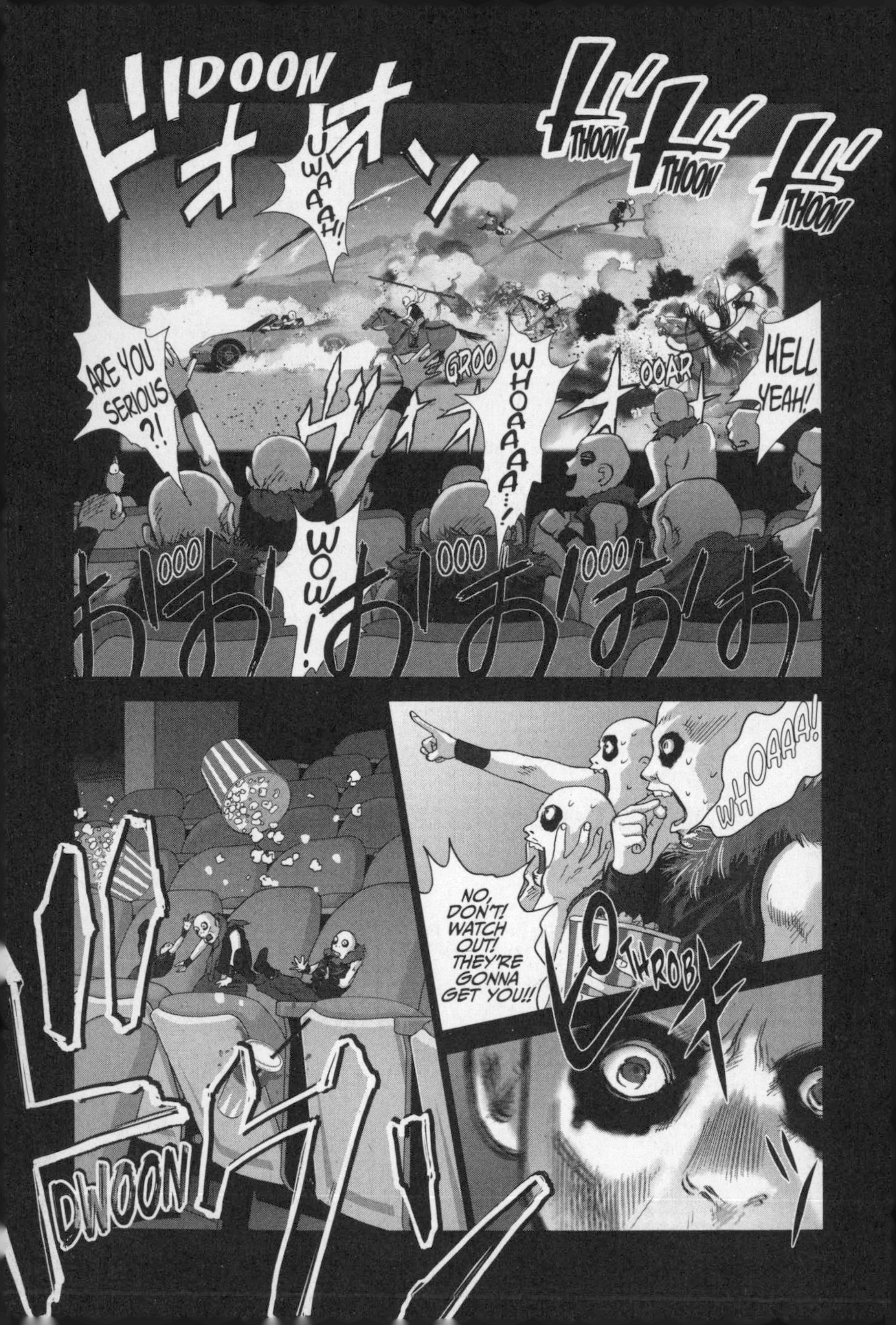
THOON
THOON
THOON
DOON
UWAAAH!!
HELL YEAH!
OOAR
WHOAAAA...!
GROO
ARE YOU SERIOUS?!
OOO
OOO
WOW!!
OOO
WHOAAA!!
NO, DON'T! WATCH OUT! THEY'RE GONNA GET YOU!!
THROB
DWOON

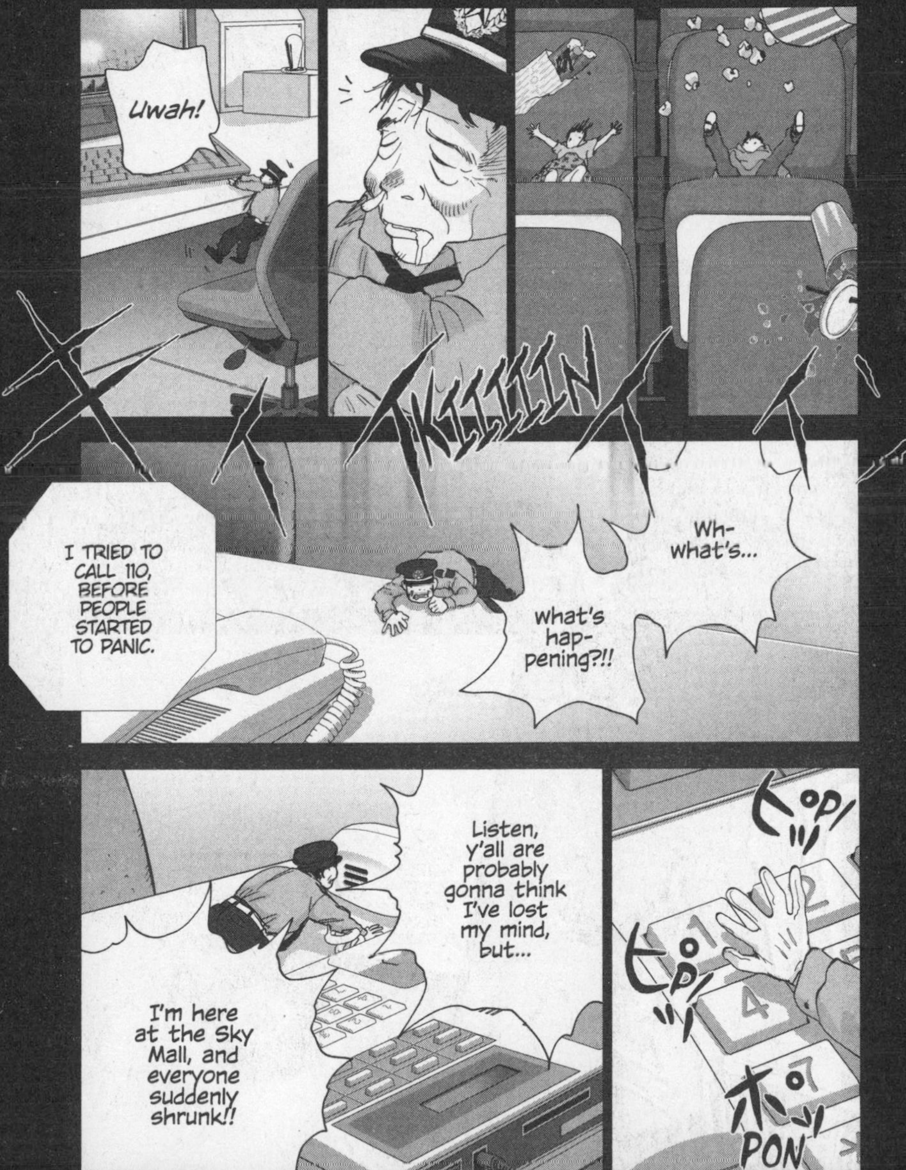

Uwah!
TKIIIIIN
Wh-what's...
what's hap-pening?!!
I TRIED TO CALL 110, BEFORE PEOPLE STARTED TO PANIC.
PON
Listen, y'all are probably gonna think I've lost my mind, but...
I'm here at the Sky Mall, and everyone suddenly shrunk!!

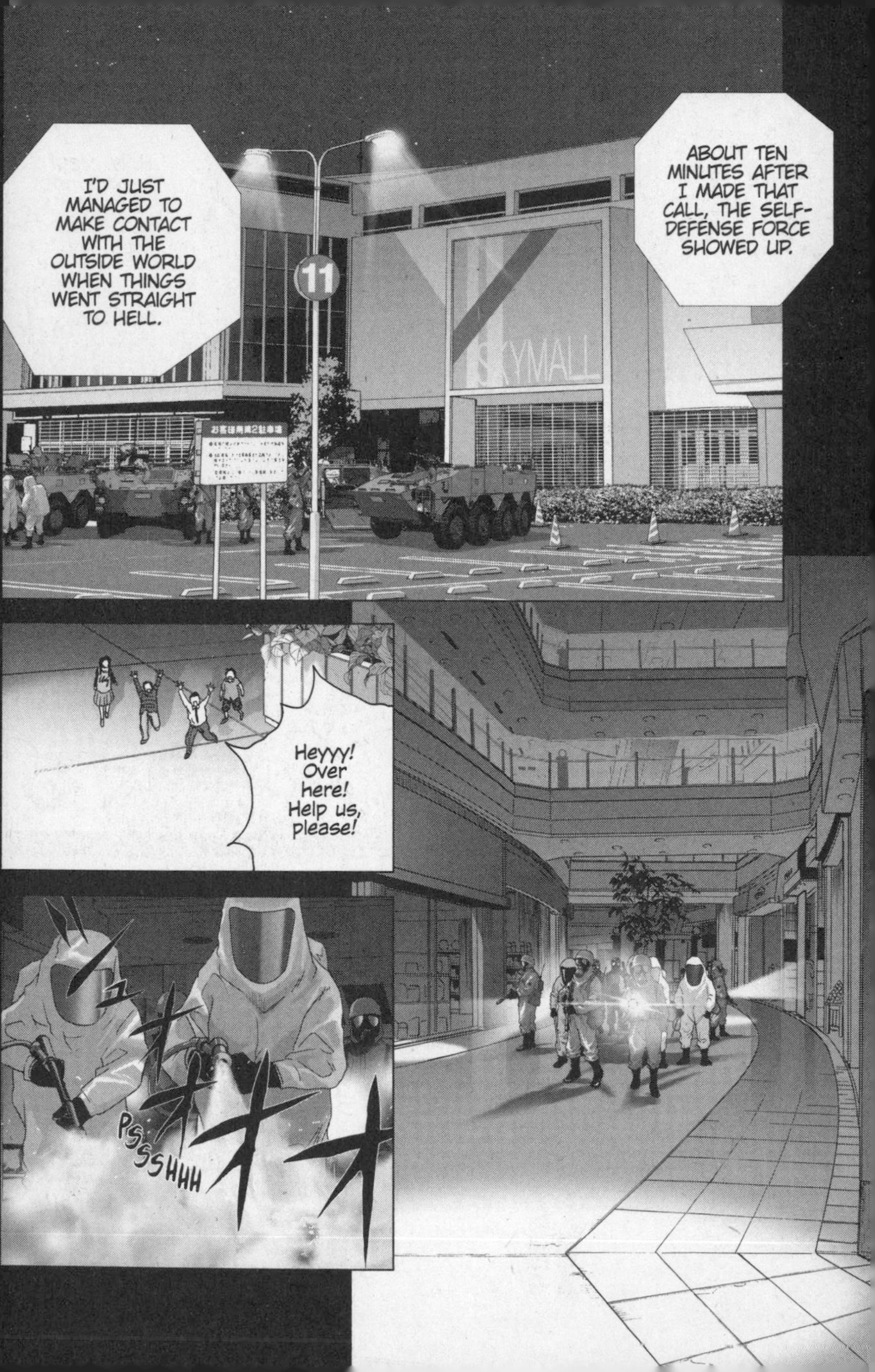
I'D JUST MANAGED TO MAKE CONTACT WITH THE OUTSIDE WORLD WHEN THINGS WENT STRAIGHT TO HELL.
ABOUT TEN MINUTES AFTER I MADE THAT CALL, THE SELF-DEFENSE FORCE SHOWED UP.
SKYMALL
Heyyy! Over here! Help us, please!
PSSSHHH

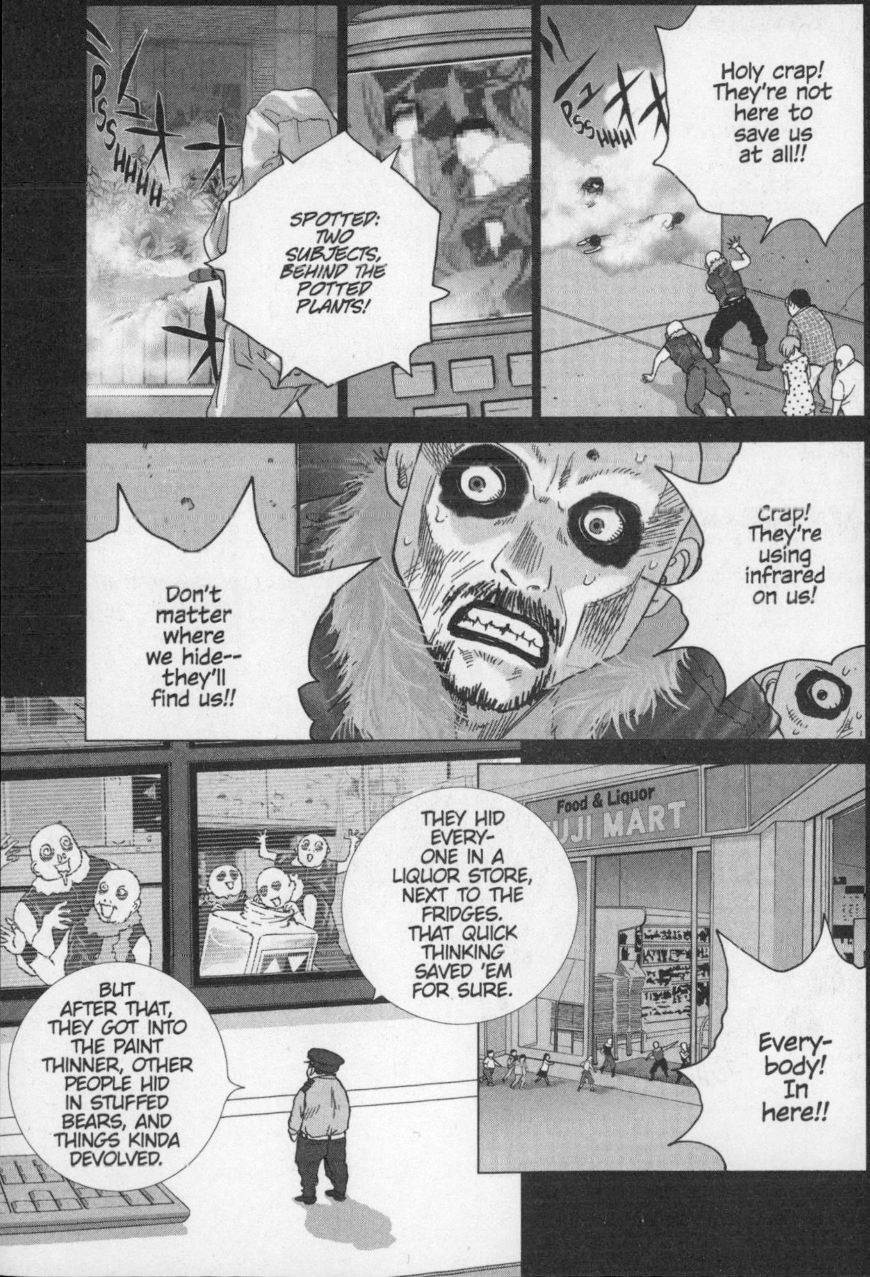
PSSHHH
Holy crap! They're not here to save us at all!!
PSSHHHH
SPOTTED: TWO SUBJECTS, BEHIND THE POTTED PLANTS!
Crap! They're using infrared on us!
Don't matter where we hide-- they'll find us!!
Food & Liquor
UJI MART
Every-body! In here!!
THEY HID EVERY-ONE IN A LIQUOR STORE, NEXT TO THE FRIDGES. THAT QUICK THINKING SAVED 'EM FOR SURE.
BUT AFTER THAT, THEY GOT INTO THE PAINT THINNER, OTHER PEOPLE HID IN STUFFED BEARS, AND THINGS KINDA DEVOLVED.

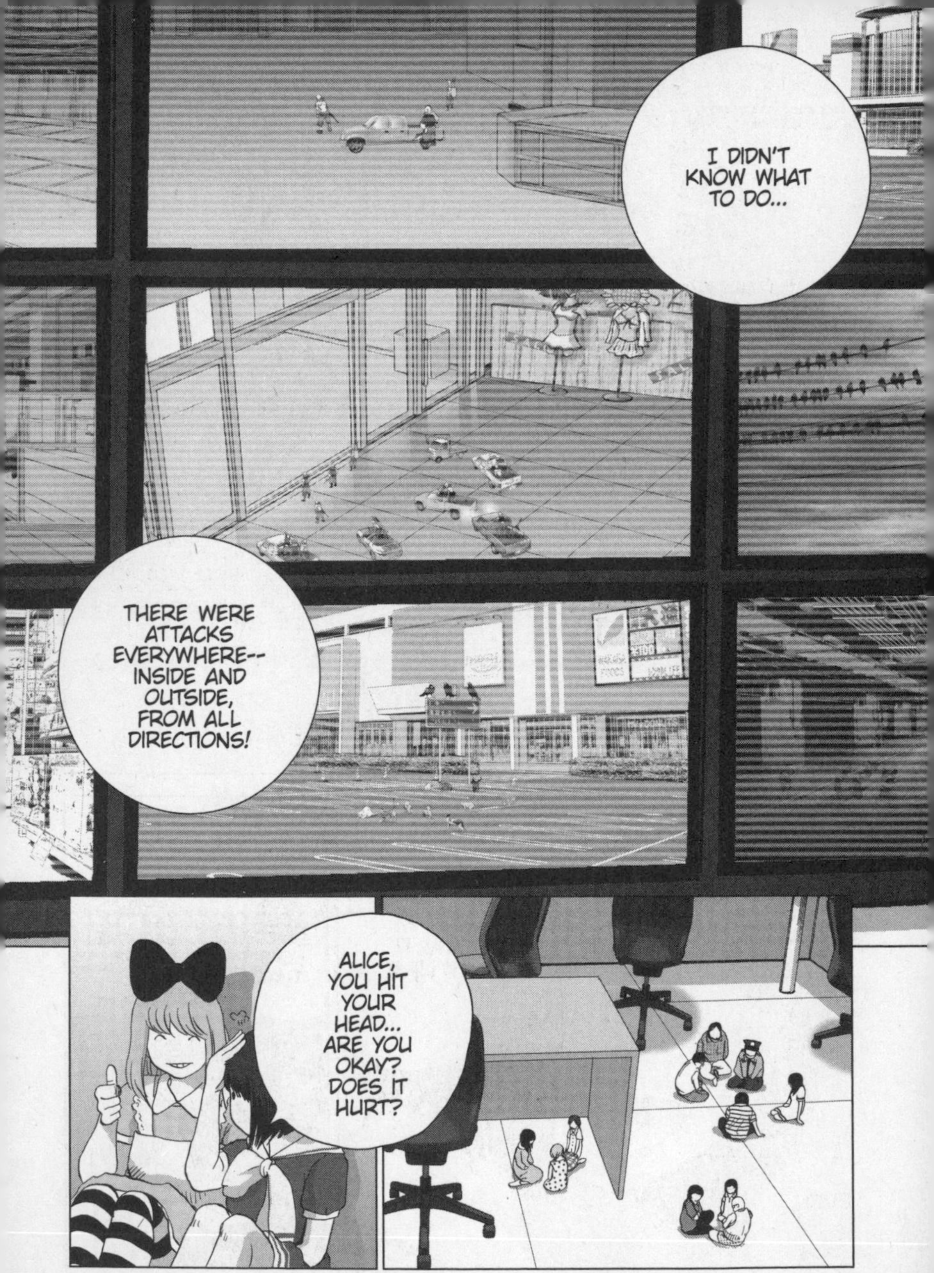
I DIDN'T KNOW WHAT TO DO...
THERE WERE ATTACKS EVERYWHERE-- INSIDE AND OUTSIDE, FROM ALL DIRECTIONS!
ALICE, YOU HIT YOUR HEAD... ARE YOU OKAY? DOES IT HURT?

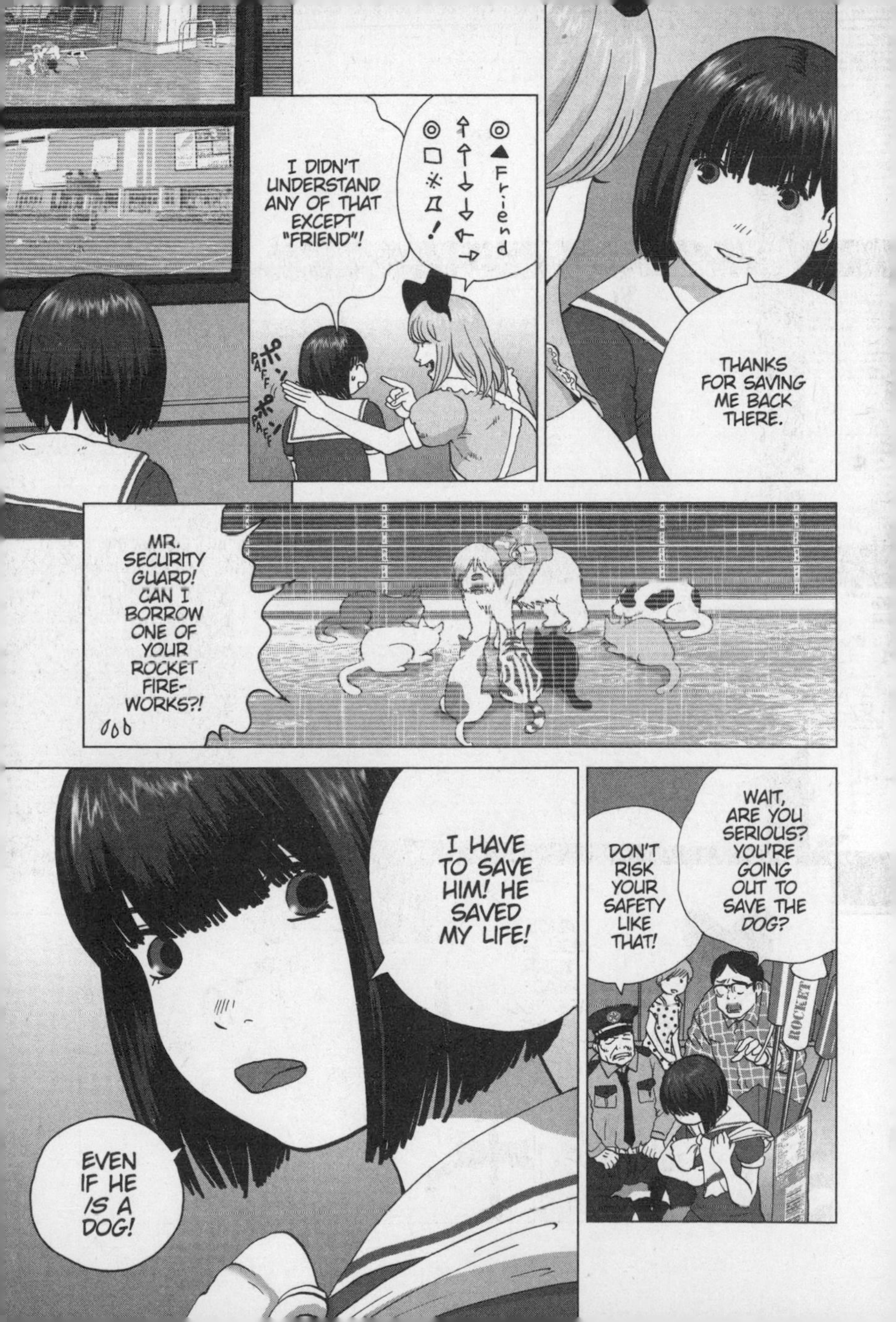
THANKS FOR SAVING ME BACK THERE.
◎▲ Friend ◎↑↑↓↓←→ ◎□※ロ!
I DIDN'T UNDERSTAND ANY OF THAT EXCEPT "FRIEND"!
PAFF PAFF
MR. SECURITY GUARD! CAN I BORROW ONE OF YOUR ROCKET FIRE-WORKS?!
WAIT, ARE YOU SERIOUS? YOU'RE GOING OUT TO SAVE THE DOG?
DON'T RISK YOUR SAFETY LIKE THAT!
ROCKET
ROCKET
I HAVE TO SAVE HIM! HE SAVED MY LIFE!
EVEN IF HE IS A DOG!

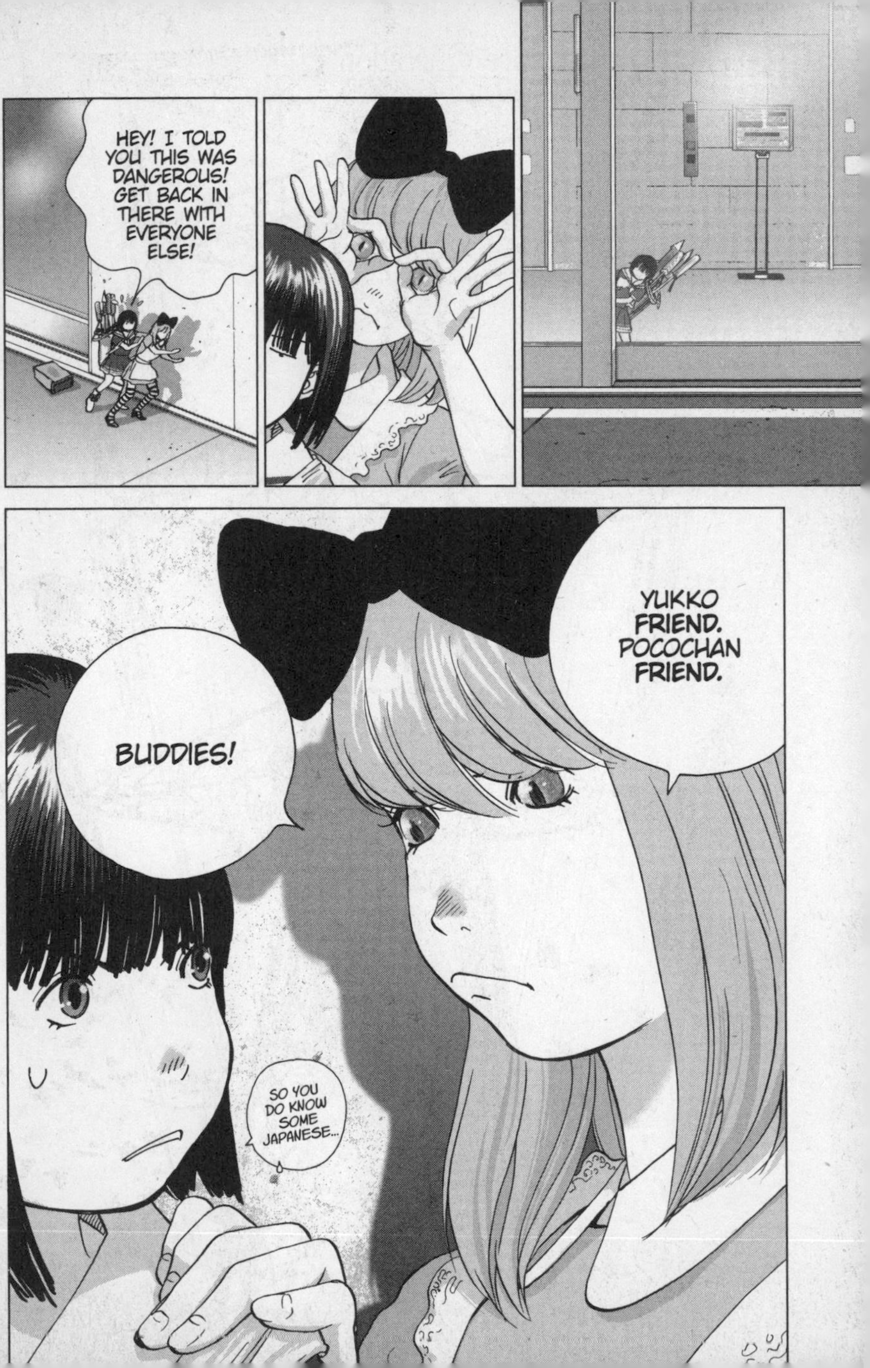
HEY! I TOLD YOU THIS WAS DANGEROUS! GET BACK IN THERE WITH EVERYONE ELSE!
YUKKO FRIEND. POCOCHAN FRIEND.
BUDDIES!
SO YOU DO KNOW SOME JAPANESE...

Chapter 11: Commence Operation

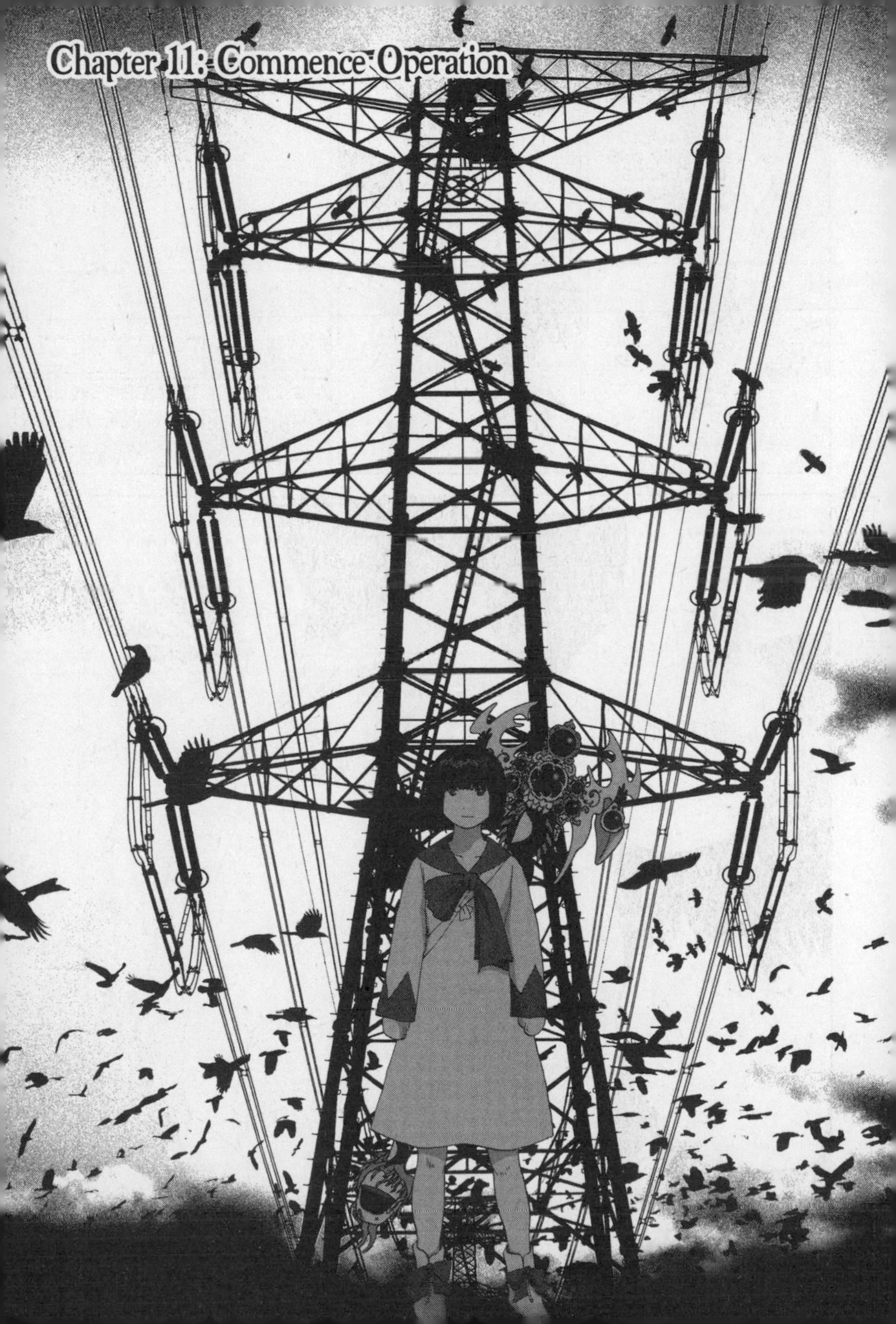

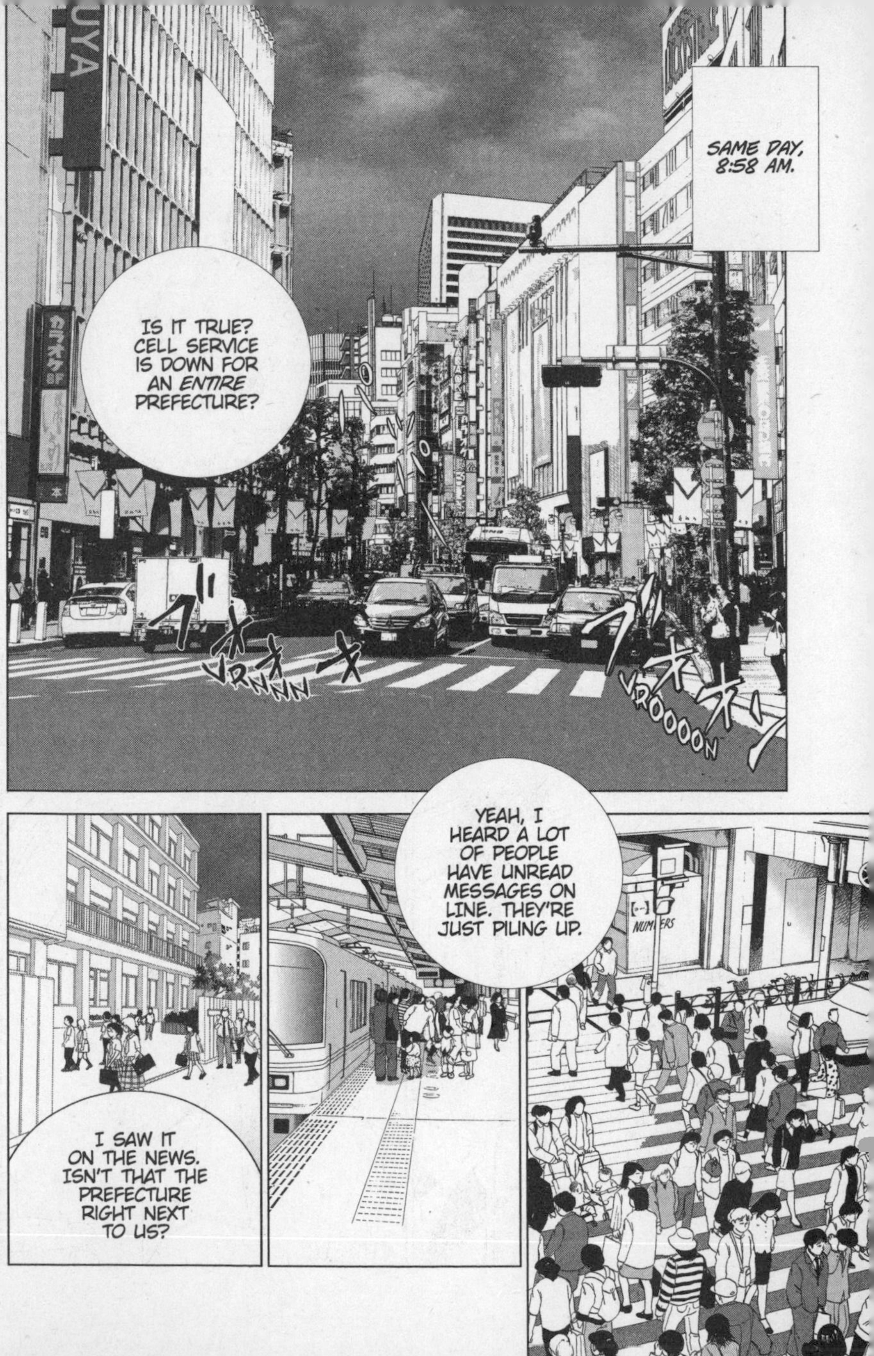
SAME DAY, 8:58 AM.
IS IT TRUE? CELL SERVICE IS DOWN FOR AN *ENTIRE* PREFECTURE?
VROOOOON
VRNNNN
YEAH, I HEARD A LOT OF PEOPLE HAVE UNREAD MESSAGES ON LINE. THEY'RE JUST PILING UP.
I SAW IT ON THE NEWS. ISN'T THAT THE PREFECTURE RIGHT NEXT TO US?

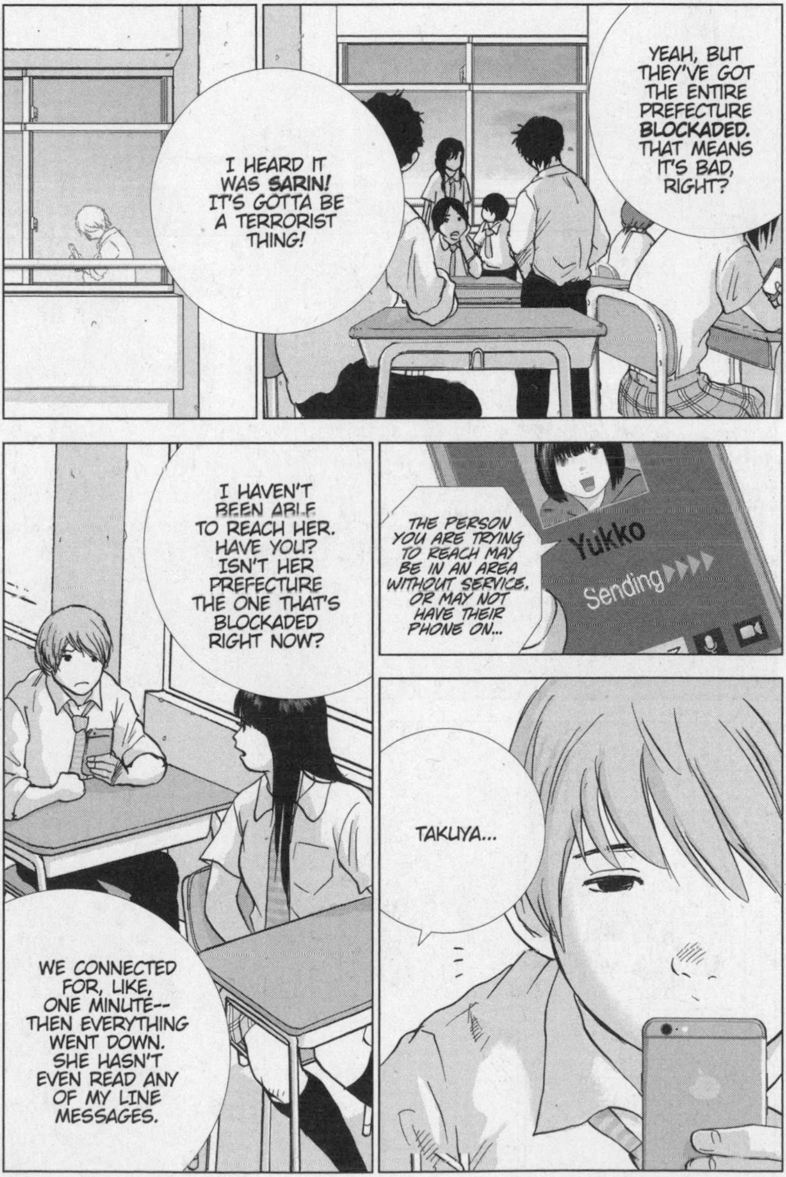
YEAH, BUT THEY'VE GOT THE ENTIRE PREFECTURE BLOCKADED. THAT MEANS IT'S BAD, RIGHT?
I HEARD IT WAS SARIN! IT'S GOTTA BE A TERRORIST THING!
Yukko
Sending
THE PERSON YOU ARE TRYING TO REACH MAY BE IN AN AREA WITHOUT SERVICE, OR MAY NOT HAVE THEIR PHONE ON...
TAKUYA...
I HAVEN'T BEEN ABLE TO REACH HER. HAVE YOU? ISN'T HER PREFECTURE THE ONE THAT'S BLOCKADED RIGHT NOW?
WE CONNECTED FOR, LIKE, ONE MINUTE-- THEN EVERYTHING WENT DOWN. SHE HASN'T EVEN READ ANY OF MY LINE MESSAGES.

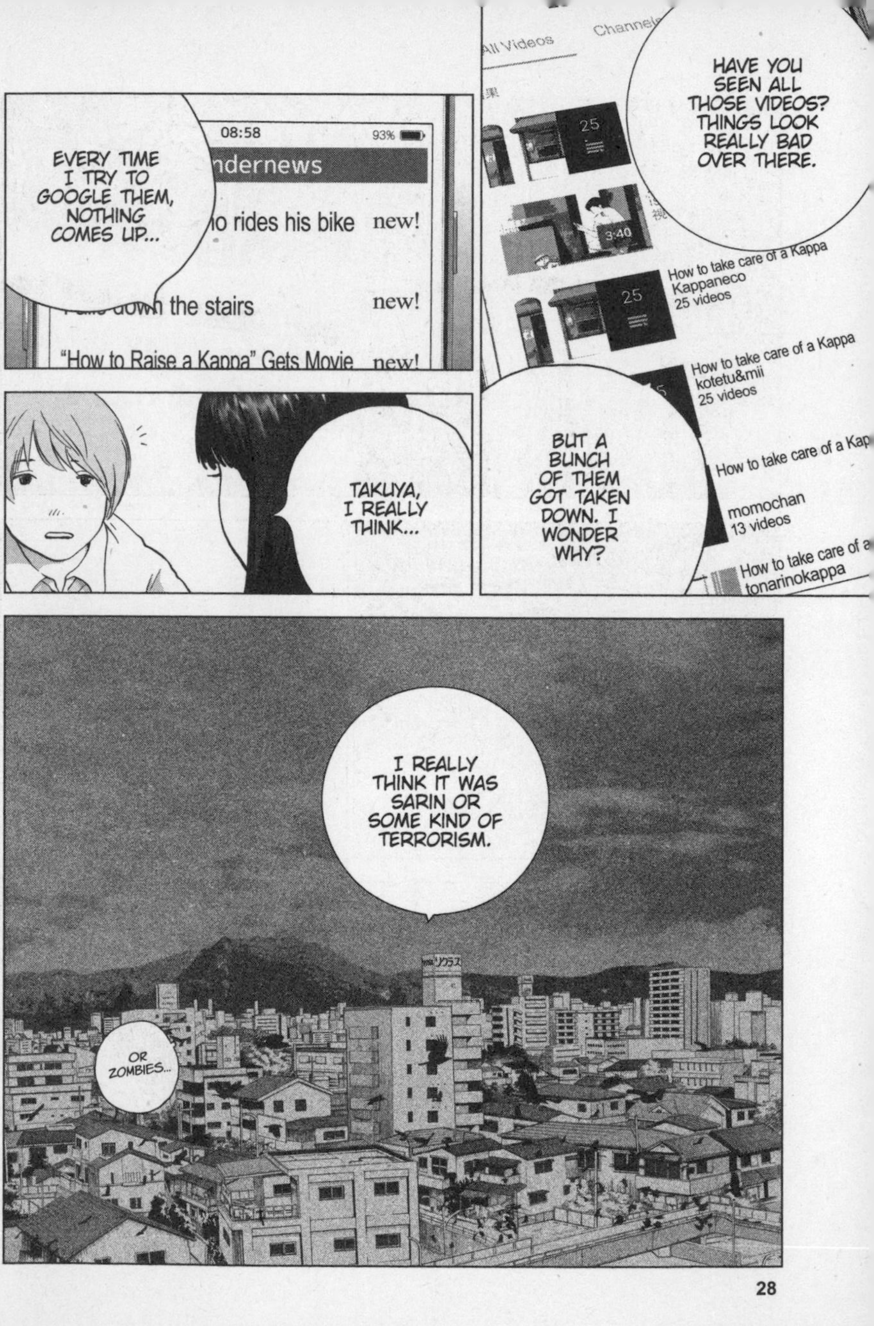
All Videos
HAVE YOU SEEN ALL THOSE VIDEOS? THINGS LOOK REALLY BAD OVER THERE.
How to take care of a Kappa
Kappaneco
25 videos
How to take care of a Kappa
kotetu&mii
25 videos
How to take care of a Kap
momochan
13 videos
How to take care of a
tonarinokappa
BUT A BUNCH OF THEM GOT TAKEN DOWN. I WONDER WHY?
08:58
93%
EVERY TIME I TRY TO GOOGLE THEM, NOTHING COMES UP...
new!
new!
"How to Raise a Kappa" Gets Movie new!
TAKUYA, I REALLY THINK...
I REALLY THINK IT WAS SARIN OR SOME KIND OF TERRORISM.
OR ZOMBIES...

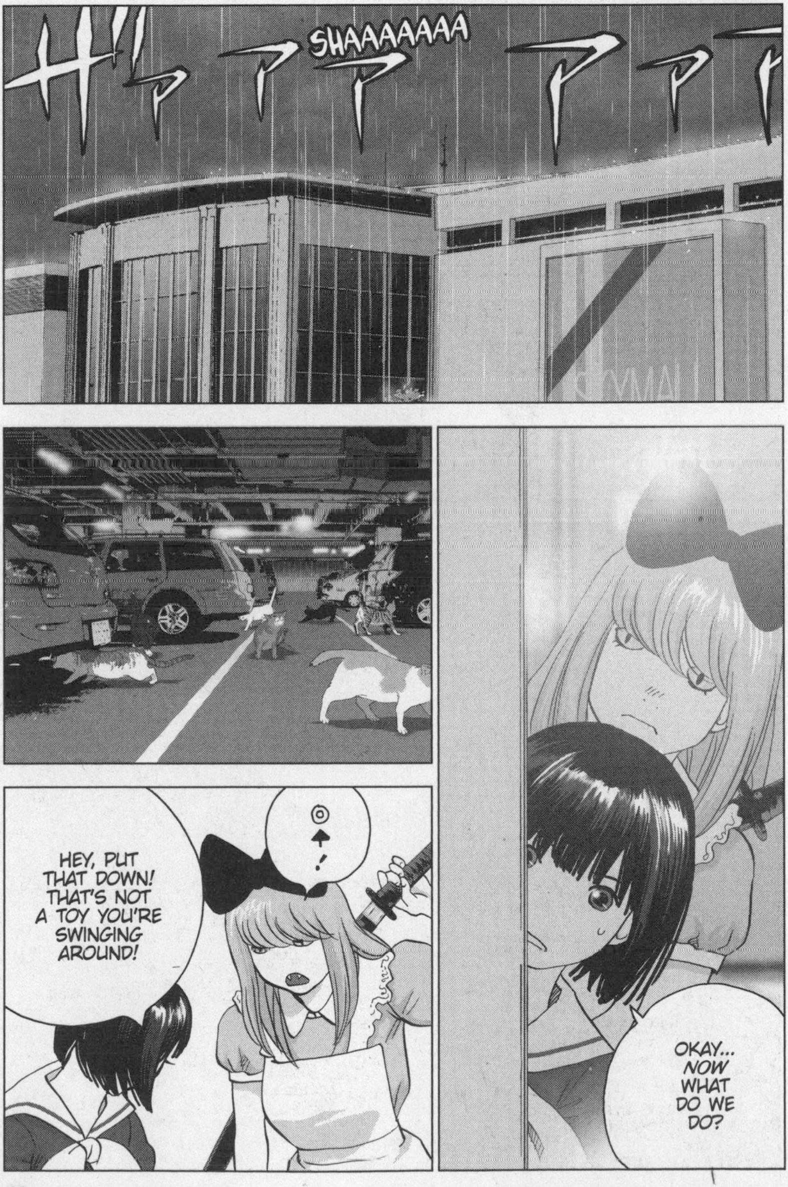
SHAAAAAAA
OKAY... NOW WHAT DO WE DO?
HEY, PUT THAT DOWN! THAT'S NOT A TOY YOU'RE SWINGING AROUND!

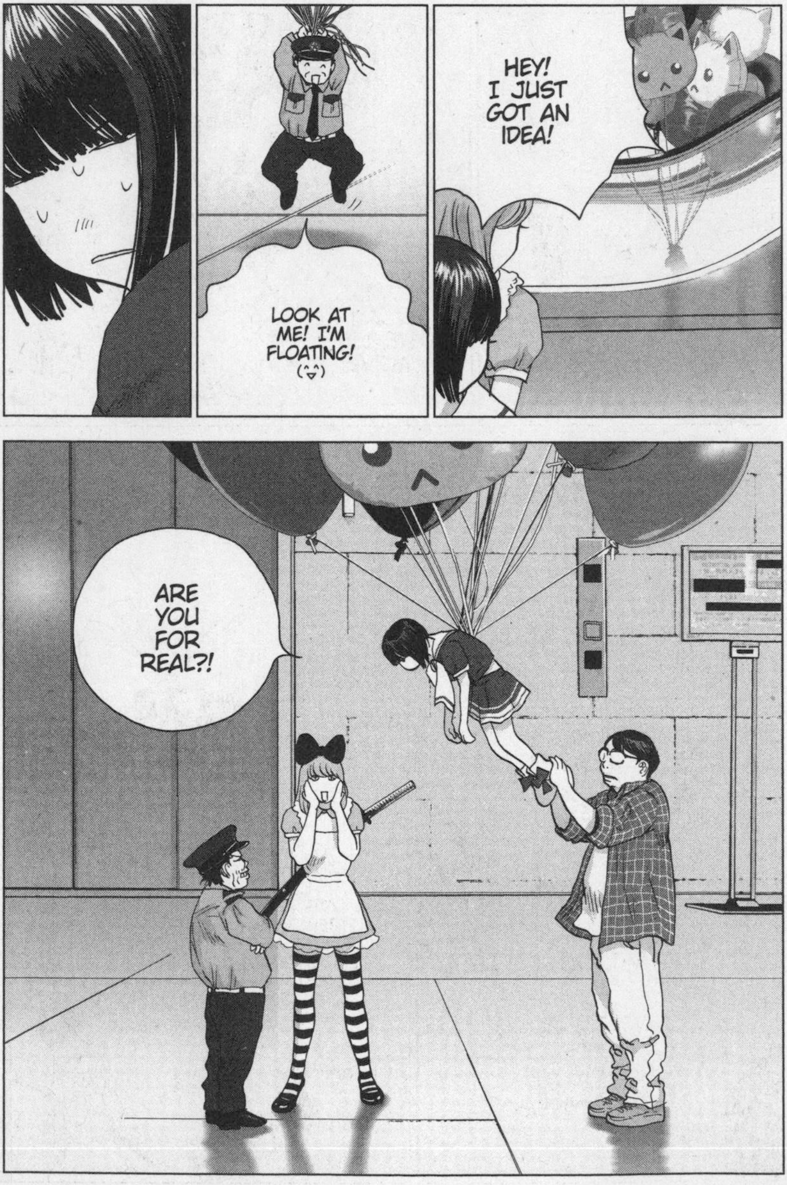
HEY! I JUST GOT AN IDEA!
LOOK AT ME! I'M FLOATING! (^▽^)
ARE YOU FOR REAL?!

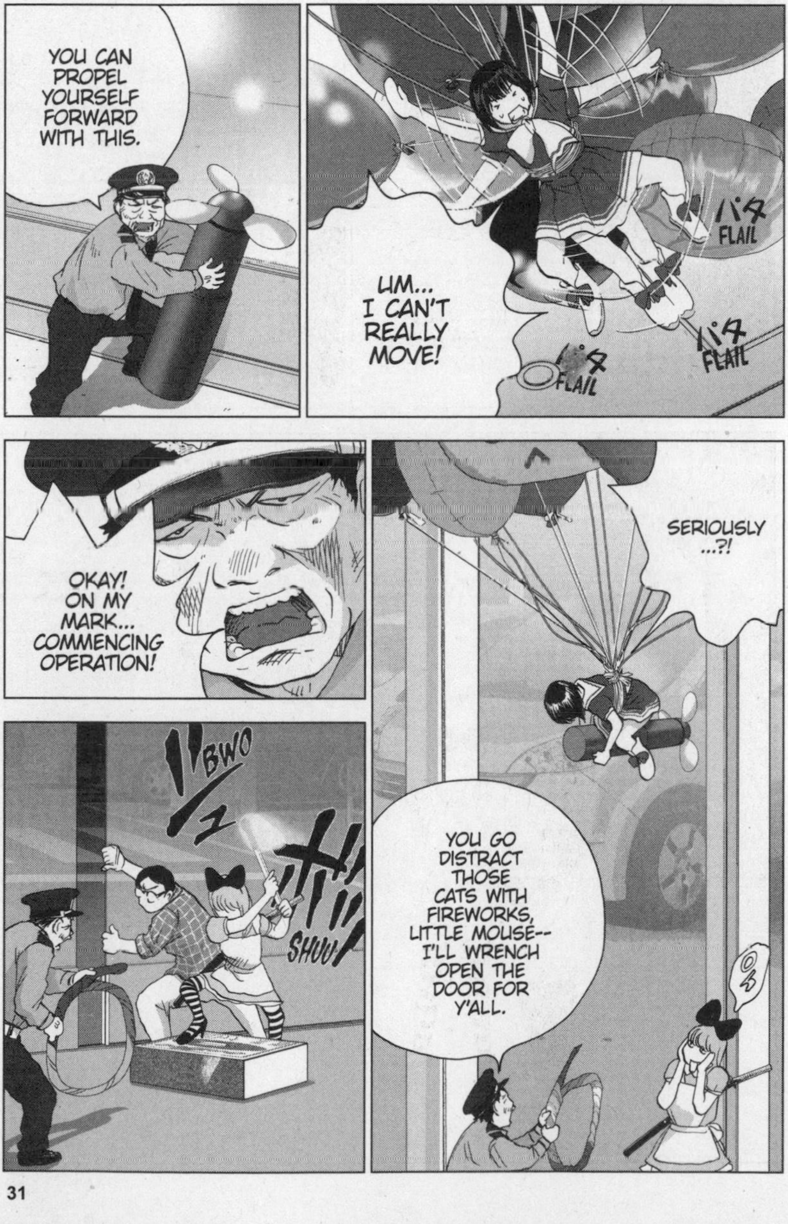
UM... I CAN'T REALLY MOVE!
パタ FLAIL
パタ FLAIL
パタ FLAIL
YOU CAN PROPEL YOURSELF FORWARD WITH THIS.
SERIOUSLY ...?!
YOU GO DISTRACT THOSE CATS WITH FIREWORKS, LITTLE MOUSE-- I'LL WRENCH OPEN THE DOOR FOR Y'ALL.
OKAY! ON MY MARK... COMMENCING OPERATION!
BWO
SHUU

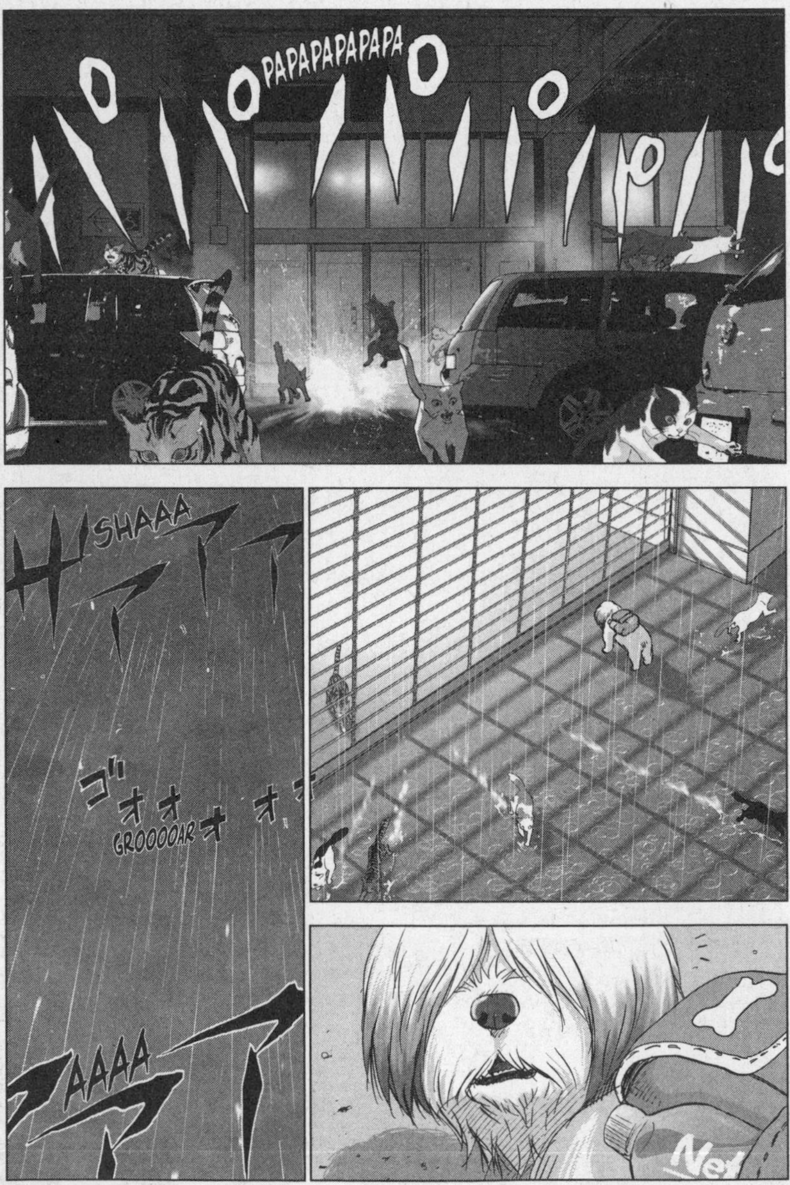
PAPAPAPAPAPA
SHAAA
ゴオオオオ
GROOOOAR
AAAA

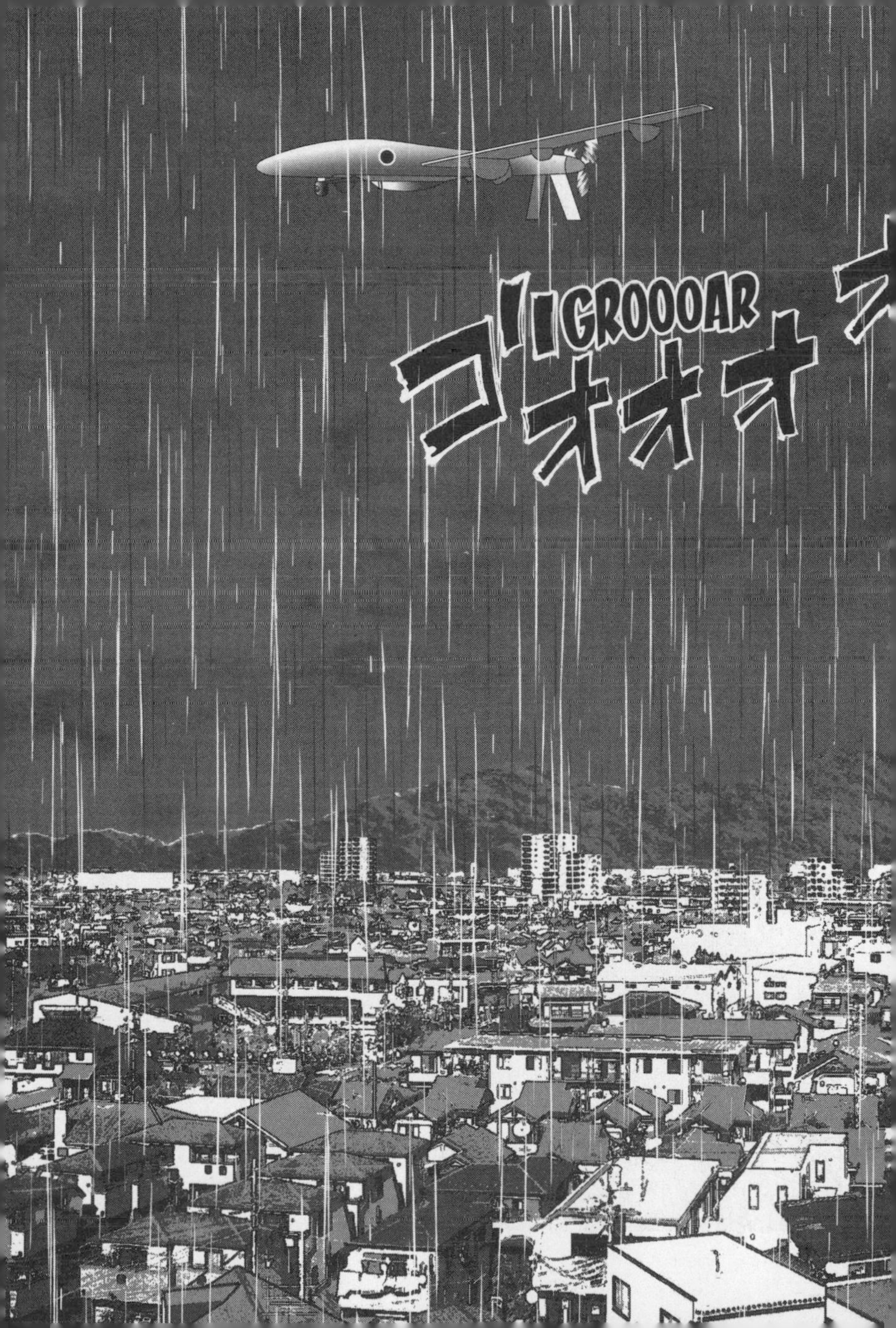
GROOOAR
ゴオオオ

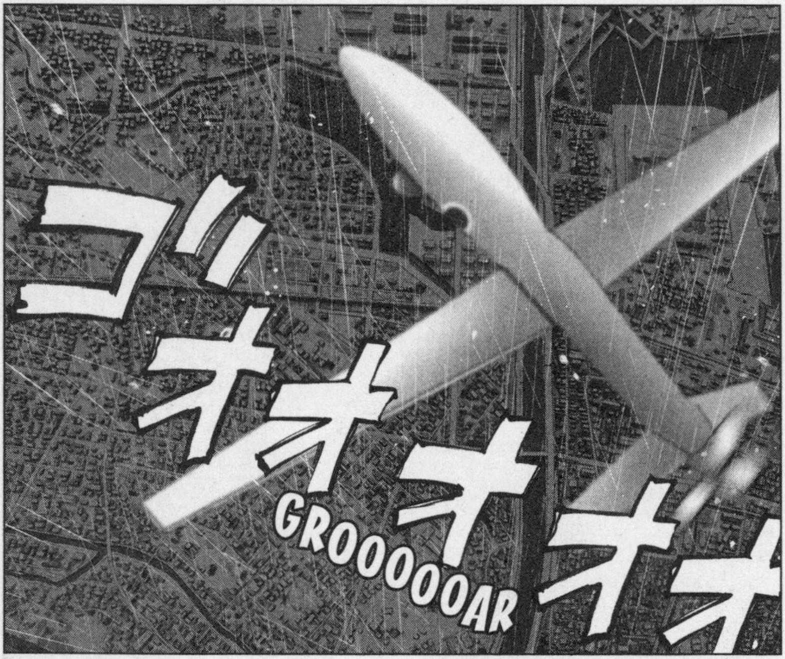
ゴオオオオ
GROOOOOOAR

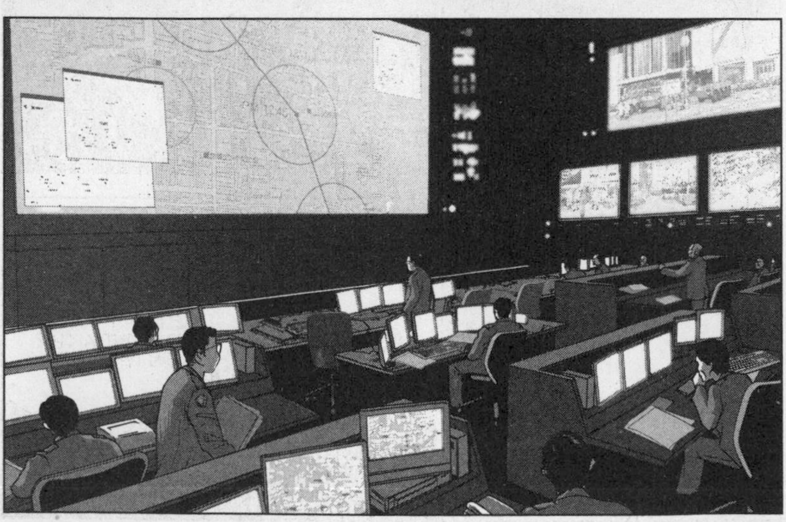

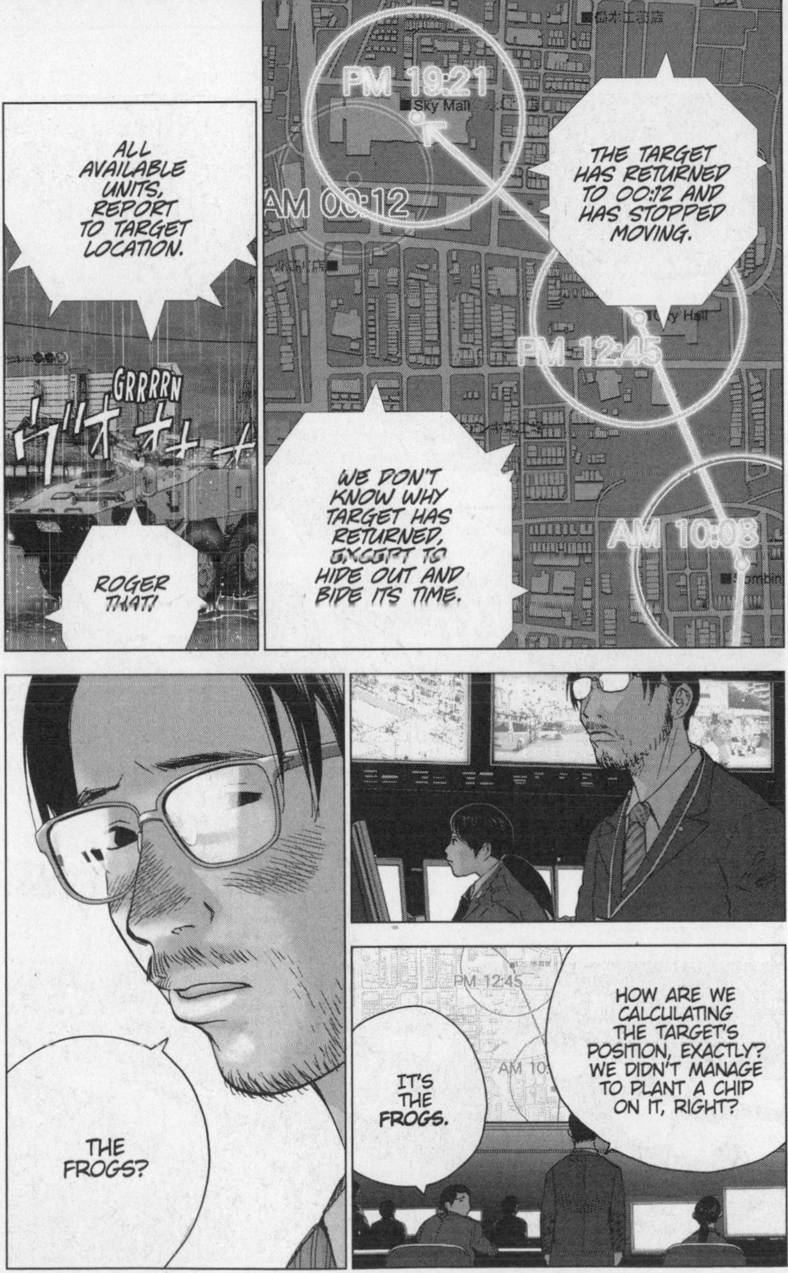
PM 19:21
Sky Mall
AM 00:12
PM 12:45
AM 10:08
THE TARGET HAS RETURNED TO 00:12 AND HAS STOPPED MOVING.
WE DON'T KNOW WHY TARGET HAS RETURNED, EXCEPT TO HIDE OUT AND BIDE ITS TIME.
ALL AVAILABLE UNITS, REPORT TO TARGET LOCATION.
GRRRRN
ヴオオォォ
ROGER THAT!
PM 12:45
HOW ARE WE CALCULATING THE TARGET'S POSITION, EXACTLY? WE DIDN'T MANAGE TO PLANT A CHIP ON IT, RIGHT?
IT'S THE FROGS.
THE FROGS?

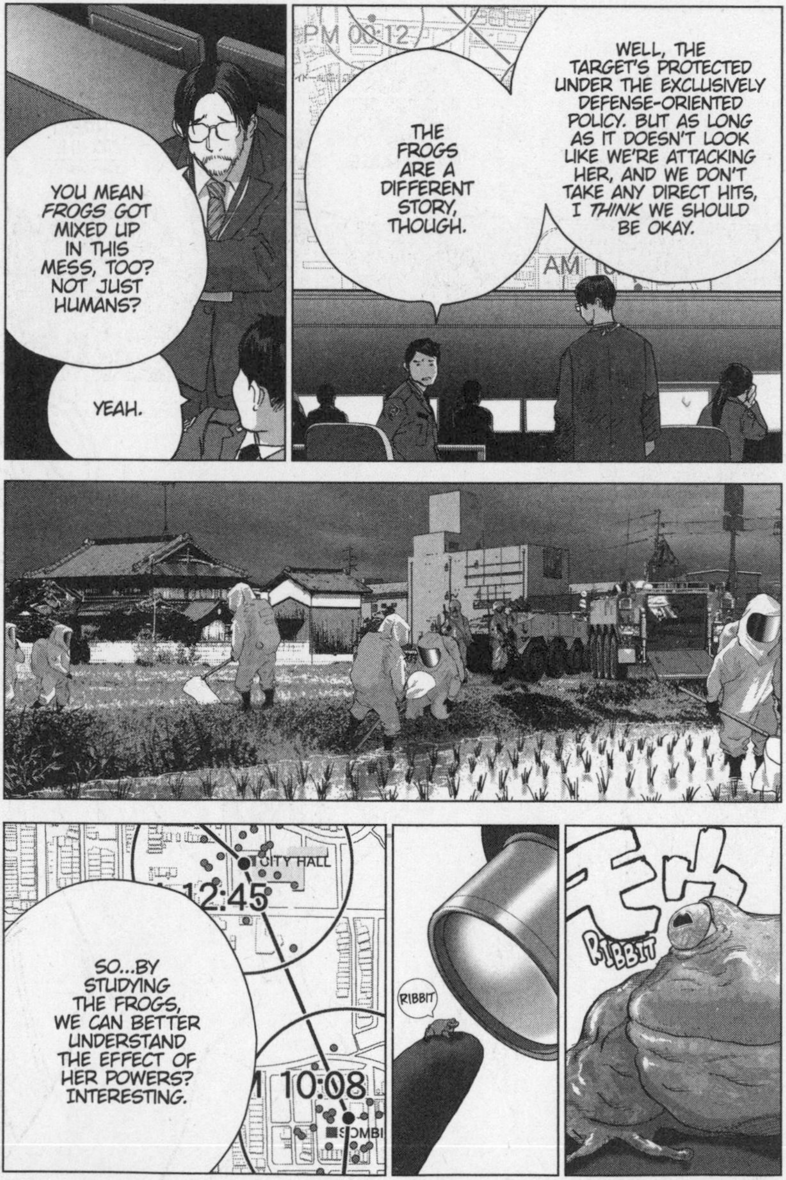

WELL, THE TARGET'S PROTECTED UNDER THE EXCLUSIVELY DEFENSE-ORIENTED POLICY. BUT AS LONG AS IT DOESN'T LOOK LIKE WE'RE ATTACKING HER, AND WE DON'T TAKE ANY DIRECT HITS, I *THINK* WE SHOULD BE OKAY.
PM 00:12
THE FROGS ARE A DIFFERENT STORY, THOUGH.
YOU MEAN *FROGS* GOT MIXED UP IN THIS MESS, TOO? NOT JUST HUMANS?
YEAH.
RIBBIT
RIBBIT
CITY HALL
12:45
SO...BY STUDYING THE FROGS, WE CAN BETTER UNDERSTAND THE EFFECT OF HER POWERS? INTERESTING.
10:08

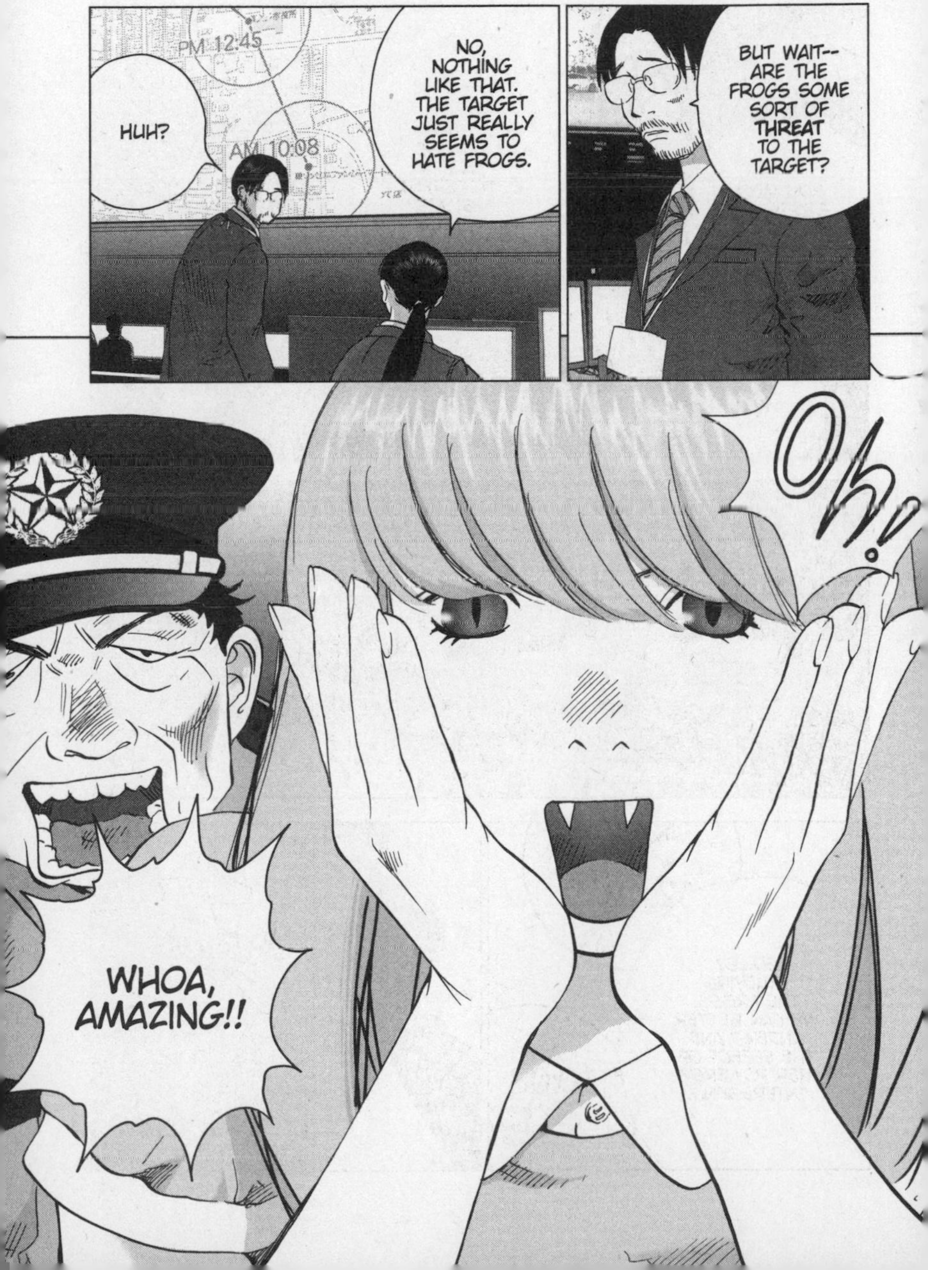
BUT WAIT-- ARE THE FROGS SOME SORT OF THREAT TO THE TARGET?
NO, NOTHING LIKE THAT. THE TARGET JUST REALLY SEEMS TO HATE FROGS.
PM 12:45
AM 10:08
HUH?
Oh!!
WHOA, AMAZING!!

BWEE EEEN

AND HERE I THOUGHT IT WOULDN'T WORK! I'LL BE DAMNED!

OKAY, MADE IT TO THE SWITCH-BOARD! I'M OPENING THE GATE!

EEK!

BWEEEEN

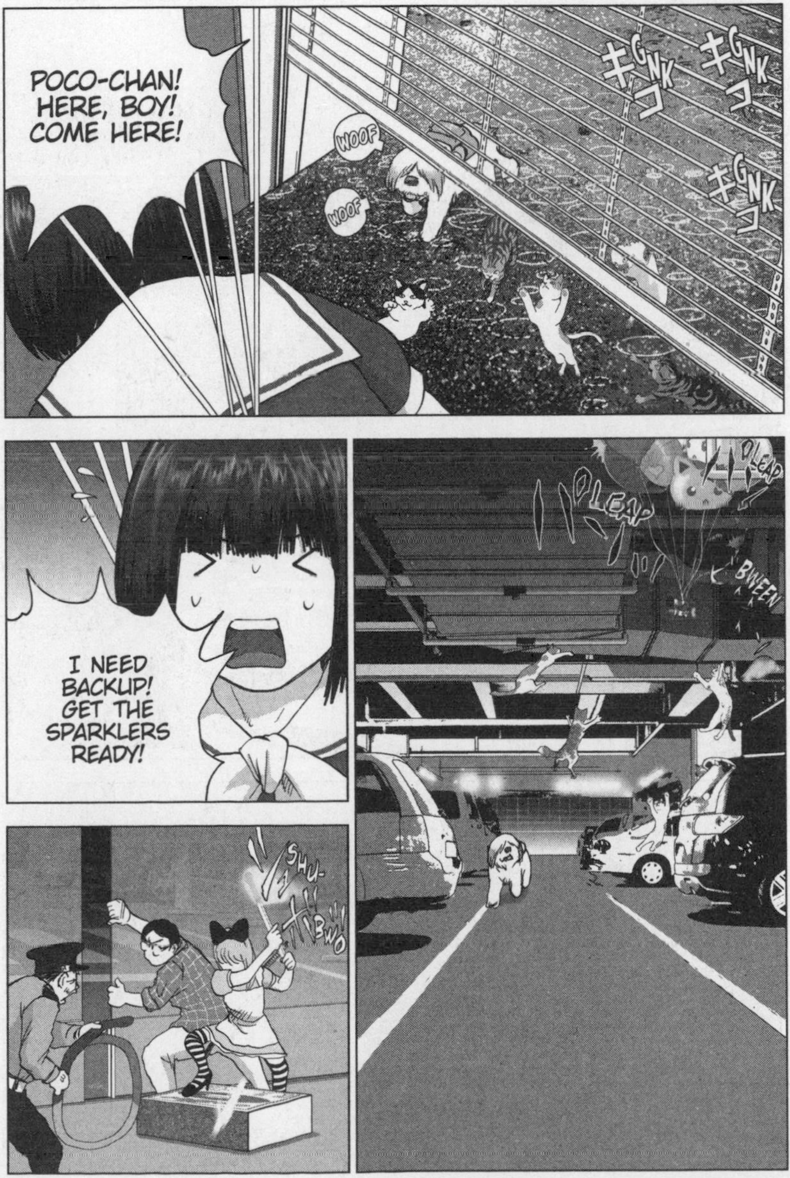
GNK
GNK
POCO-CHAN! HERE, BOY! COME HERE!
WOOF
GNK
WOOF
LEAP
LEAP
BWEEN
I NEED BACKUP! GET THE SPARKLERS READY!
SHU-
BWO

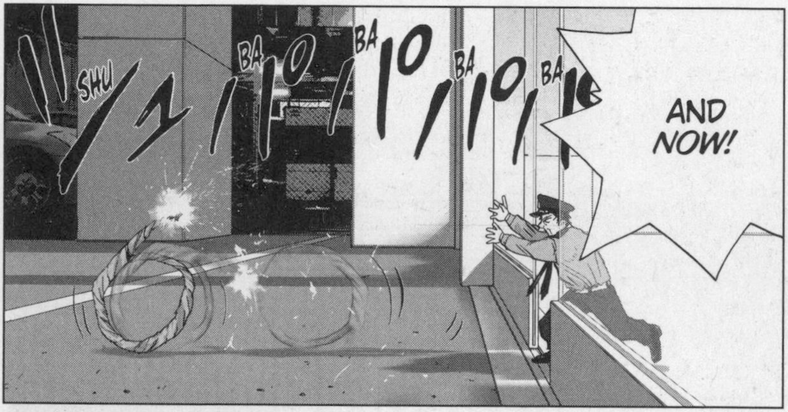
AND NOW!
BA
BA
BA
BA
SHU

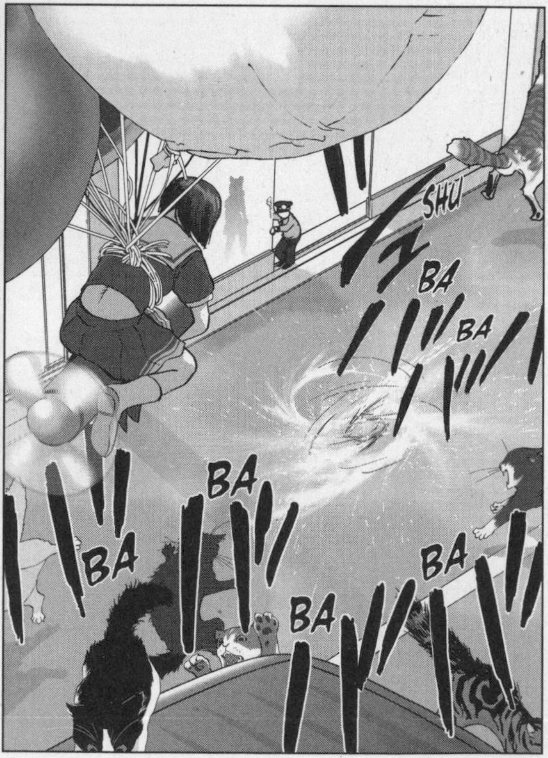
SHU
BA
BA
BA
BA
BA
BA

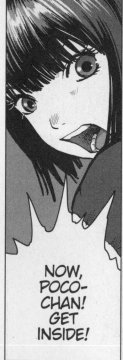

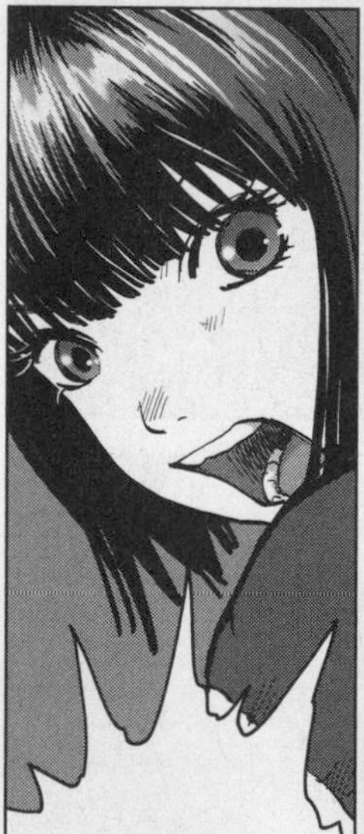
NOW, POCO-CHAN! GET INSIDE!

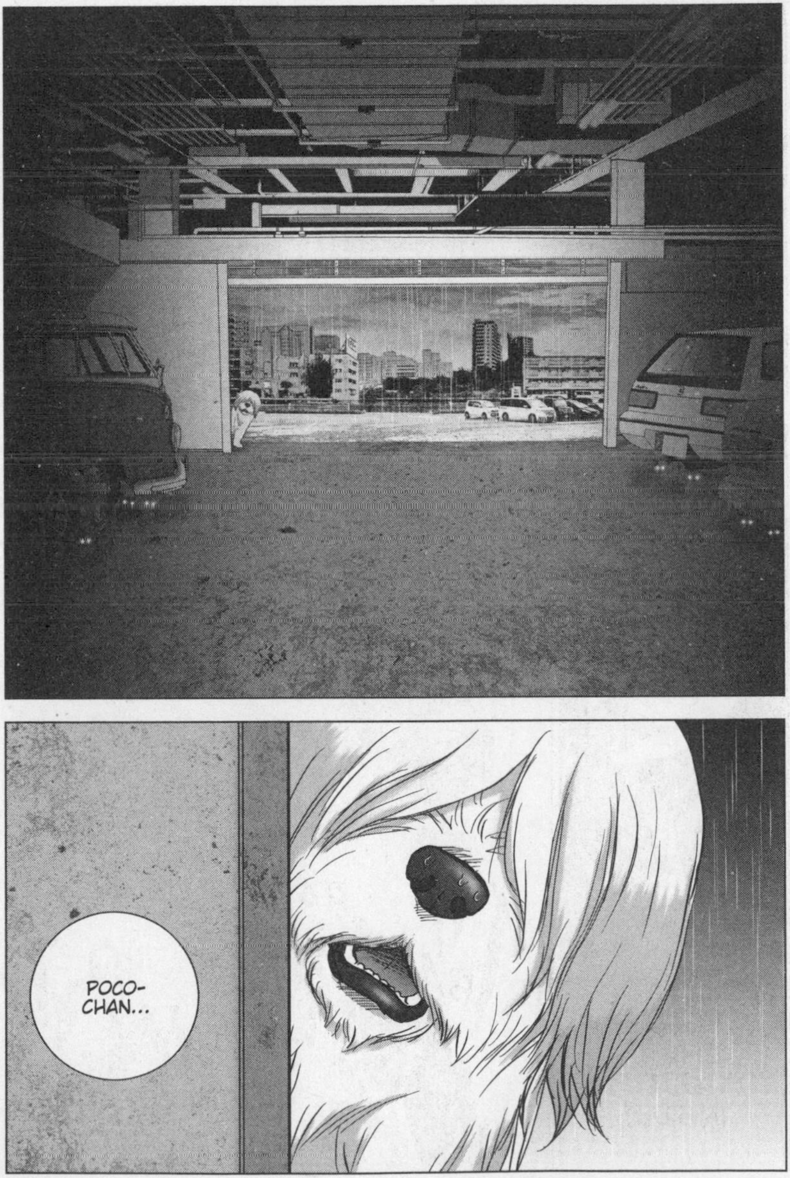
POCO-
CHAN...

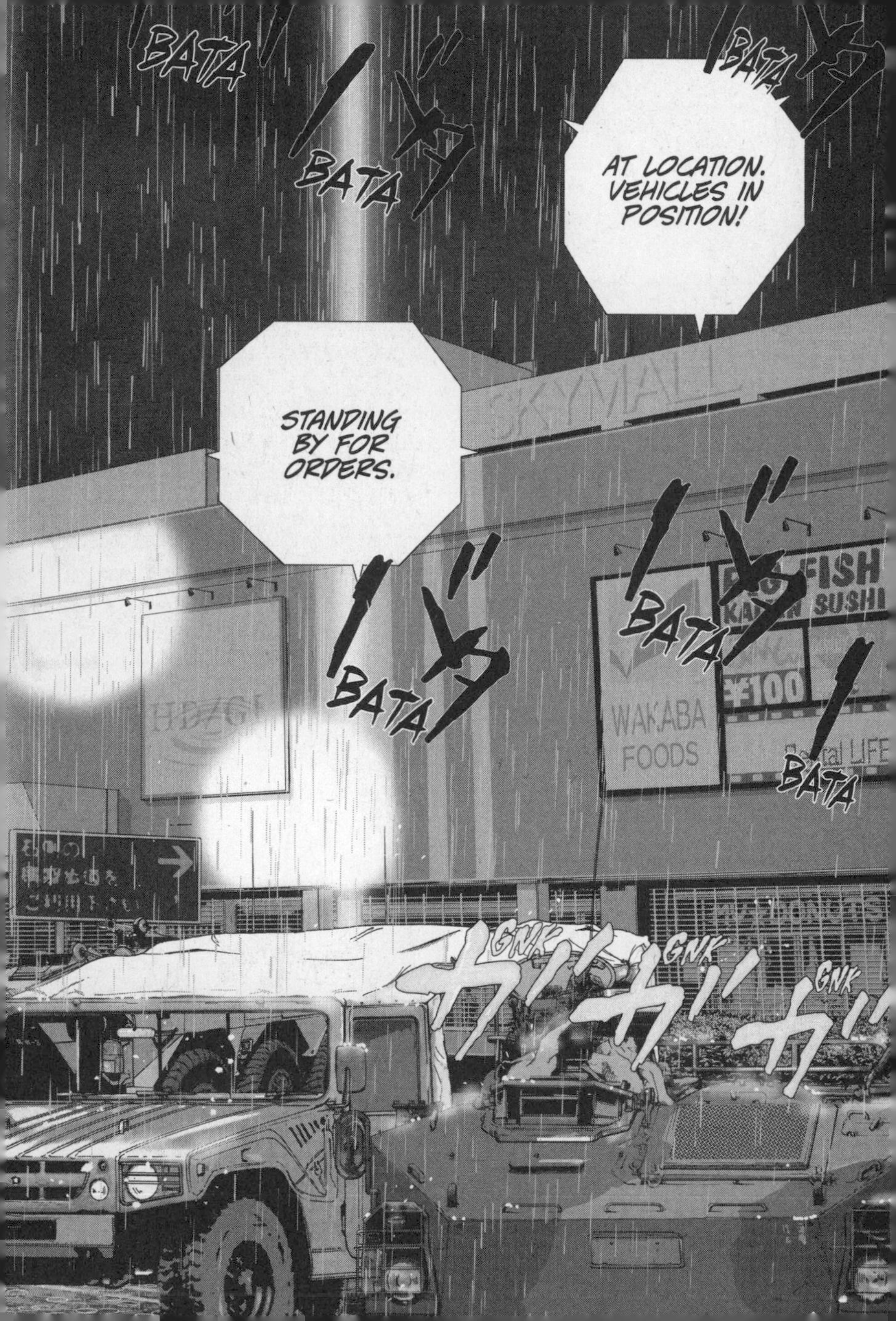
BATA
AT LOCATION. VEHICLES IN POSITION!
BATA
BATA
SKYMALL
STANDING BY FOR ORDERS.
BATA
BATA
BATA
FISH
SUSHI
¥100
WAKABA FOODS
GNK
GNK
GNK

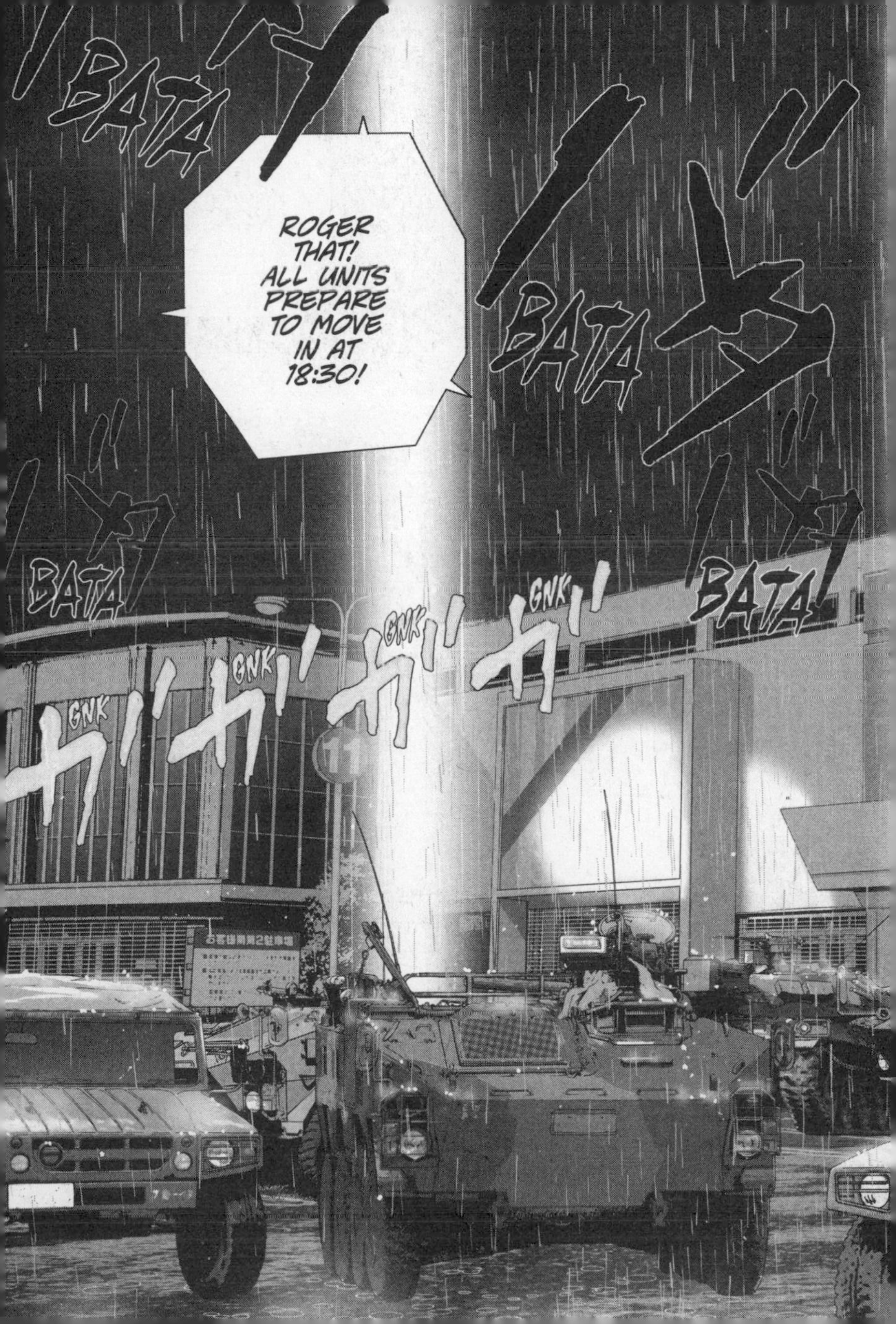
BATA
ROGER THAT! ALL UNITS PREPARE TO MOVE IN AT 18:30!
BATA
BATA
BATA
GNK
GNK
GNK
GNK
GNK

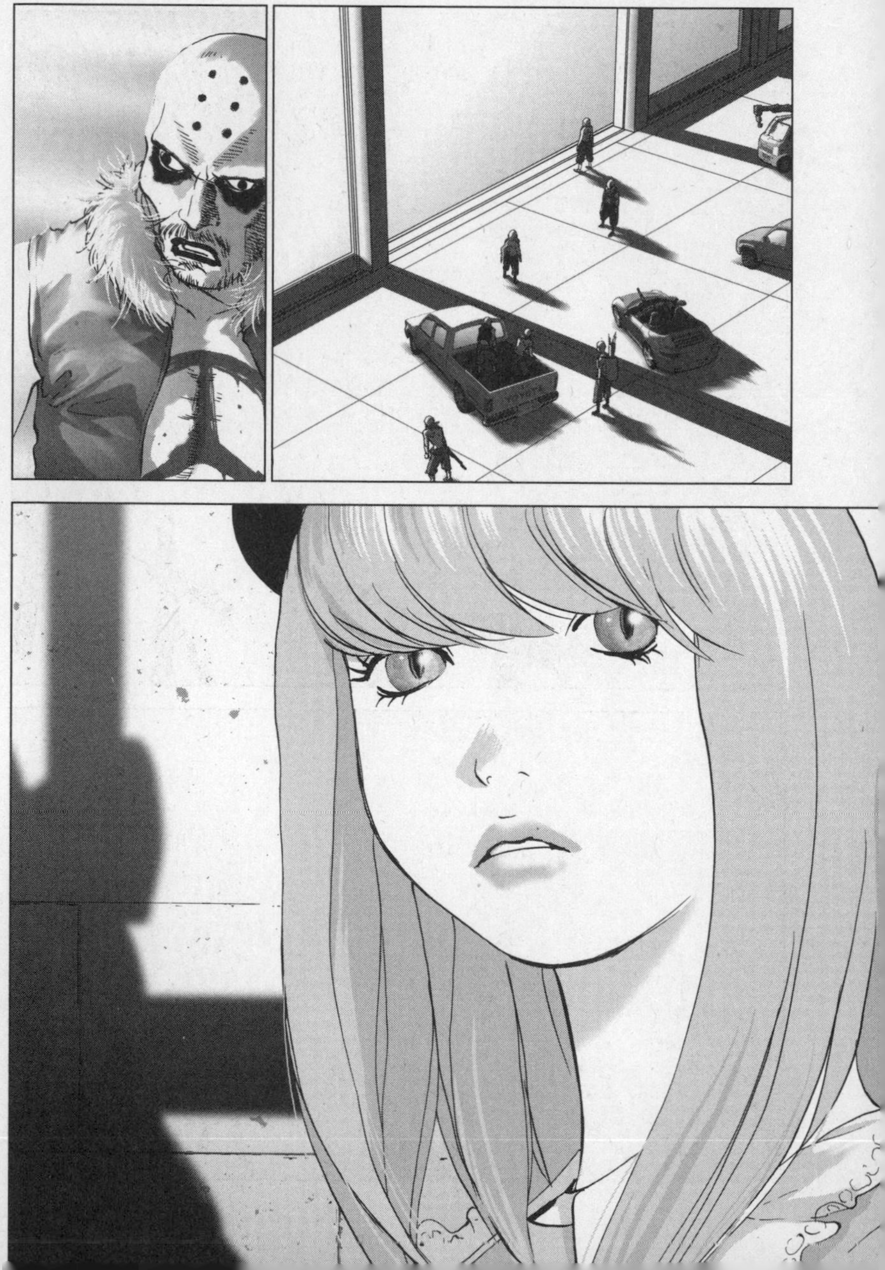

Chapter 12: Chaos

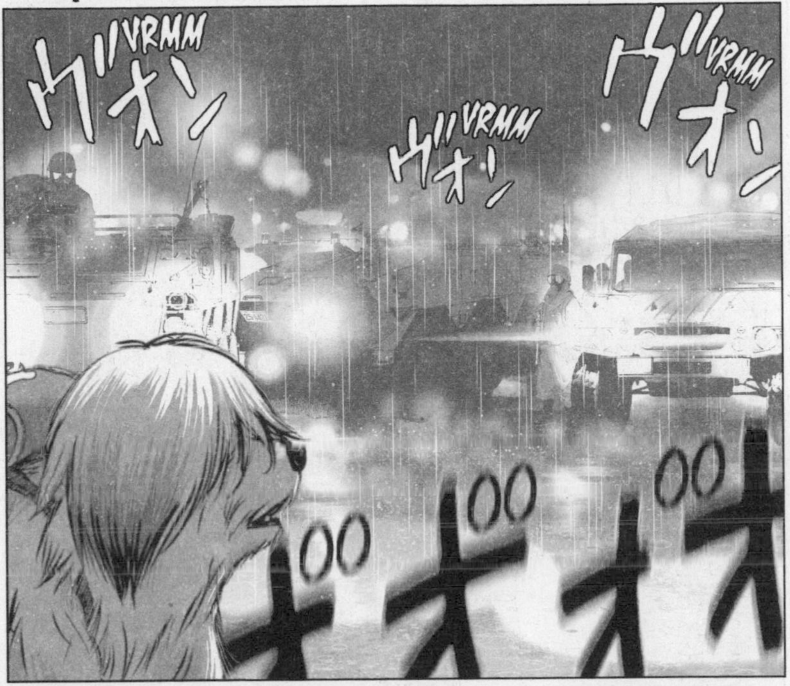
VRMM
VRMM
VRMM
OO
OO
OO

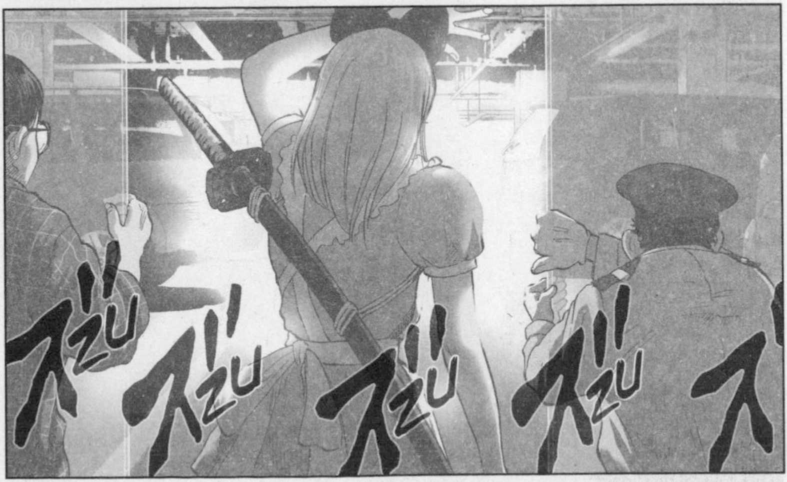
ZU
ZU
ZU

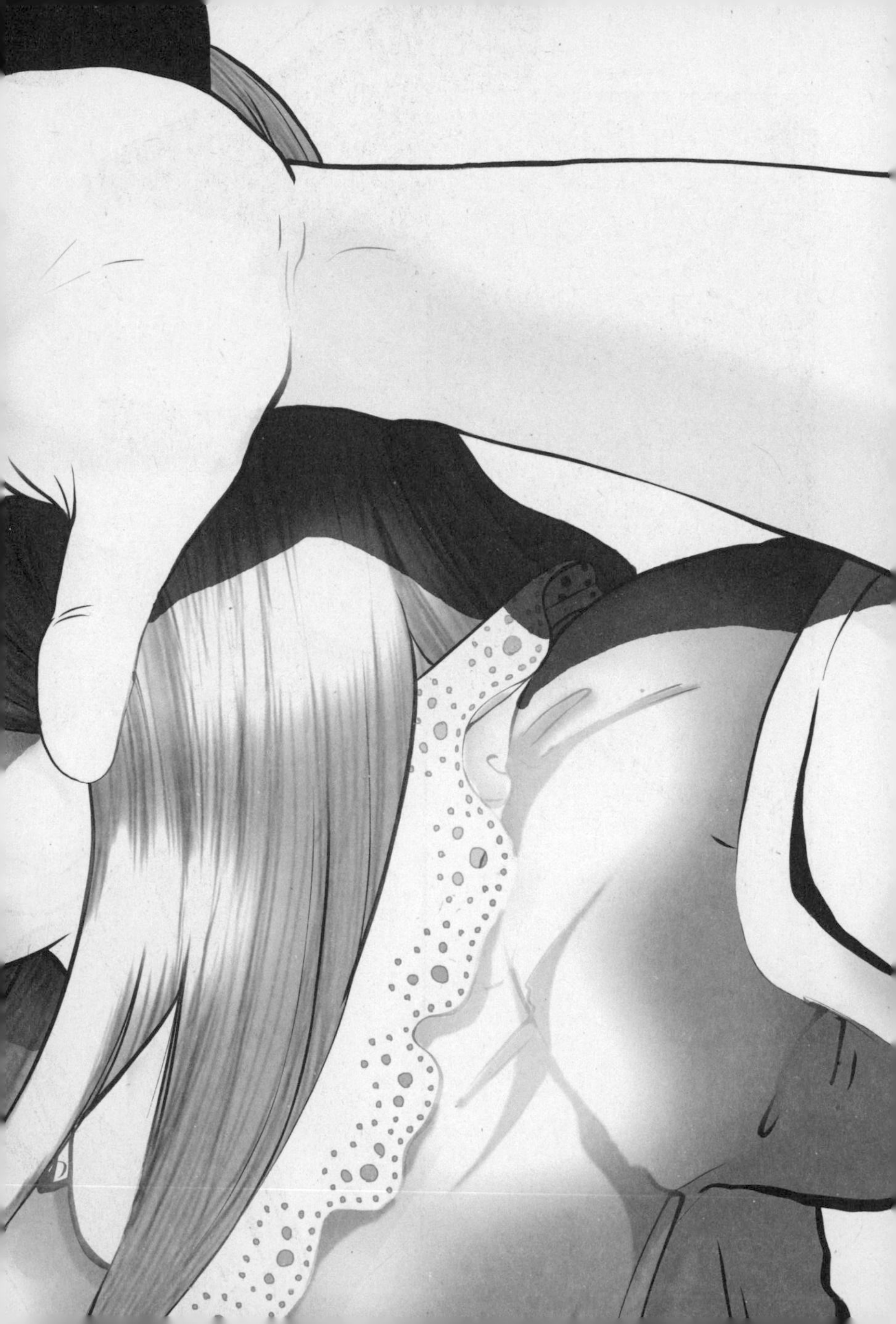

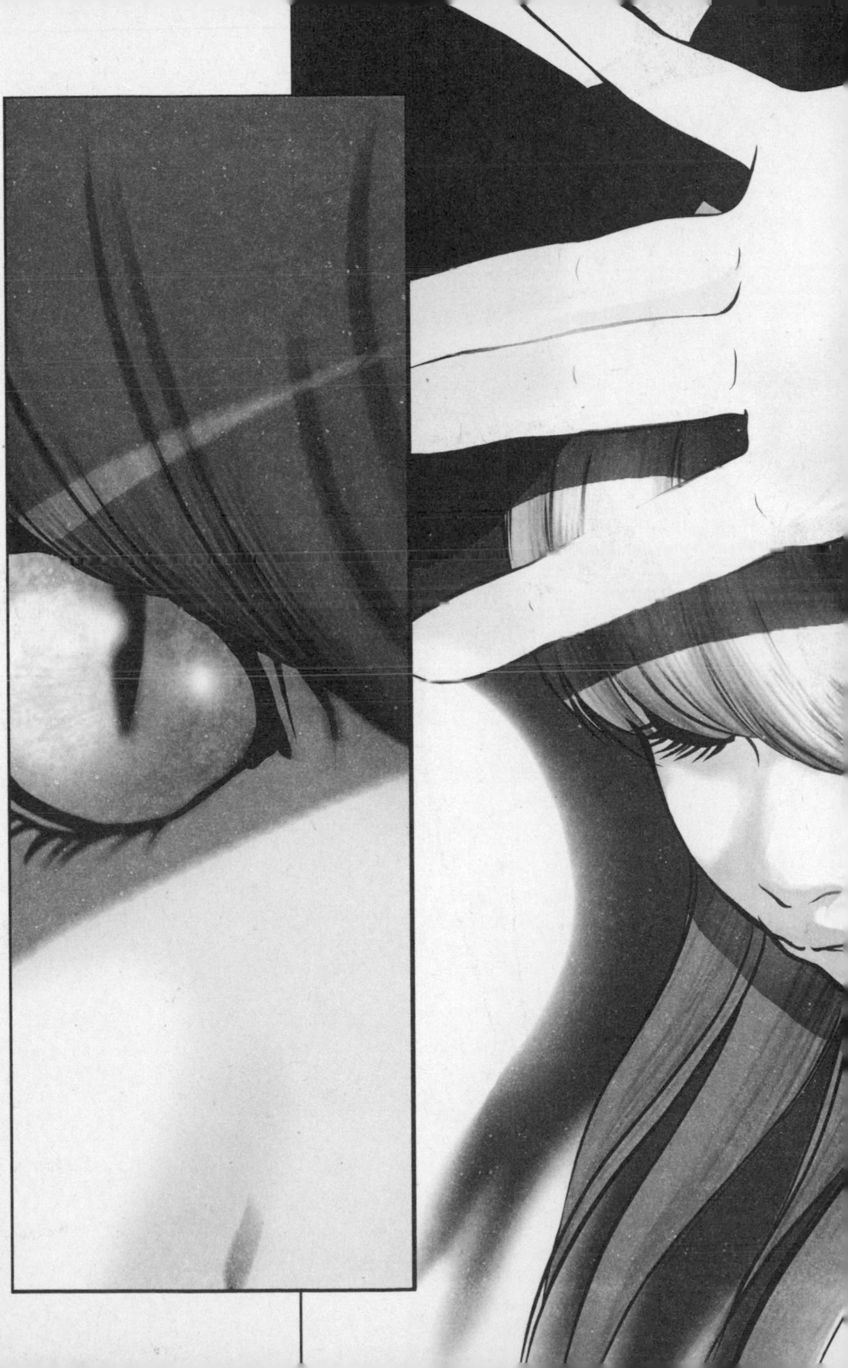

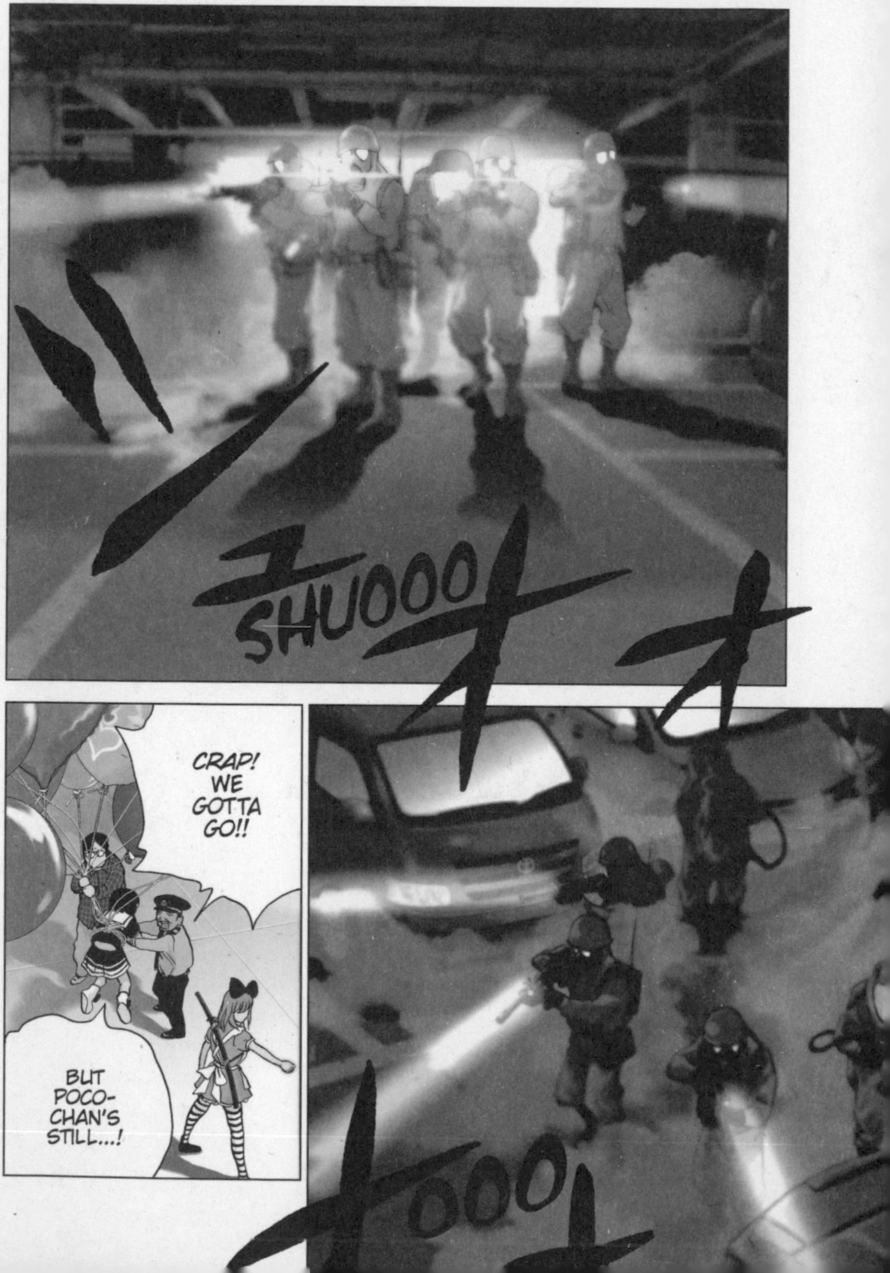
SHUOOO
OOO
CRAP! WE GOTTA GO!!
BUT POCO-CHAN'S STILL...!

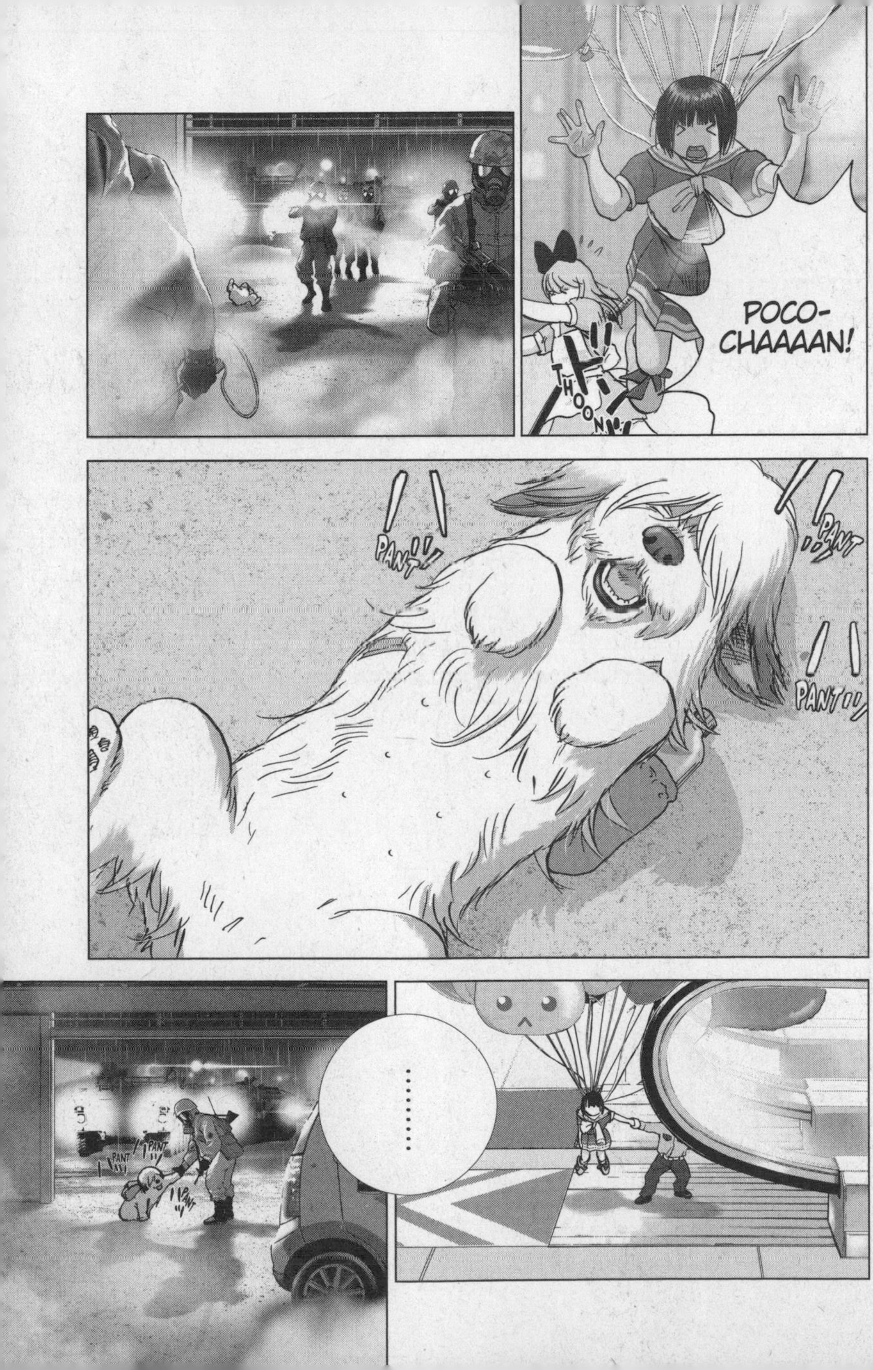
POCO-CHAAAAN!
THOON!!
PANT!!
PANT!!
PANT!!
......
PANT!!
PANT!!
PANT!!

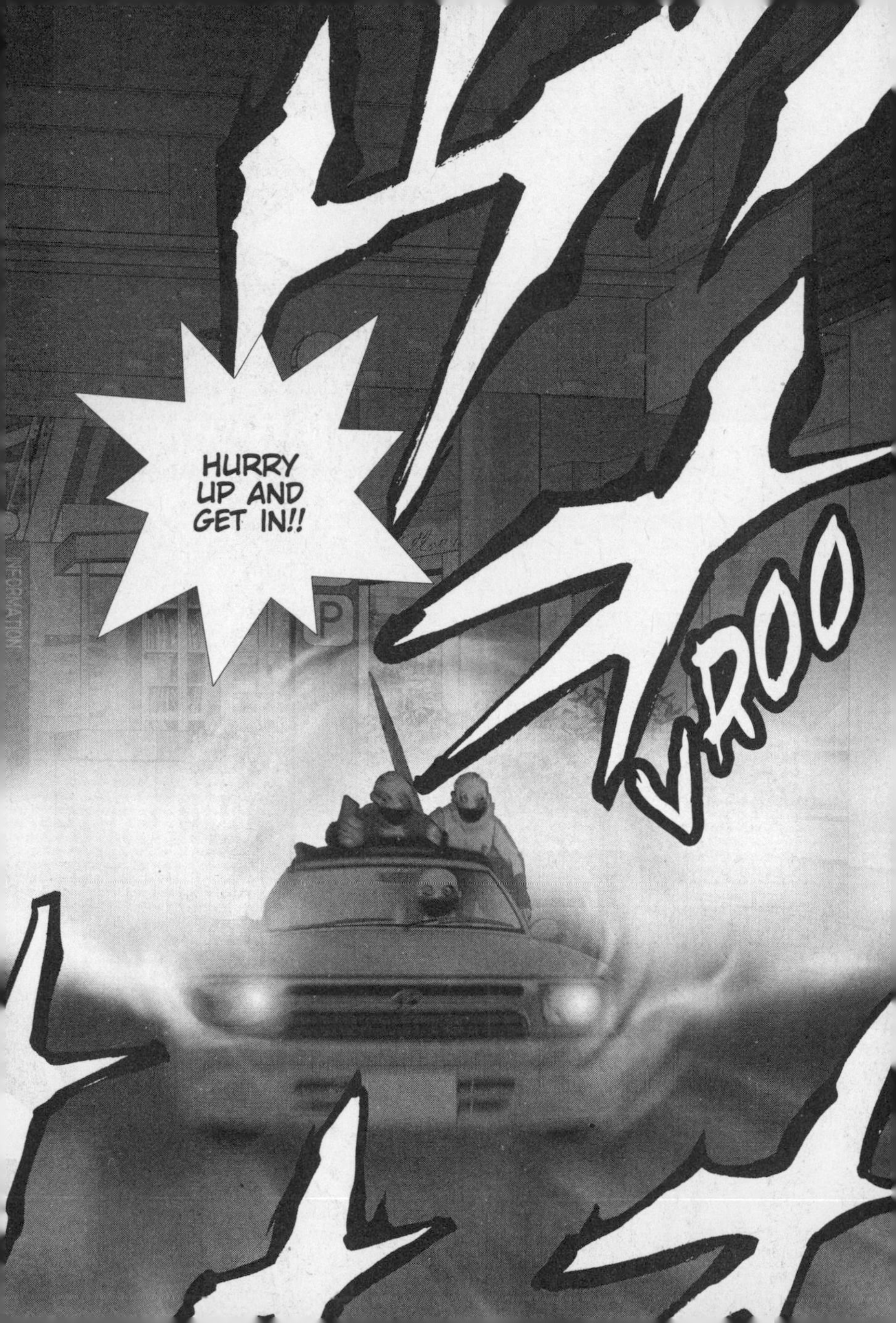
HURRY UP AND GET IN!!
VROO

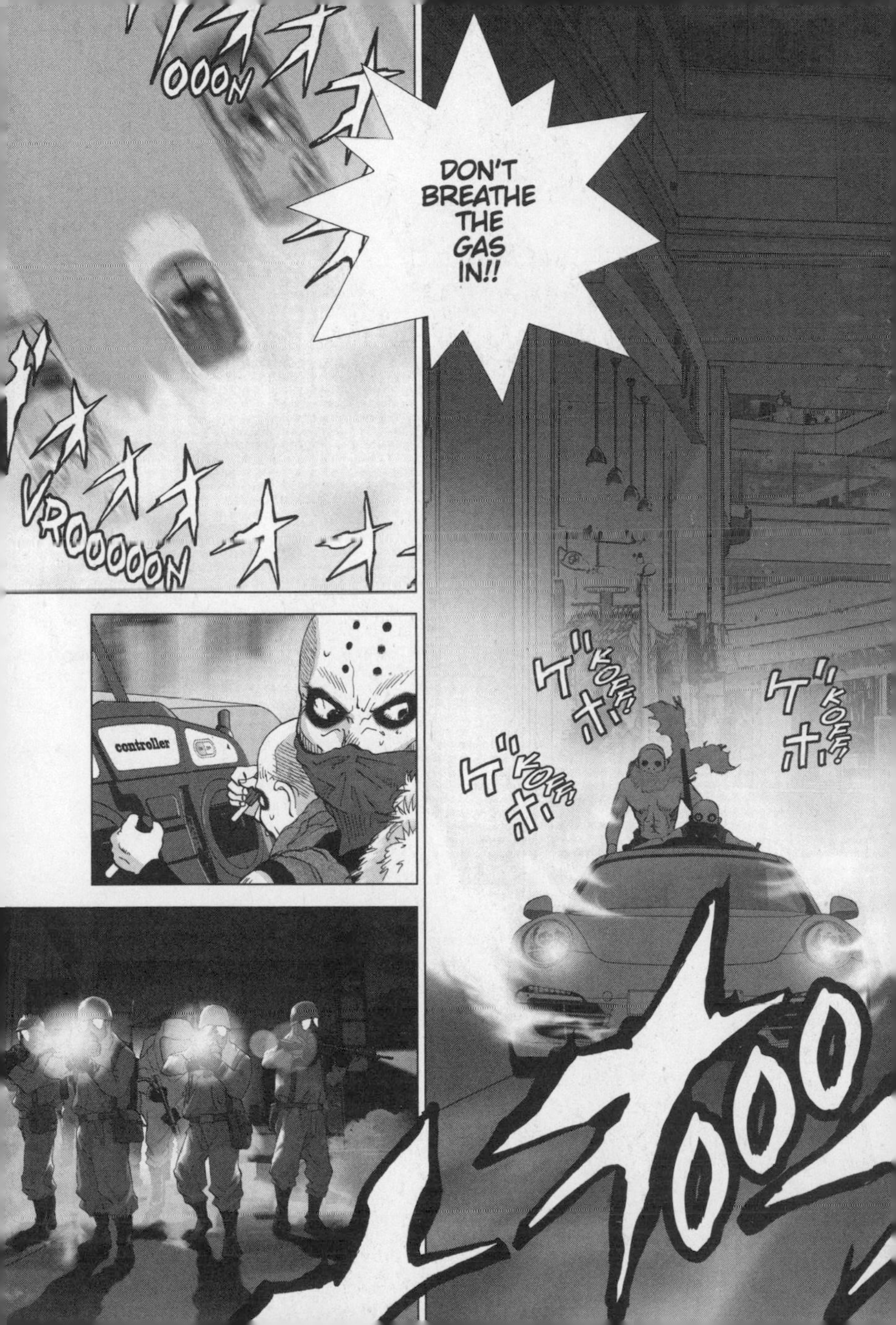
DON'T BREATHE THE GAS IN!!
KOFF KOFF
KOFF KOFF
KOFF KOFF
OOON
VROOOOOON
controller

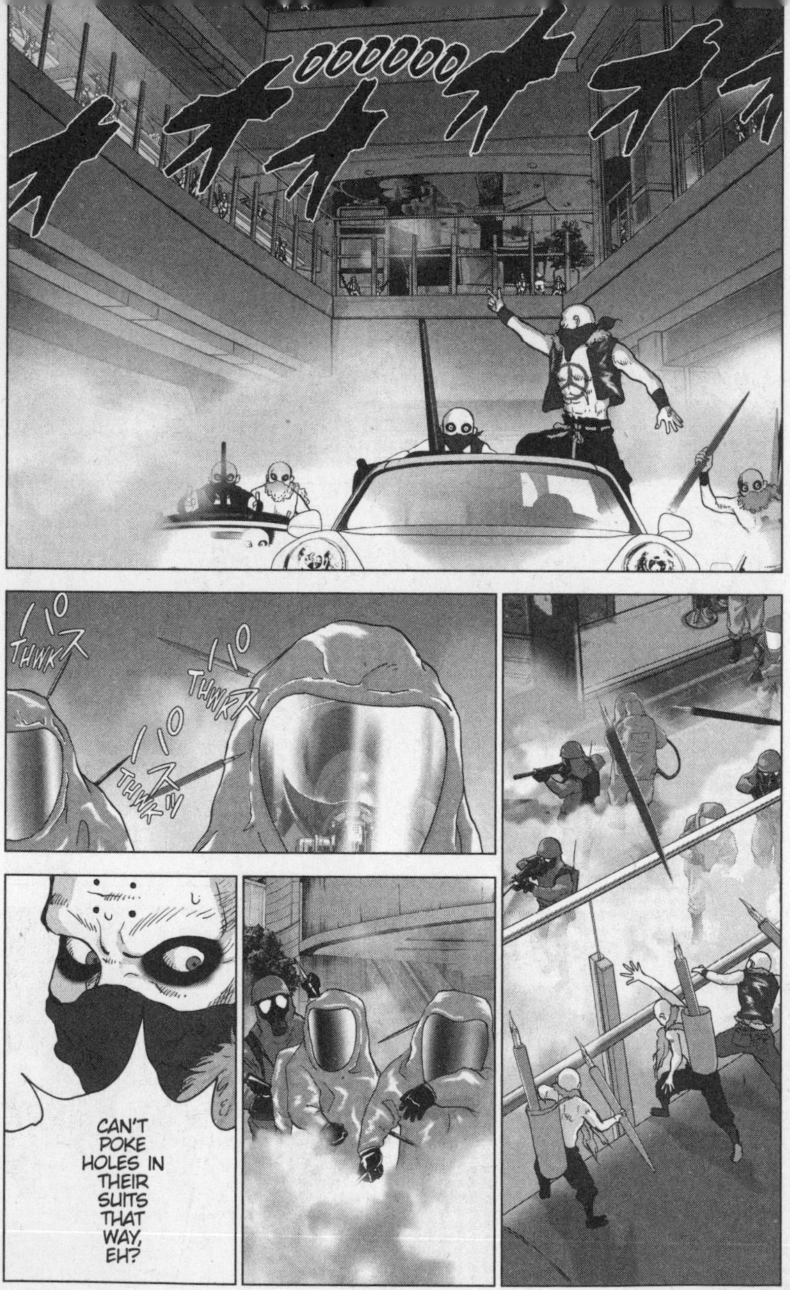
OOOOOOO
THWK
THWK
THWK
CAN'T POKE HOLES IN THEIR SUITS THAT WAY, EH?

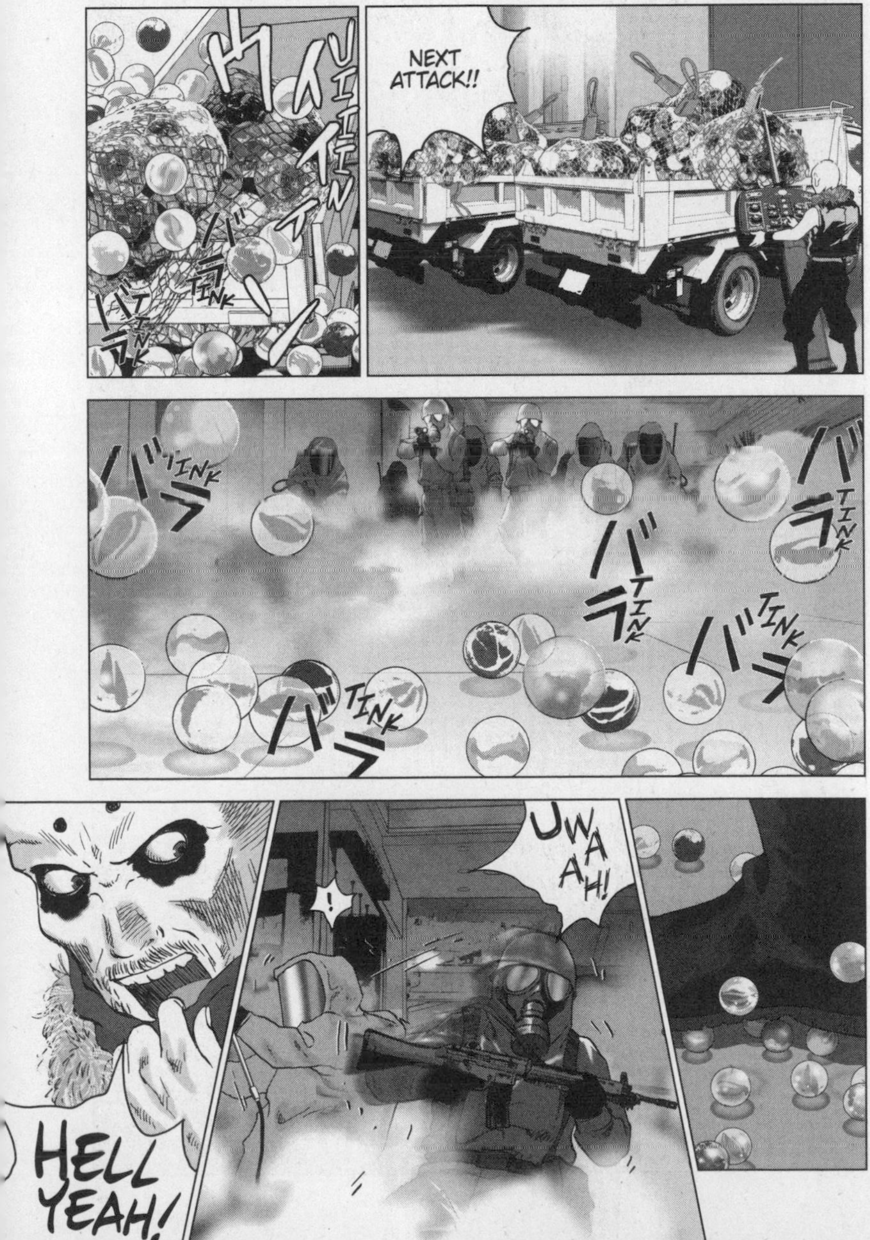
NEXT ATTACK!!
ウイイイーン
UIIIN
バラ
TINK
バラ
TINK
バラ
TINK
バラ
TINK
バラ
TINK
バラ
TINK
バラ
TINK
UWAAH!
!
HELL YEAH!

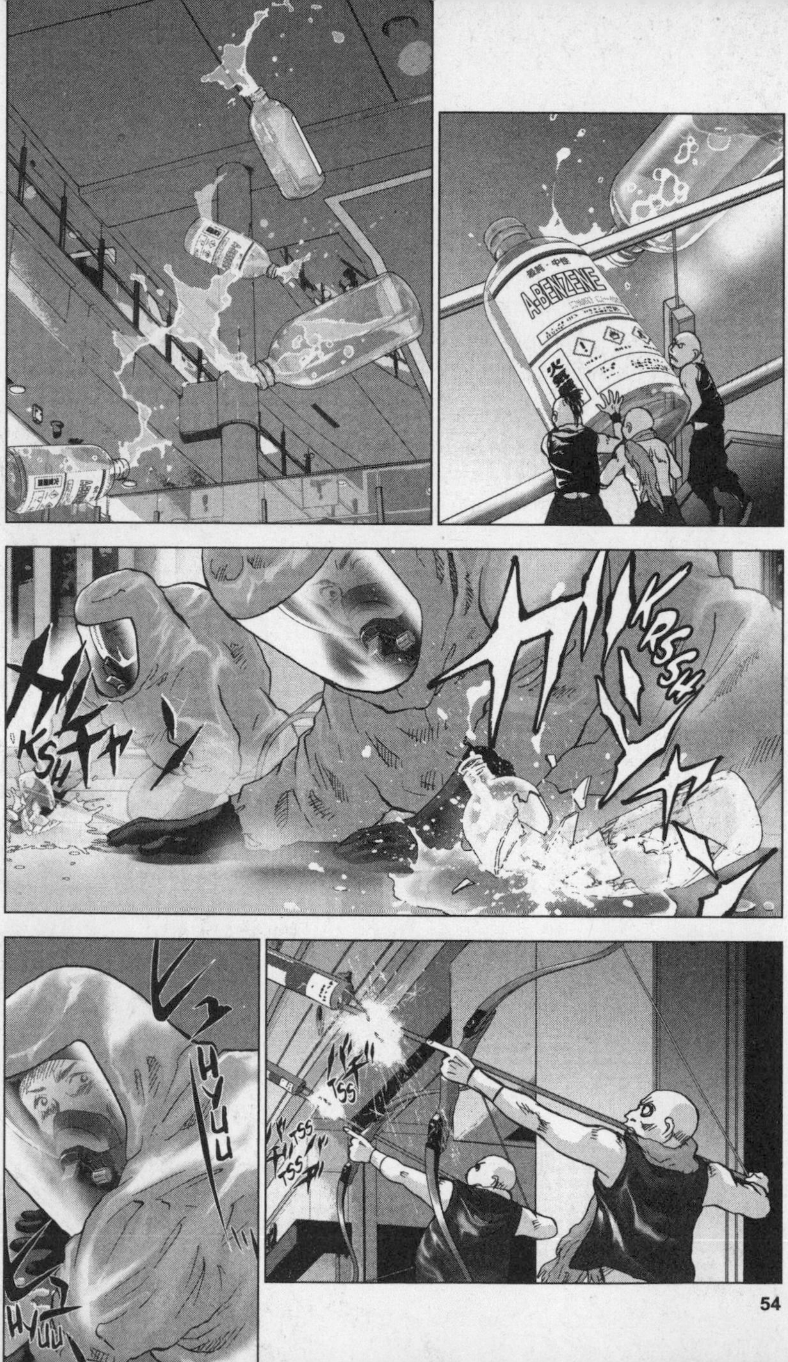
A-BENZENE
KRSSH
KSH
TSS
TSS
TSS
HYUU
HYUU

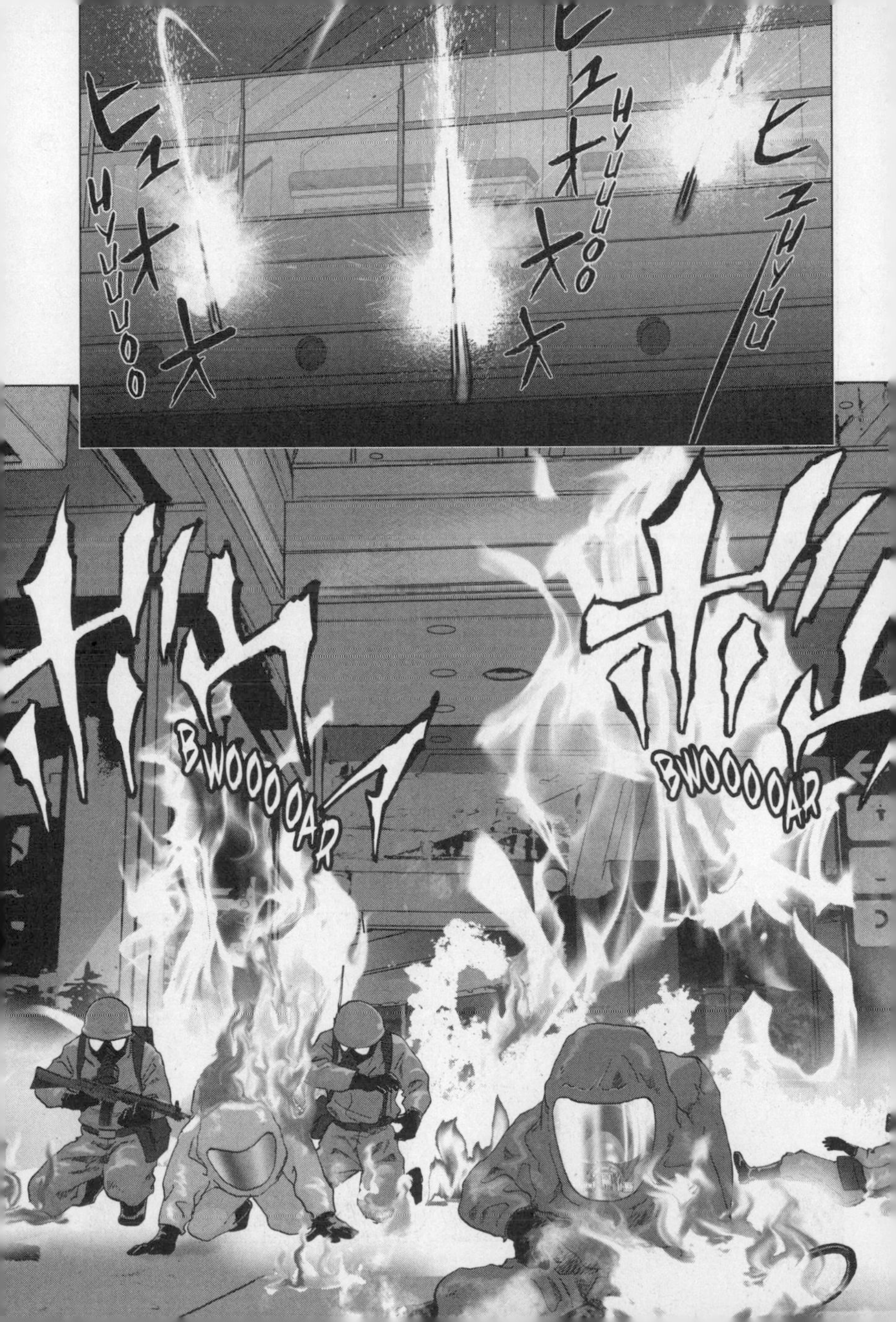
HYUUUU
HYUUUUOO
HYUUUUOO
BWOOOOAR
BWOOOOAR

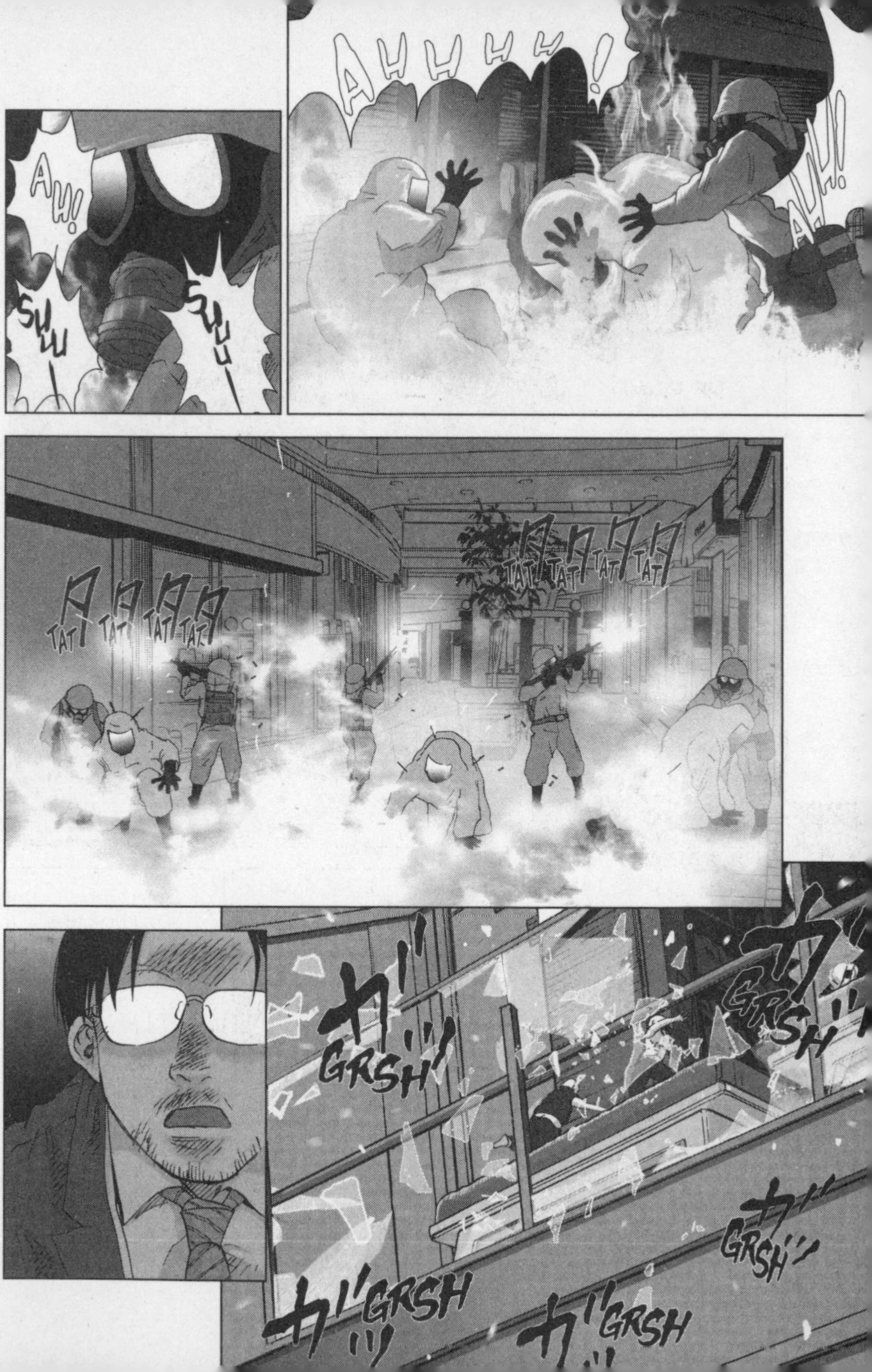
AHHHHH!
AH!
AH!
SHUU
SHUU
TAT TAT TAT TAT
TAT TAT TAT TAT
GRSH!
GRSH
GRSH
GRSH
GRSH

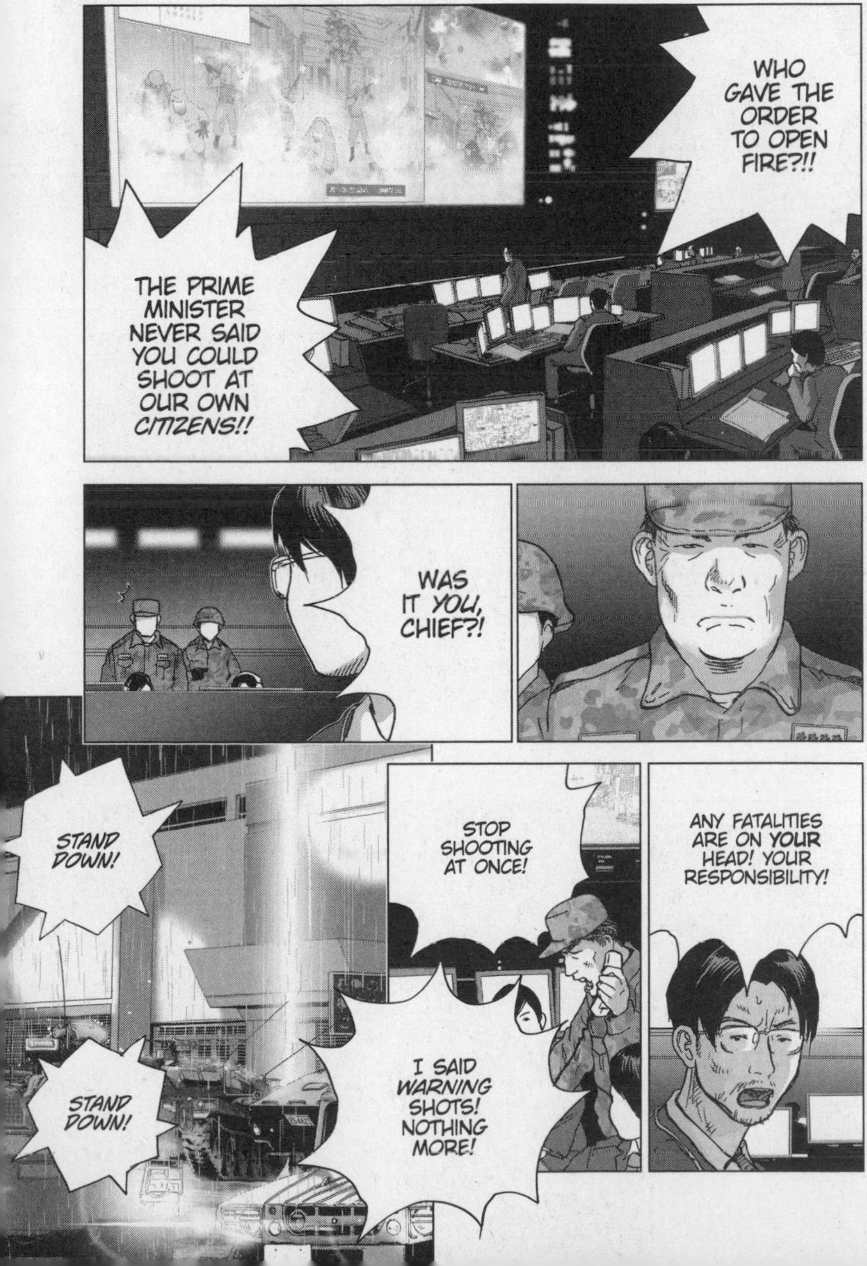
WHO GAVE THE ORDER TO OPEN FIRE?!!
THE PRIME MINISTER NEVER SAID YOU COULD SHOOT AT OUR OWN *CITIZENS!!*
WAS IT *YOU*, CHIEF?!
ANY FATALITIES ARE ON **YOUR** HEAD! YOUR RESPONSIBILITY!
STOP SHOOTING AT ONCE!
I SAID *WARNING* SHOTS! NOTHING MORE!
STAND DOWN!
STAND DOWN!

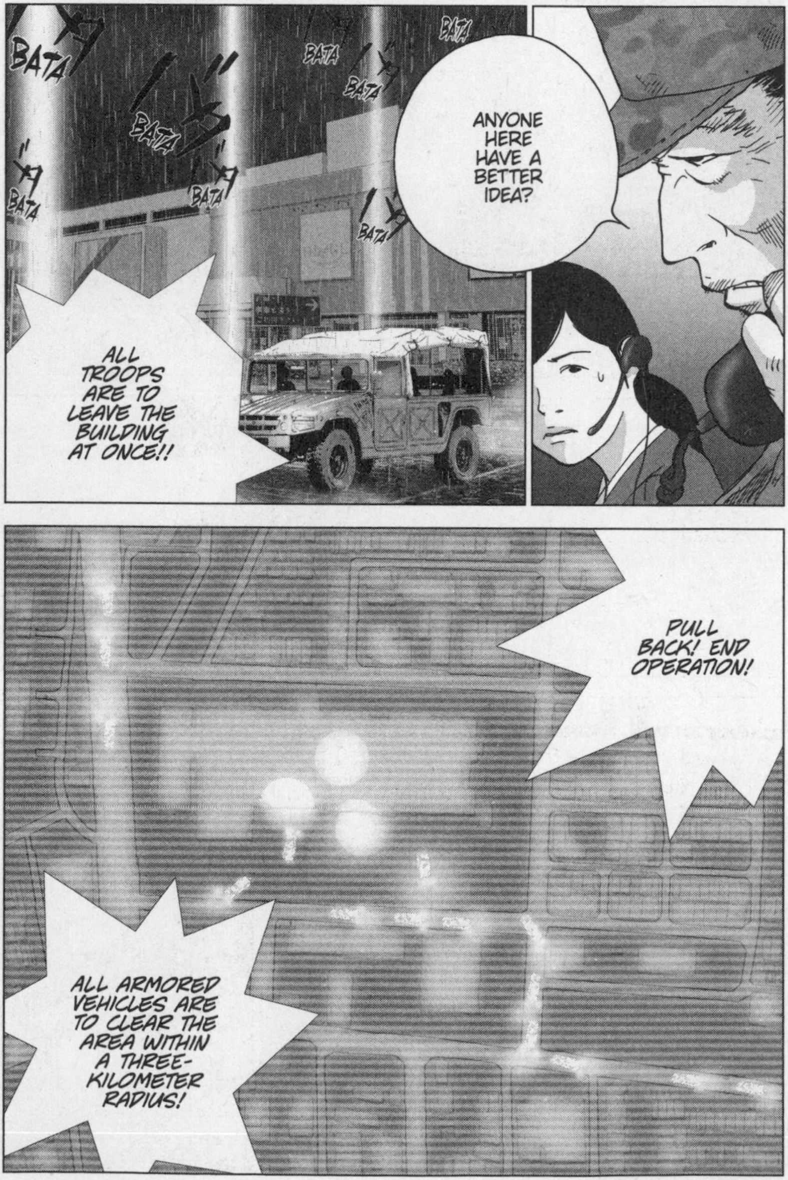
ANYONE HERE HAVE A BETTER IDEA?
BATA
BATA
BATA
BATA
BATA
BATA
BATA
BATA
ALL TROOPS ARE TO LEAVE THE BUILDING AT ONCE!!
PULL BACK! END OPERATION!
ALL ARMORED VEHICLES ARE TO CLEAR THE AREA WITHIN A THREE-KILOMETER RADIUS!

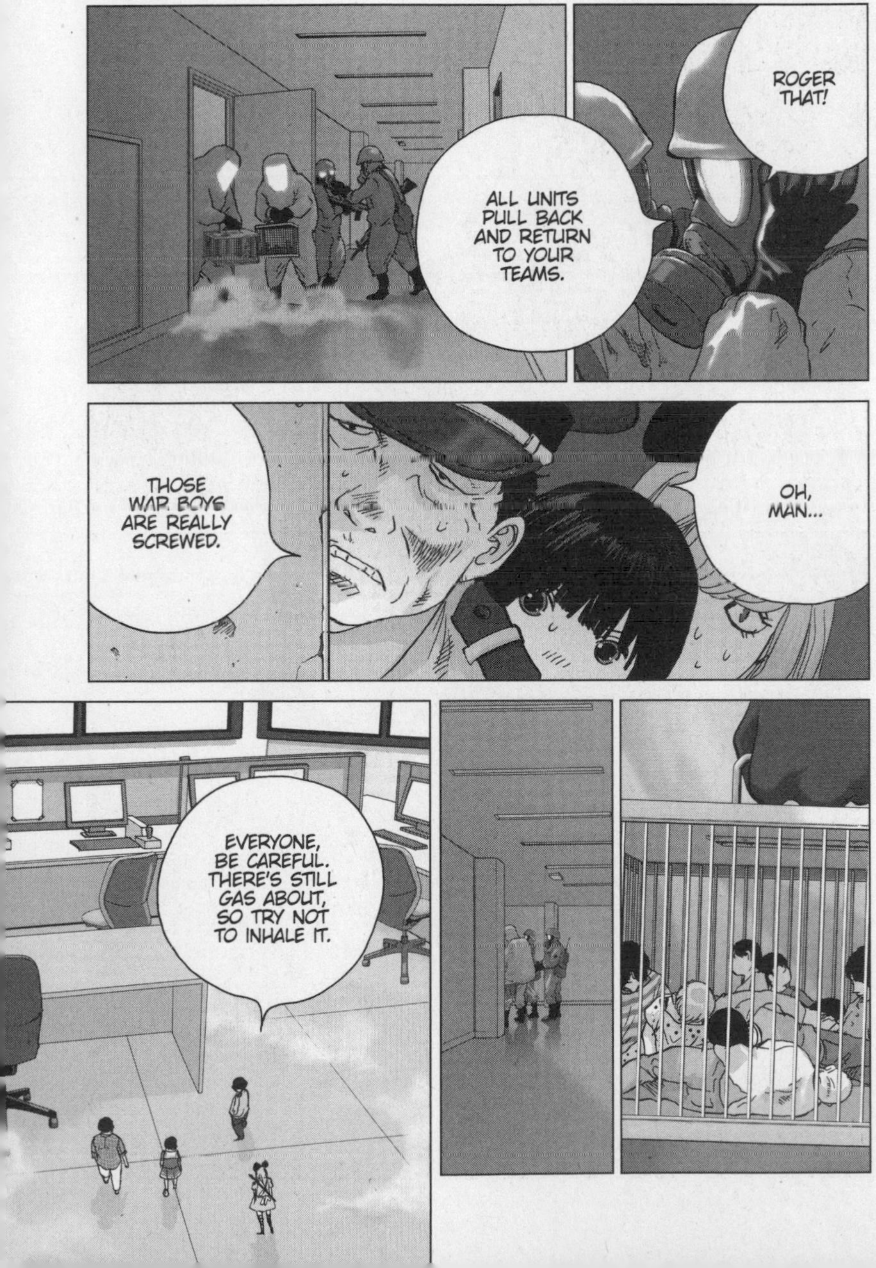
ROGER THAT!
ALL UNITS PULL BACK AND RETURN TO YOUR TEAMS.
OH, MAN...
THOSE WAR BOYS ARE REALLY SCREWED.
EVERYONE, BE CAREFUL. THERE'S STILL GAS ABOUT, SO TRY NOT TO INHALE IT.

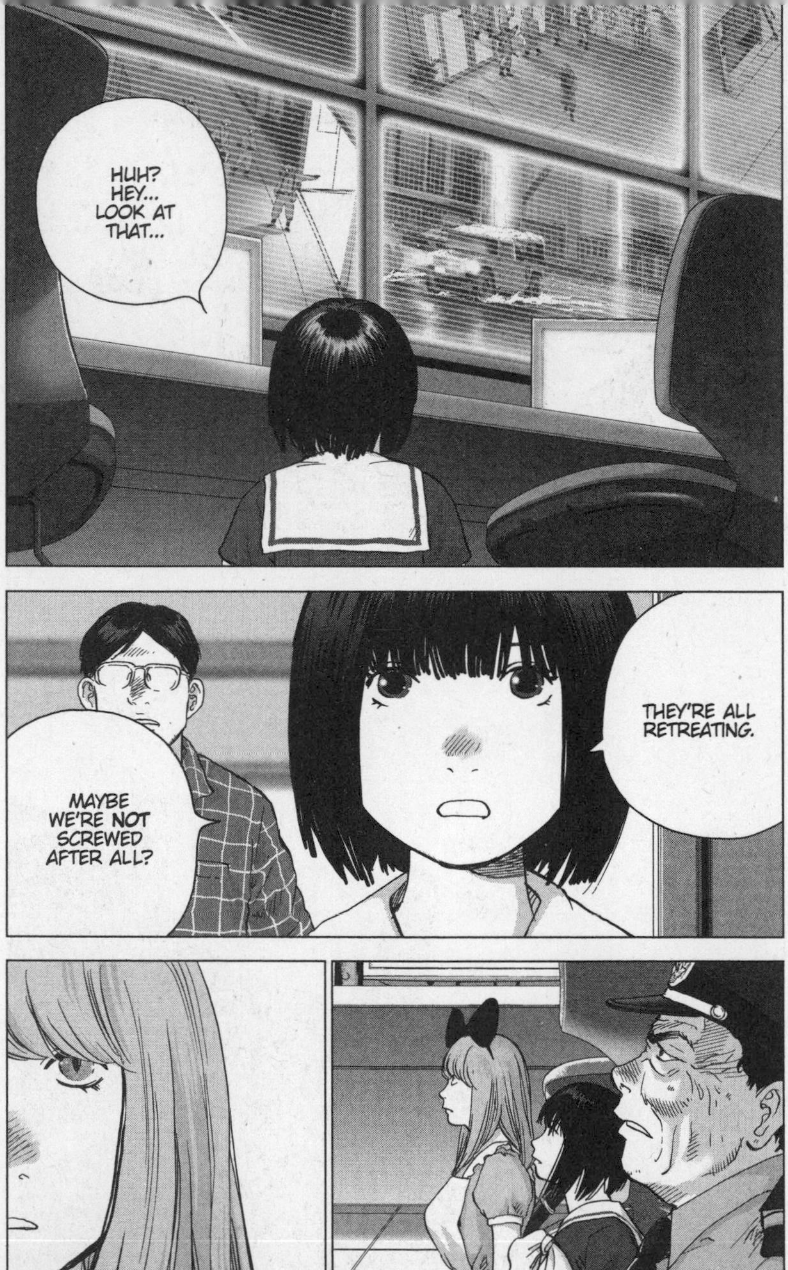
HUH? HEY... LOOK AT THAT...
THEY'RE ALL RETREATING.
MAYBE WE'RE NOT SCREWED AFTER ALL?

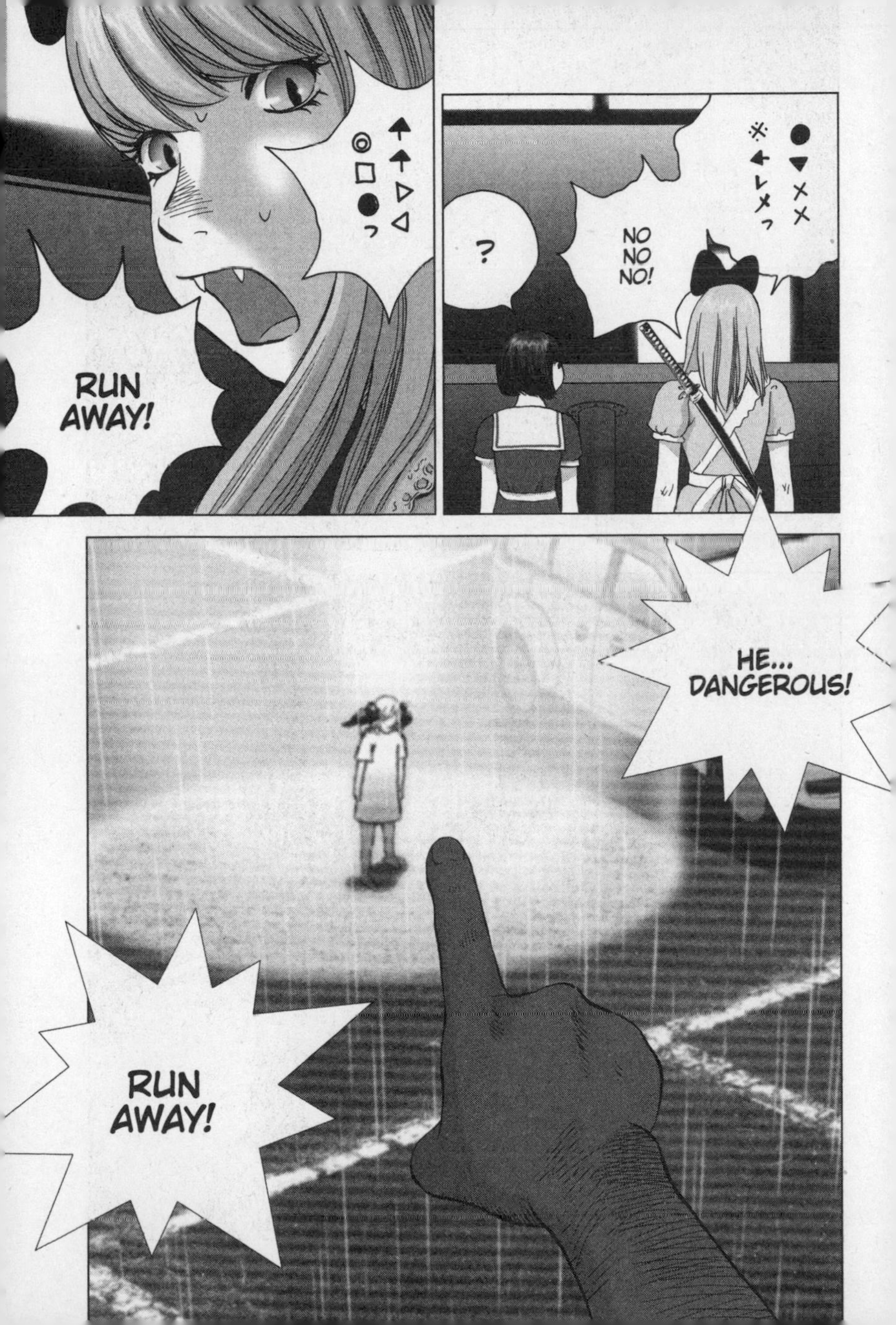
NO NO NO!
?
RUN AWAY!
HE... DANGEROUS!
RUN AWAY!

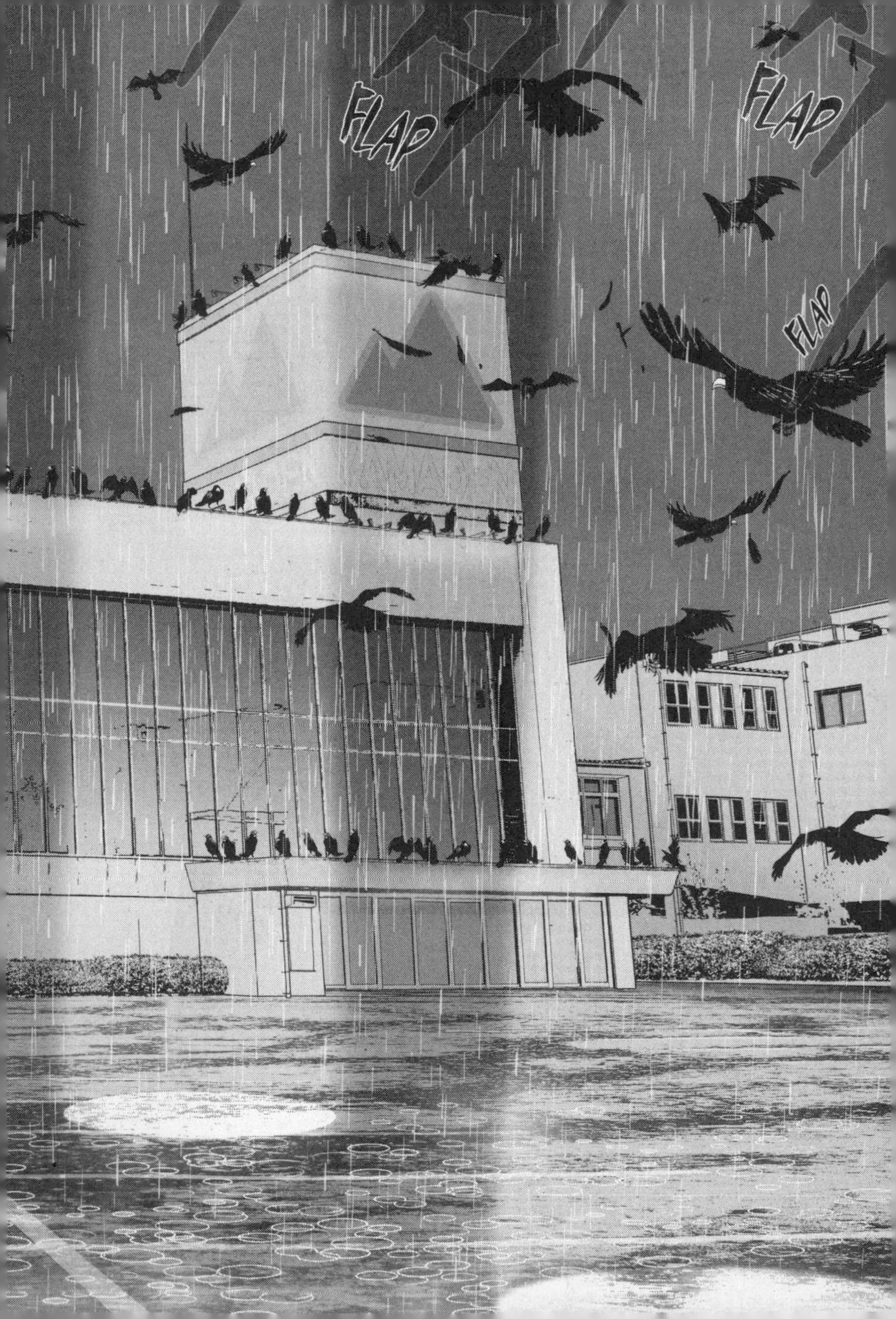
FLAP
FLAP
FLAP

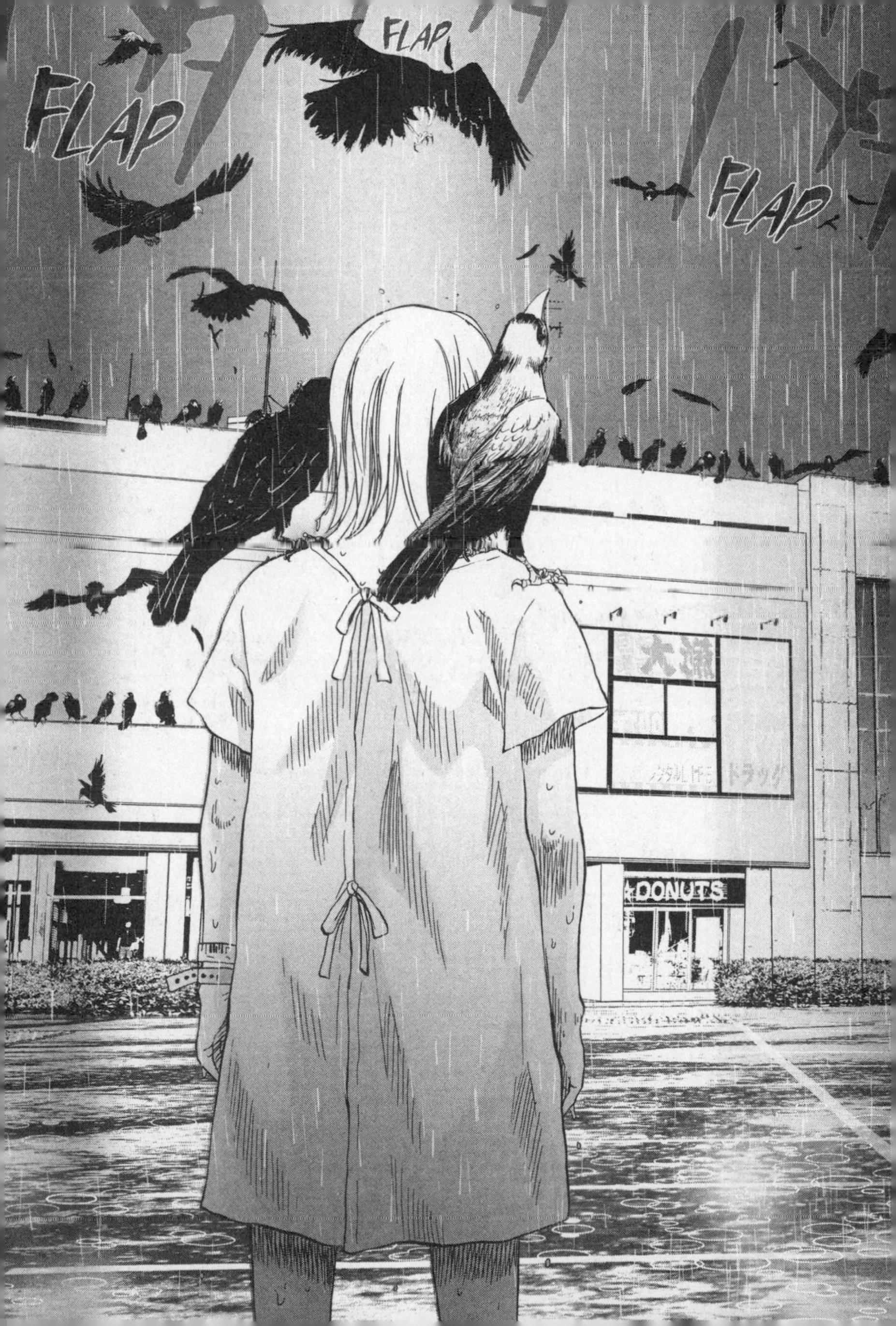
FLAP
FLAP
FLAP
DONUTS

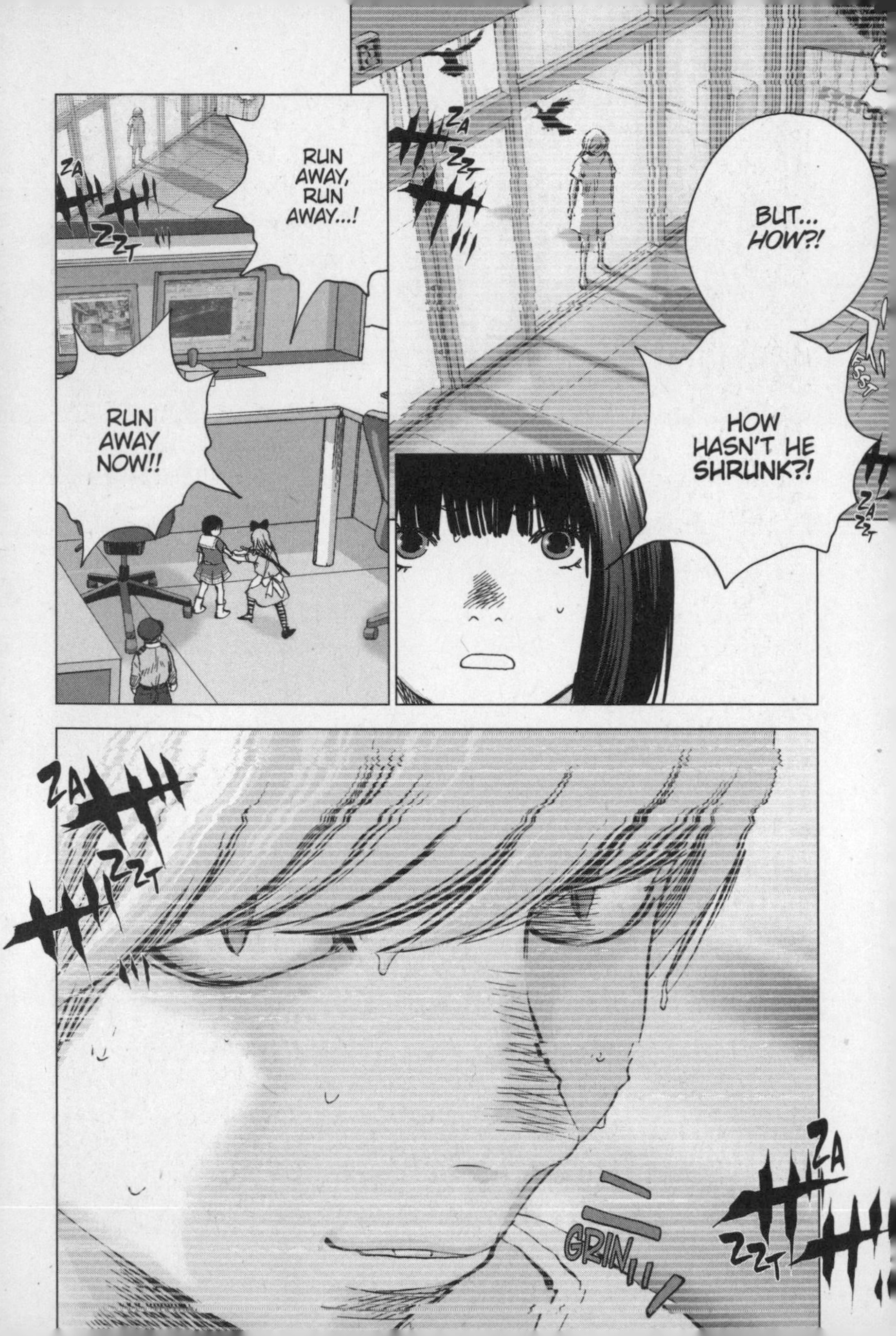
BUT... HOW?!
HOW HASN'T HE SHRUNK?!
ZA ZZZT
FSST
ZA ZZZT
ZA ZZZT
RUN AWAY, RUN AWAY...!
RUN AWAY NOW!!
ZA ZZZT
GRIN
ZA ZZZT

Chapter 13: A Boy

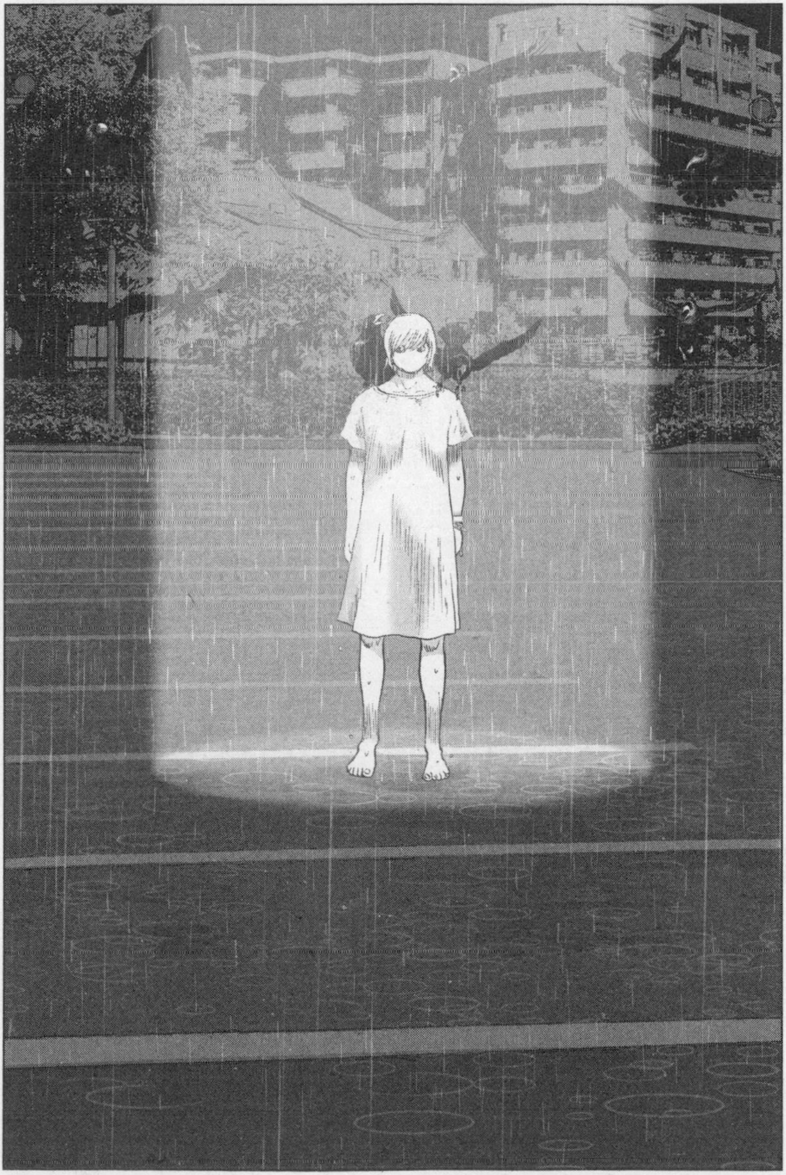

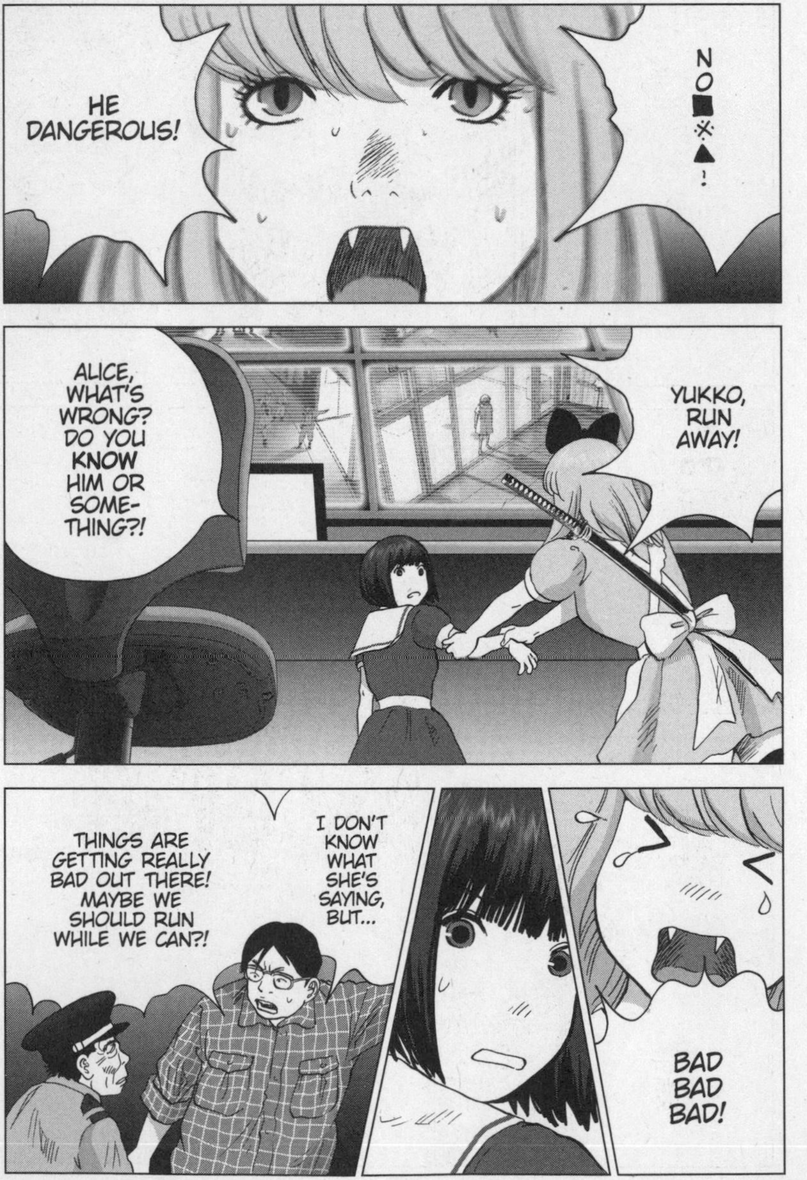
NO■※▲!
HE DANGEROUS!
YUKKO, RUN AWAY!
ALICE, WHAT'S WRONG? DO YOU KNOW HIM OR SOME-THING?!
BAD BAD BAD!
I DON'T KNOW WHAT SHE'S SAYING, BUT...
THINGS ARE GETTING REALLY BAD OUT THERE! MAYBE WE SHOULD RUN WHILE WE CAN?!

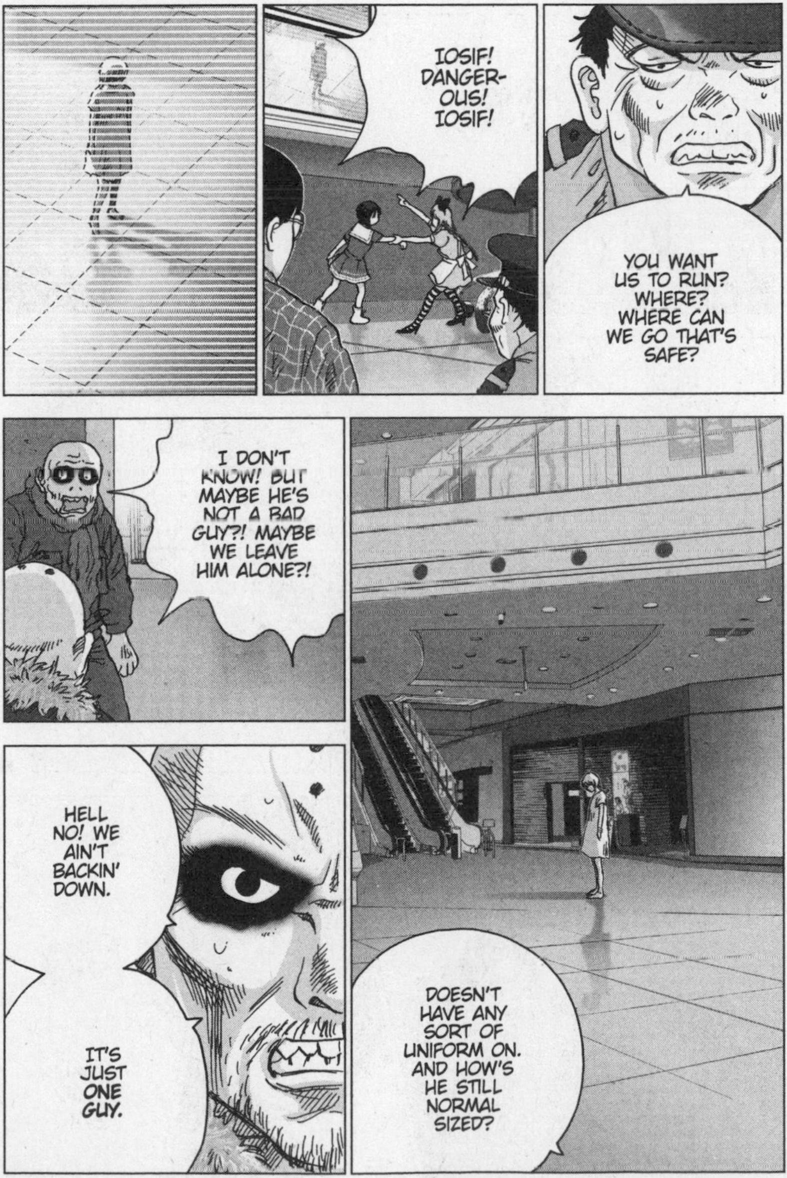
YOU WANT US TO RUN? WHERE? WHERE CAN WE GO THAT'S SAFE?
IOSIF! DANGER-OUS! IOSIF!
DOESN'T HAVE ANY SORT OF UNIFORM ON. AND HOW'S HE STILL NORMAL SIZED?
I DON'T KNOW! BUT MAYBE HE'S NOT A BAD GUY?! MAYBE WE LEAVE HIM ALONE?!
HELL NO! WE AIN'T BACKIN' DOWN.
IT'S JUST ONE GUY.

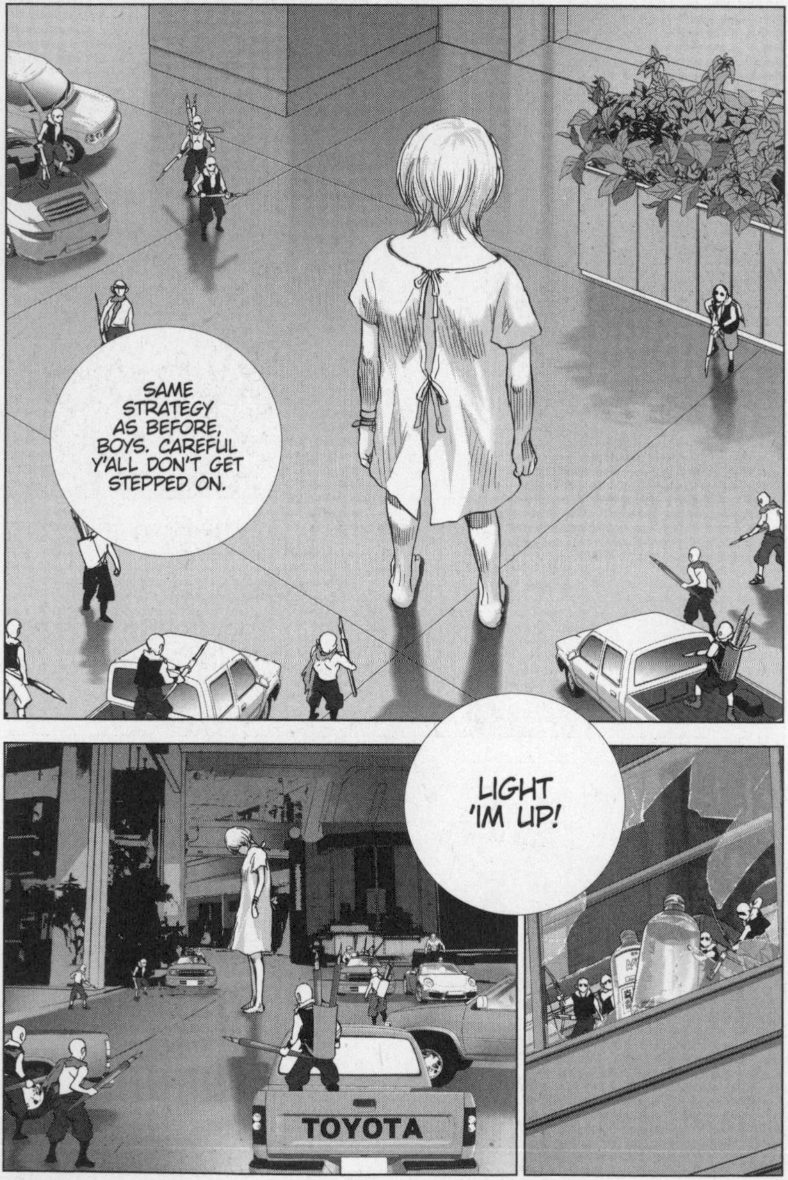
SAME STRATEGY AS BEFORE, BOYS. CAREFUL Y'ALL DON'T GET STEPPED ON.
LIGHT 'IM UP!
TOYOTA

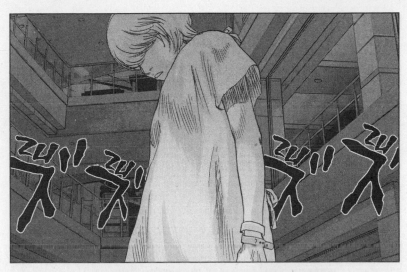

YOU THROW YOURS FIRST!

COME ON-- HURRY UP AND THROW THE DAMN SPEAR!

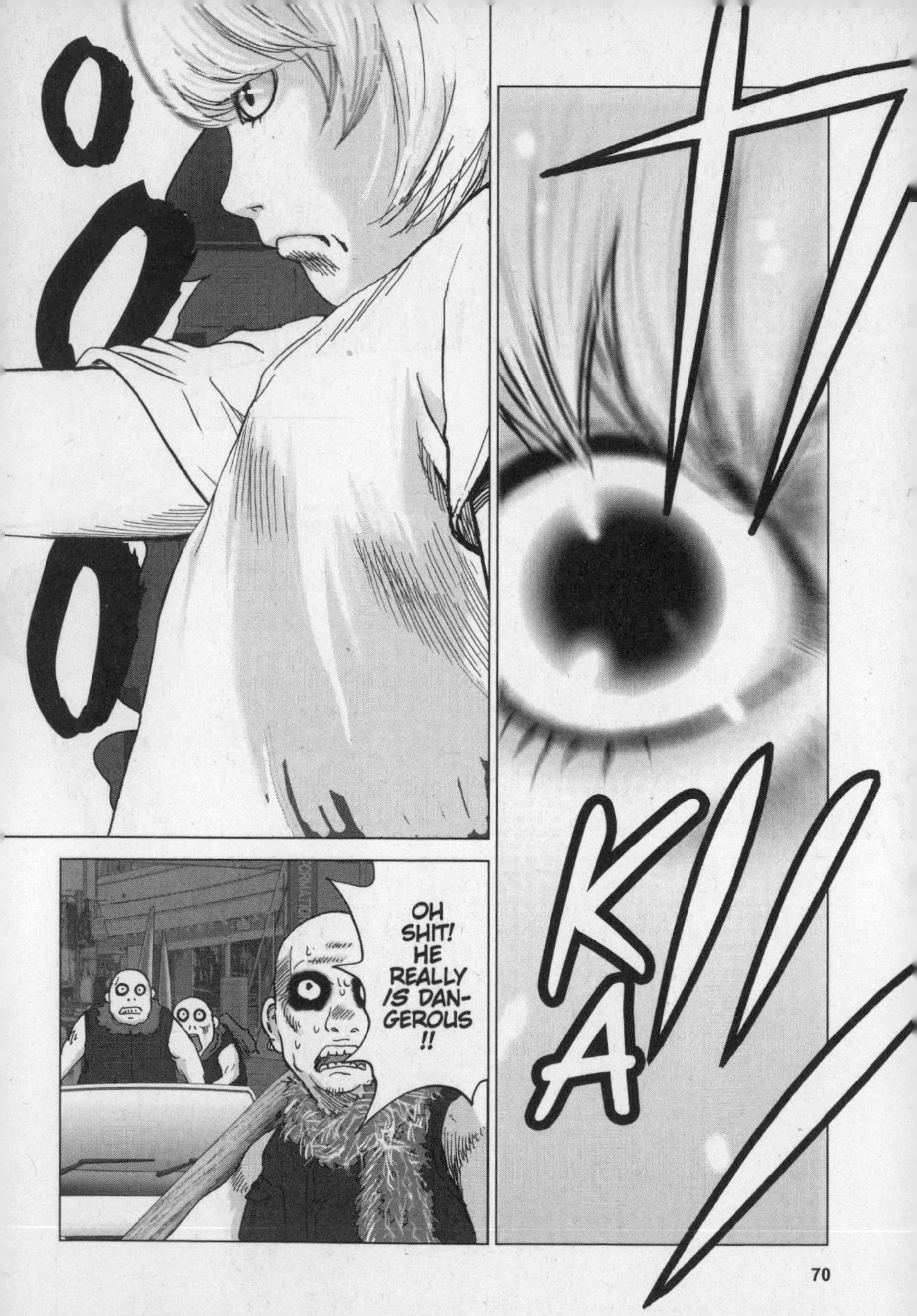
KA
OOO
OH SHIT! HE REALLY IS DANGEROUS!!

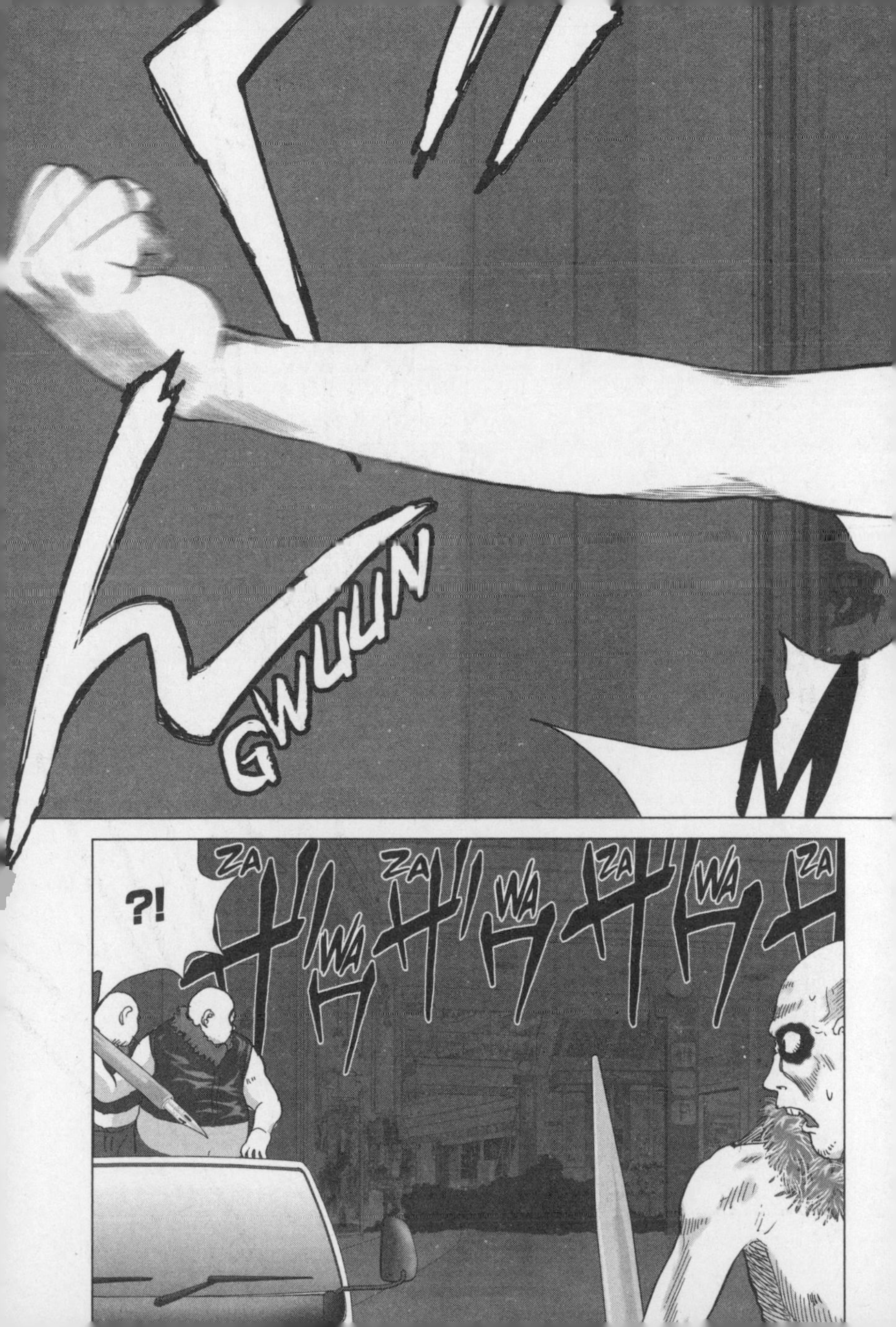
GWUUN
ZA WA ZA WA ZA WA ZA WA ZA
?!

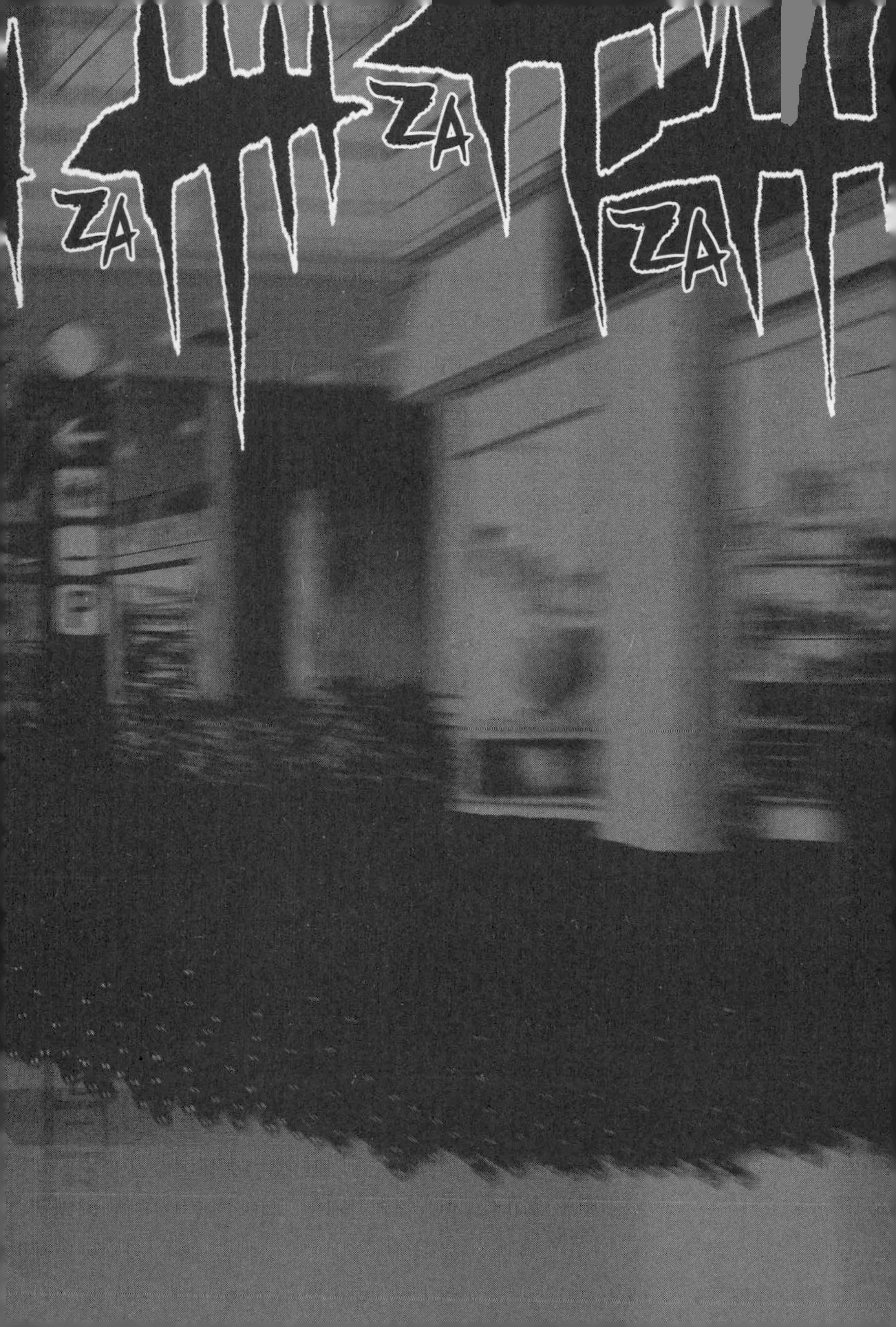
ZA
ZA
ZA

ZA
ZA
ZA

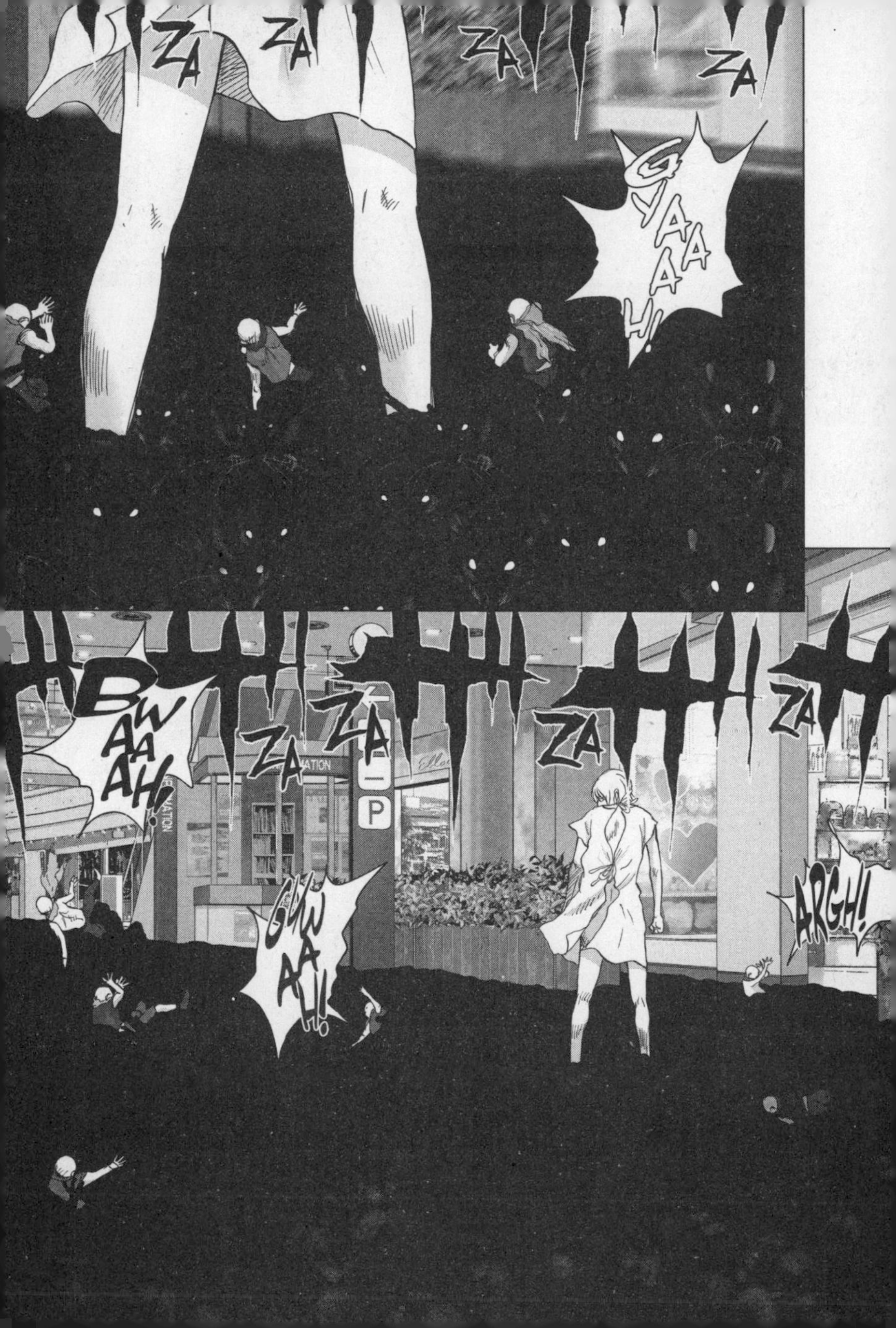
ZA
GYAAAAH!
ZA
ZA
ZA
ZA
ARGH!
ZA
ZA
ZA
BWAAAH!
GWAAAH!

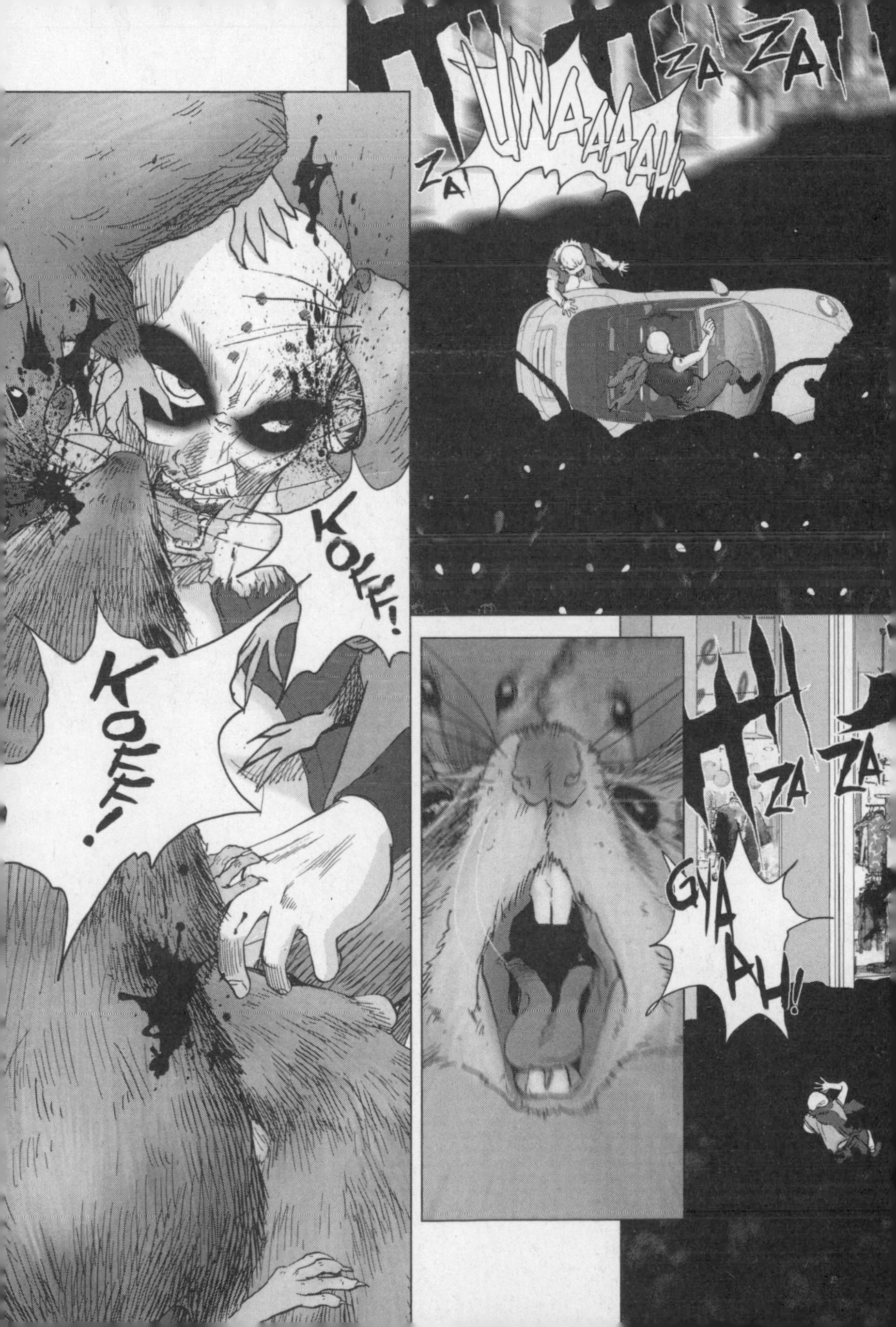
ZA ZA
UWAAAAH!!
ZA
ZA ZA
GYAAAH!
KOFF!
KOFF!

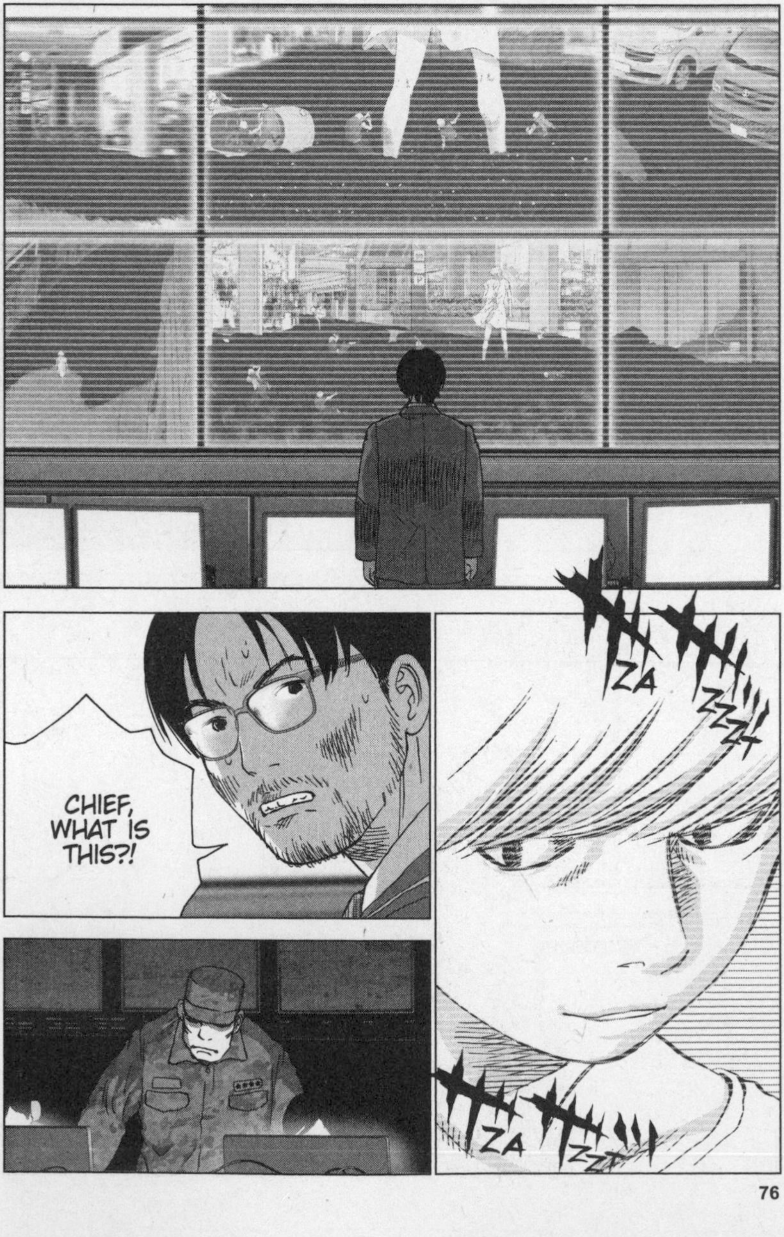
ZA
ZZZT
ZA
ZZZT
CHIEF, WHAT IS THIS?!

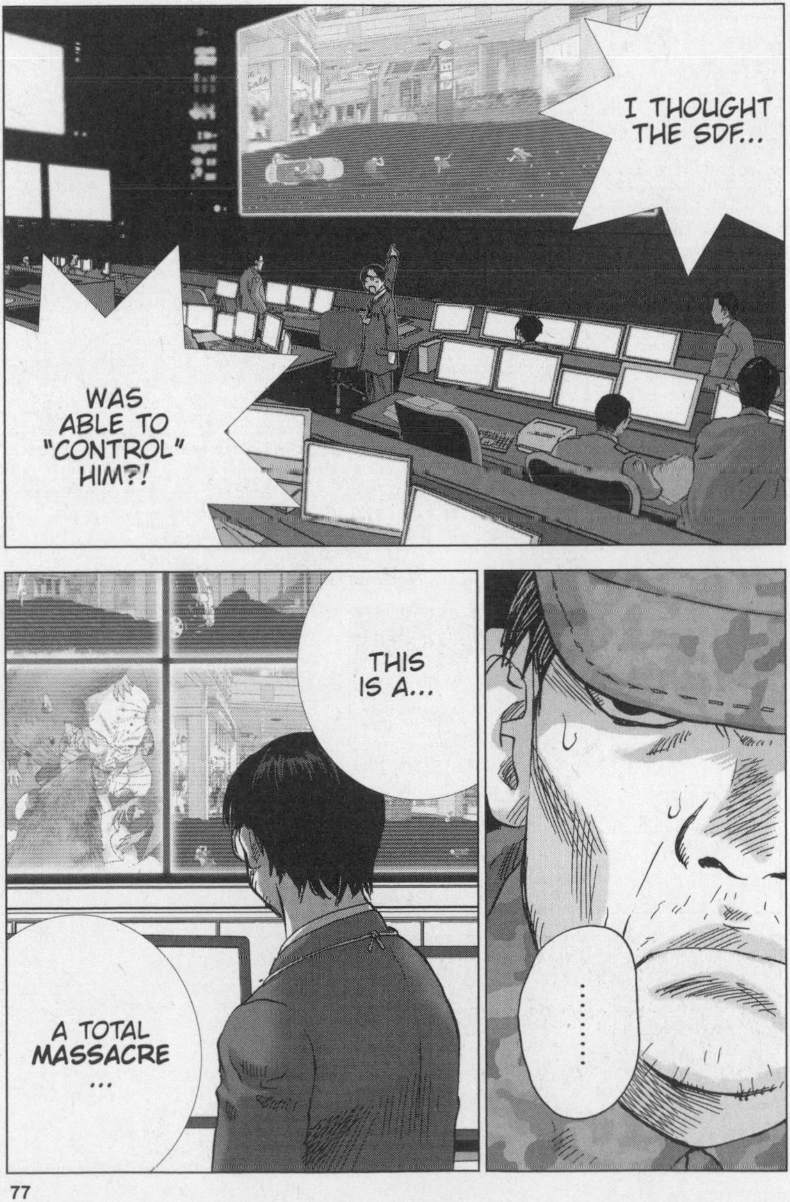
I THOUGHT THE SDF...
WAS ABLE TO "CONTROL" HIM?!
......
THIS IS A...
A TOTAL MASSACRE ...

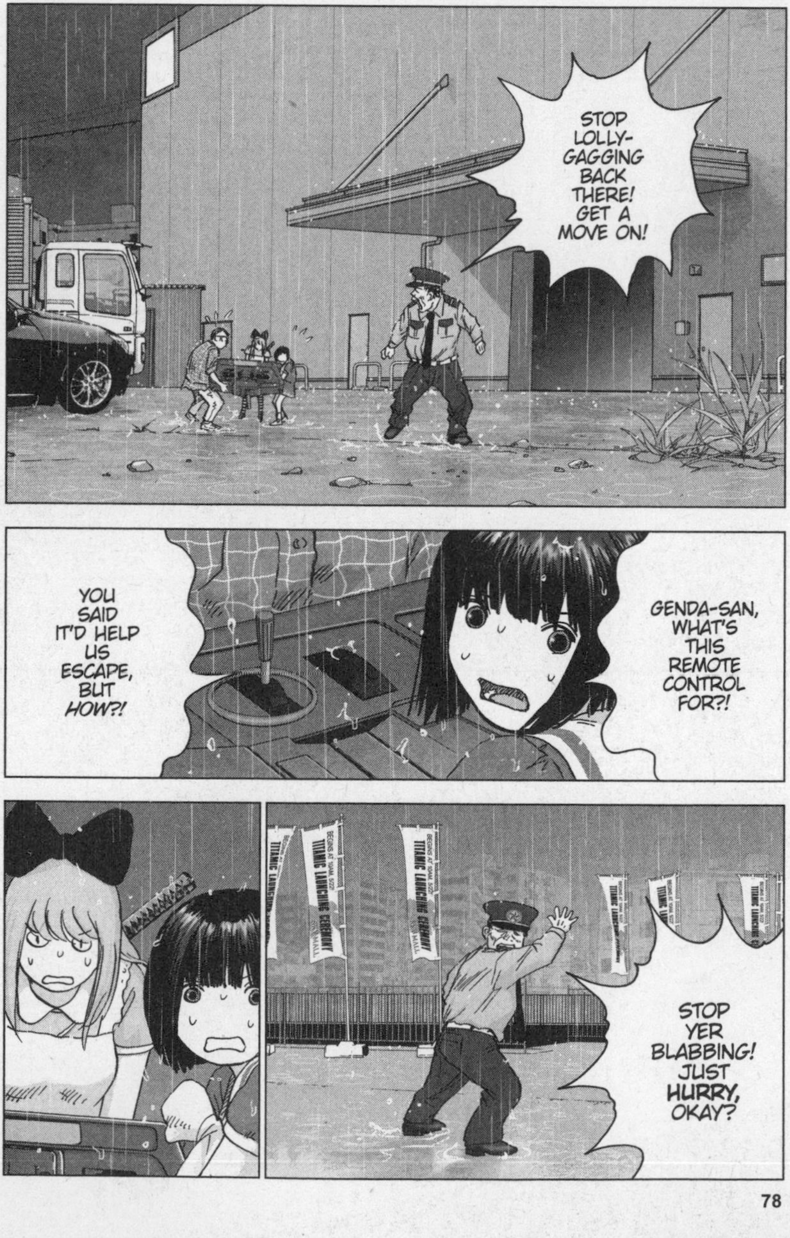
STOP LOLLY-GAGGING BACK THERE! GET A MOVE ON!
GENDA-SAN, WHAT'S THIS REMOTE CONTROL FOR?!
YOU SAID IT'D HELP US ESCAPE, BUT *HOW*?!
TITANIC LAUNCHING CEREMONY
STOP YER BLABBING! JUST **HURRY**, OKAY?

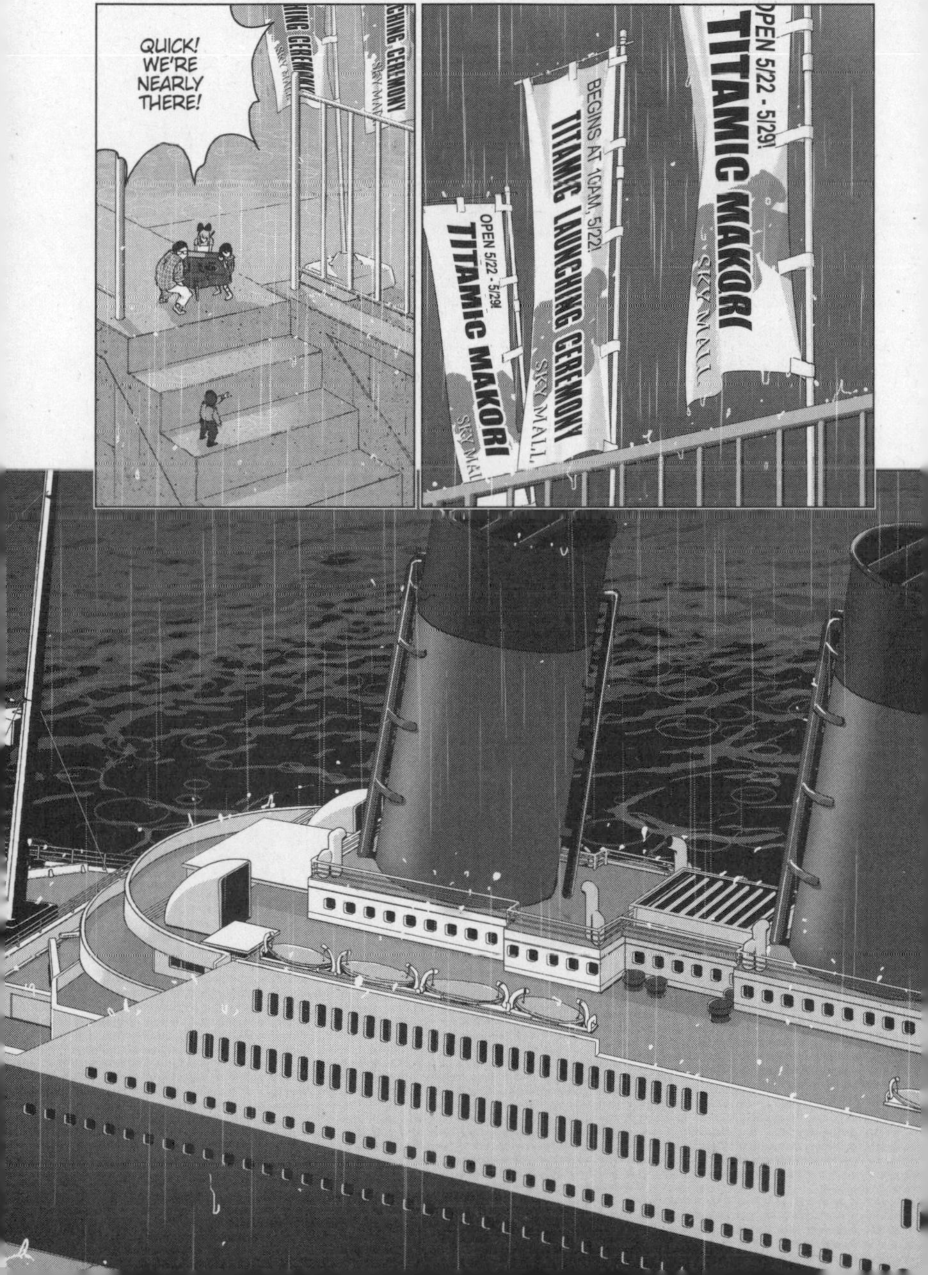
OPEN 5/22 - 5/29!
TITAMIC MAKORI
SKY MALL
BEGINS AT 10AM, 5/22!
TITAMIC LAUNCHING CEREMONY
SKY MALL
OPEN 5/22 - 5/29!
TITAMIC MAKORI
SKY MALL
QUICK! WE'RE NEARLY THERE!

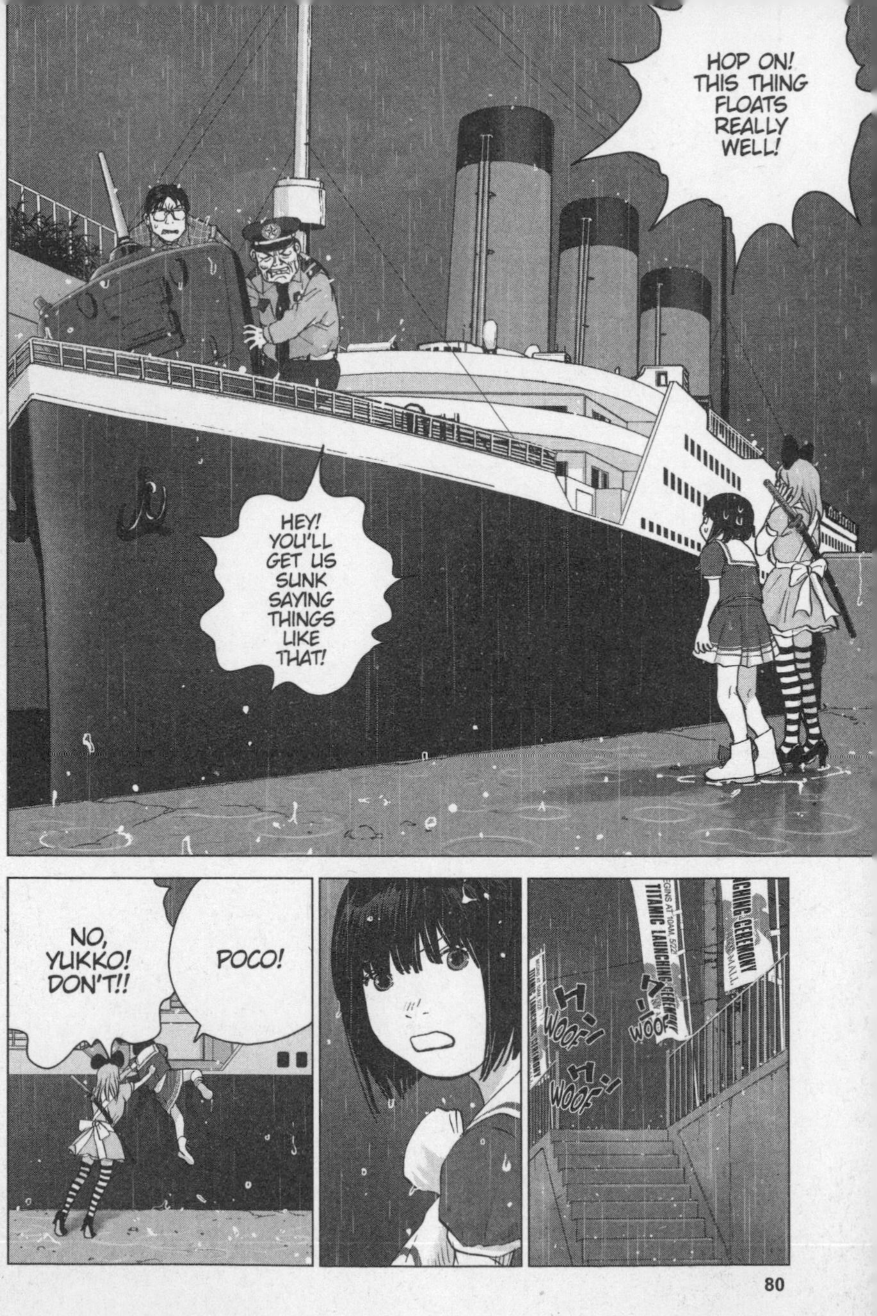
HOP ON! THIS THING FLOATS REALLY WELL!
HEY! YOU'LL GET US SUNK SAYING THINGS LIKE THAT!
CHING CEREMONY
MALL
EGINS AT 10AM, 5/22!
TITAMIC LAUNCHING CEREMONY
WOOF
WOOF
WOOF
POCO!
NO, YUKKO! DON'T!!

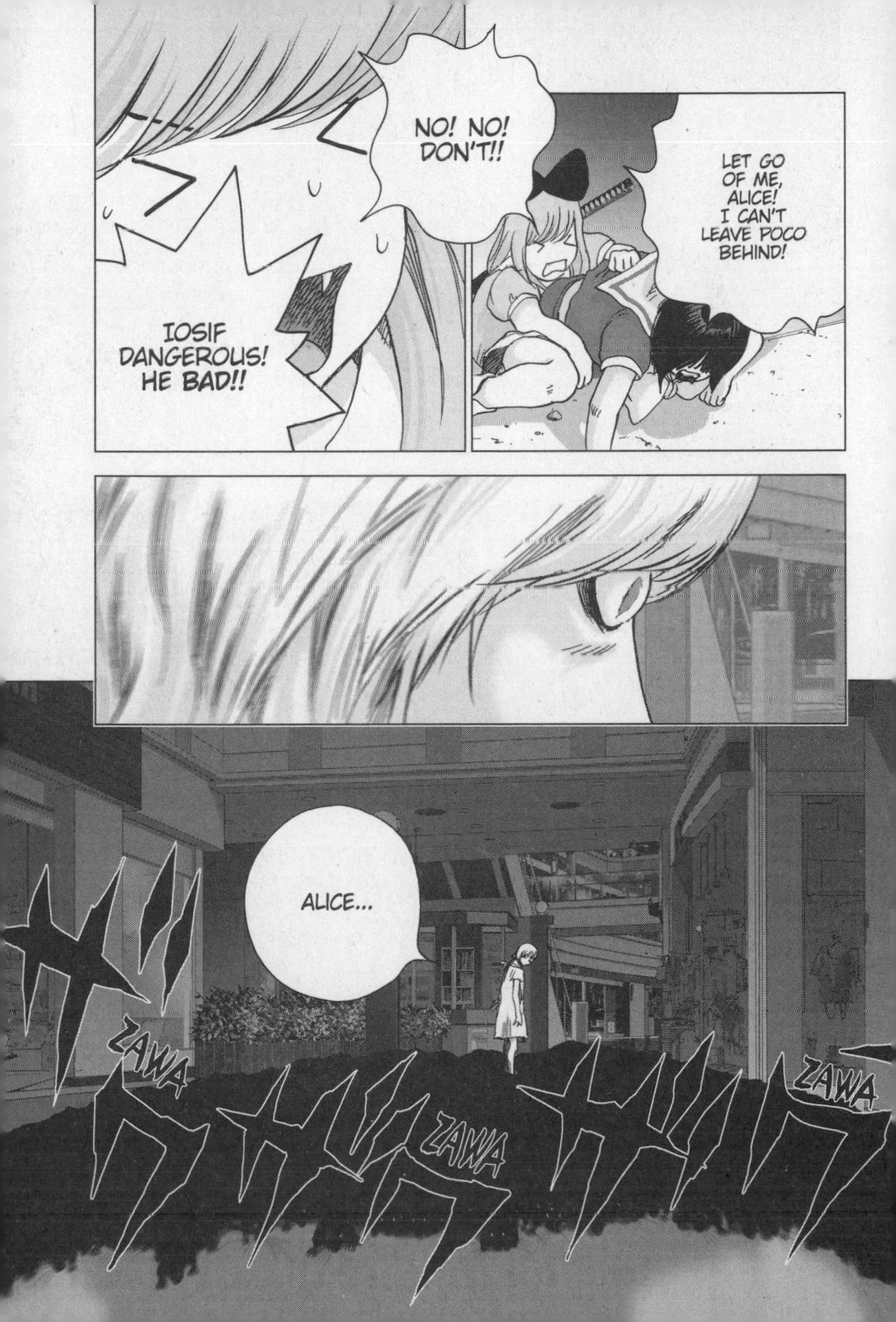
LET GO OF ME, ALICE! I CAN'T LEAVE POCO BEHIND!
NO! NO! DON'T!!
IOSIF DANGEROUS! HE BAD!!
ALICE...
ZAWA
ZAWA
ZAWA

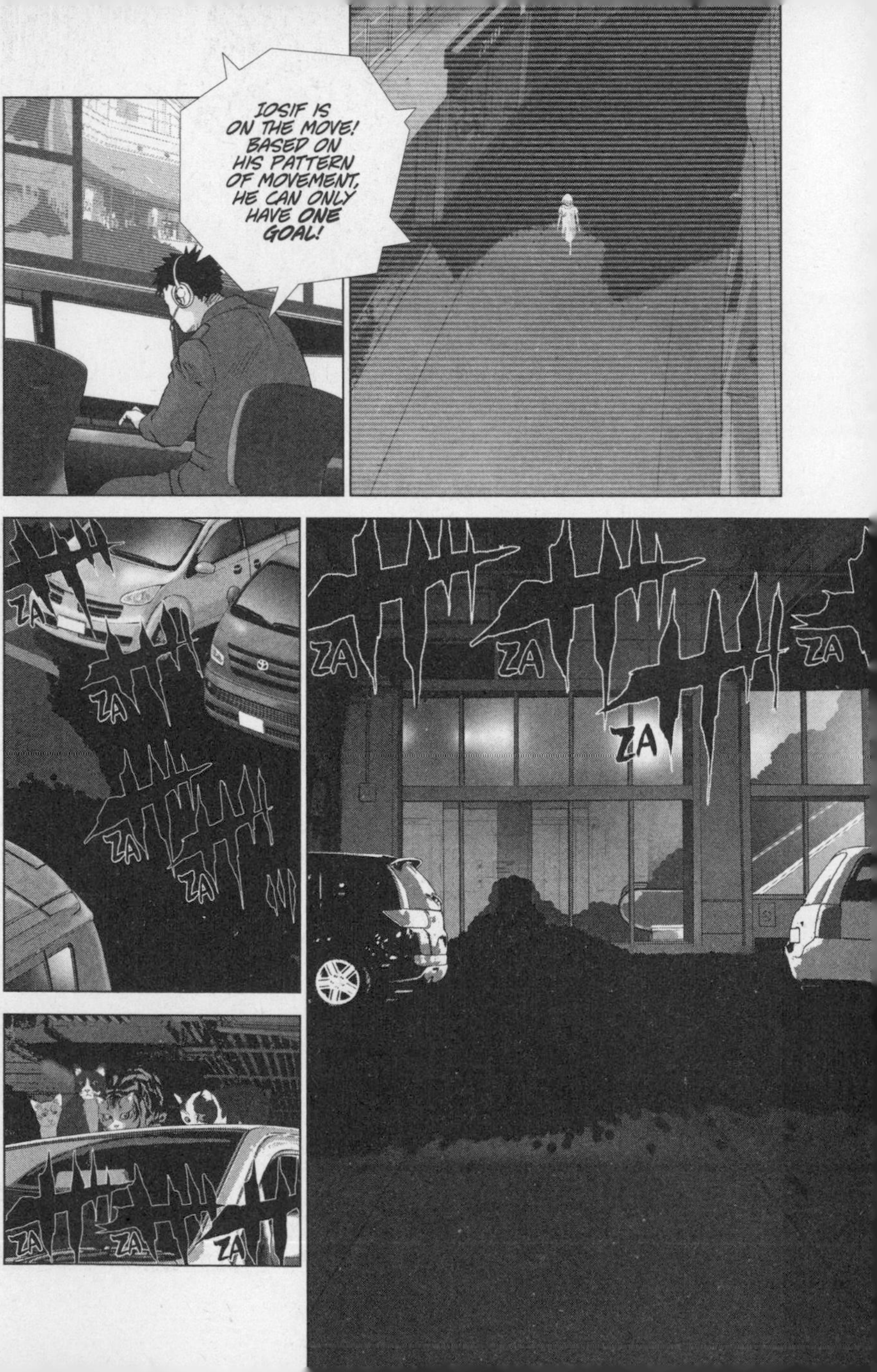
IOSIF IS ON THE MOVE! BASED ON HIS PATTERN OF MOVEMENT, HE CAN ONLY HAVE ONE GOAL!
ZA
ZA
ZA
ZA
ZA
ZA
ZA
ZA
ZA
ZA
ZA
ZA

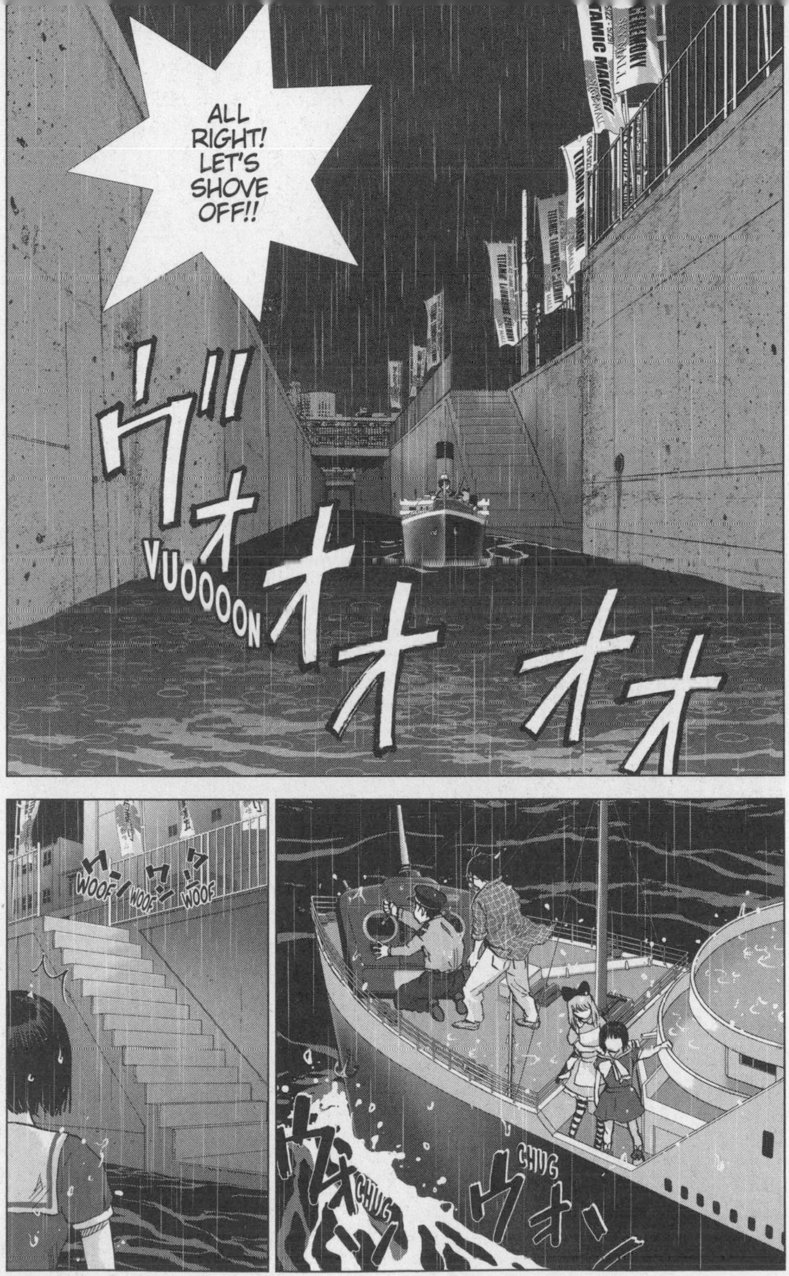
ALL RIGHT! LET'S SHOVE OFF!!
ヴォオオオオ
VUOOOON
ウォン
CHUG
ウォン
CHUG
ワン! ワン! ワン!
WOOF WOOF WOOF

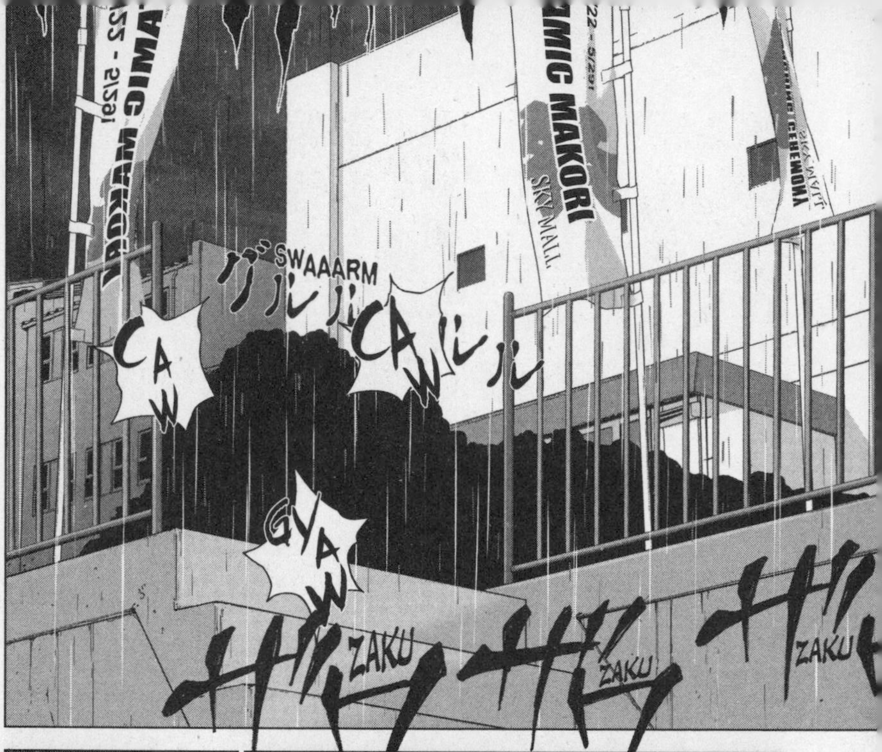
SWAAARM
CAW
CAW
GYAAW
ZAKU
ZAKU
ZAKU

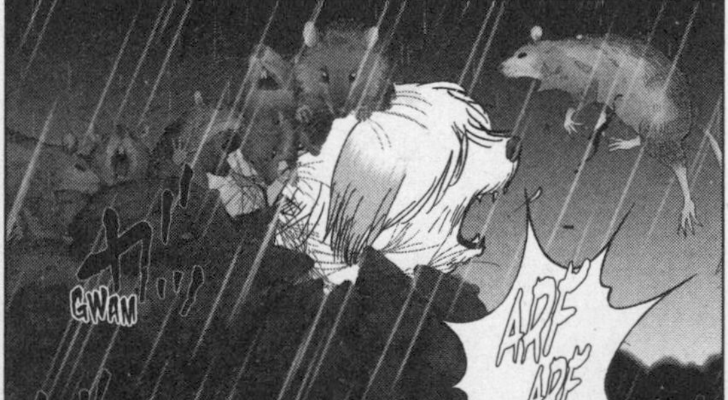
ARF
ARF
ARF
ARF
ARF
GWAM
GWAM
GWAM
GWAM
GWAM
GWAM

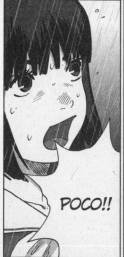

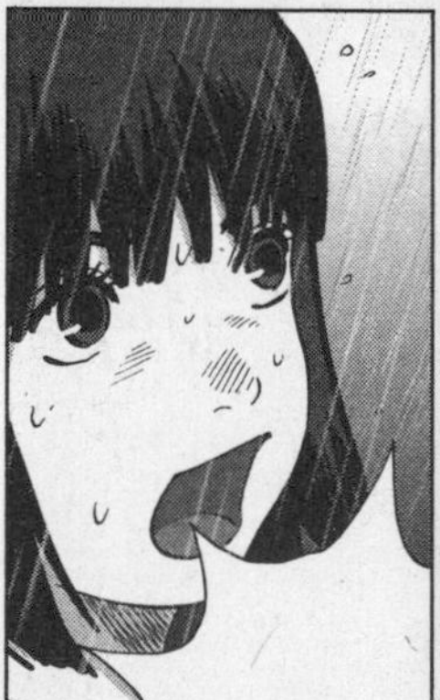
POCO!!

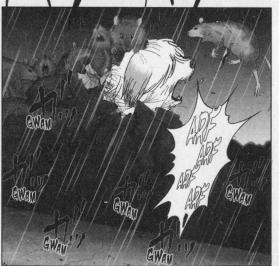

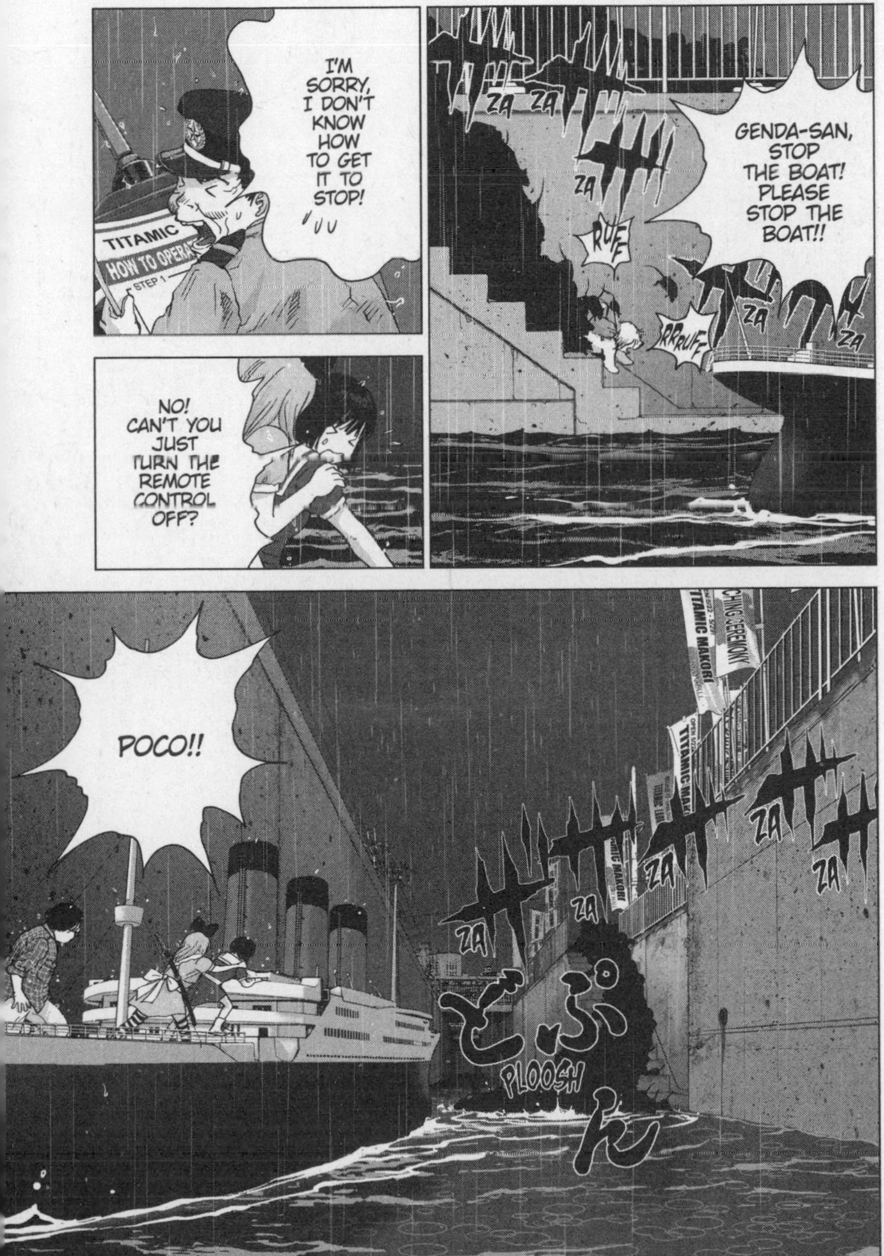
ZA ZA
ZA
GENDA-SAN, STOP THE BOAT! PLEASE STOP THE BOAT!!
RUFF
RRRUFF
ZA
ZA
I'M SORRY, I DON'T KNOW HOW TO GET IT TO STOP!
TITAMIC
HOW TO OPERA
STEP 1
NO! CAN'T YOU JUST TURN THE REMOTE CONTROL OFF?
TITAMIC MAKORI
POCO!!
ZA
ZA
ZA
ZA
ZA
どぷん
PLOOSH

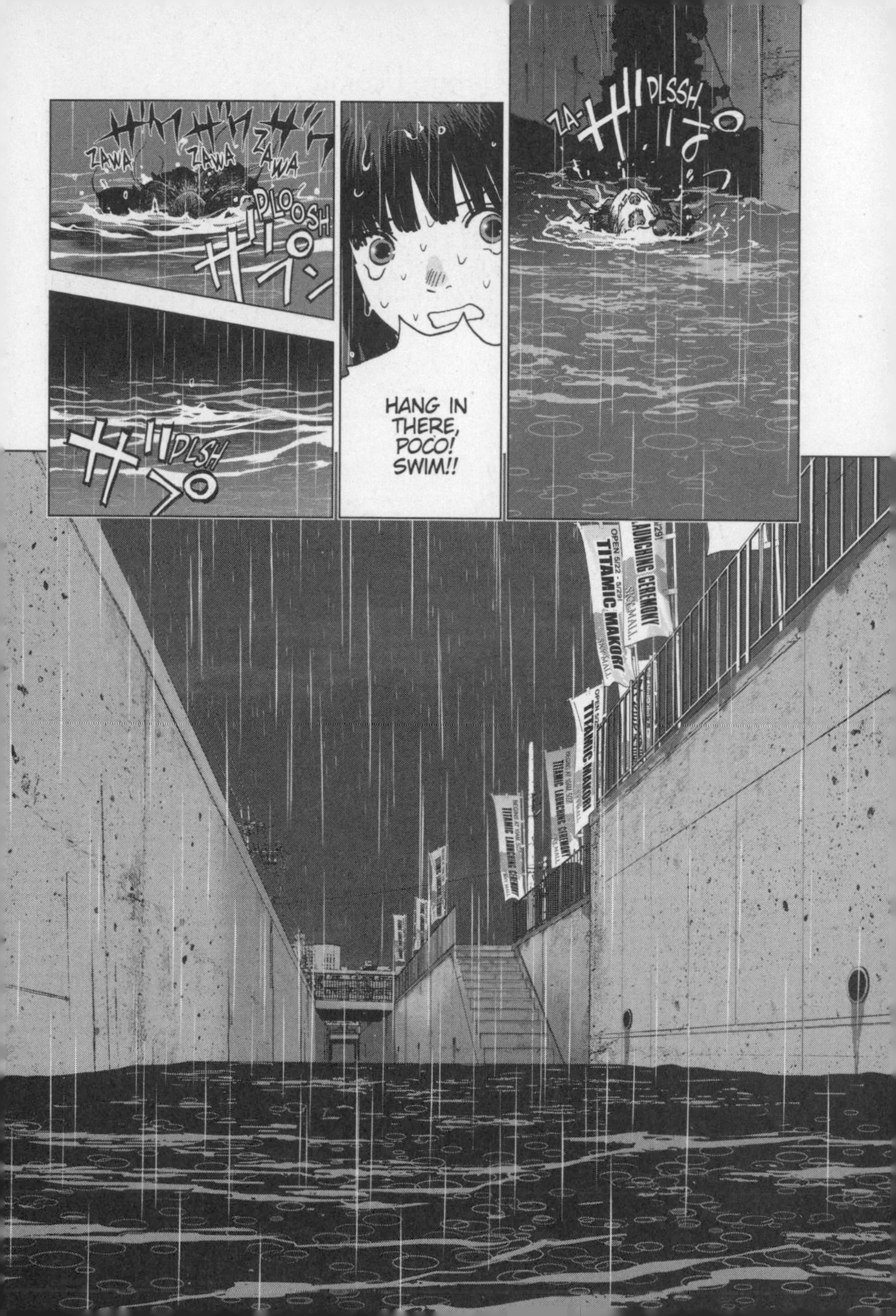
ZA-
PLSSH
HANG IN THERE, POCO! SWIM!!
ZAWA ZAWA ZAWA
PLOOSH
PLSH
OPEN 5/22 - 5/29!
TITAMIC MAKORI
SKYMALL
TITAMIC MAKORI
TITAMIC LAUNCHING CEREMONY

Chapter 14: An Underground Canal

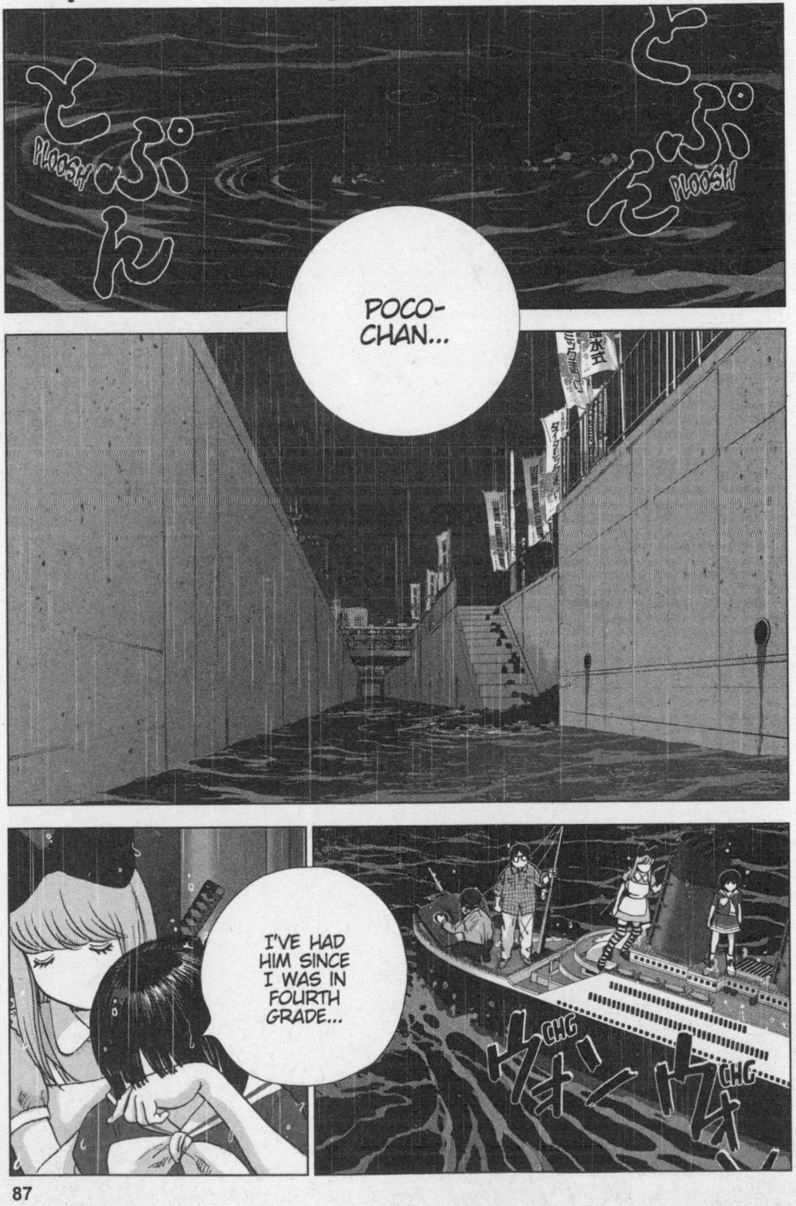
どぷん
PLOOSH
どぷん
PLOOSH
POCO-CHAN...
CHG
CHG
I'VE HAD HIM SINCE I WAS IN FOURTH GRADE...

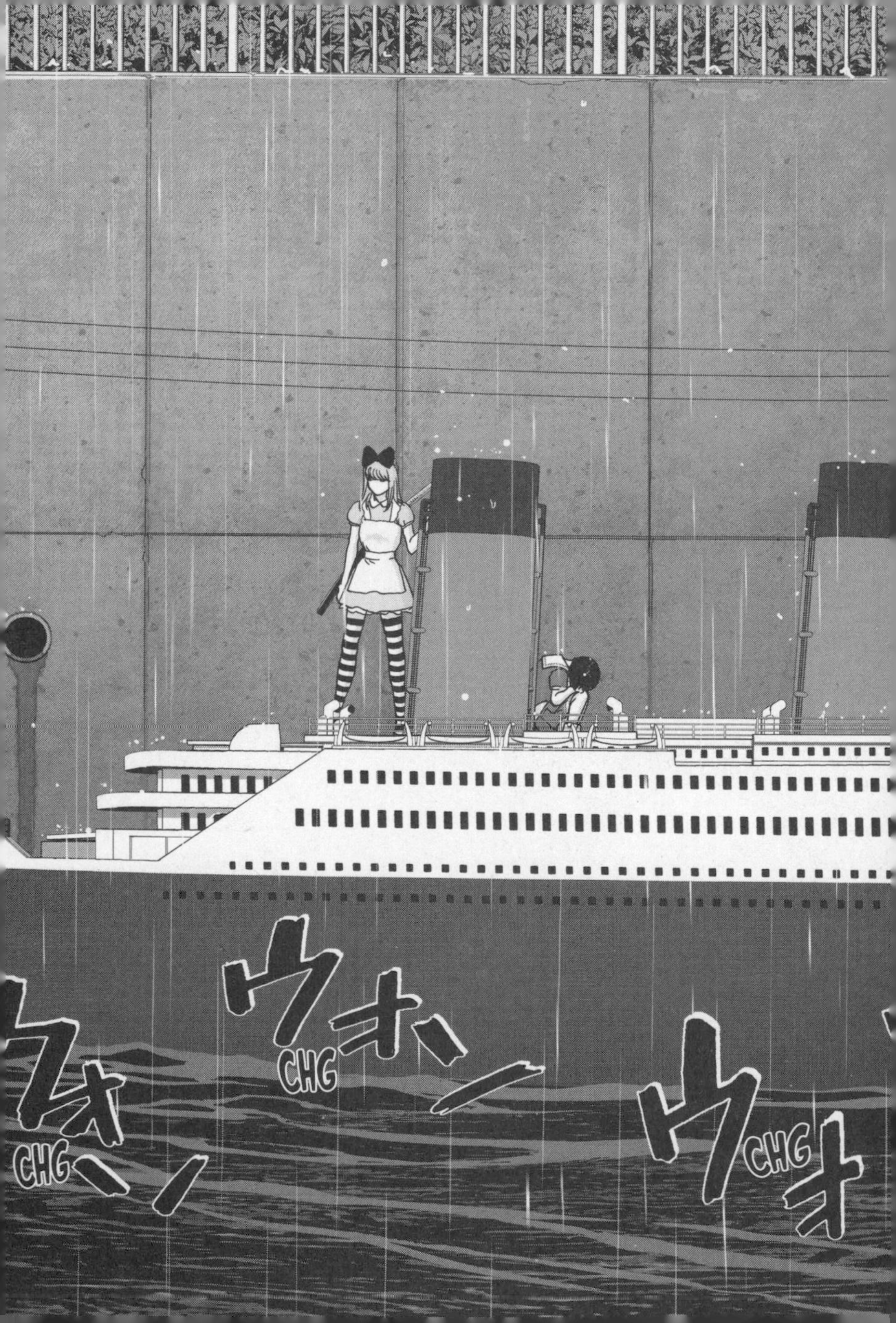
CHG
CHG
CHG

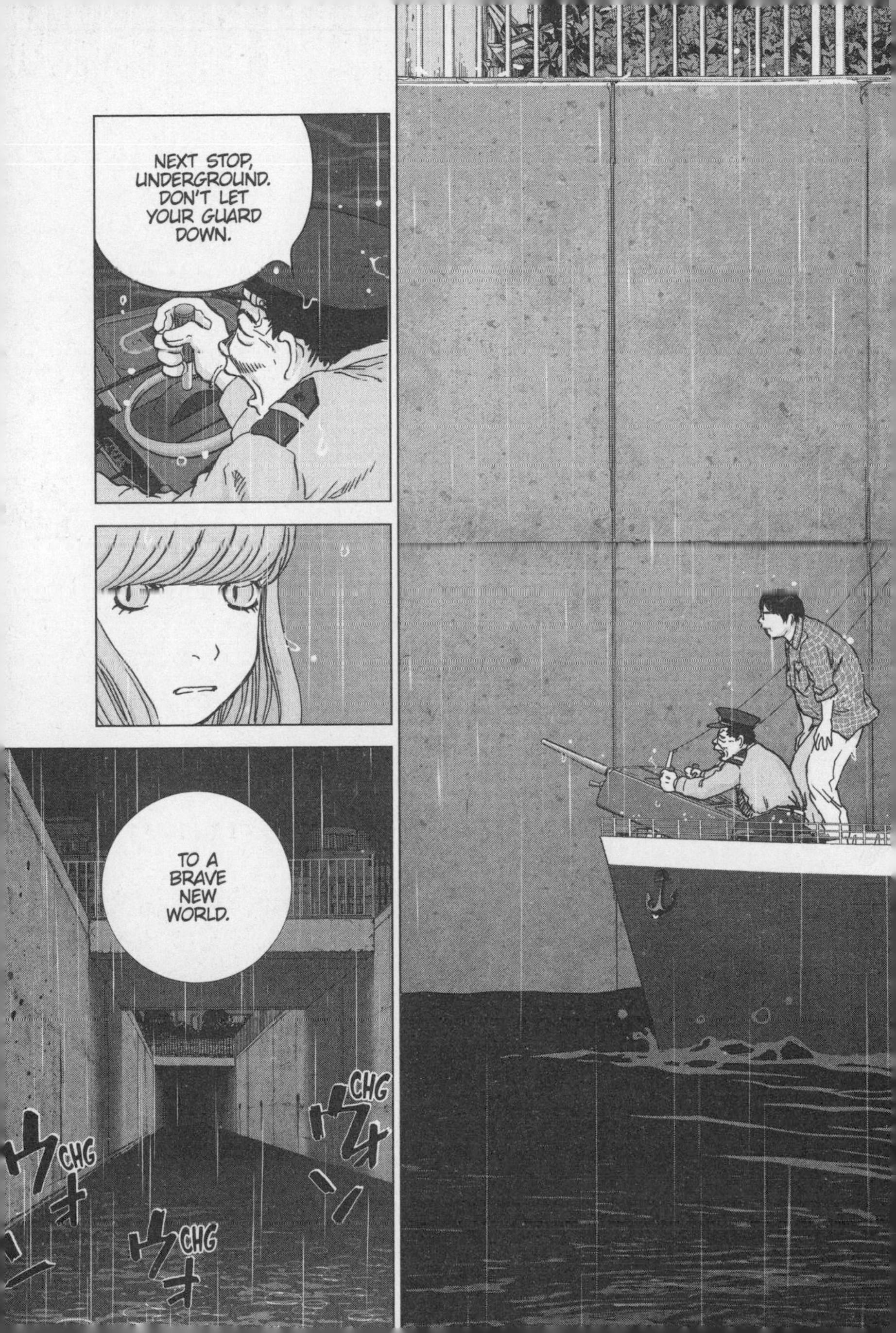
NEXT STOP, UNDERGROUND. DON'T LET YOUR GUARD DOWN.
TO A BRAVE NEW WORLD.
CHG
CHG
CHG

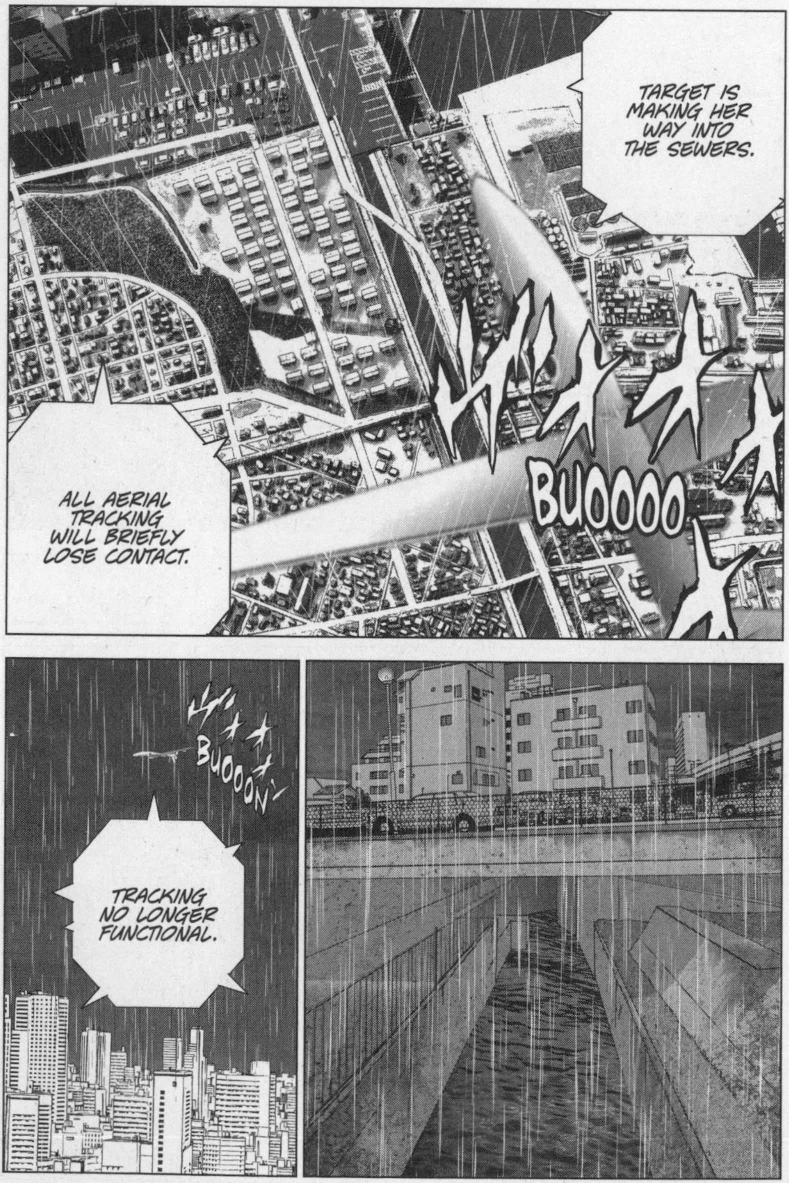
TARGET IS MAKING HER WAY INTO THE SEWERS.
BUOOOO
ALL AERIAL TRACKING WILL BRIEFLY LOSE CONTACT.
BUOOON
TRACKING NO LONGER FUNCTIONAL.

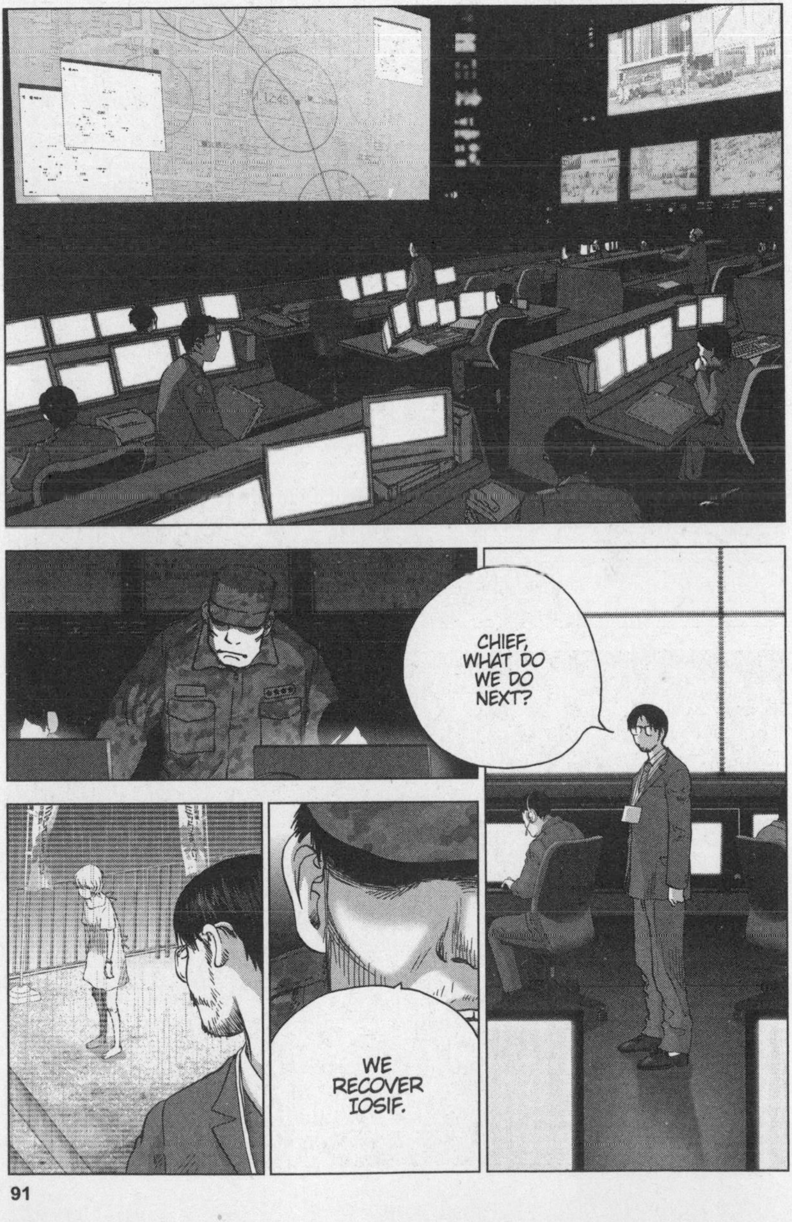
CHIEF, WHAT DO WE DO NEXT?
WE RECOVER IOSIF.

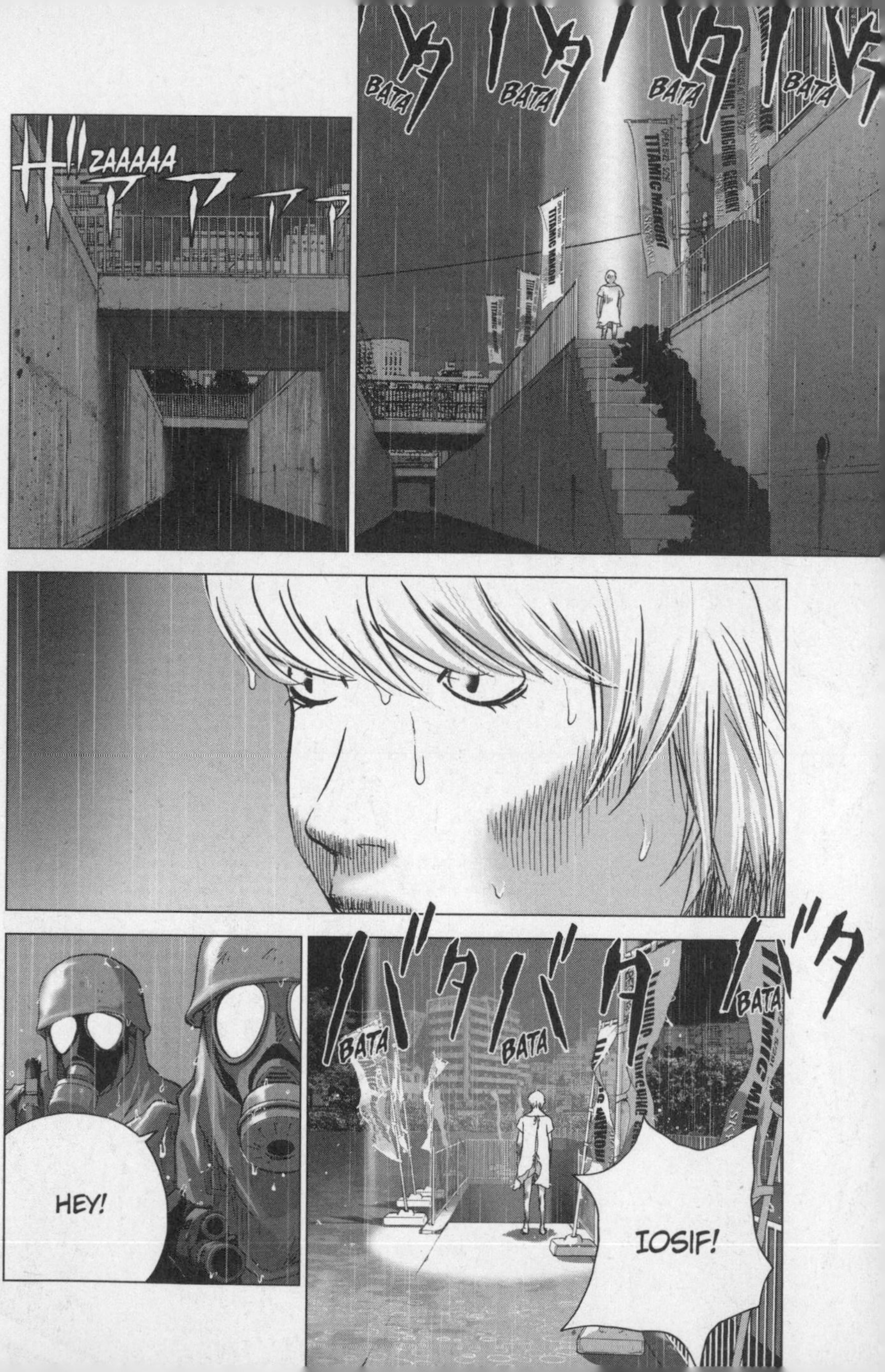
BATA
BATA
BATA
BATA
ZAAAAA
BATA
BATA
BATA
IOSIF!
HEY!

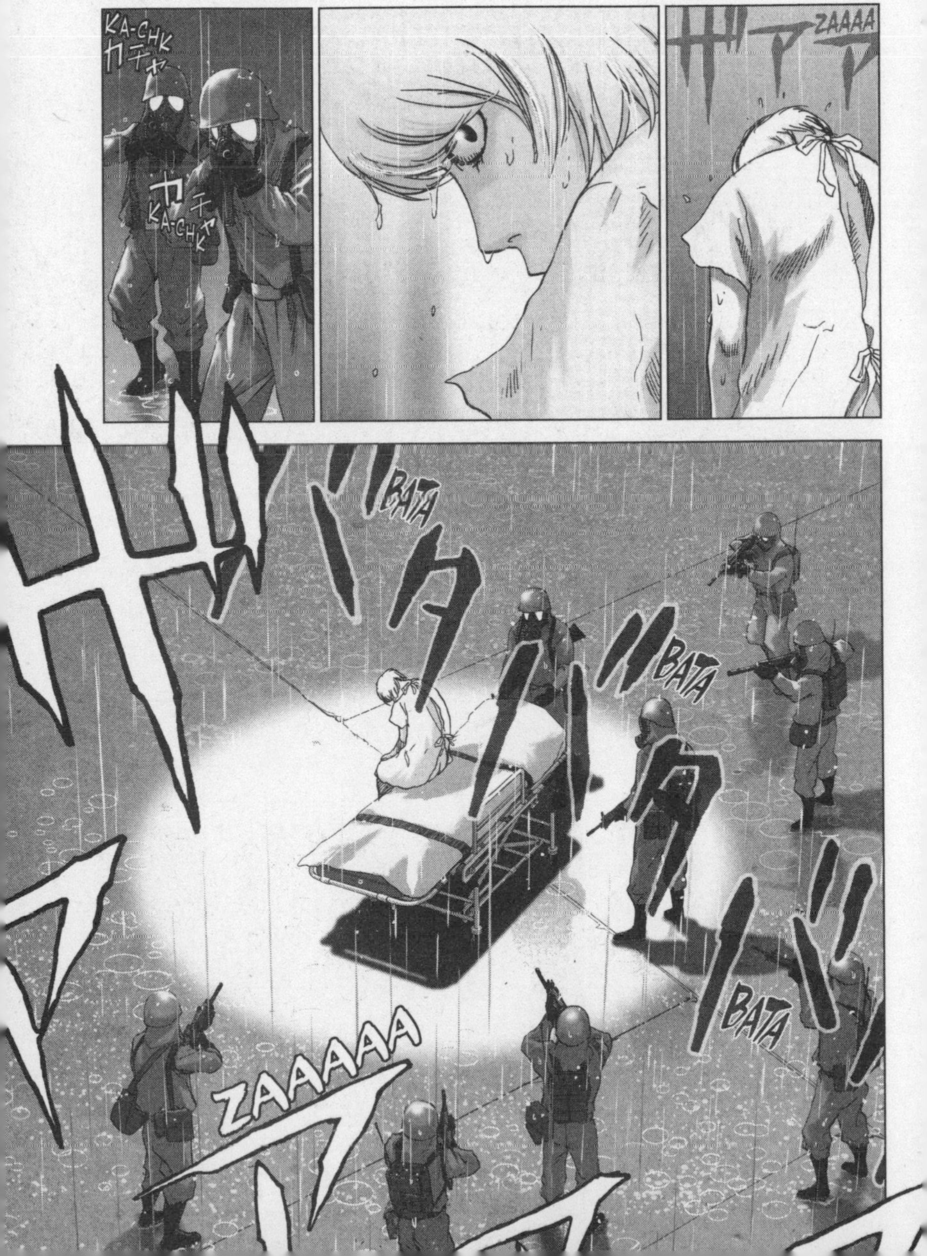
ZAAAA
KA-CHK
カチャ
カチャ
KA-CHK
BATA
BATA
BATA
ZAAAAA

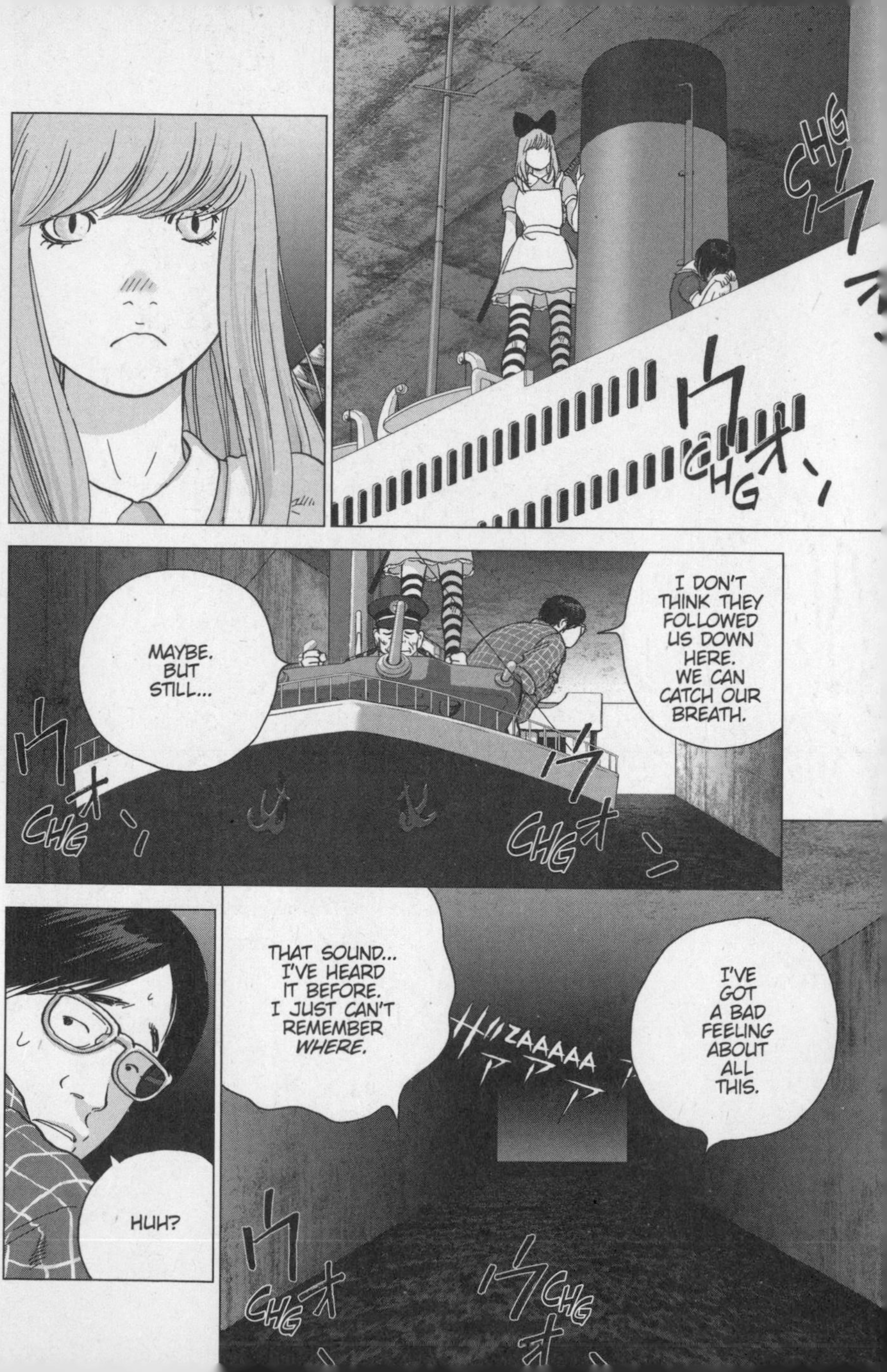
CHG
CHG
I DON'T THINK THEY FOLLOWED US DOWN HERE. WE CAN CATCH OUR BREATH.
MAYBE. BUT STILL...
CHG
CHG
I'VE GOT A BAD FEELING ABOUT ALL THIS.
THAT SOUND... I'VE HEARD IT BEFORE. I JUST CAN'T REMEMBER WHERE.
ZAAAAA
CHG
CHG
HUH?

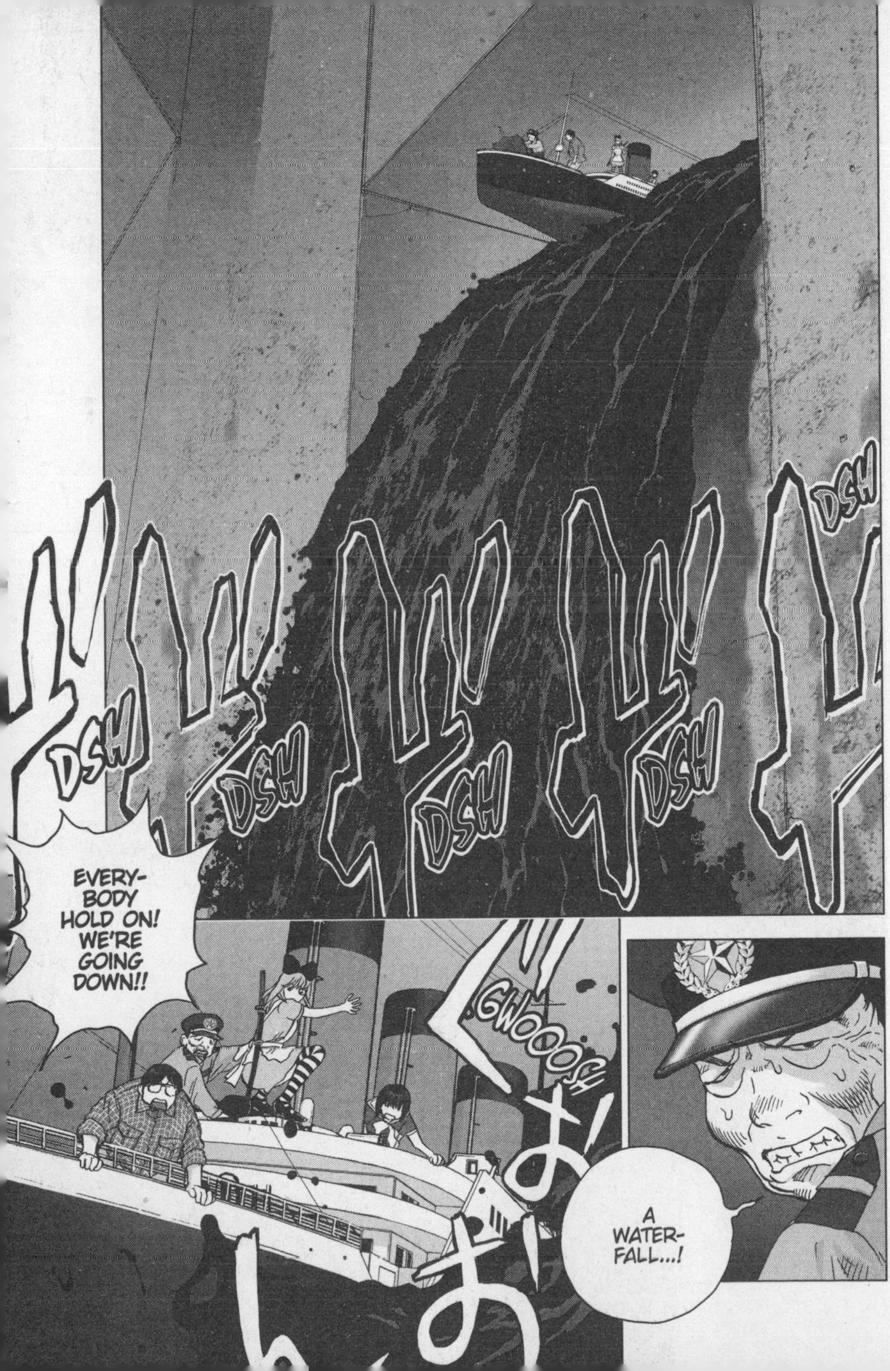
DSH
DSH
DSH
DSH
DSH
DSH
A WATER-FALL...!
EVERY-BODY HOLD ON! WE'RE GOING DOWN!!
GWOOOOSH
お!
お!

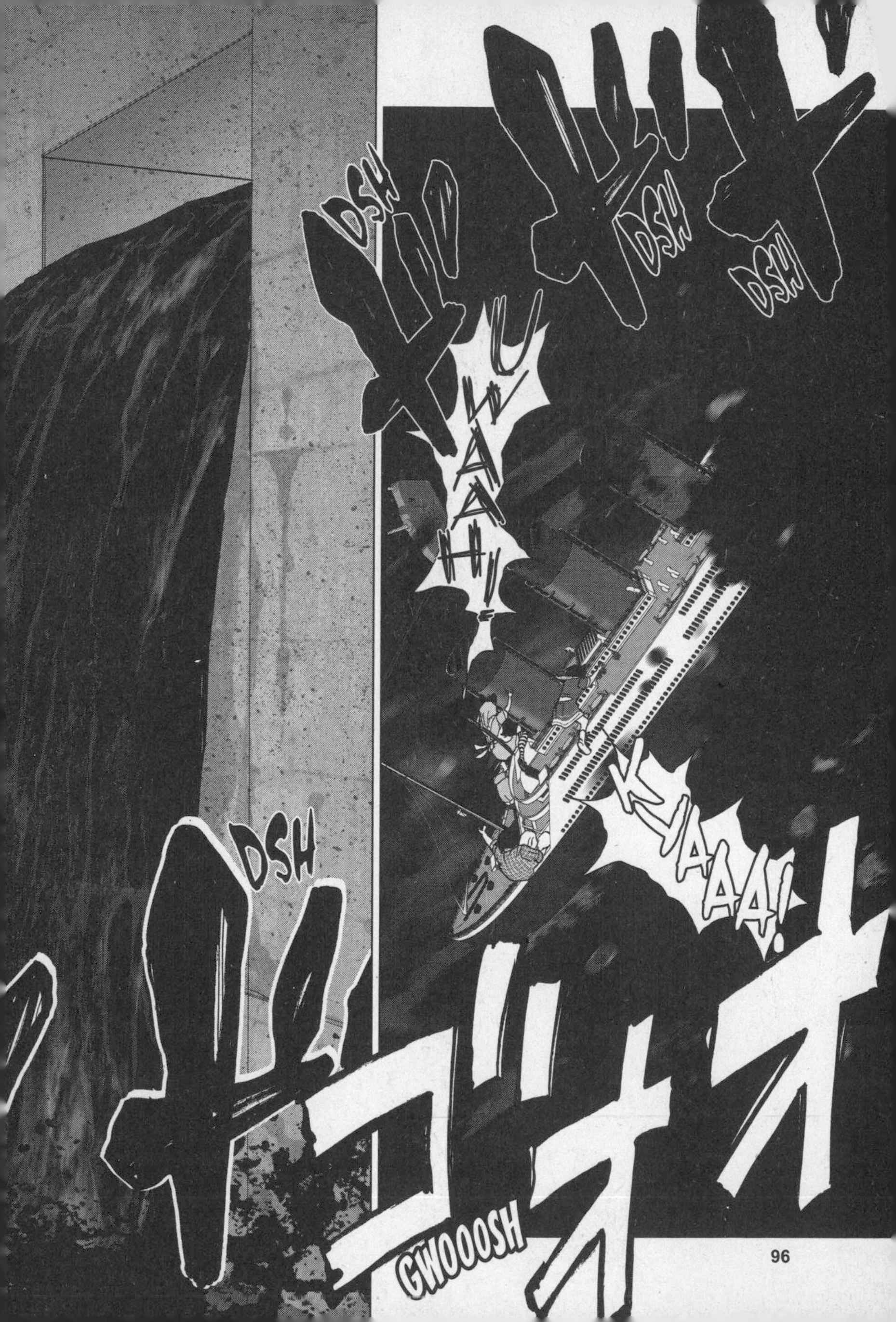
DSH
DSH
DSH
DSH
UWAAAHH!
KYAAAA!
DSH
GWOOOSH

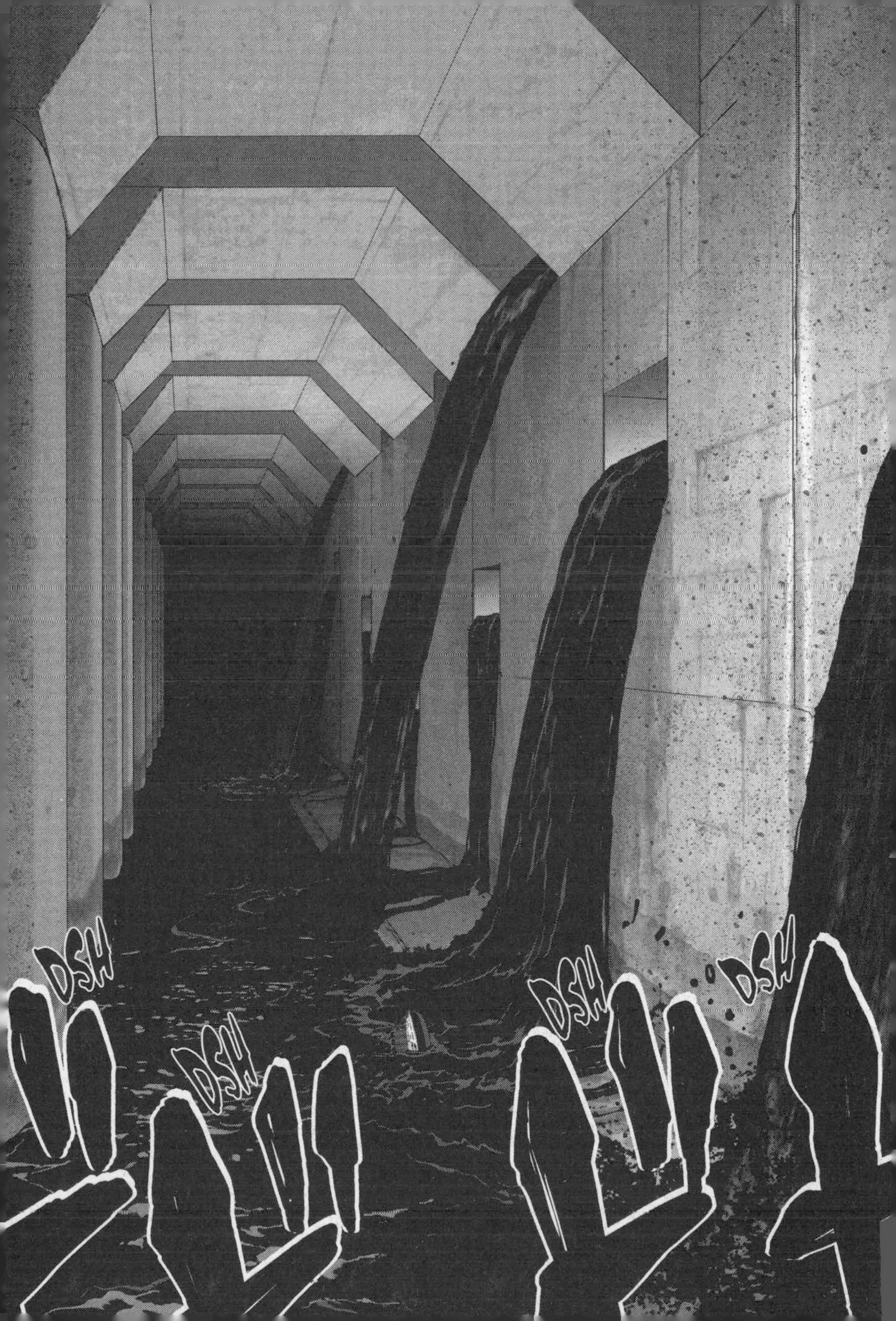
DSH
DSH
DSH
DSH

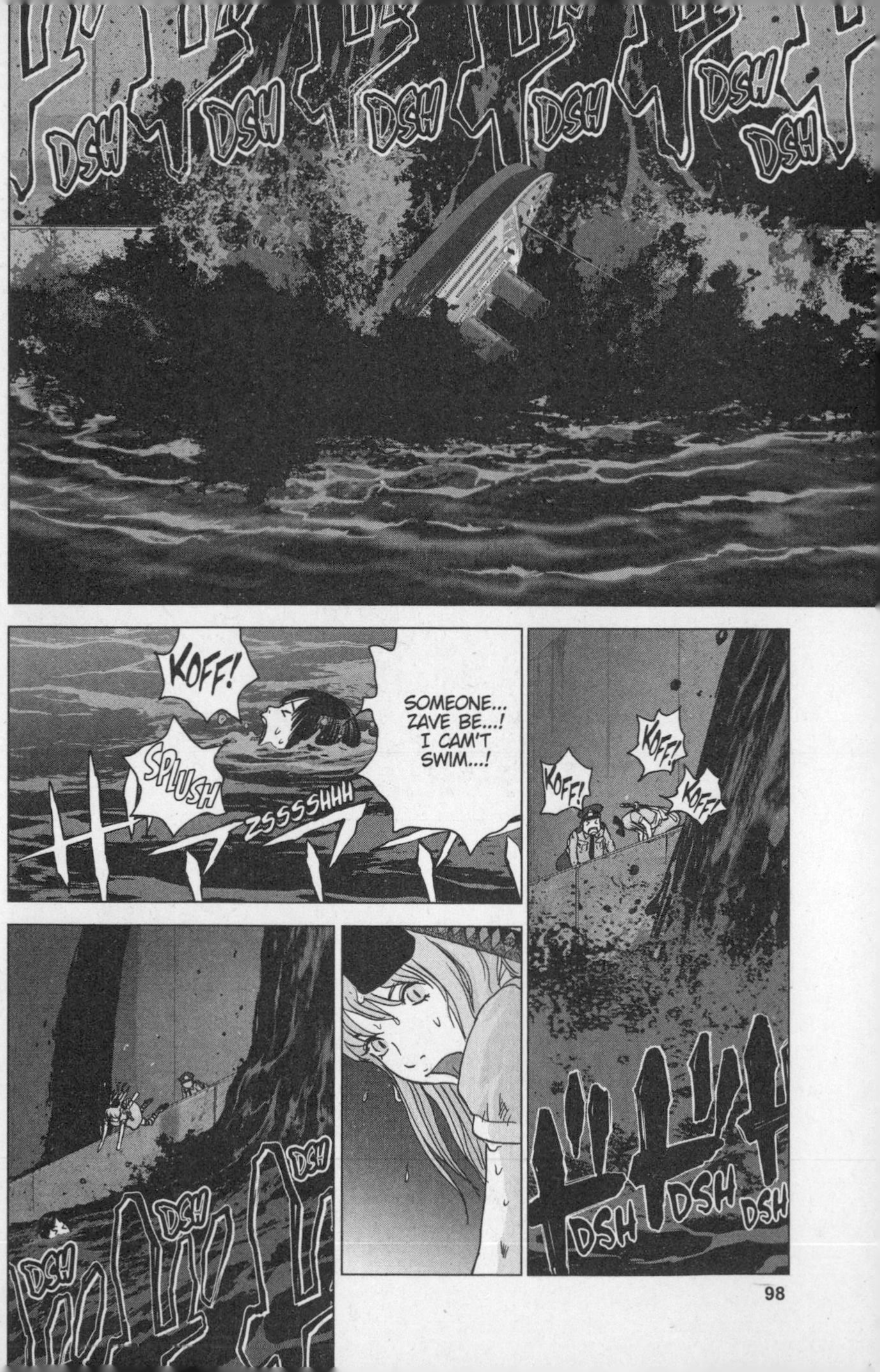
DSH
DSH
DSH
DSH
DSH
DSH
KOFF!
KOFF!
KOFF!
DSH
DSH
DSH
KOFF!
SOMEONE... ZAVE BE...! I CAM'T SWIM...!
SPLUSH
ZSSSSHHH
DSH
DSH
DSH

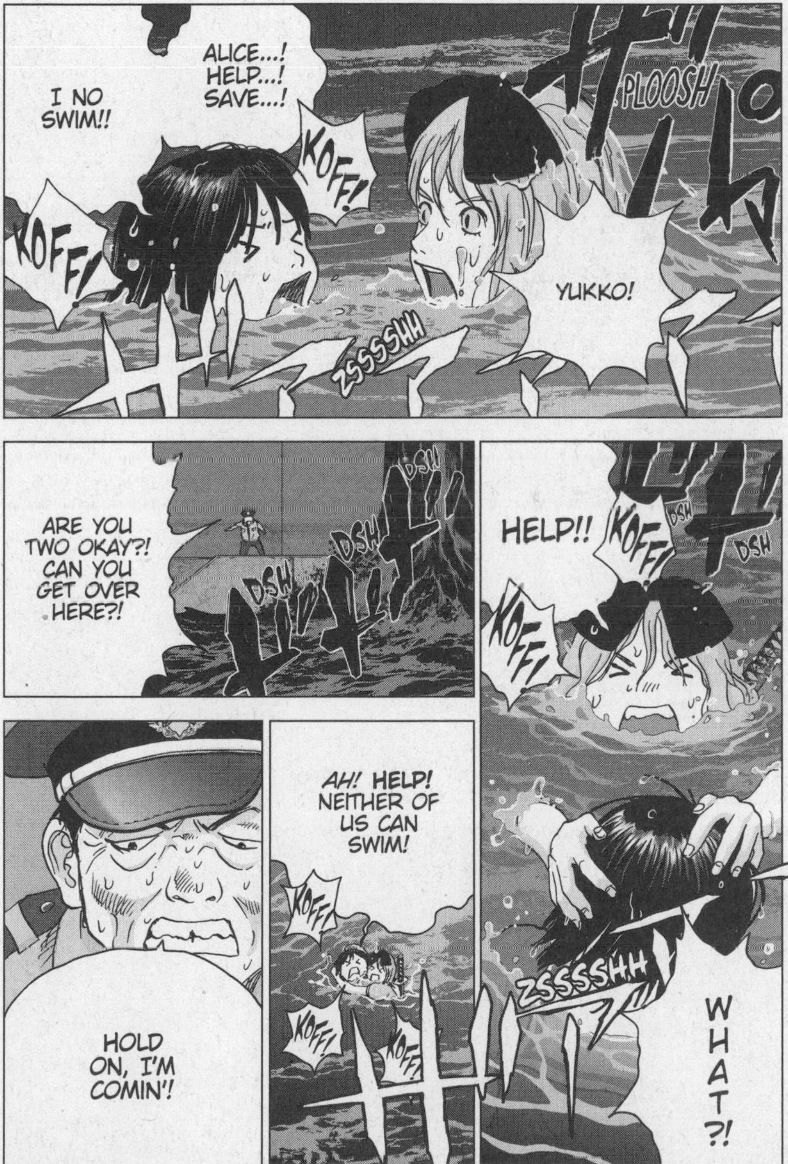
PLOOSH
YUKKO!
ALICE...! HELP...! SAVE...!
KOFF!
I NO SWIM!!
KOFF!
ZSSSSHH
DSH
HELP!!
KOFF!
DSH
KOFF!
DSH
DSH
DSH
ARE YOU TWO OKAY?! CAN YOU GET OVER HERE?!
WHAT?!
ZSSSSHH
AH! HELP! NEITHER OF US CAN SWIM!
KOFF!
KOFF!
KOFF!
HOLD ON, I'M COMIN'!

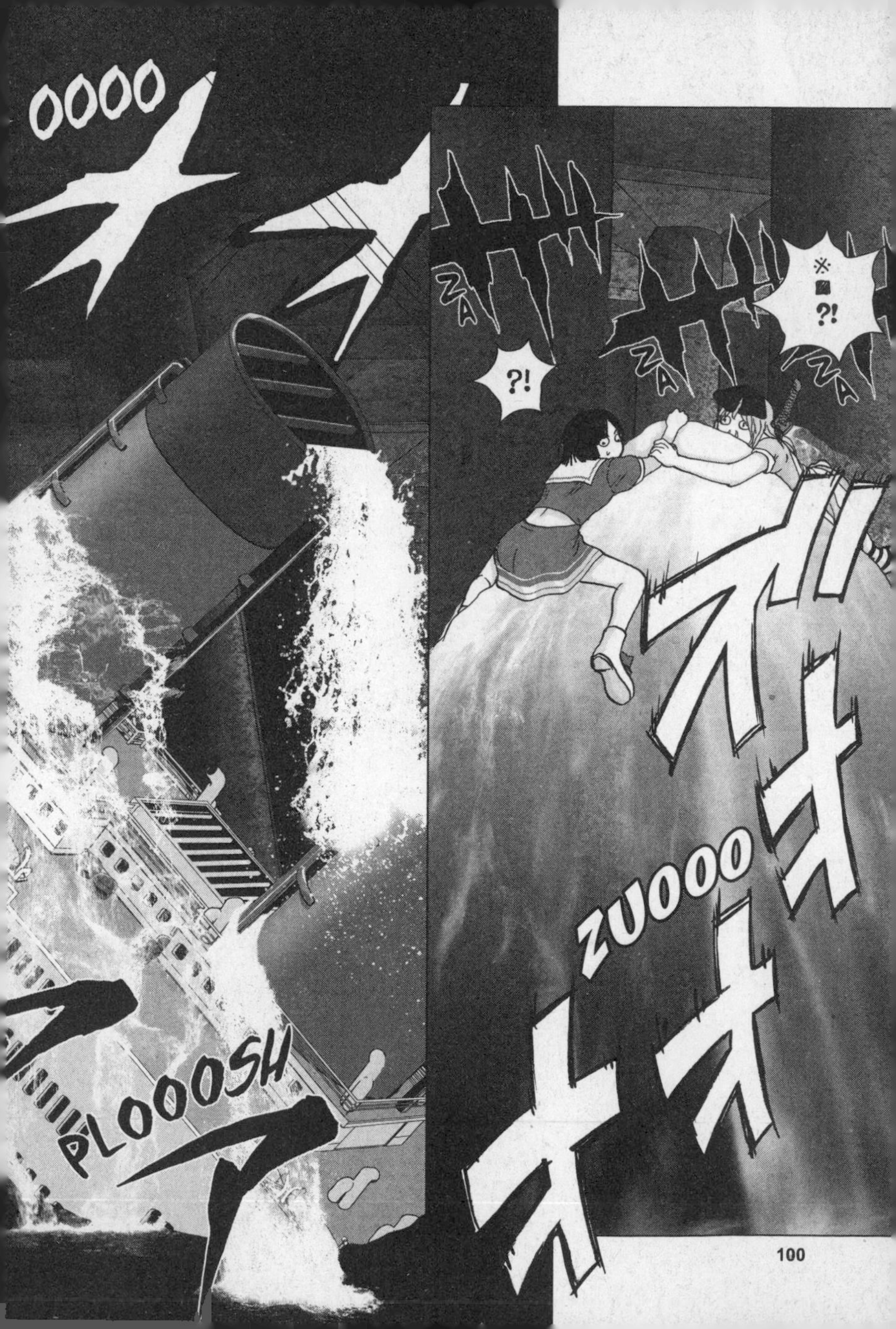
ZA
?!
ZA
ZA
?!
ZUOOO
OOOO
PLOOOSH

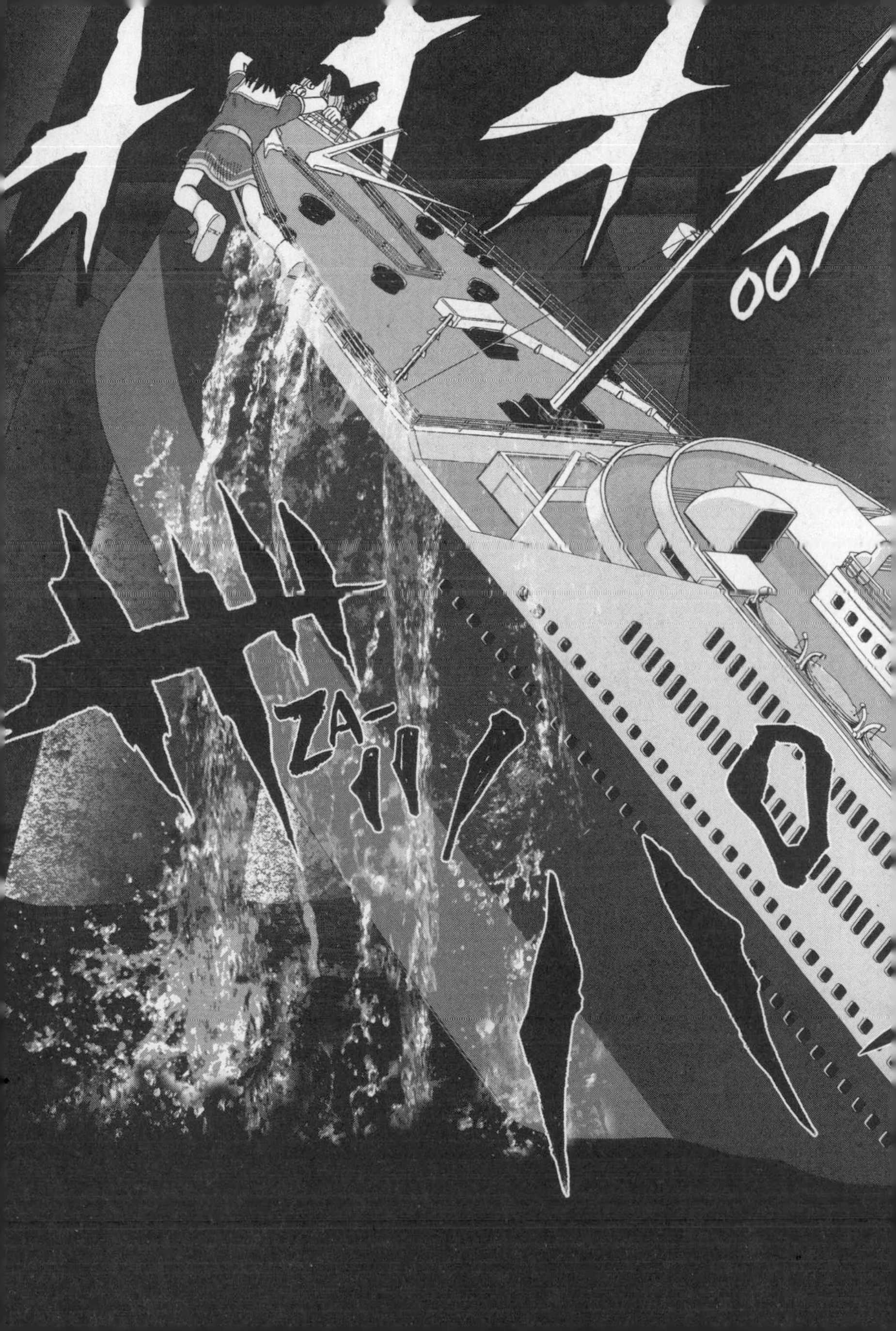
OO
ZA-
O

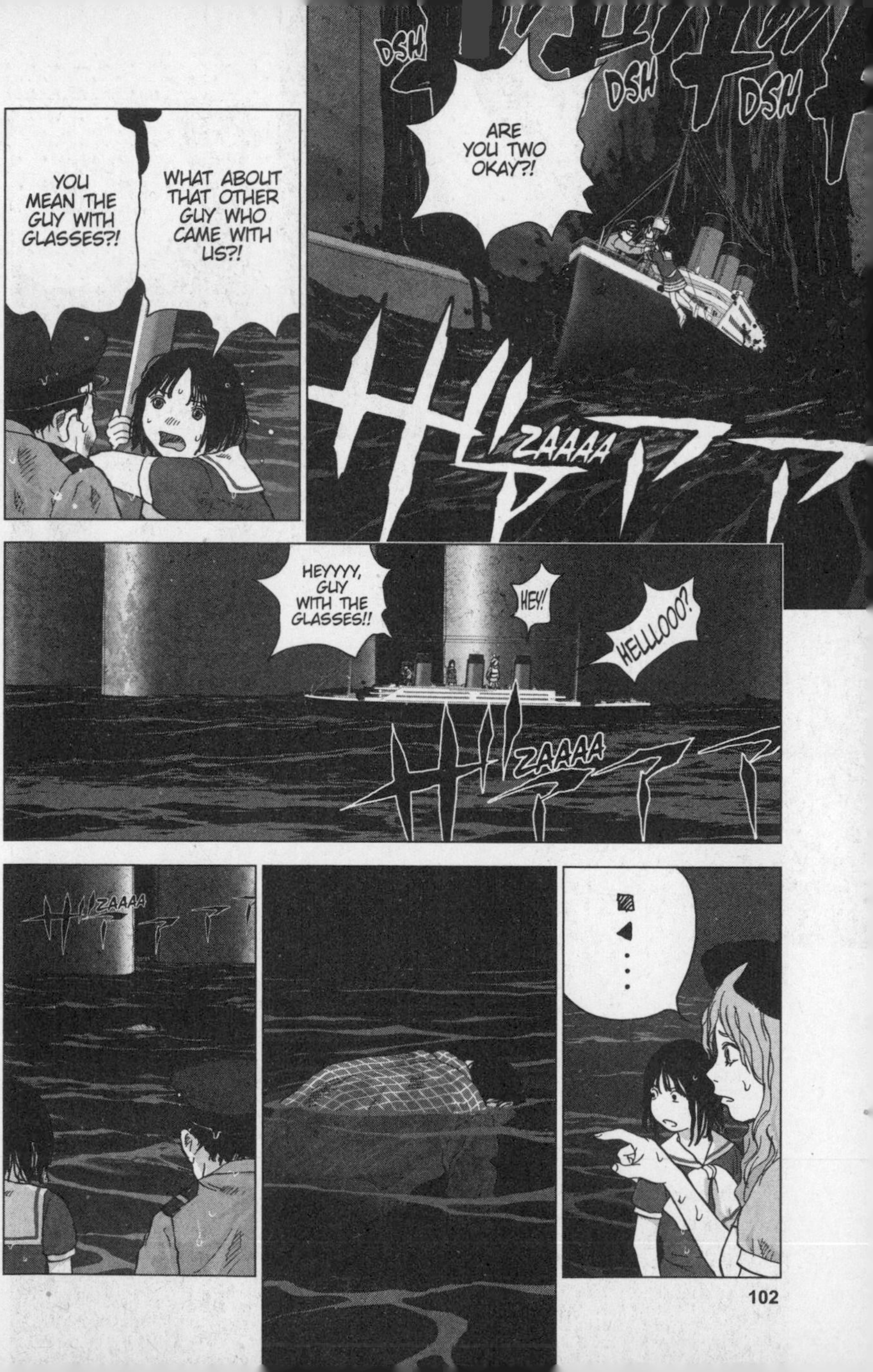
DSH
DSH
DSH
ARE YOU TWO OKAY?!
ZAAAA
WHAT ABOUT THAT OTHER GUY WHO CAME WITH US?!
YOU MEAN THE GUY WITH GLASSES?!
HEYYYY, GUY WITH THE GLASSES!!
HEY!
HELLLOOO?
ZAAAA
ZAAAA

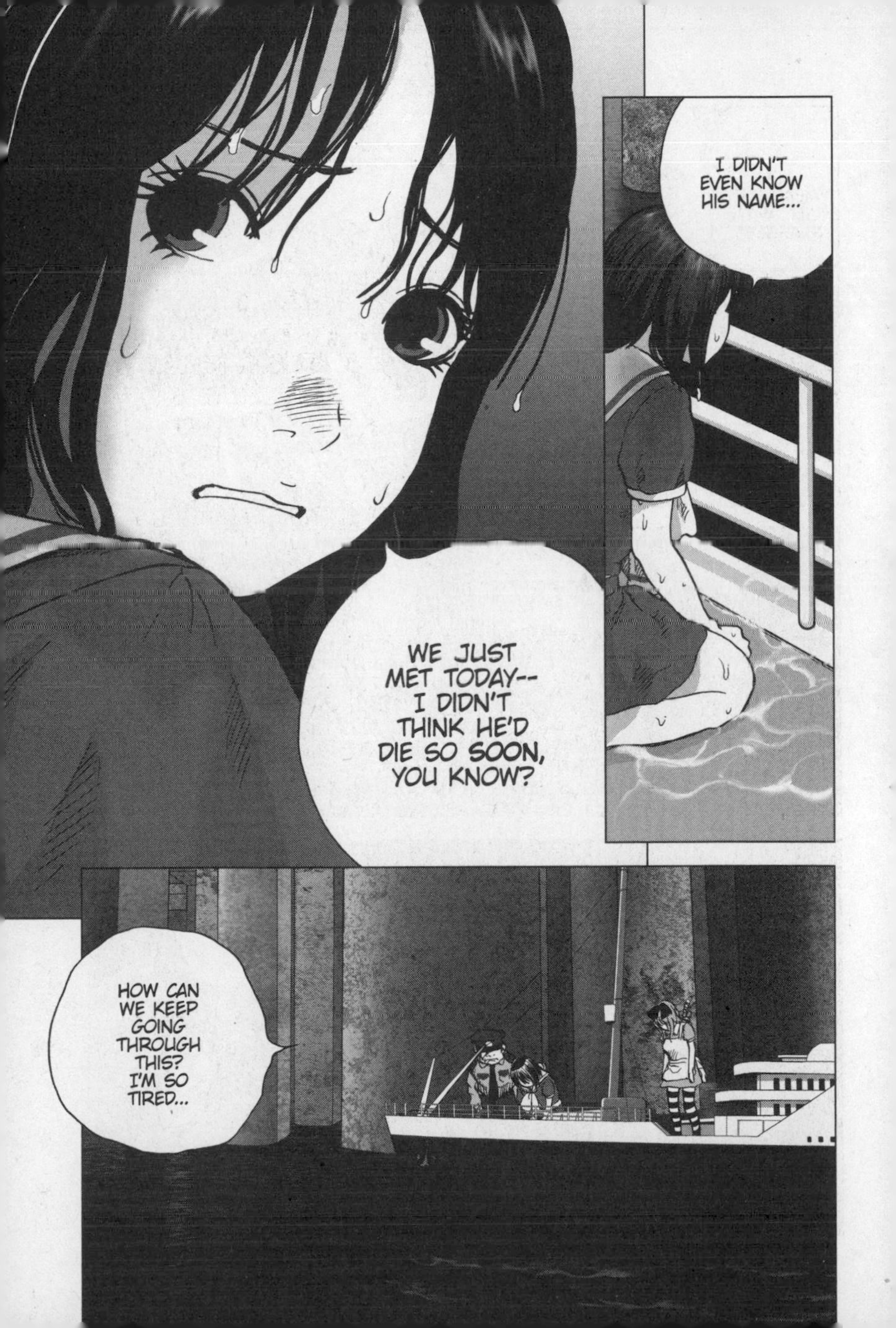
I DIDN'T EVEN KNOW HIS NAME...
WE JUST MET TODAY-- I DIDN'T THINK HE'D DIE SO SOON, YOU KNOW?
HOW CAN WE KEEP GOING THROUGH THIS? I'M SO TIRED...

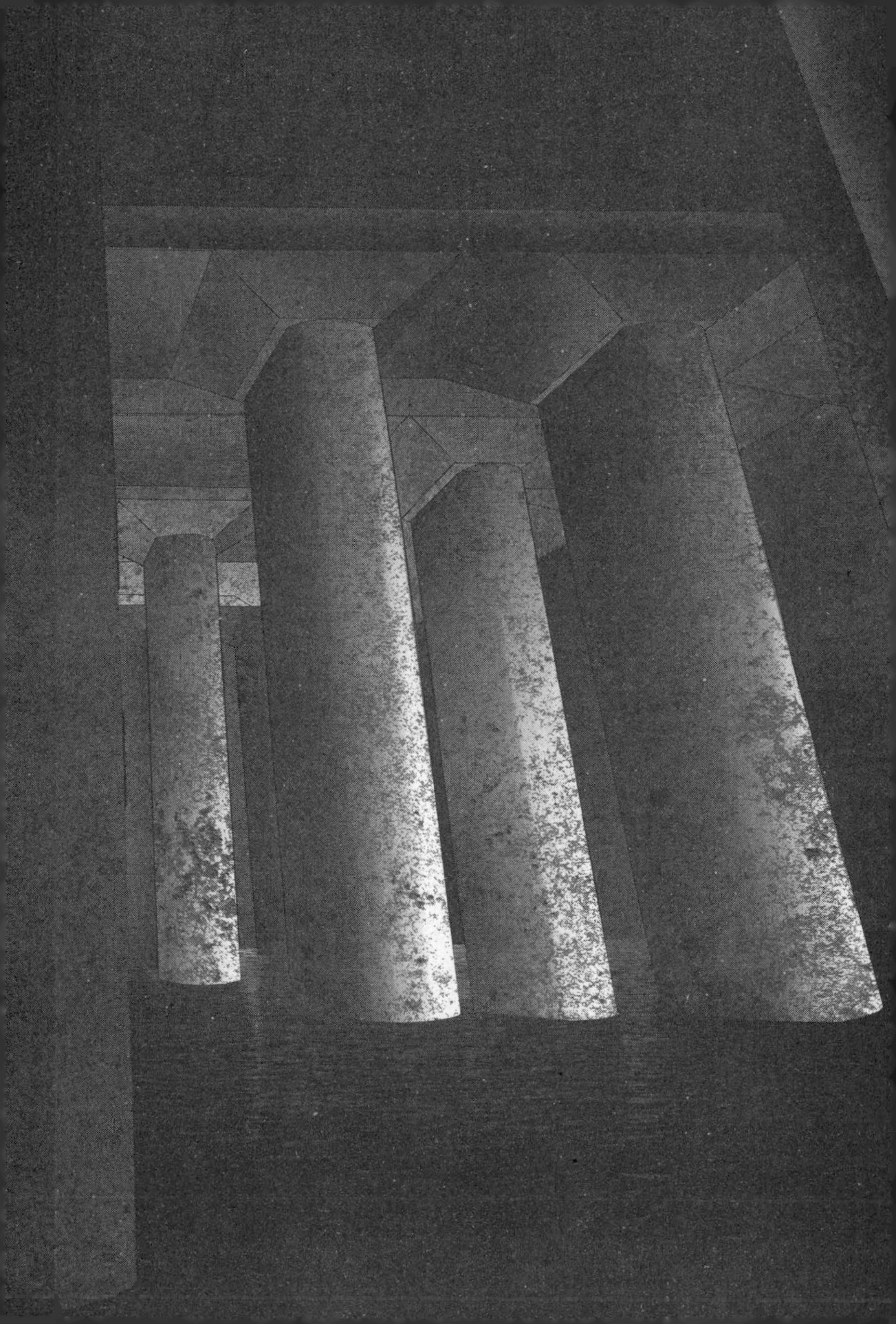

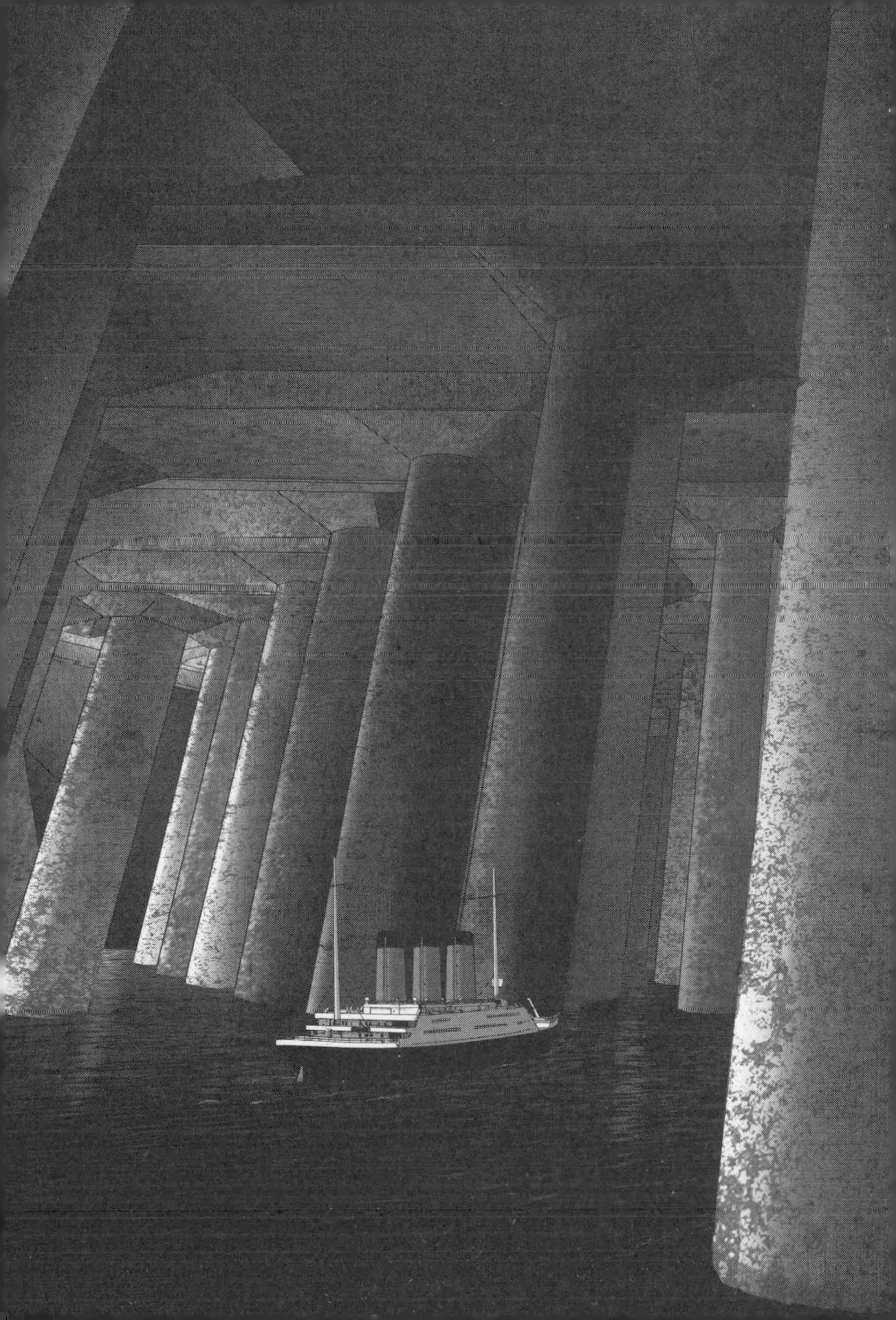

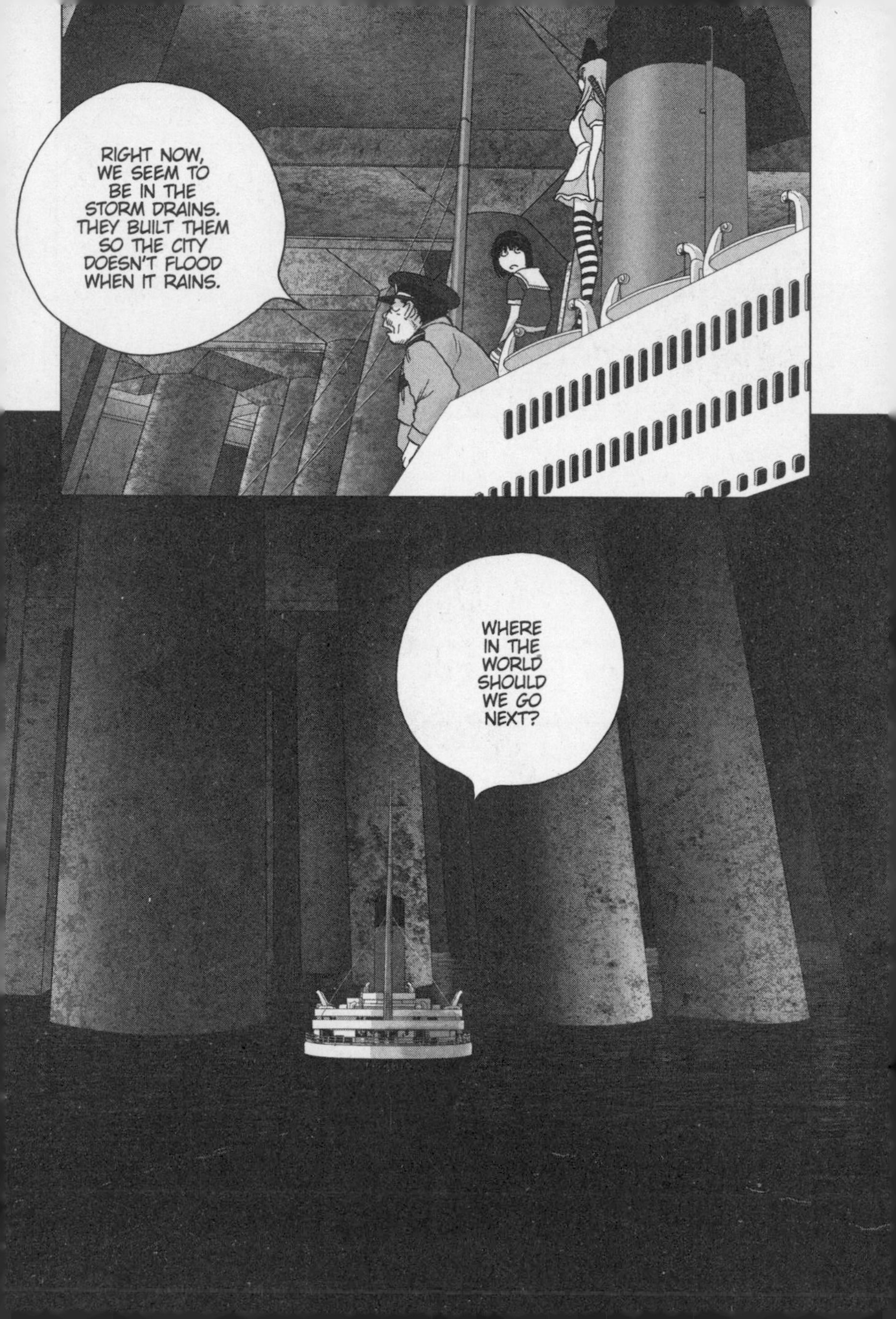
RIGHT NOW, WE SEEM TO BE IN THE STORM DRAINS. THEY BUILT THEM SO THE CITY DOESN'T FLOOD WHEN IT RAINS.
WHERE IN THE WORLD SHOULD WE GO NEXT?

Chapter 15: Awakening

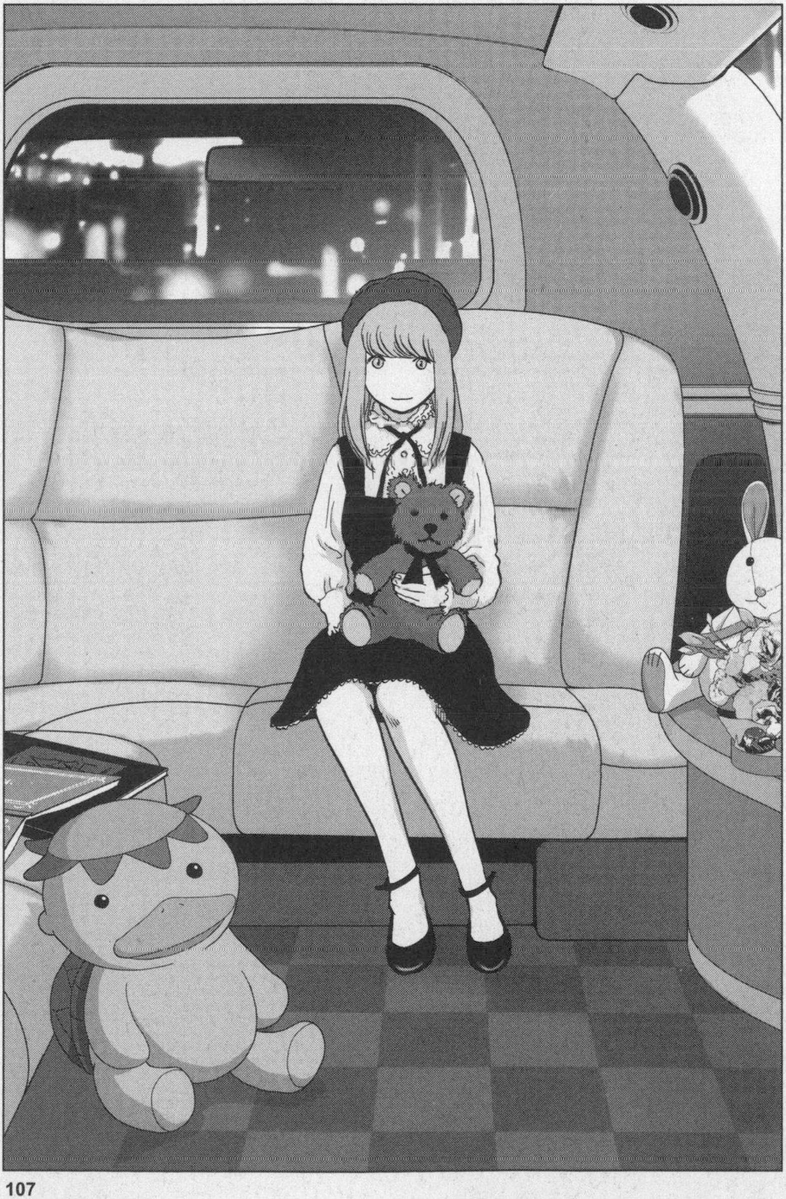

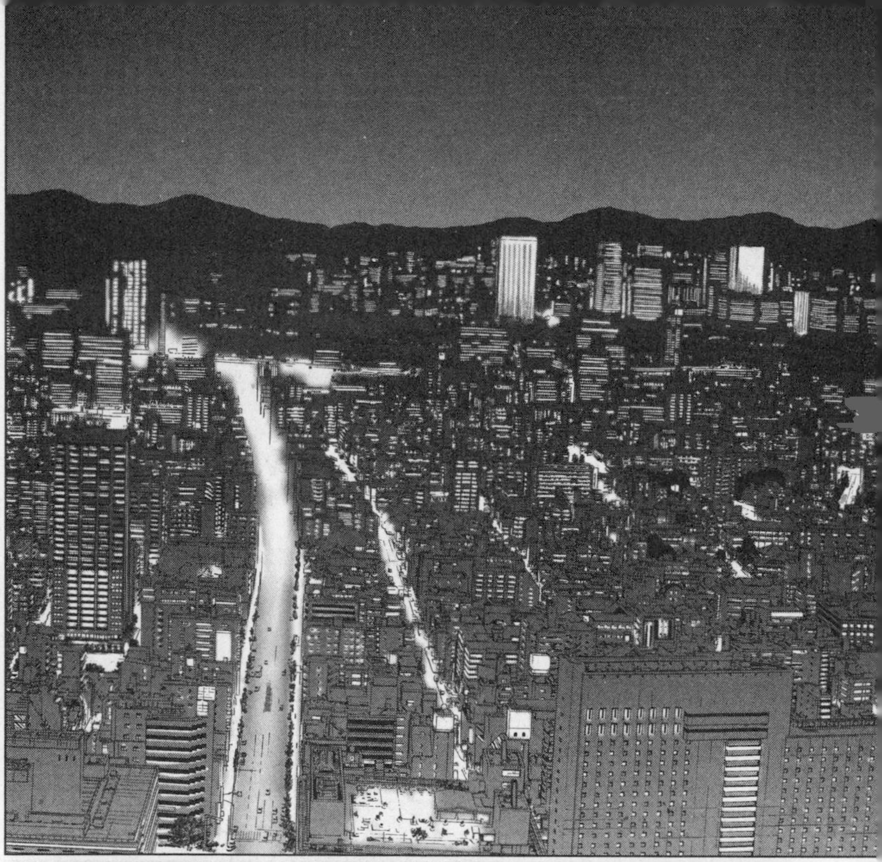
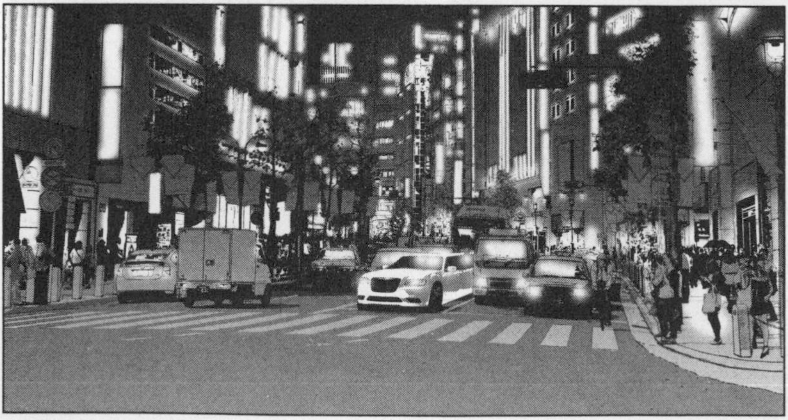

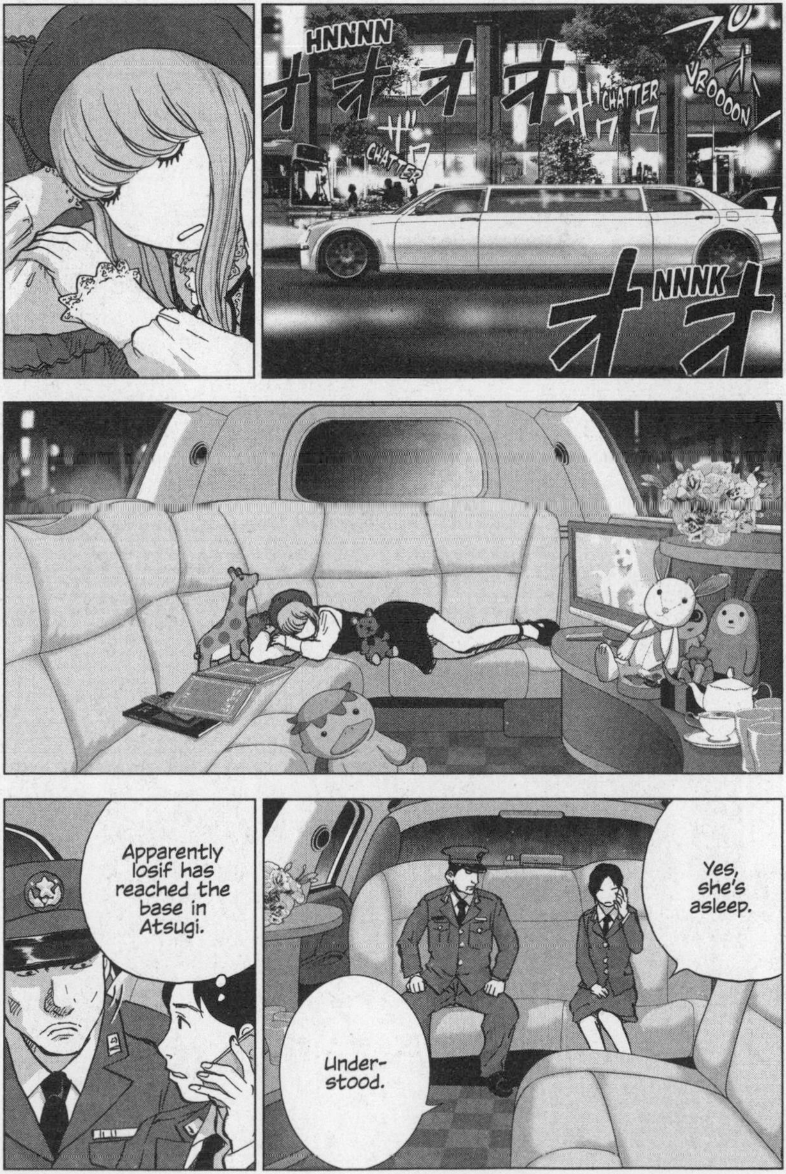
VROOOON
CHATTER
HNNNN
CHATTER
NNNK
Yes, she's asleep.
Under-stood.
Apparently Iosif has reached the base in Atsugi.

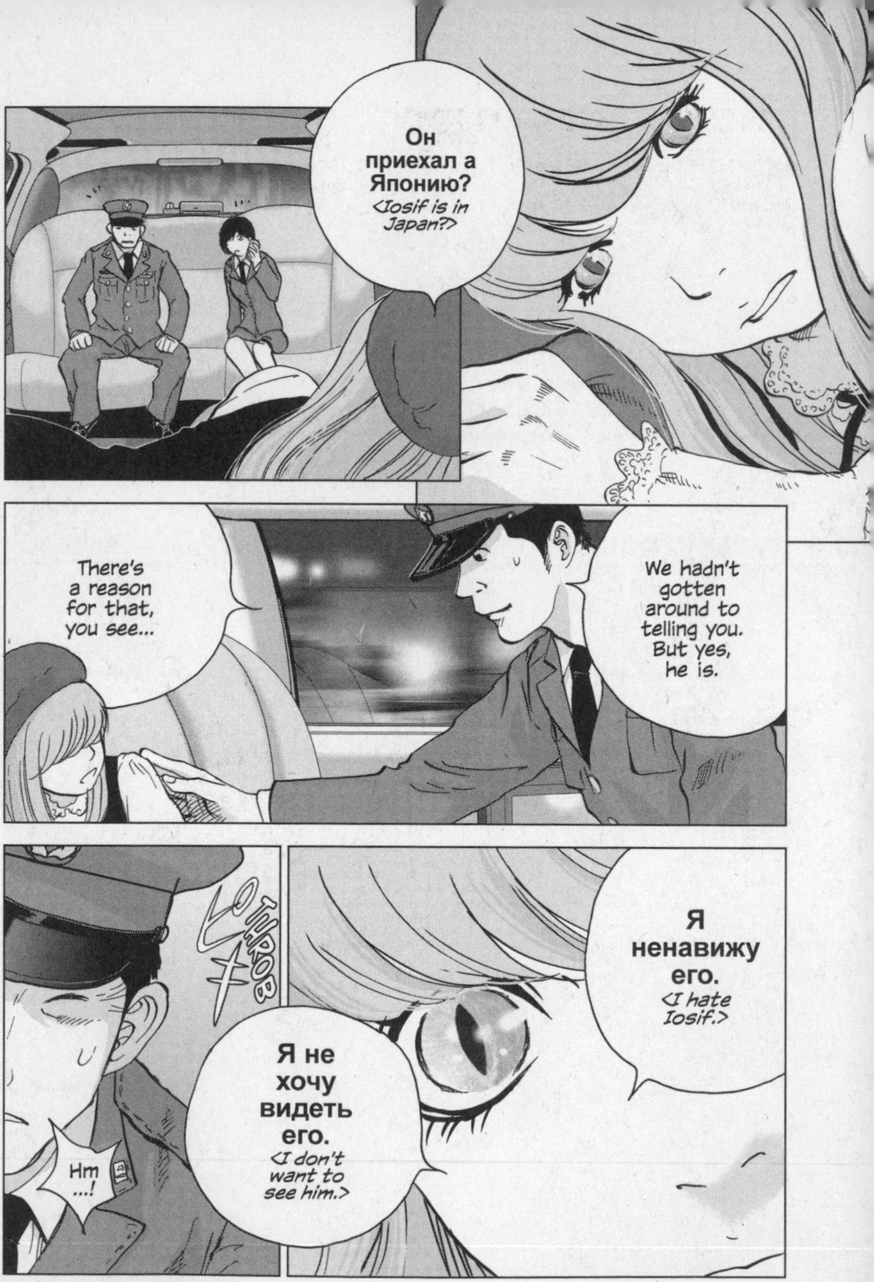
Он приехал а Японию?
<Iosif is in Japan?>
We hadn't gotten around to telling you. But yes, he is.
There's a reason for that, you see...
Я ненавижу его.
<I hate Iosif.>
Я не хочу видеть его.
<I don't want to see him.>
THROB
Hm ...!

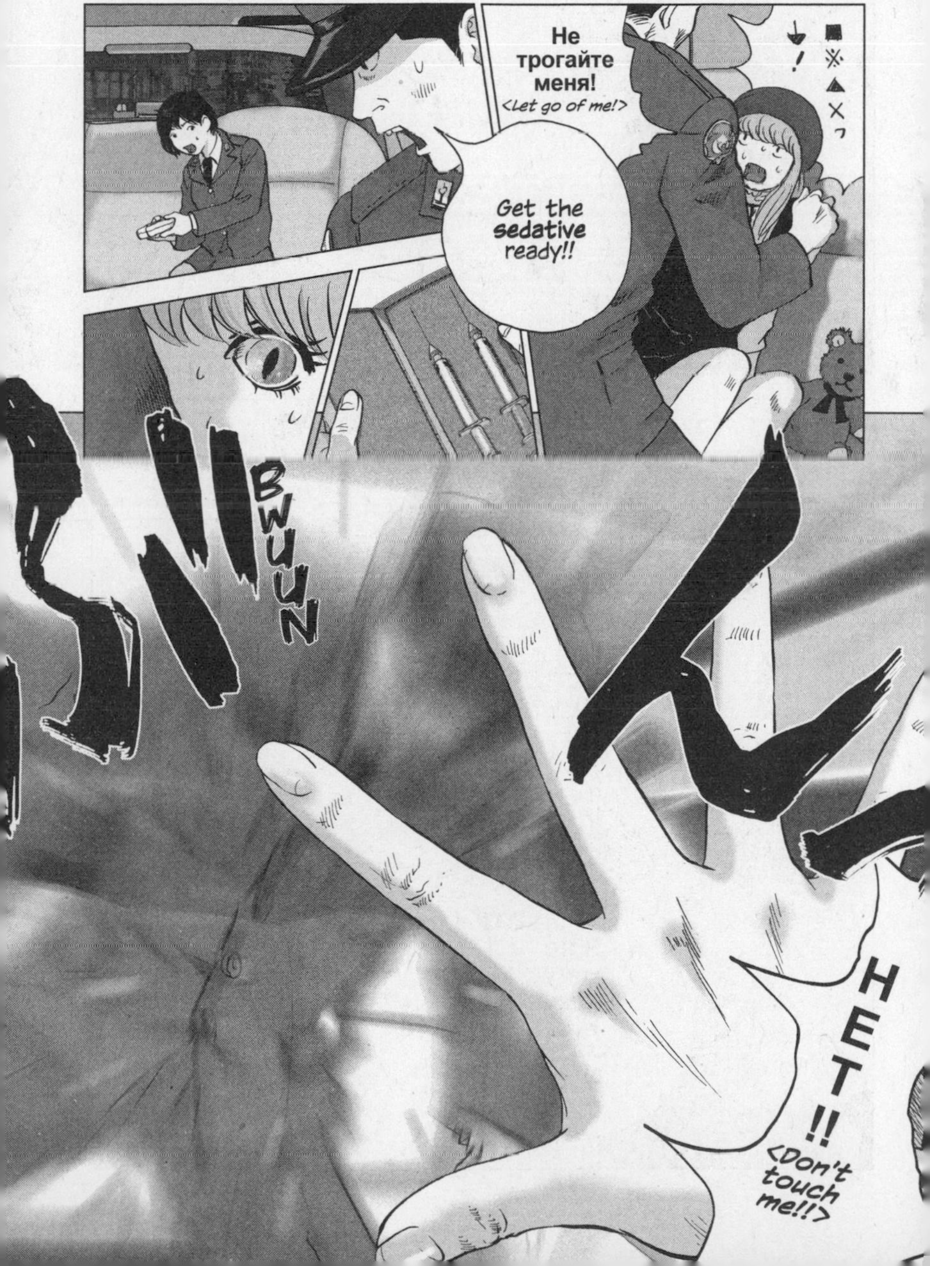

Не трогайте меня!
<Let go of me!>
Get the sedative ready!!
BWUUN
НЕТ!!
<Don't touch me!!>

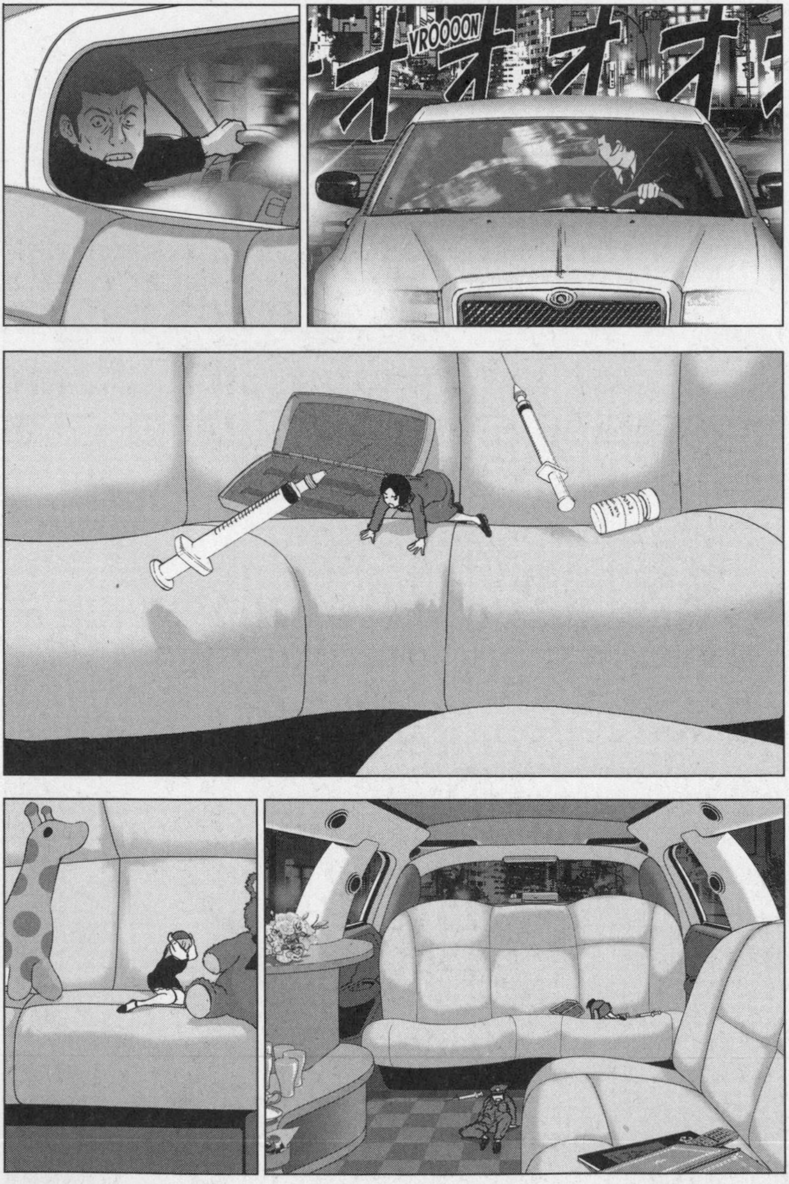
オオオオ
VROOOON

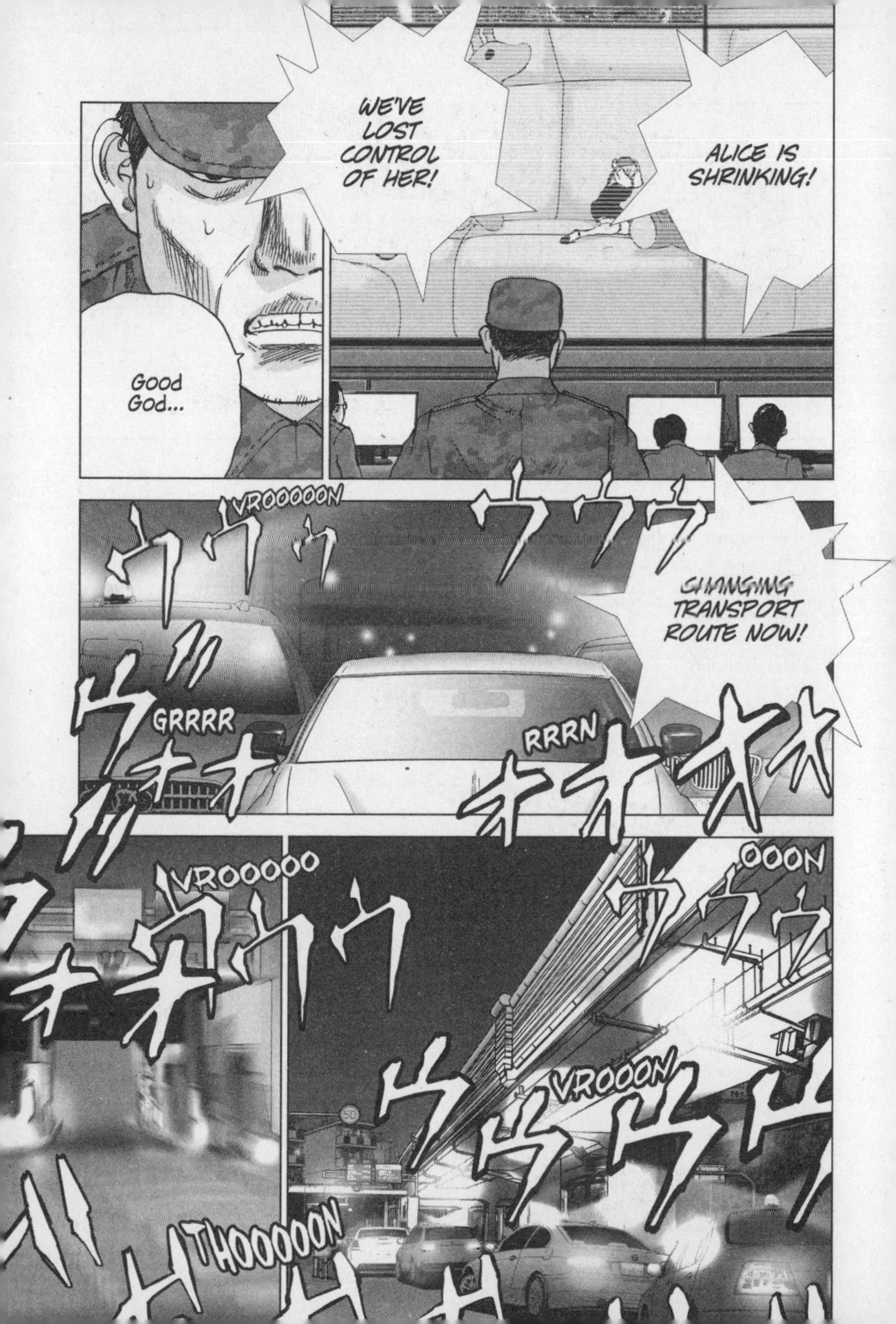
ALICE IS SHRINKING!
WE'VE LOST CONTROL OF HER!
Good God...
CHANGING TRANSPORT ROUTE NOW!
VROOOOON
RRRN
GRRRR
OOON
VROOON
THOOOOON
VROOOOO

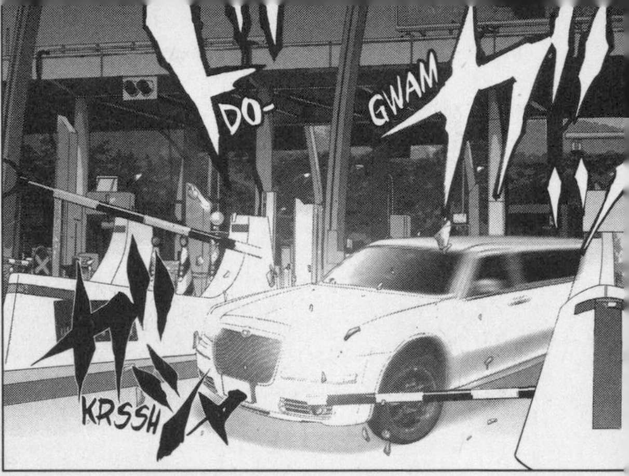
DO-GWAM
KRSSH

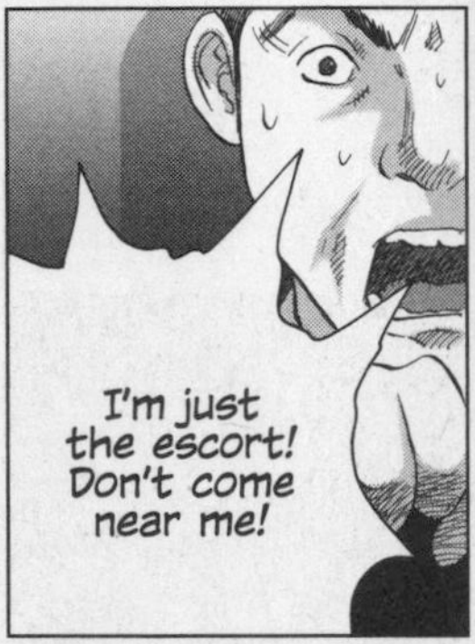
I'm just the escort! Don't come near me!

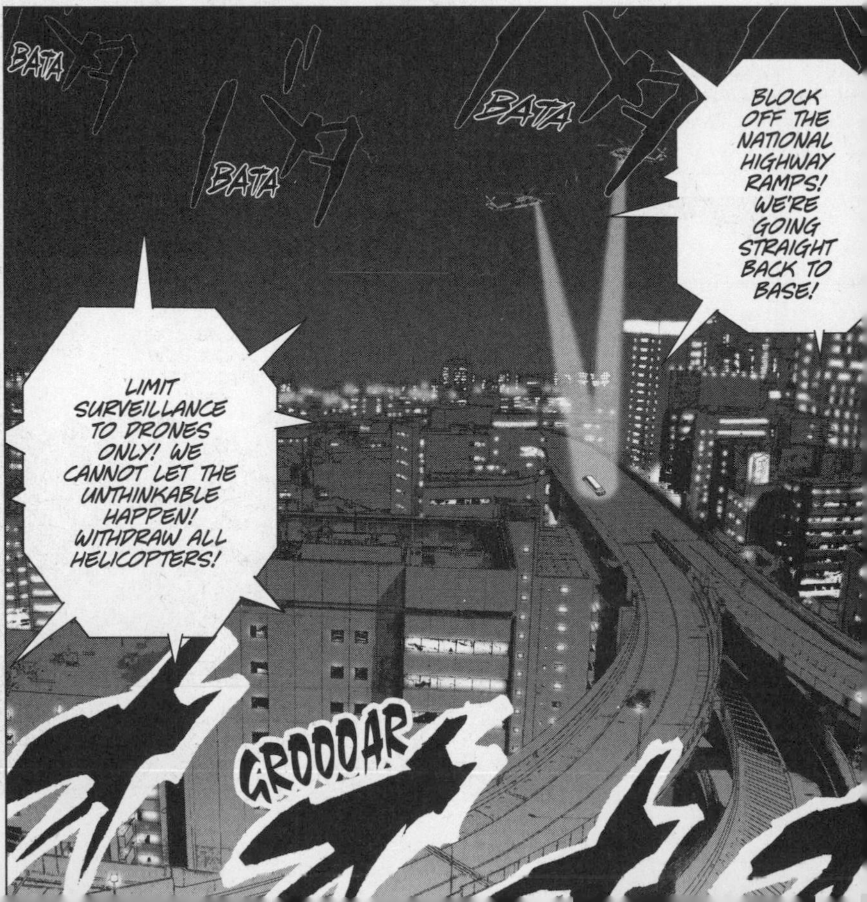
BATA
BATA
BATA
BLOCK OFF THE NATIONAL HIGHWAY RAMPS! WE'RE GOING STRAIGHT BACK TO BASE!
LIMIT SURVEILLANCE TO DRONES ONLY! WE CANNOT LET THE UNTHINKABLE HAPPEN! WITHDRAW ALL HELICOPTERS!
GROOOAR

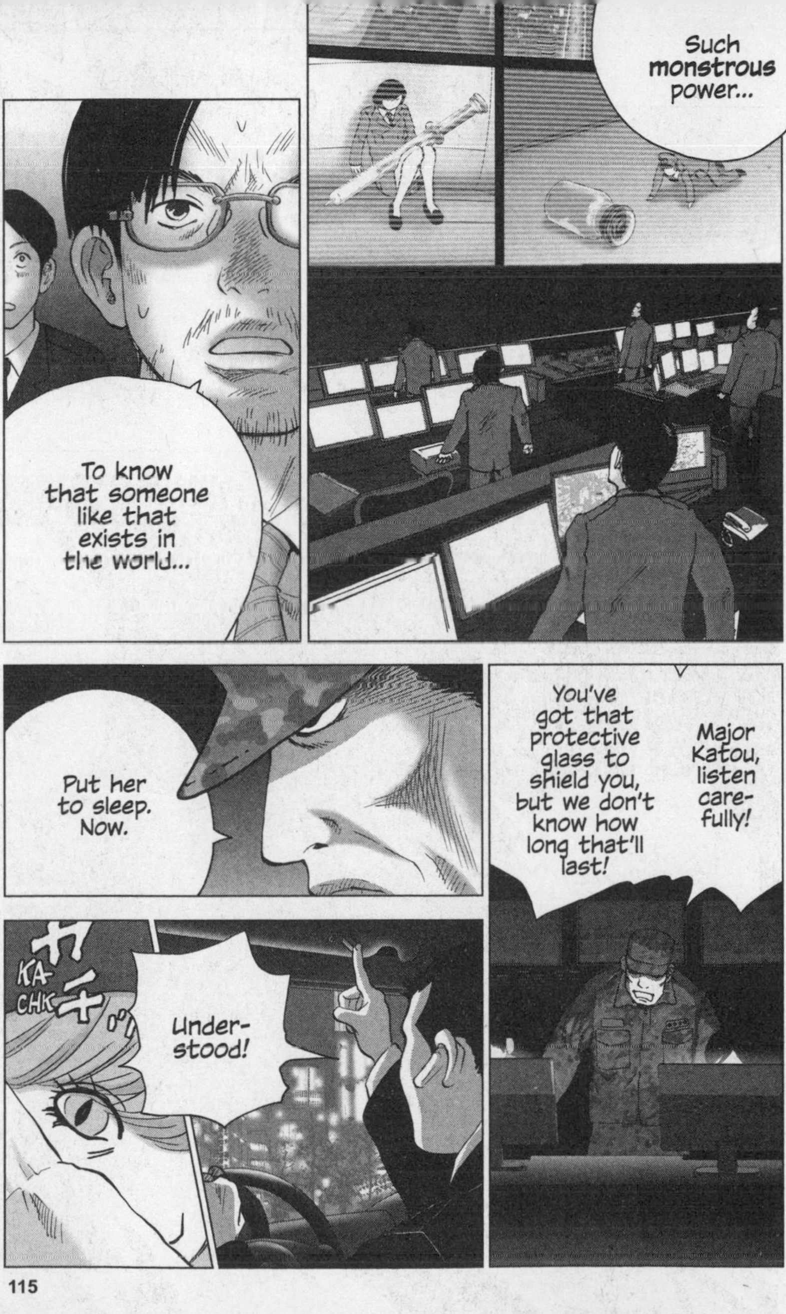
Such monstrous power...
To know that someone like that exists in the world...
Major Katou, listen carefully!
You've got that protective glass to shield you, but we don't know how long that'll last!
Put her to sleep. Now.
KA CHK
Under-stood!

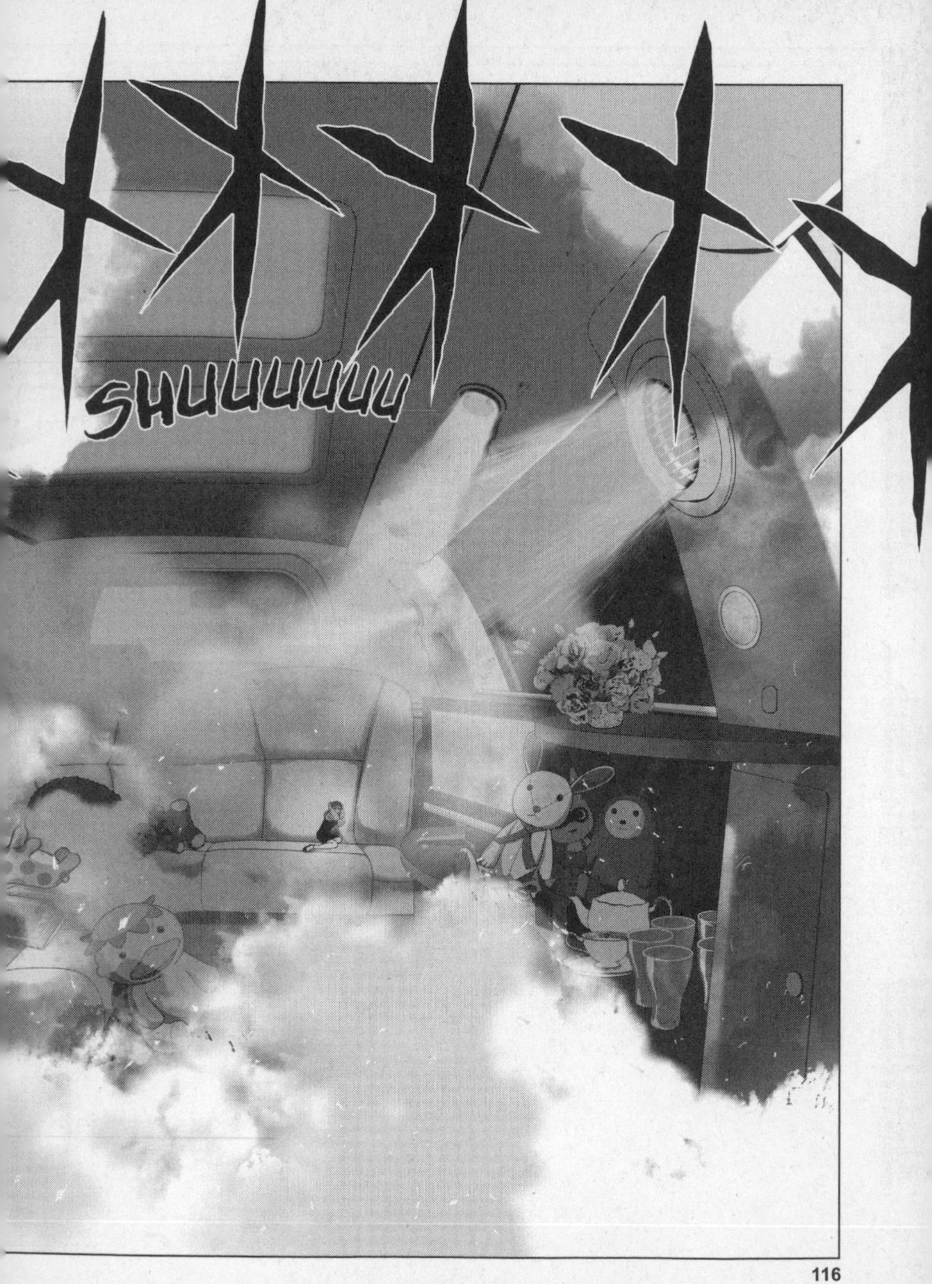
SHUUUUUU

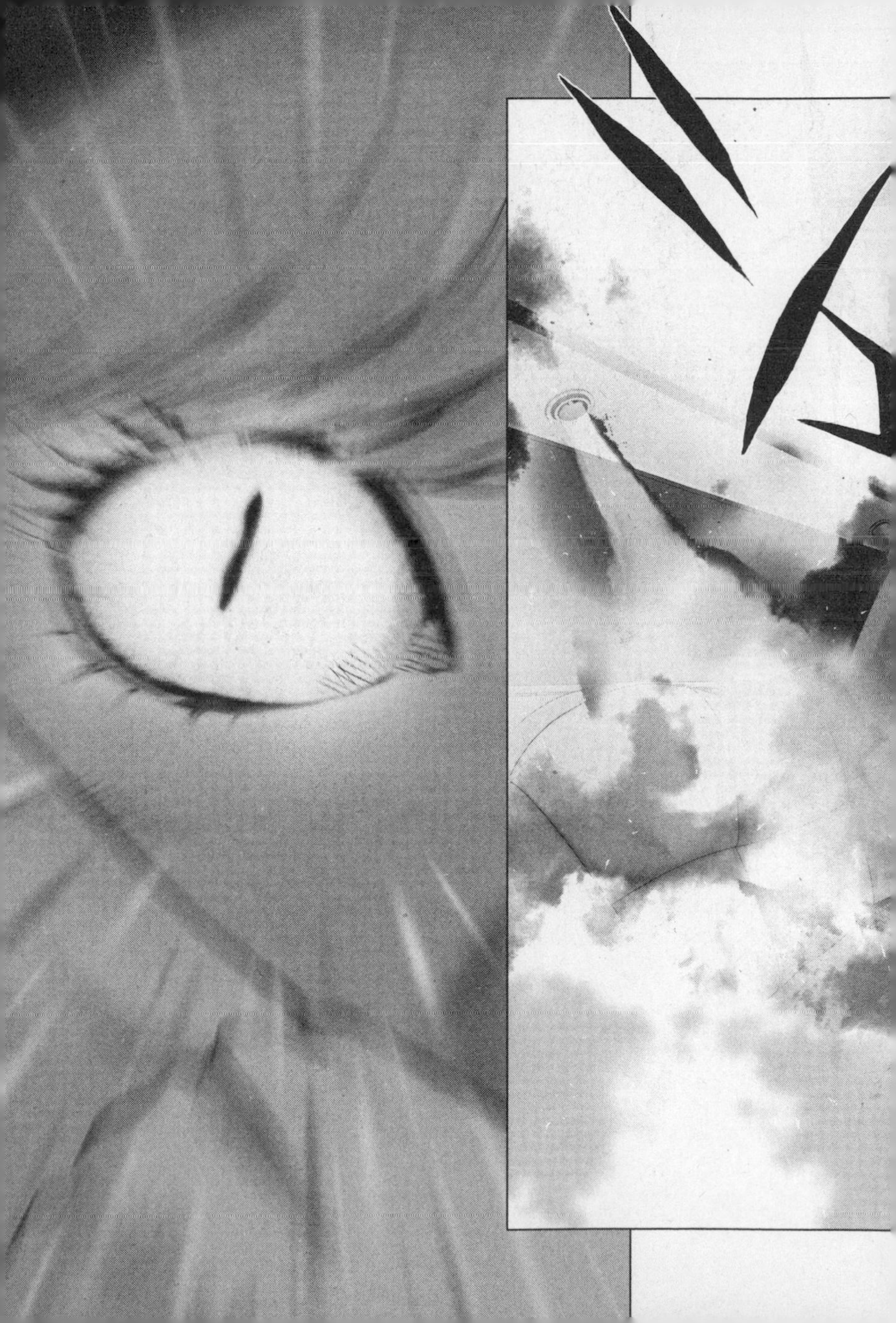

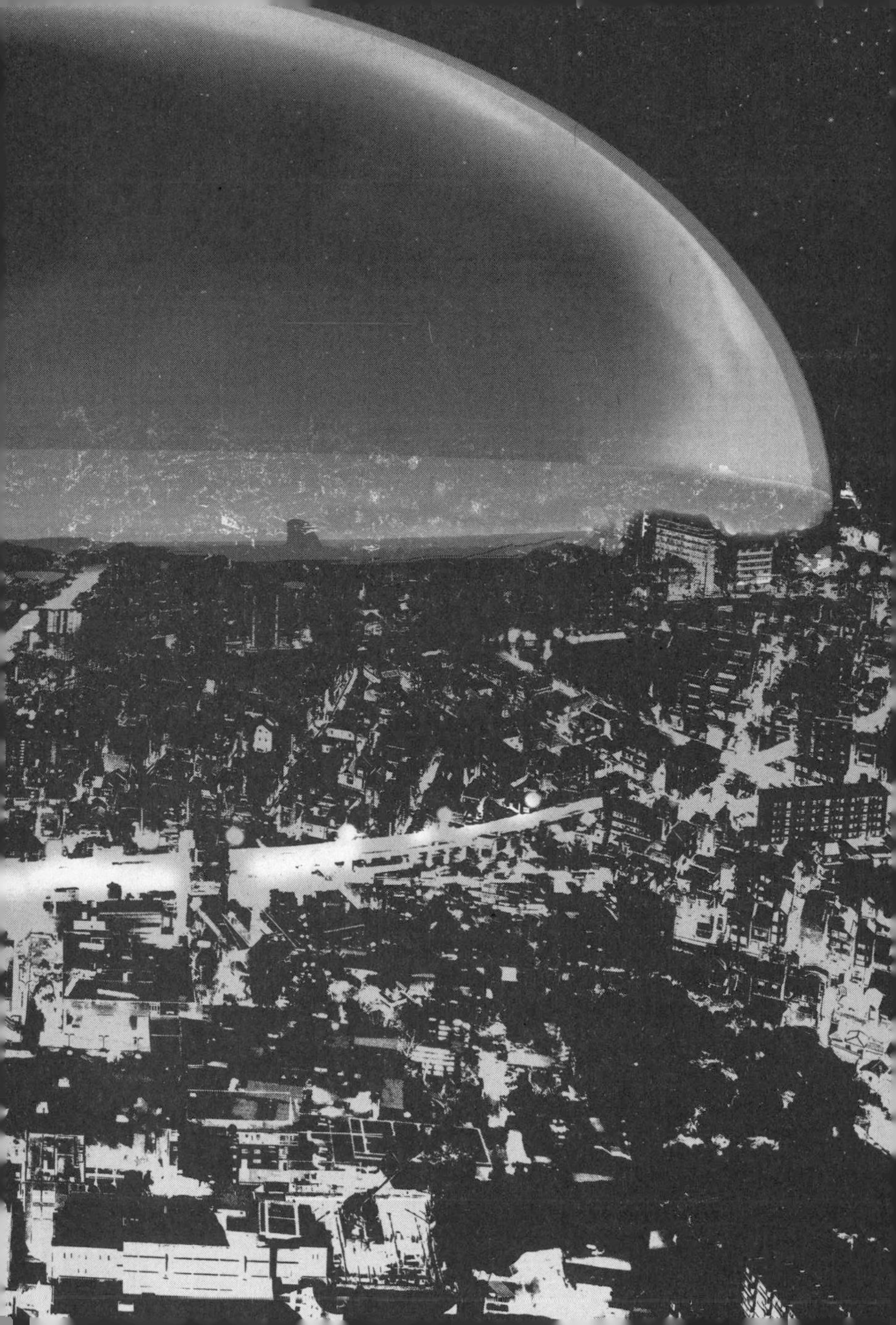

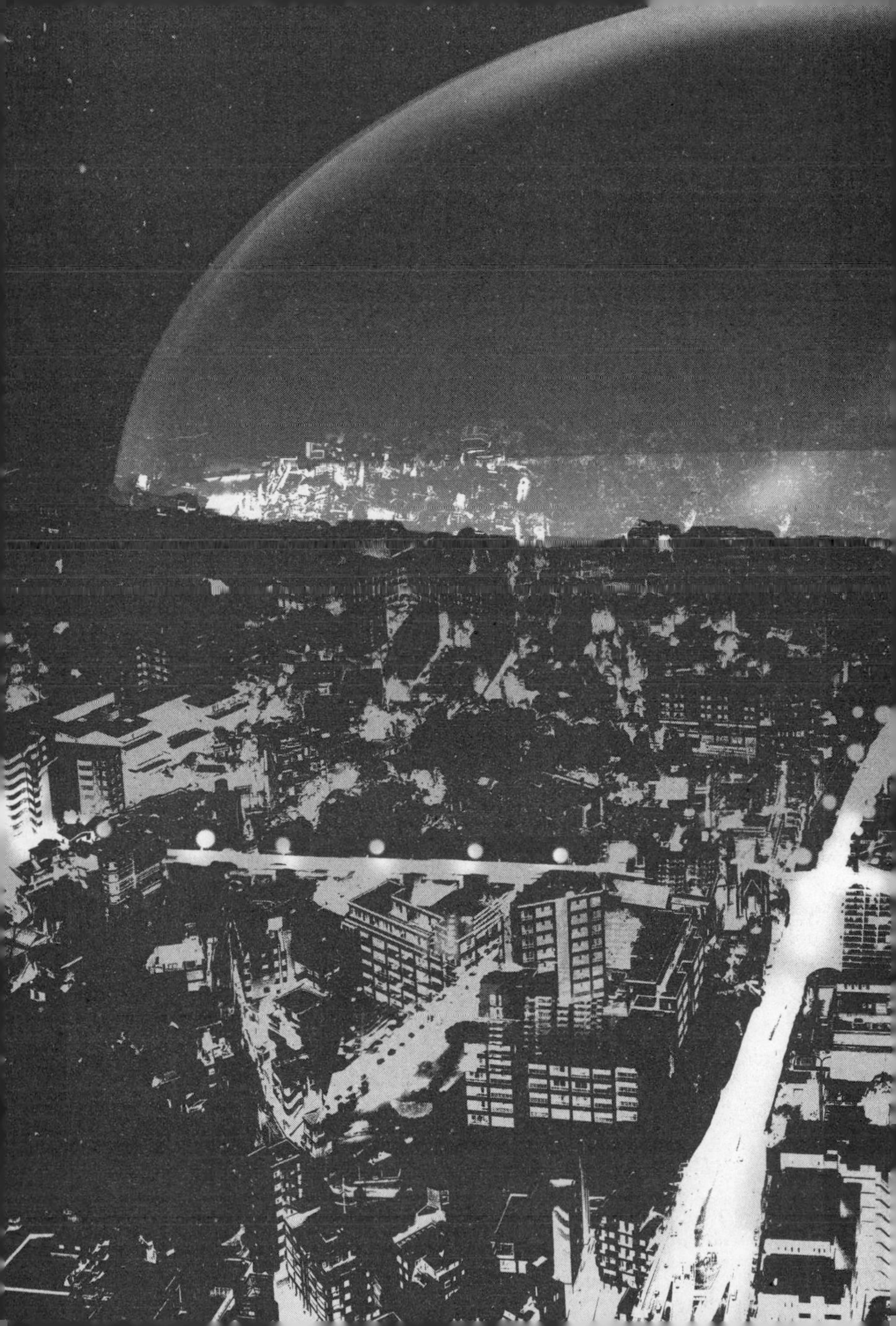

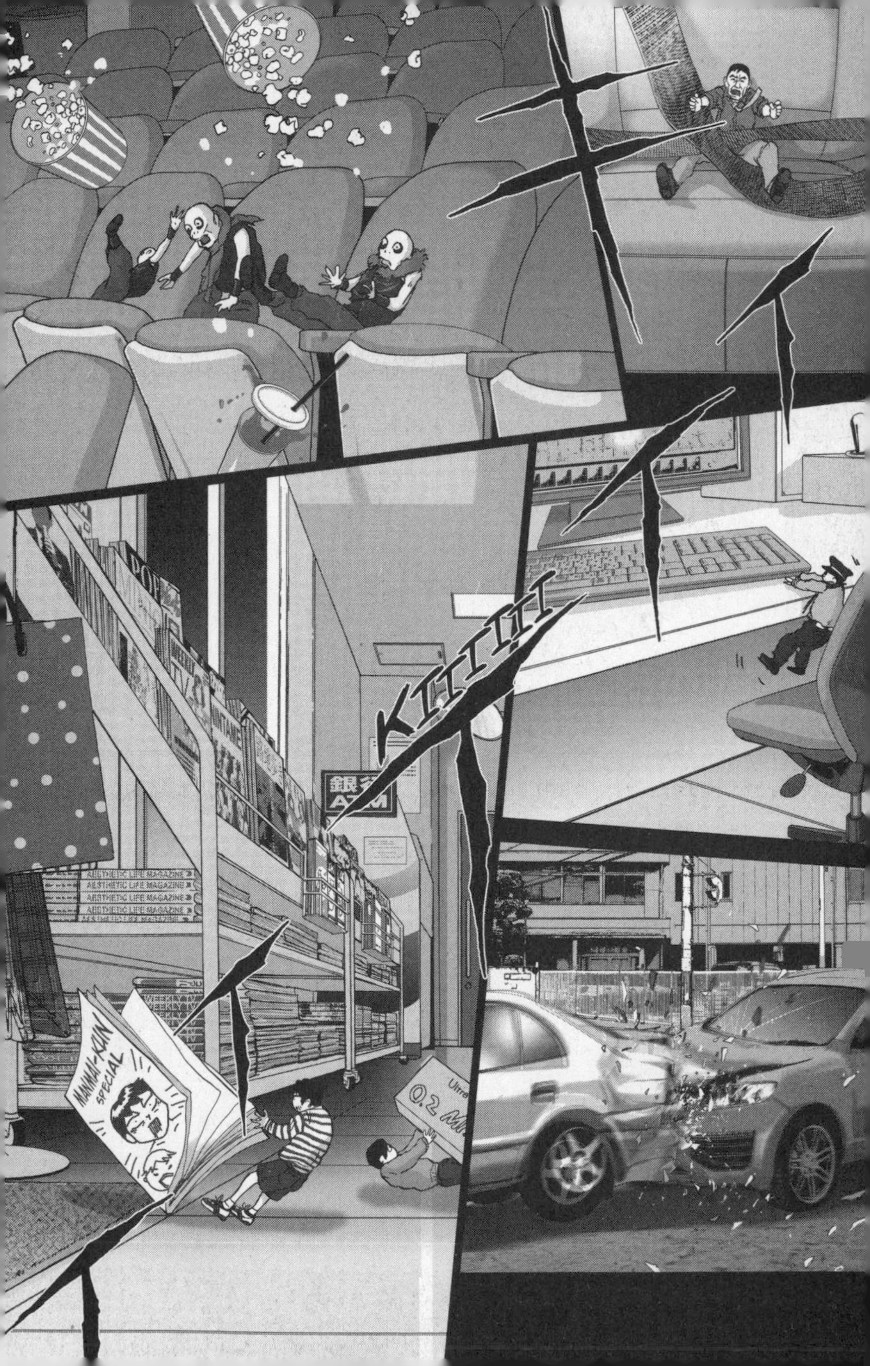

KIIIIII
銀行
ATM
POP
AESTHETIC LIFE MAGAZINE
MANMAI-KUN SPECIAL
0.2 MM

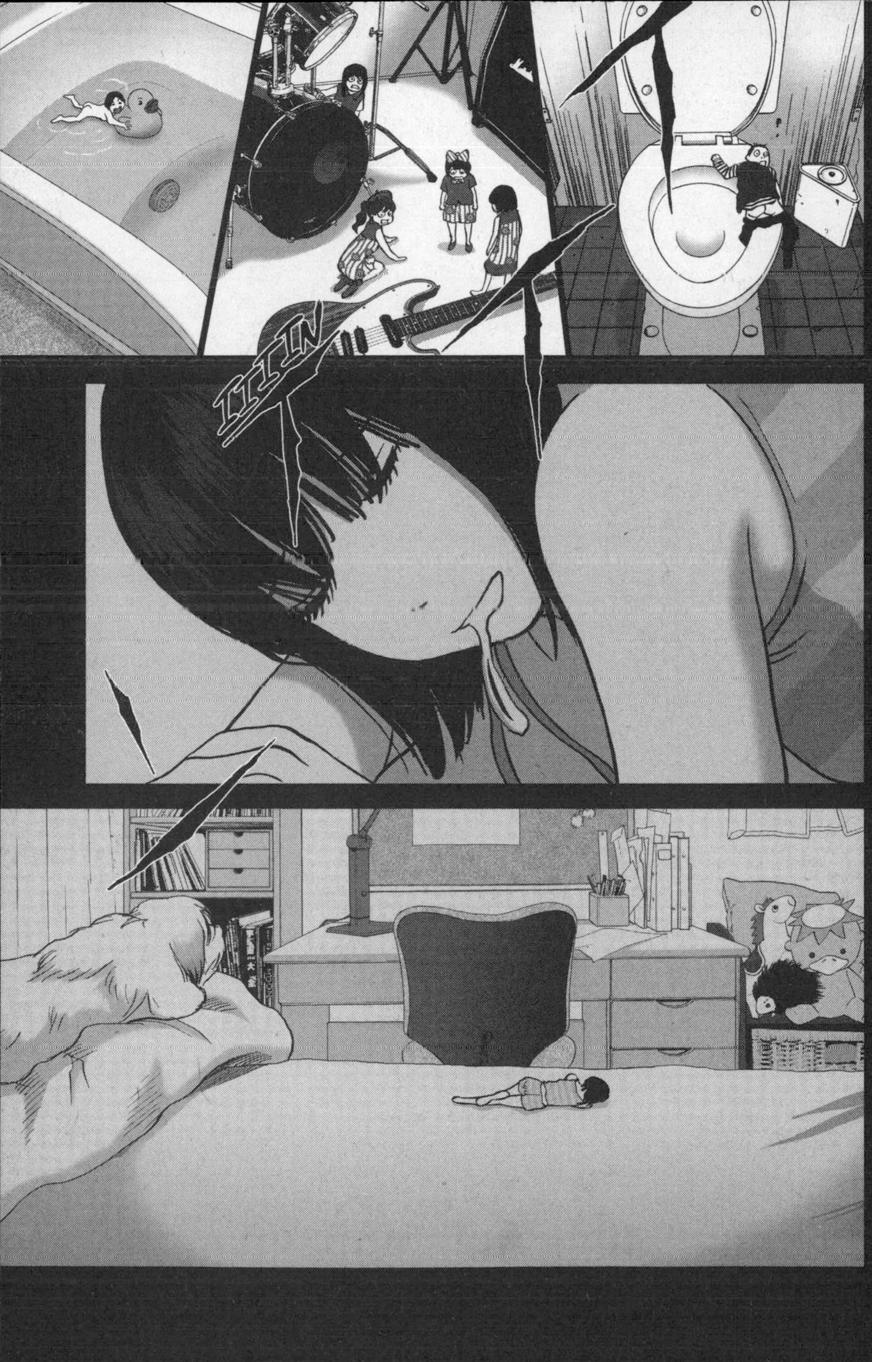
IIIIN

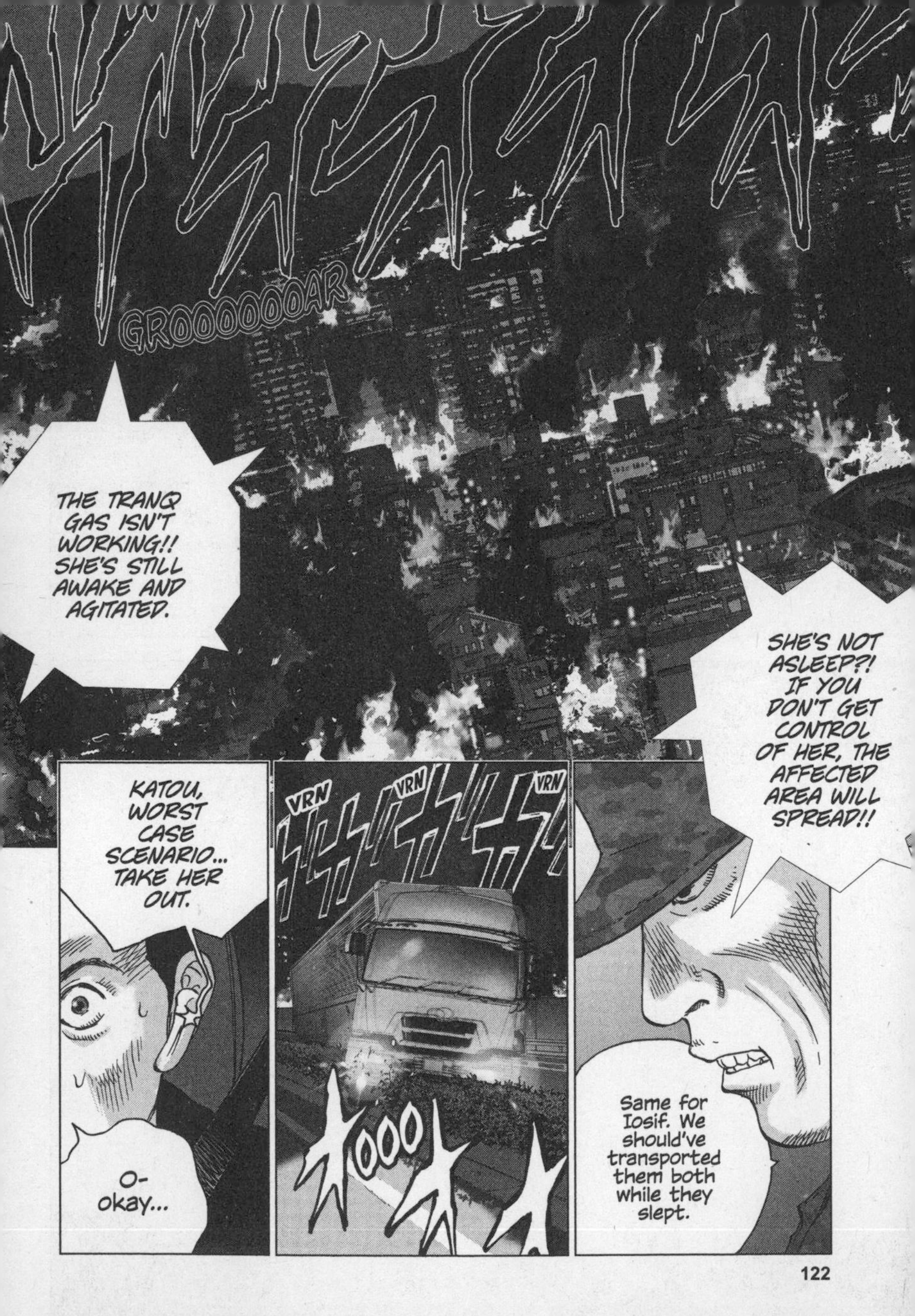
GROOOOOOAR
THE TRANQ GAS ISN'T WORKING!! SHE'S STILL AWAKE AND AGITATED.
SHE'S NOT ASLEEP?! IF YOU DON'T GET CONTROL OF HER, THE AFFECTED AREA WILL SPREAD!!
Same for Iosif. We should've transported them both while they slept.
VRN
VRN
VRN
OOO
KATOU, WORST CASE SCENARIO... TAKE HER OUT.
O-okay...

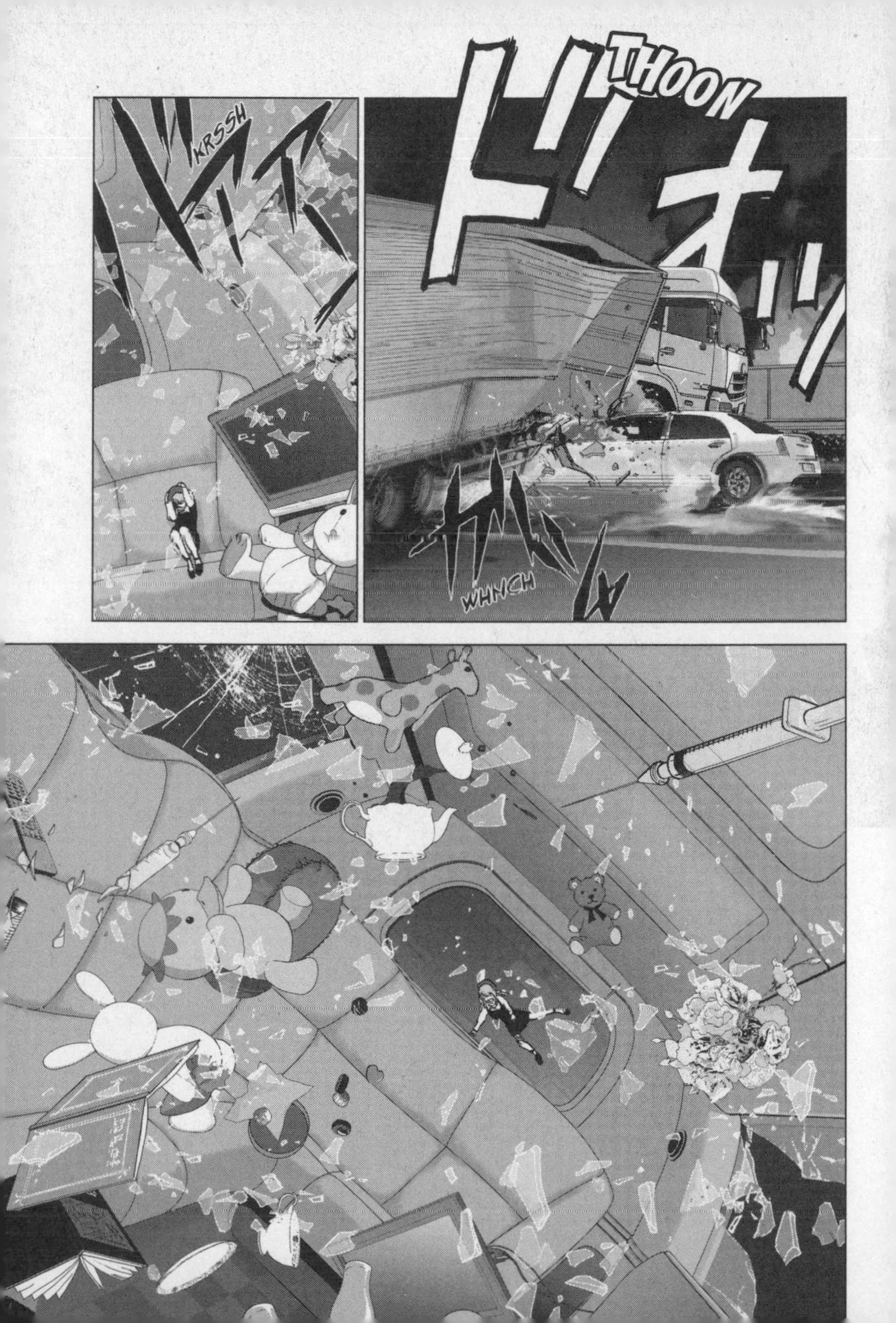
THOON
WHNCH
KRSSH

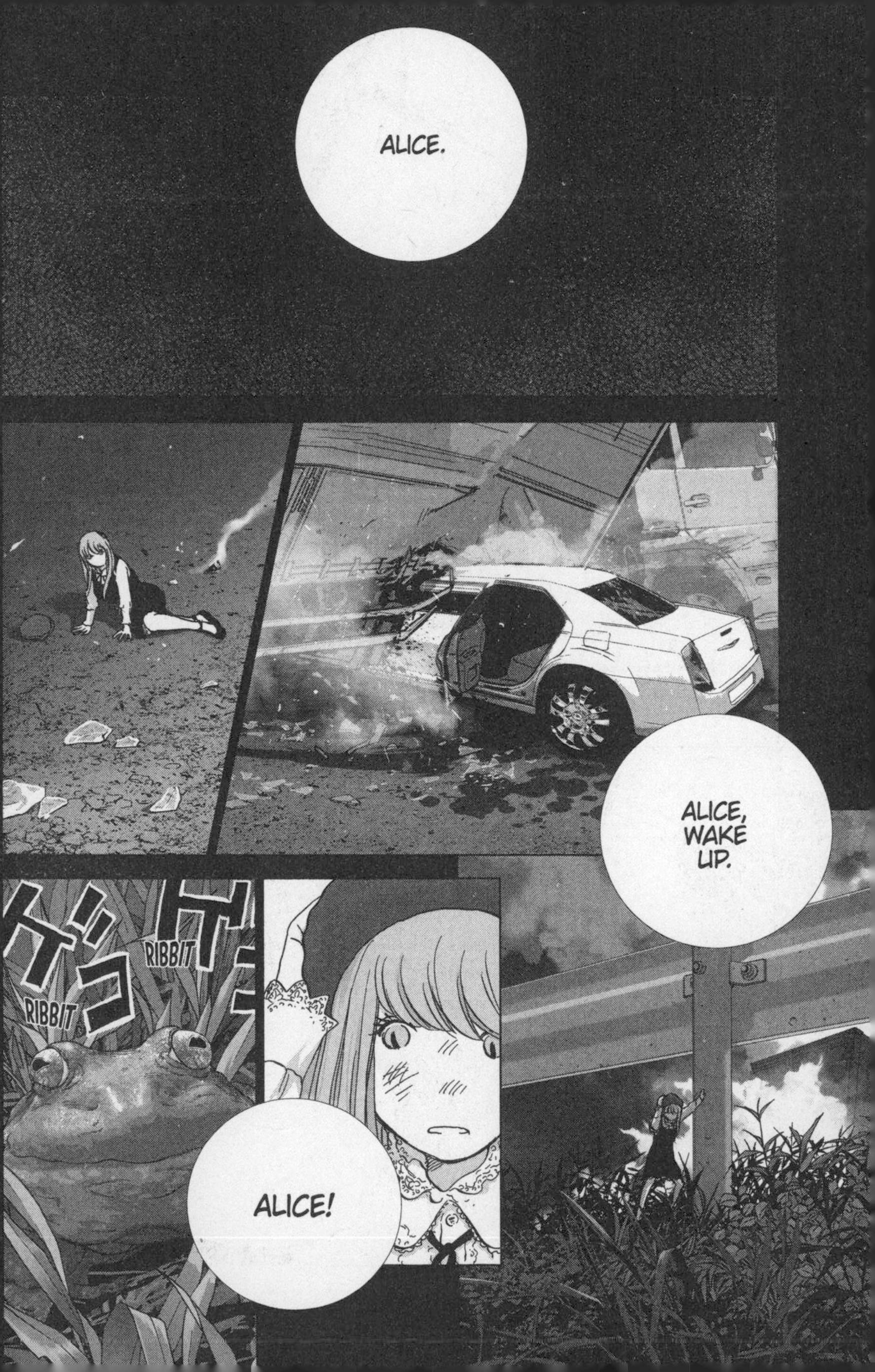
ALICE.
ALICE, WAKE UP.
ALICE!
RIBBIT
RIBBIT

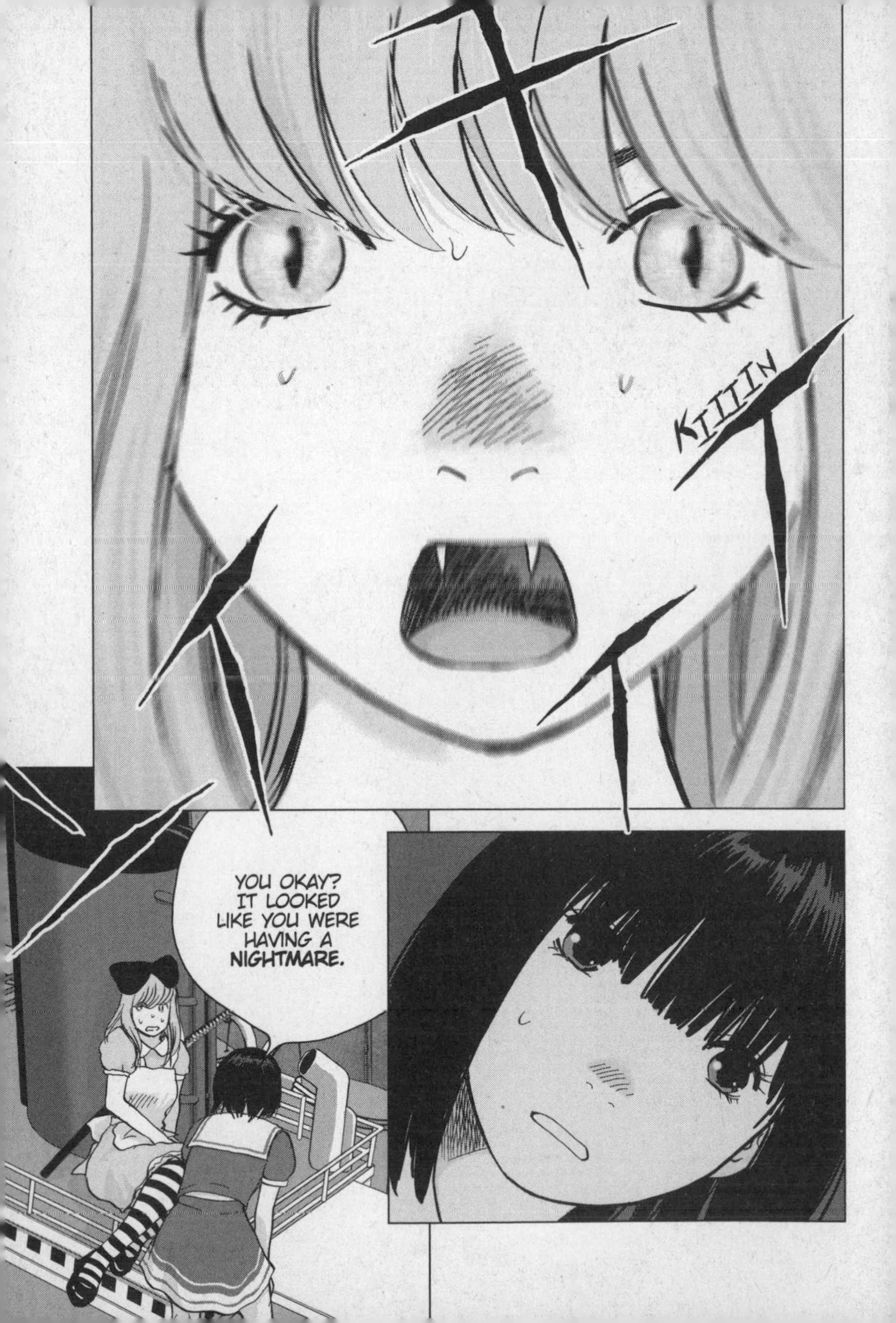
KIIIIN
YOU OKAY? IT LOOKED LIKE YOU WERE HAVING A NIGHTMARE.

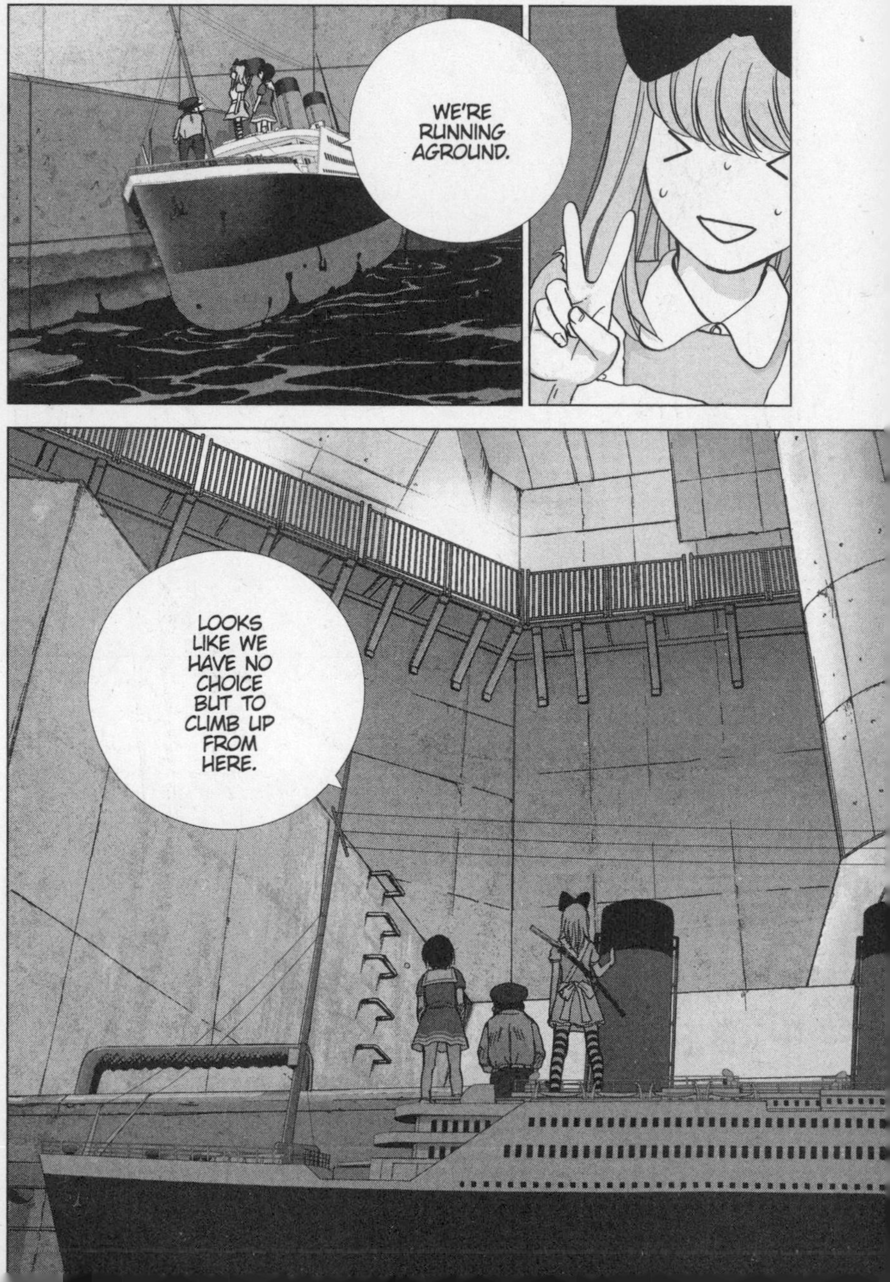
WE'RE RUNNING AGROUND.
LOOKS LIKE WE HAVE NO CHOICE BUT TO CLIMB UP FROM HERE.

Chapter 16: Alice, the Weapon

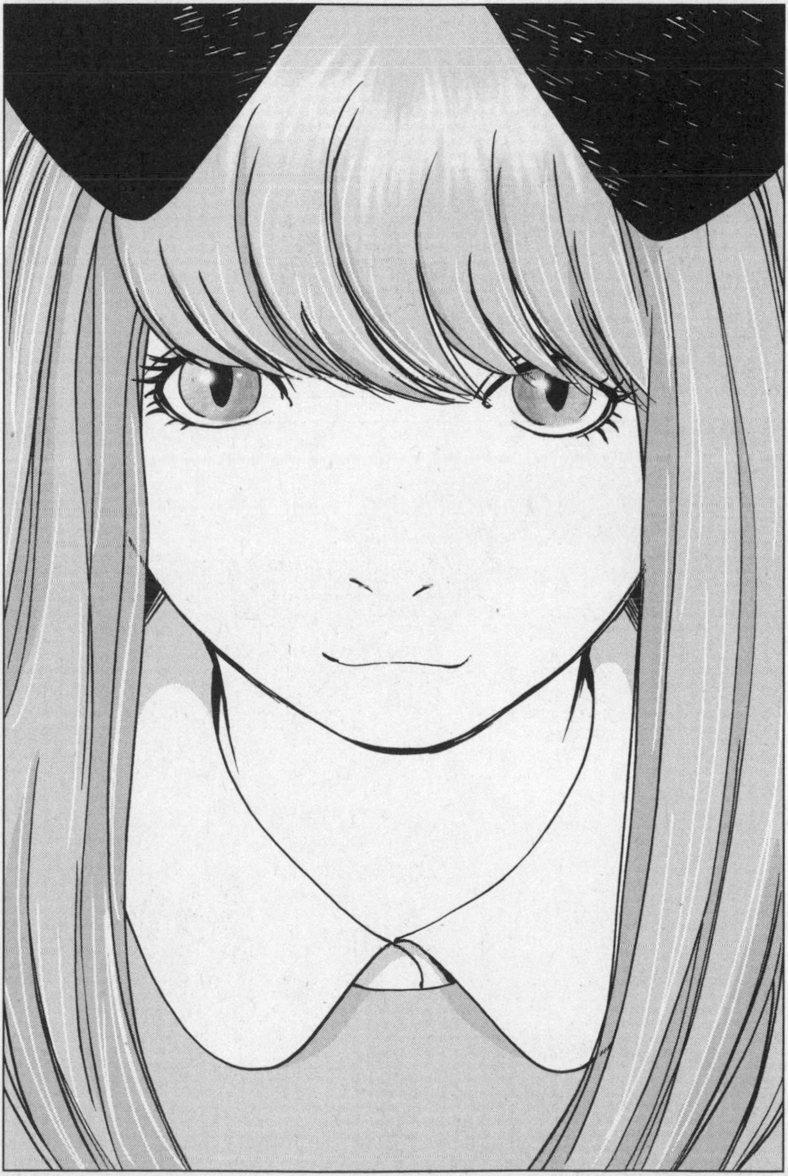

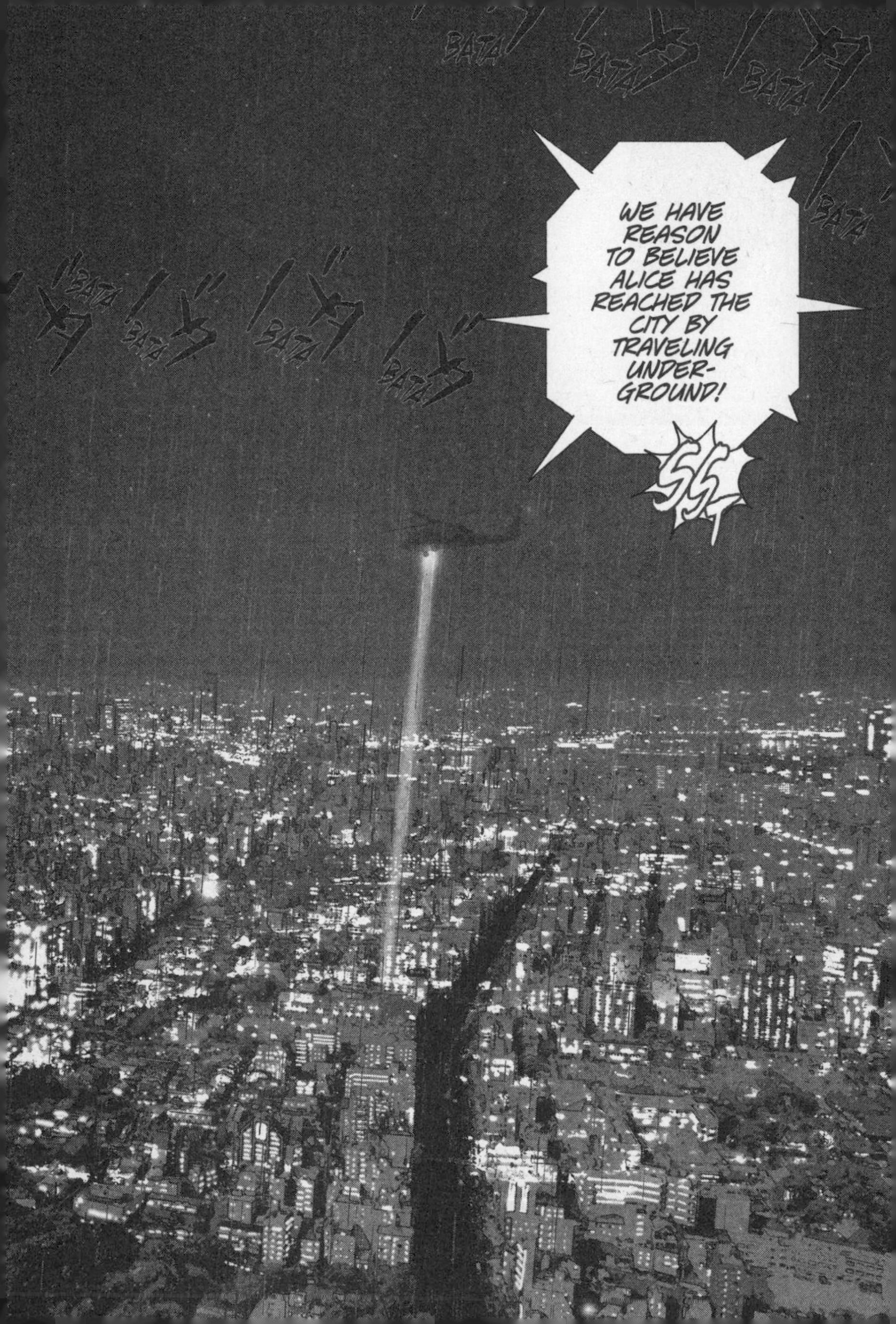
BATA BATA BATA BATA
WE HAVE REASON TO BELIEVE ALICE HAS REACHED THE CITY BY TRAVELING UNDER-GROUND!
BATA BATA BATA BATA
SSS

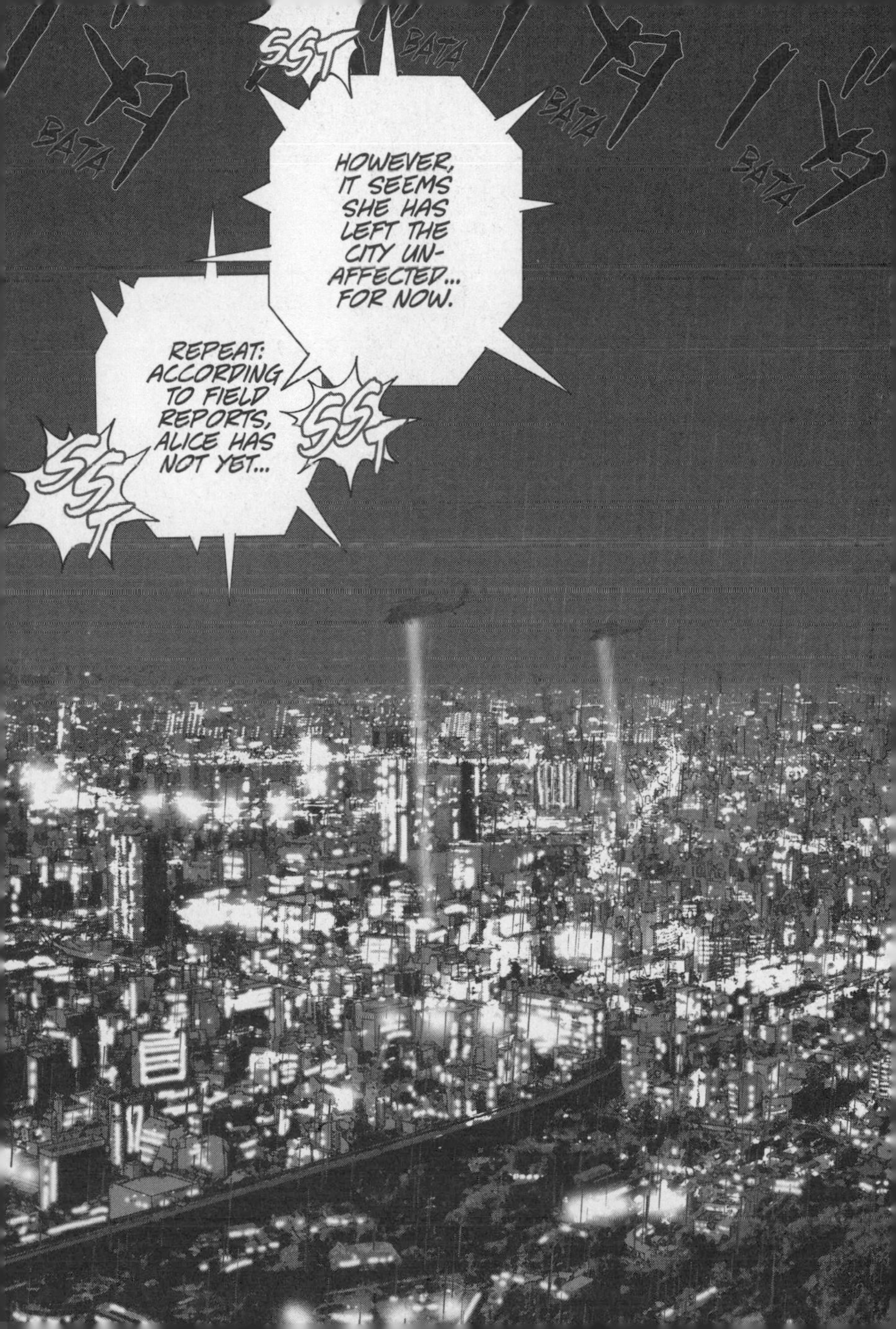
BATA
BATA
BATA
BATA
SST
REPEAT: ACCORDING TO FIELD REPORTS, ALICE HAS NOT YET...
HOWEVER, IT SEEMS SHE HAS LEFT THE CITY UN-AFFECTED... FOR NOW.
SS
SST

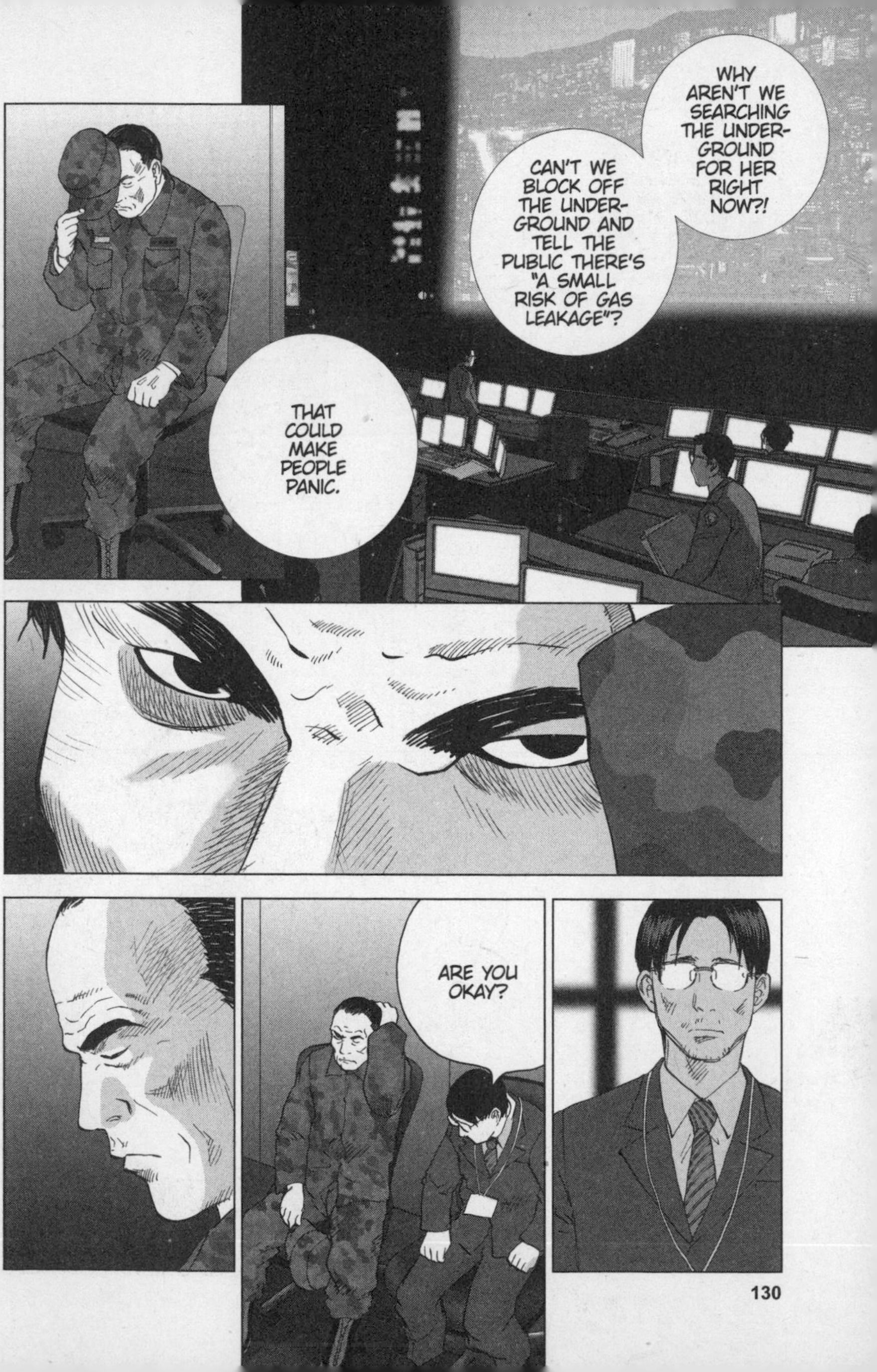
WHY AREN'T WE SEARCHING THE UNDER-GROUND FOR HER RIGHT NOW?!
CAN'T WE BLOCK OFF THE UNDER-GROUND AND TELL THE PUBLIC THERE'S "A SMALL RISK OF GAS LEAKAGE"?
THAT COULD MAKE PEOPLE PANIC.
ARE YOU OKAY?

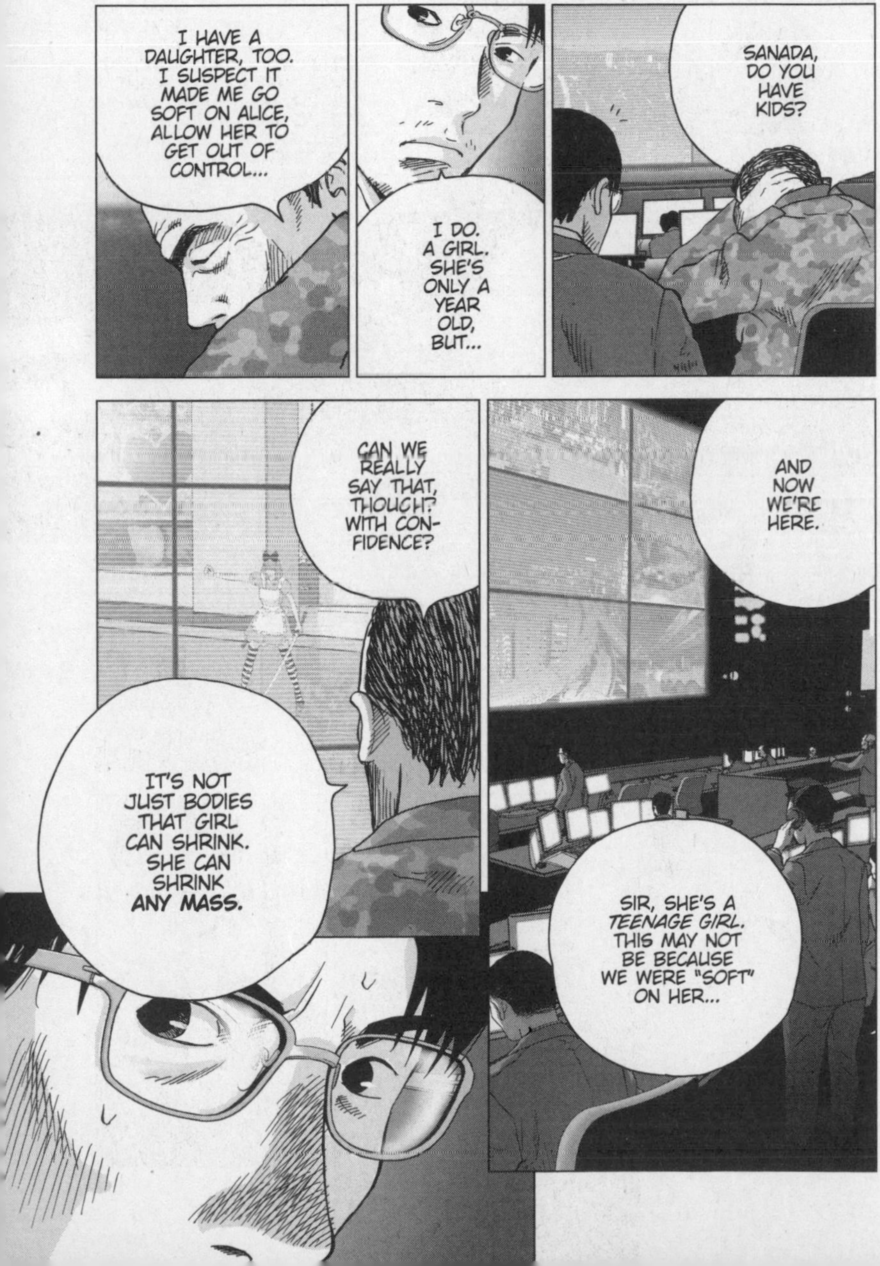
SANADA, DO YOU HAVE KIDS?
I DO. A GIRL. SHE'S ONLY A YEAR OLD, BUT...
I HAVE A DAUGHTER, TOO. I SUSPECT IT MADE ME GO SOFT ON ALICE, ALLOW HER TO GET OUT OF CONTROL...
AND NOW WE'RE HERE.
SIR, SHE'S A TEENAGE GIRL. THIS MAY NOT BE BECAUSE WE WERE "SOFT" ON HER...
CAN WE REALLY SAY THAT, THOUGH? WITH CONFIDENCE?
IT'S NOT JUST BODIES THAT GIRL CAN SHRINK. SHE CAN SHRINK ANY MASS.

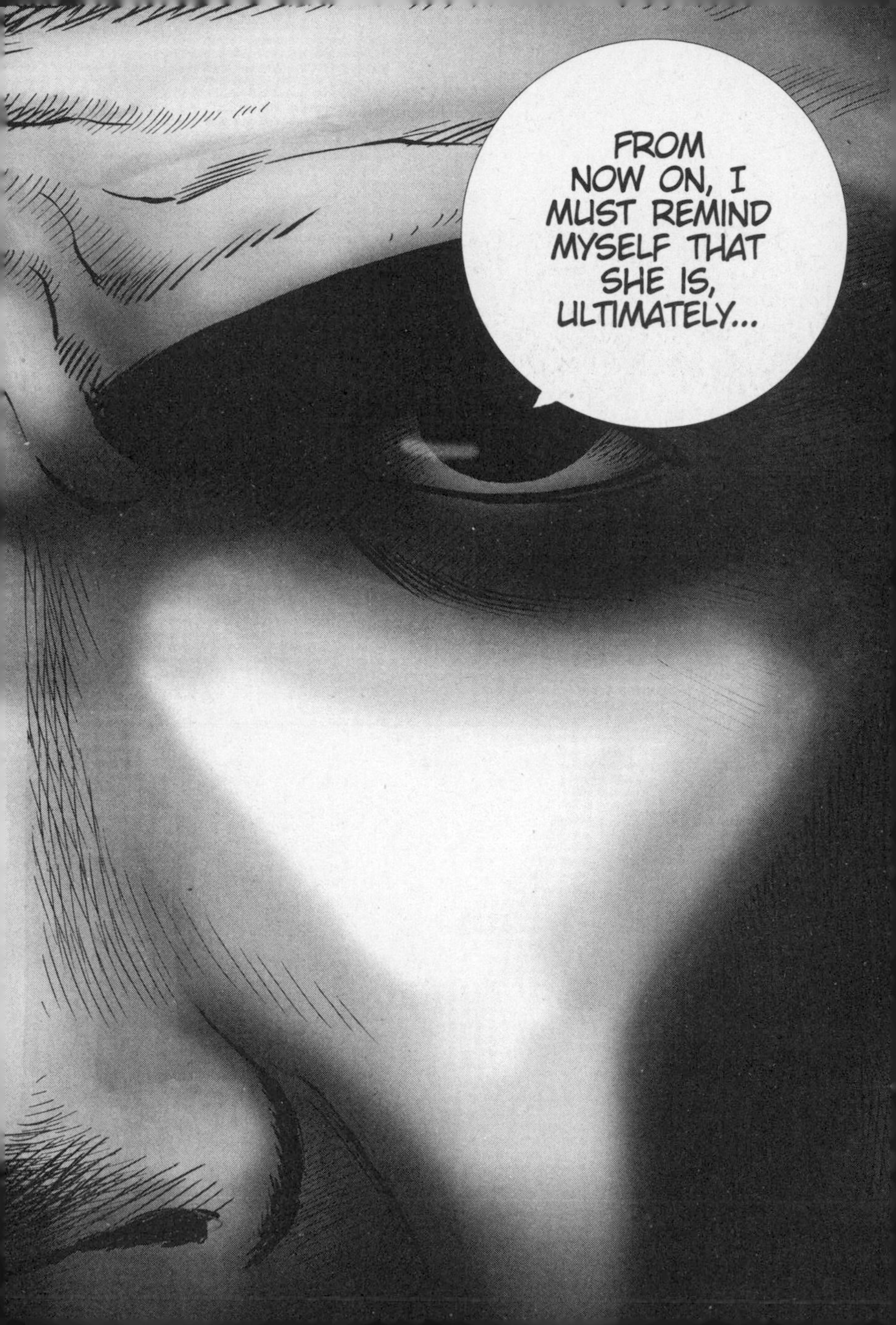
FROM NOW ON, I MUST REMIND MYSELF THAT SHE IS, ULTIMATELY...

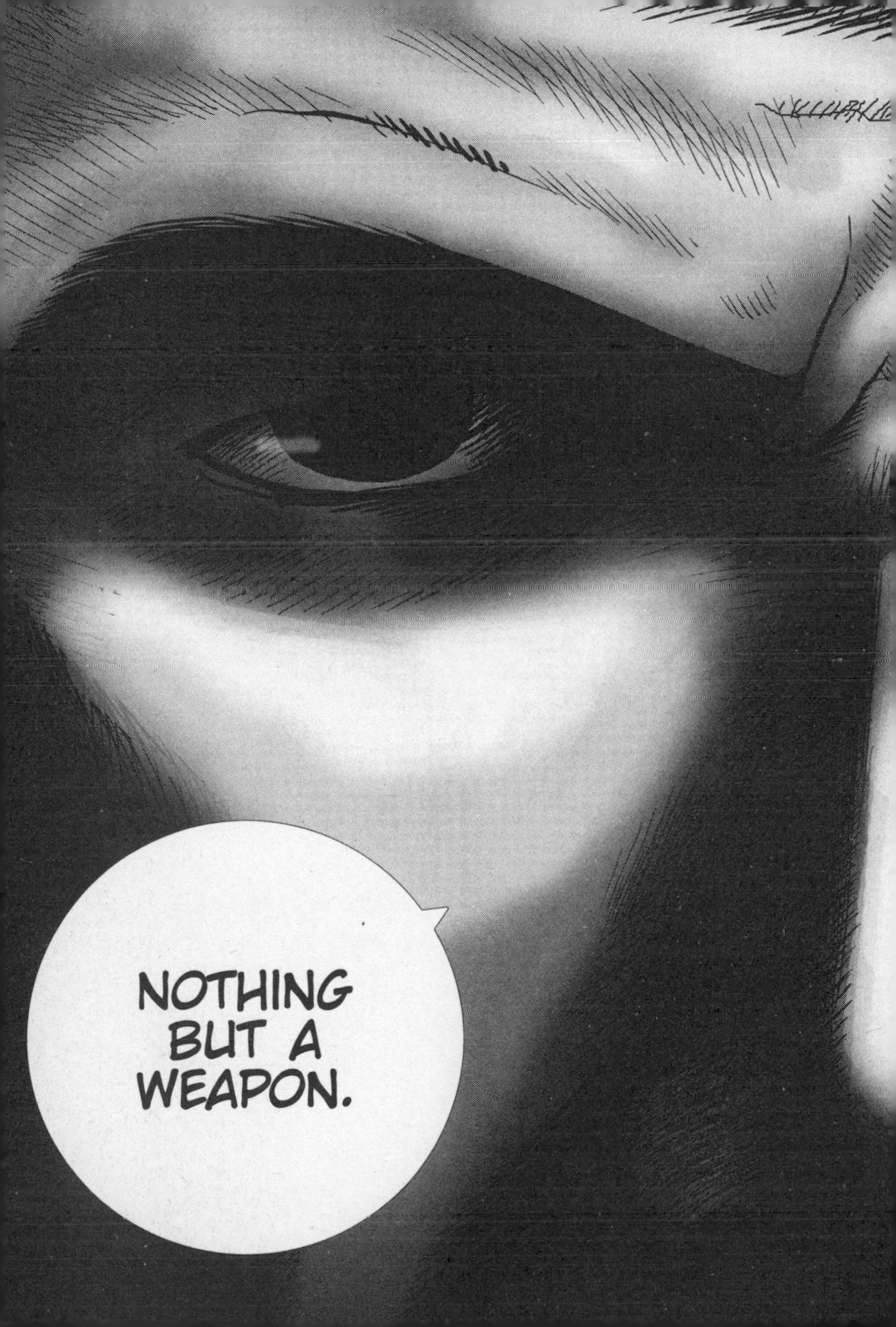
NOTHING BUT A WEAPON.

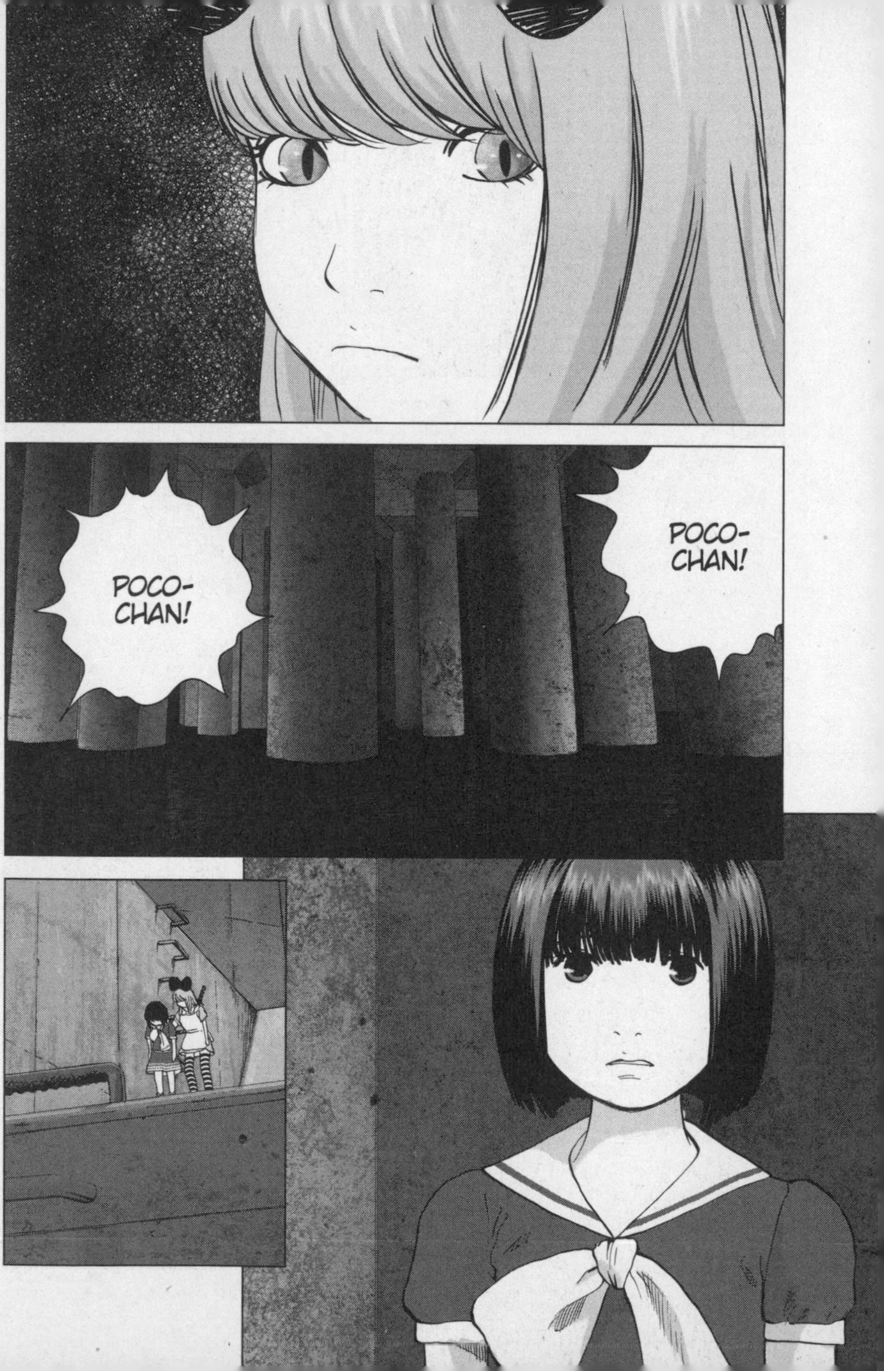
POCO-CHAN!
POCO-CHAN!

YUKKO-CHAN, I'M REALLY SORRY ABOUT YOUR DOG...

BUT THE WATER IS RISING. WE HAVE TO KEEP GOING.

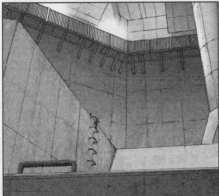

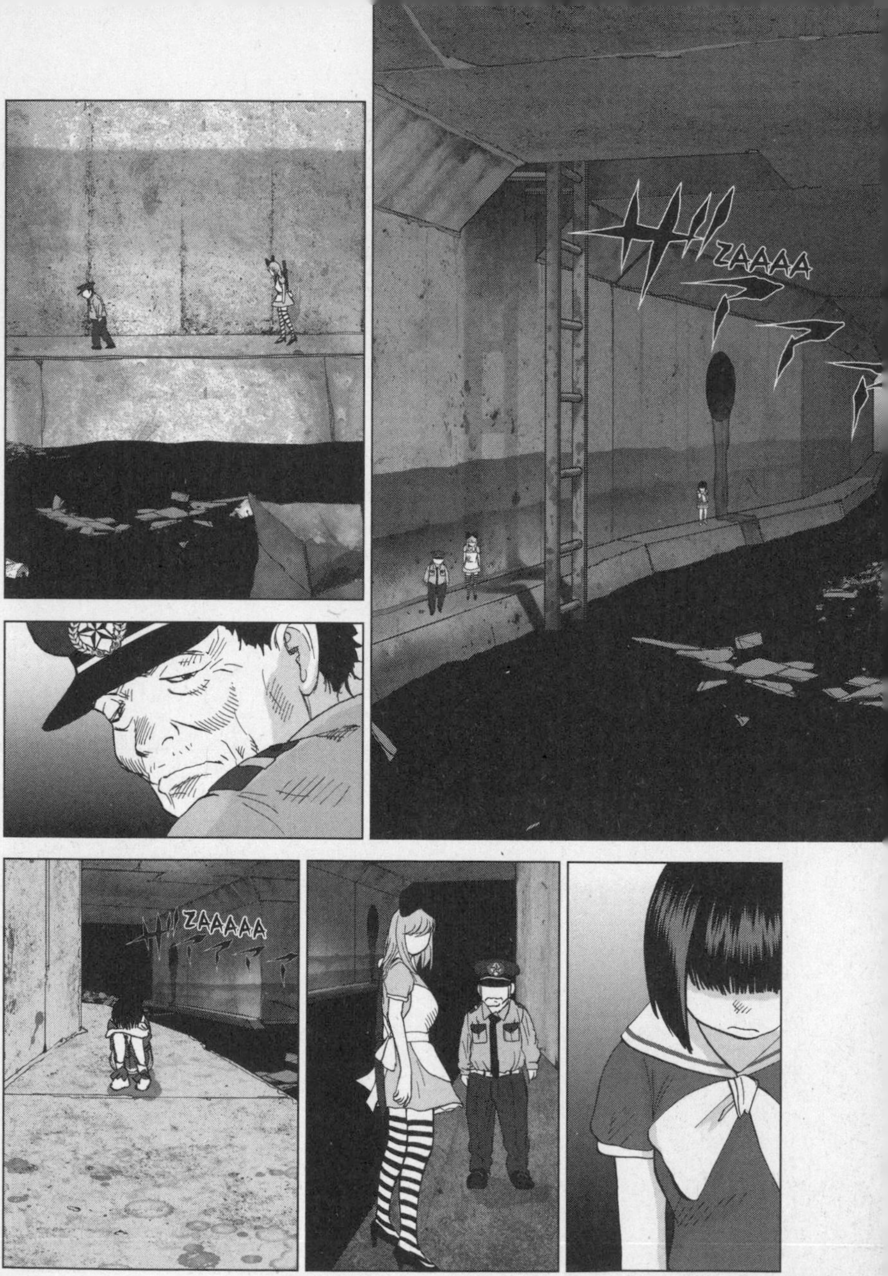
ZAAAA
ZAAAAA

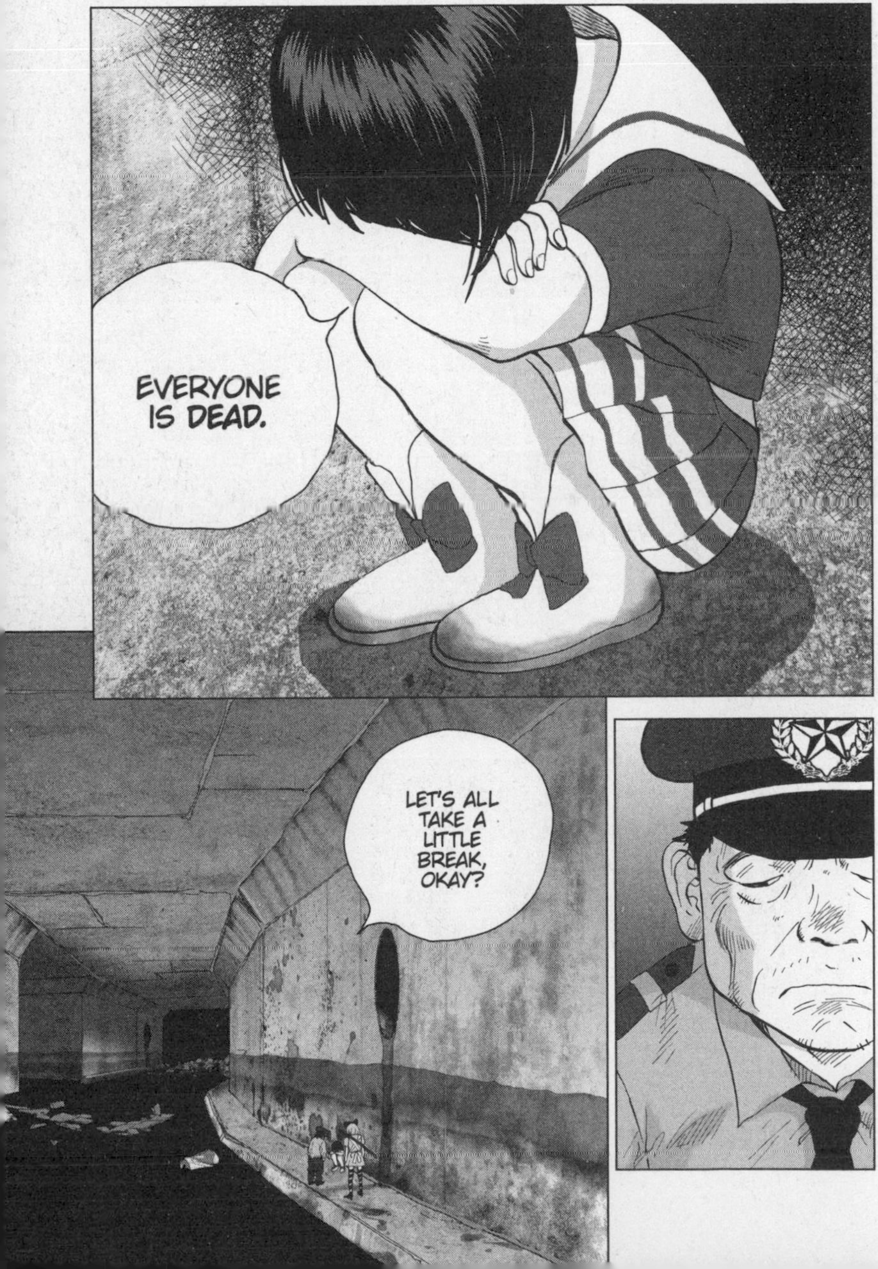
EVERYONE IS DEAD.
LET'S ALL TAKE A LITTLE BREAK, OKAY?

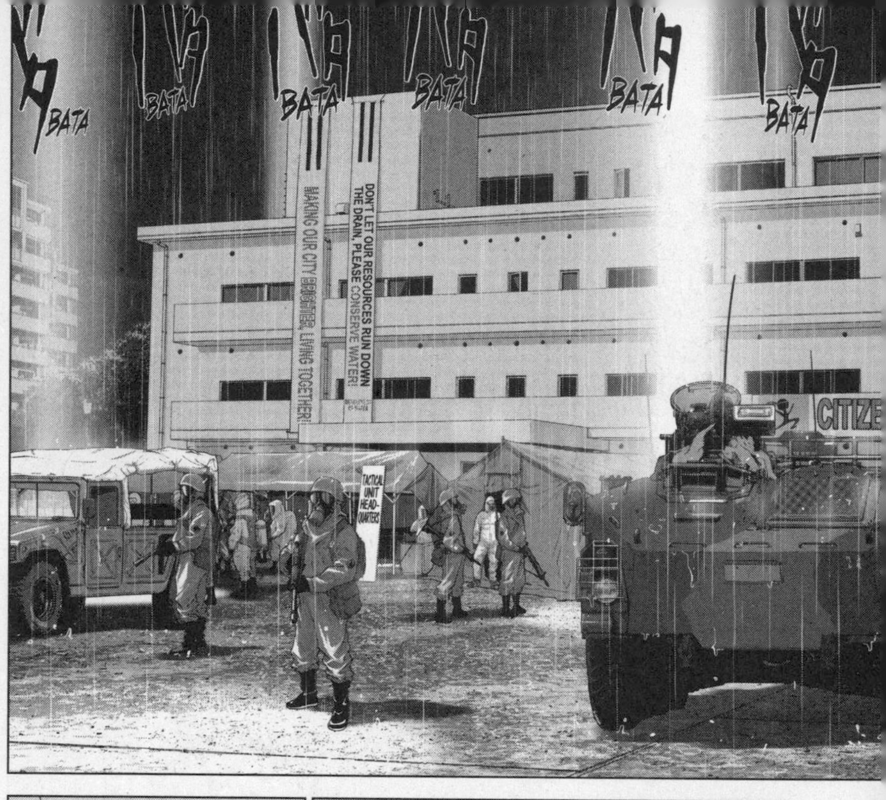
BATA
BATA
BATA
BATA
BATA
BATA
MAKING OUR CITY BRIGHTER, LIVING TOGETHER!
DON'T LET OUR RESOURCES RUN DOWN THE DRAIN, PLEASE CONSERVE WATER!
TACTICAL UNIT HEAD-QUARTERS
CITIZE

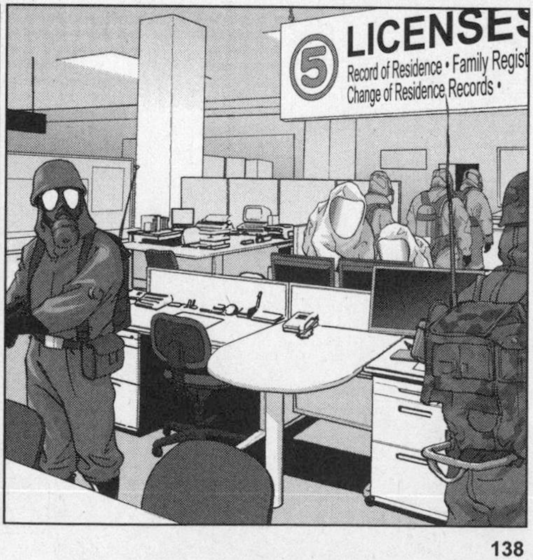
5 LICENSES
Record of Residence • Family Regist
Change of Residence Records •

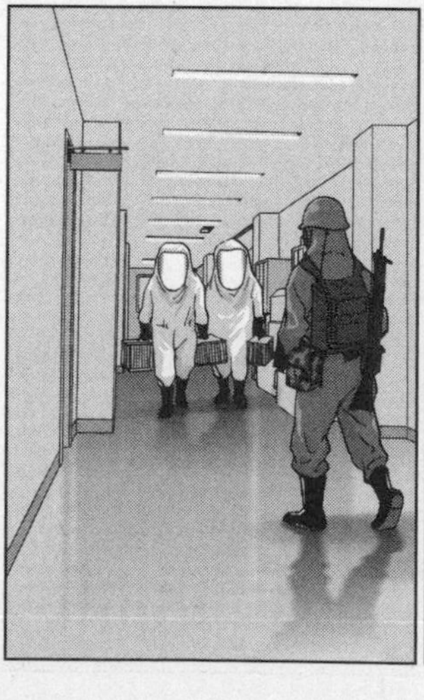

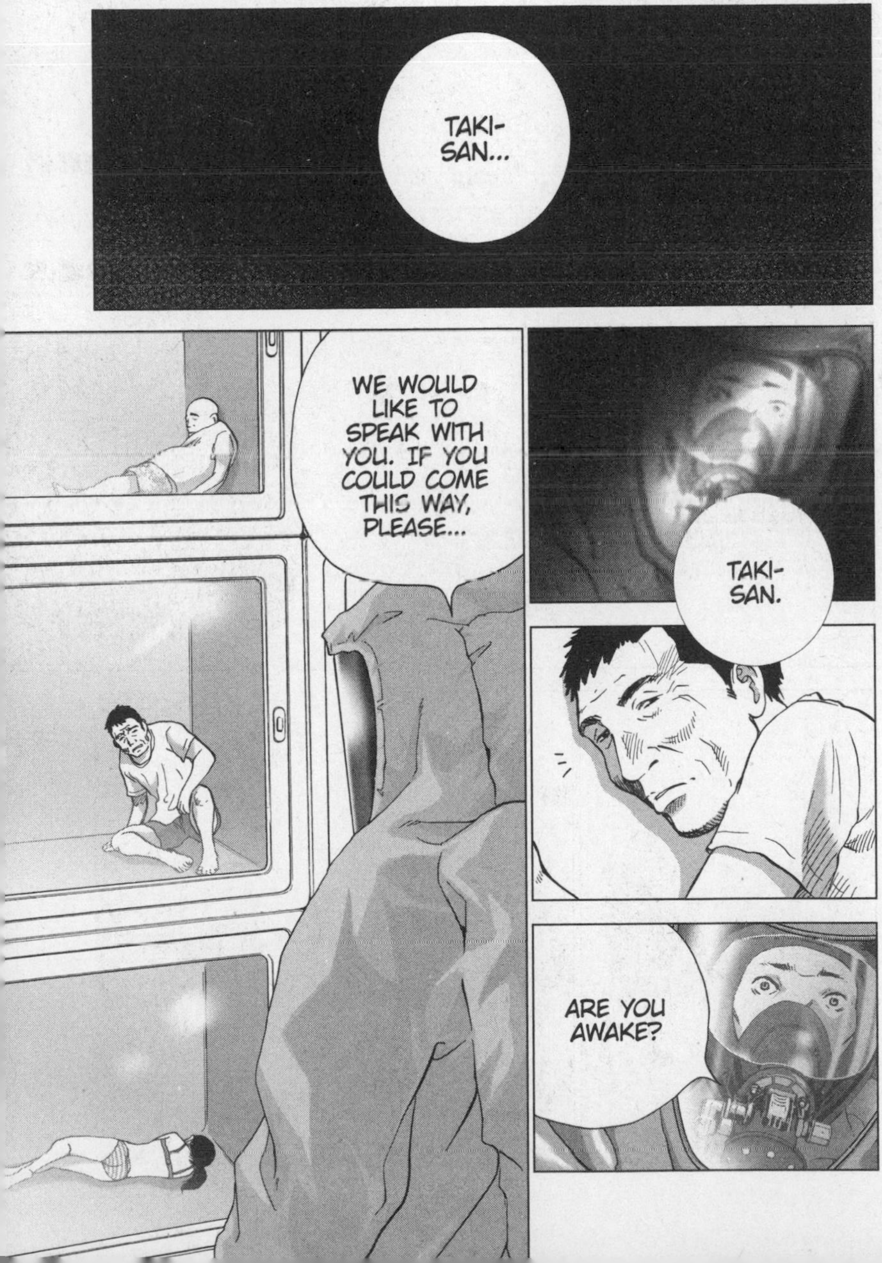
TAKI-SAN...
TAKI-SAN.
ARE YOU AWAKE?
WE WOULD LIKE TO SPEAK WITH YOU. IF YOU COULD COME THIS WAY, PLEASE...

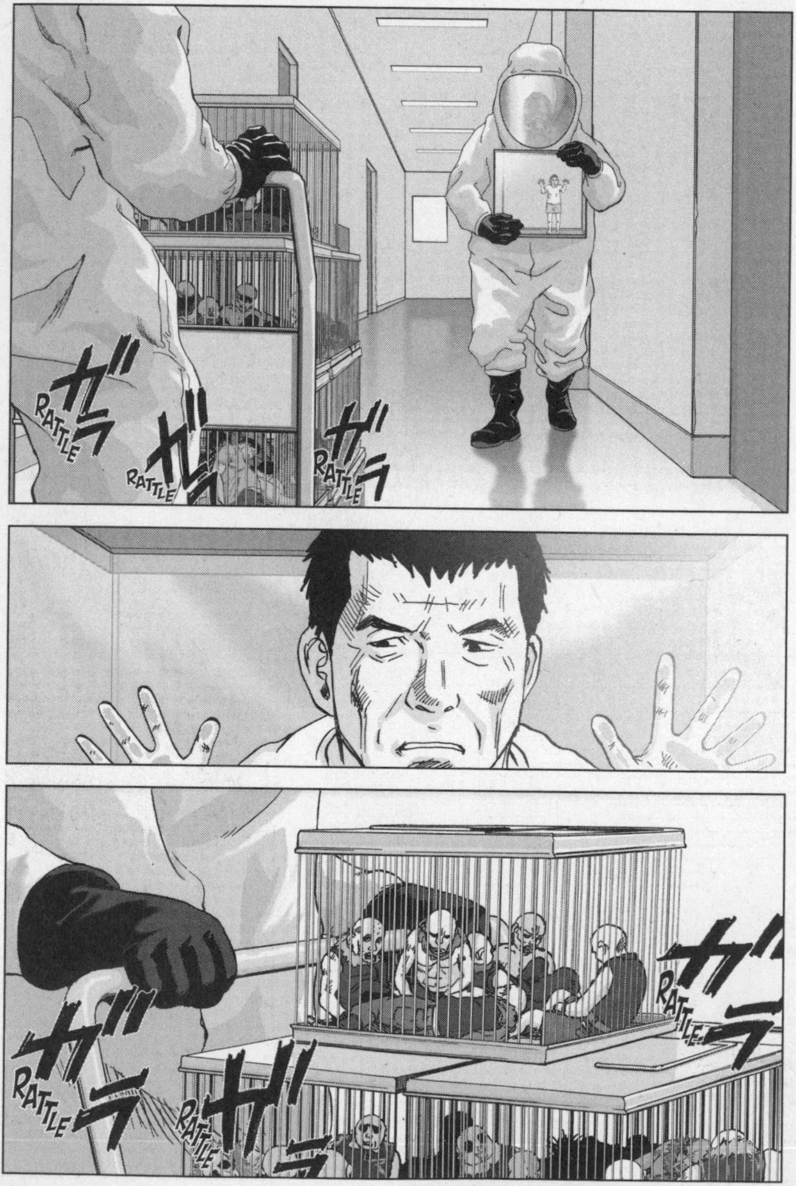
ガラ
RATTLE
ガラ
RATTLE
ガラ
RATTLE
ガラ
RATTLE
ガラ
RATTLE
ガラ
RATTLE

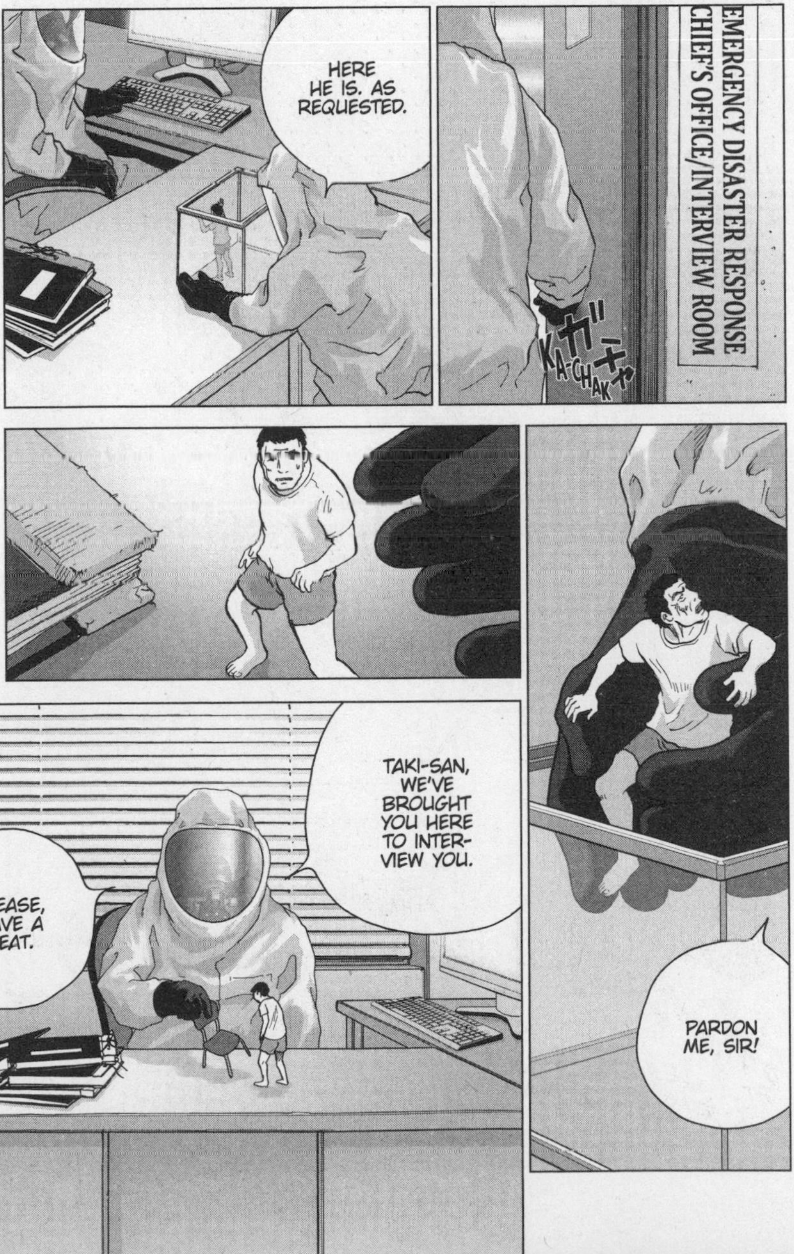
EMERGENCY DISASTER RESPONSE CHIEF'S OFFICE/INTERVIEW ROOM
KA-CHAK
HERE HE IS. AS REQUESTED.
PARDON ME, SIR!
TAKI-SAN, WE'VE BROUGHT YOU HERE TO INTER-VIEW YOU.
PLEASE, HAVE A SEAT.

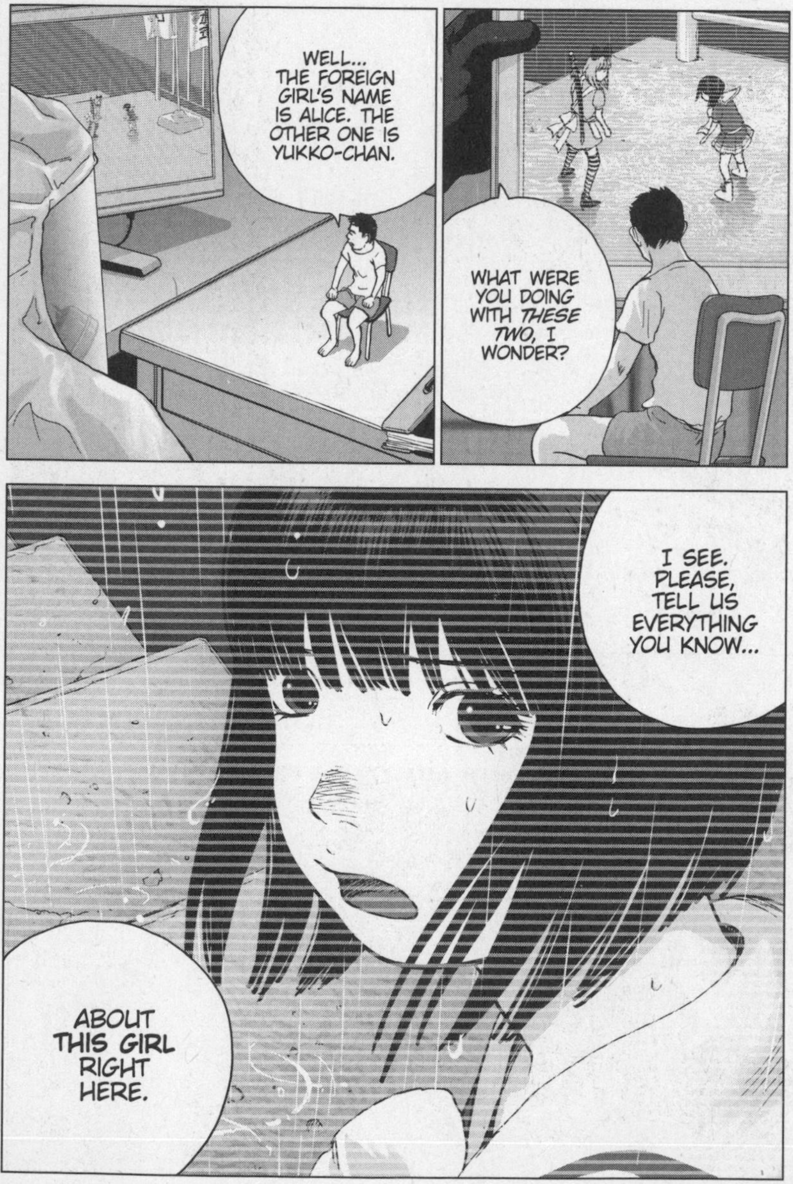
WHAT WERE YOU DOING WITH *THESE TWO*, I WONDER?
WELL... THE FOREIGN GIRL'S NAME IS ALICE. THE OTHER ONE IS YUKKO-CHAN.
I SEE. PLEASE, TELL US EVERYTHING YOU KNOW...
ABOUT THIS GIRL RIGHT HERE.

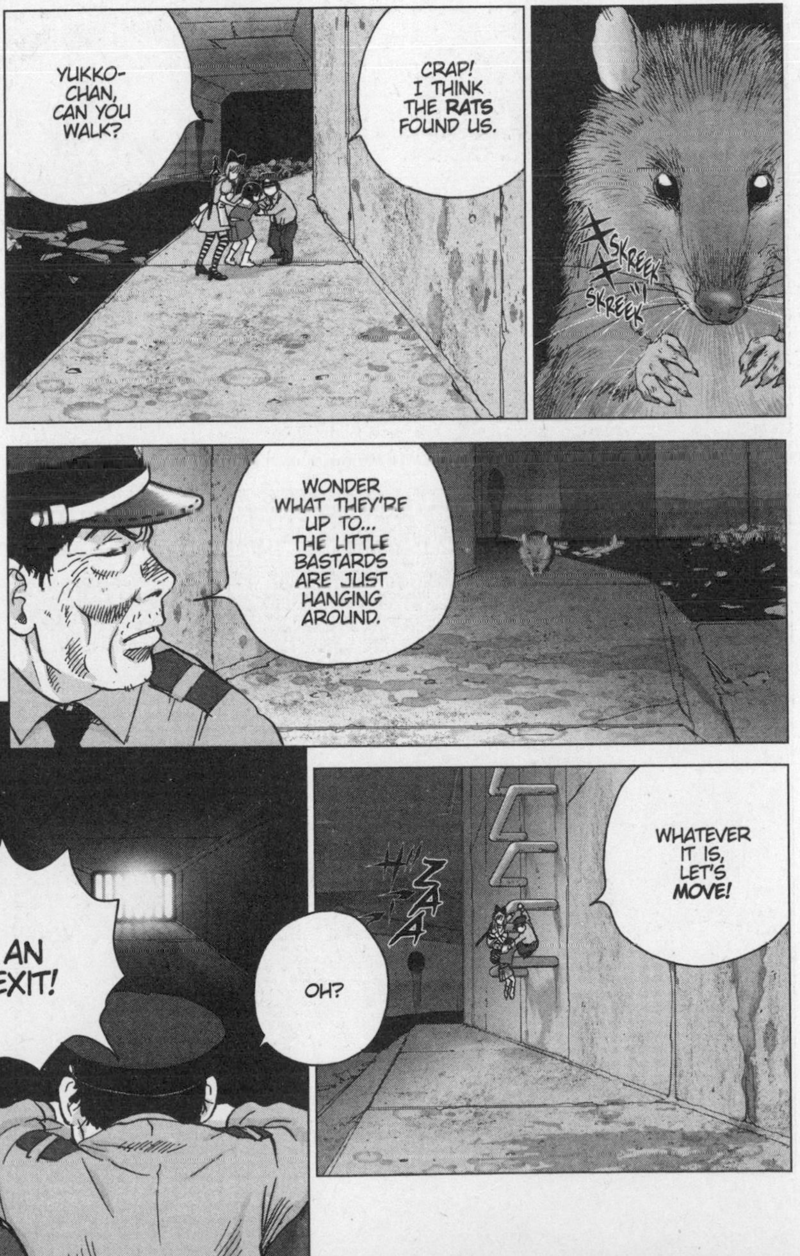
SKREEK
SKREEK
CRAP! I THINK THE RATS FOUND US.
YUKKO-CHAN, CAN YOU WALK?
WONDER WHAT THEY'RE UP TO... THE LITTLE BASTARDS ARE JUST HANGING AROUND.
WHATEVER IT IS, LET'S MOVE!
ZAA
OH?
AN EXIT!

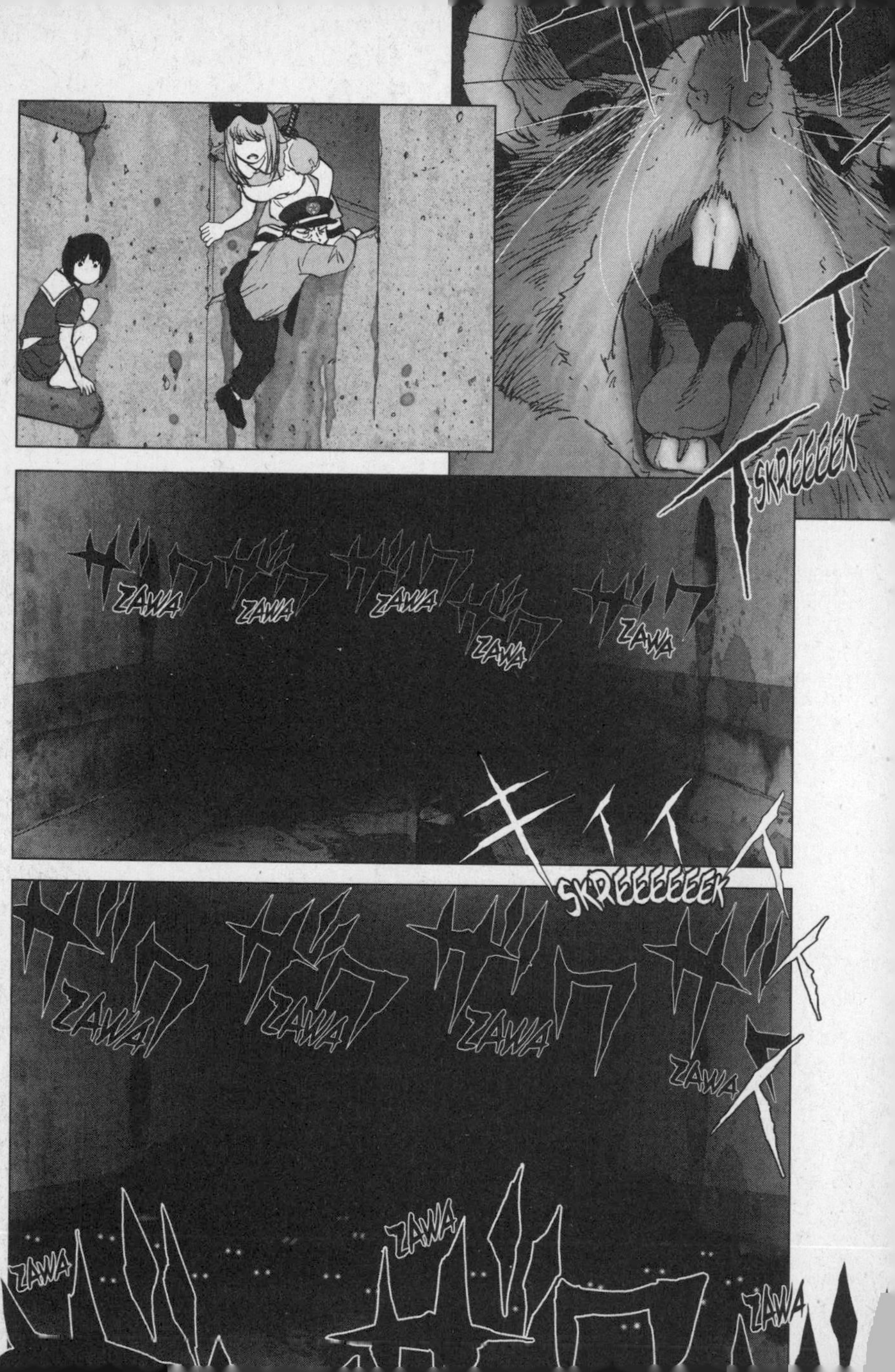
SKREEEEEK
ZAWA
ZAWA
ZAWA
ZAWA
ZAWA
SKREEEEEEEK
ZAWA
ZAWA
ZAWA
ZAWA
ZAWA
ZAWA
ZAWA

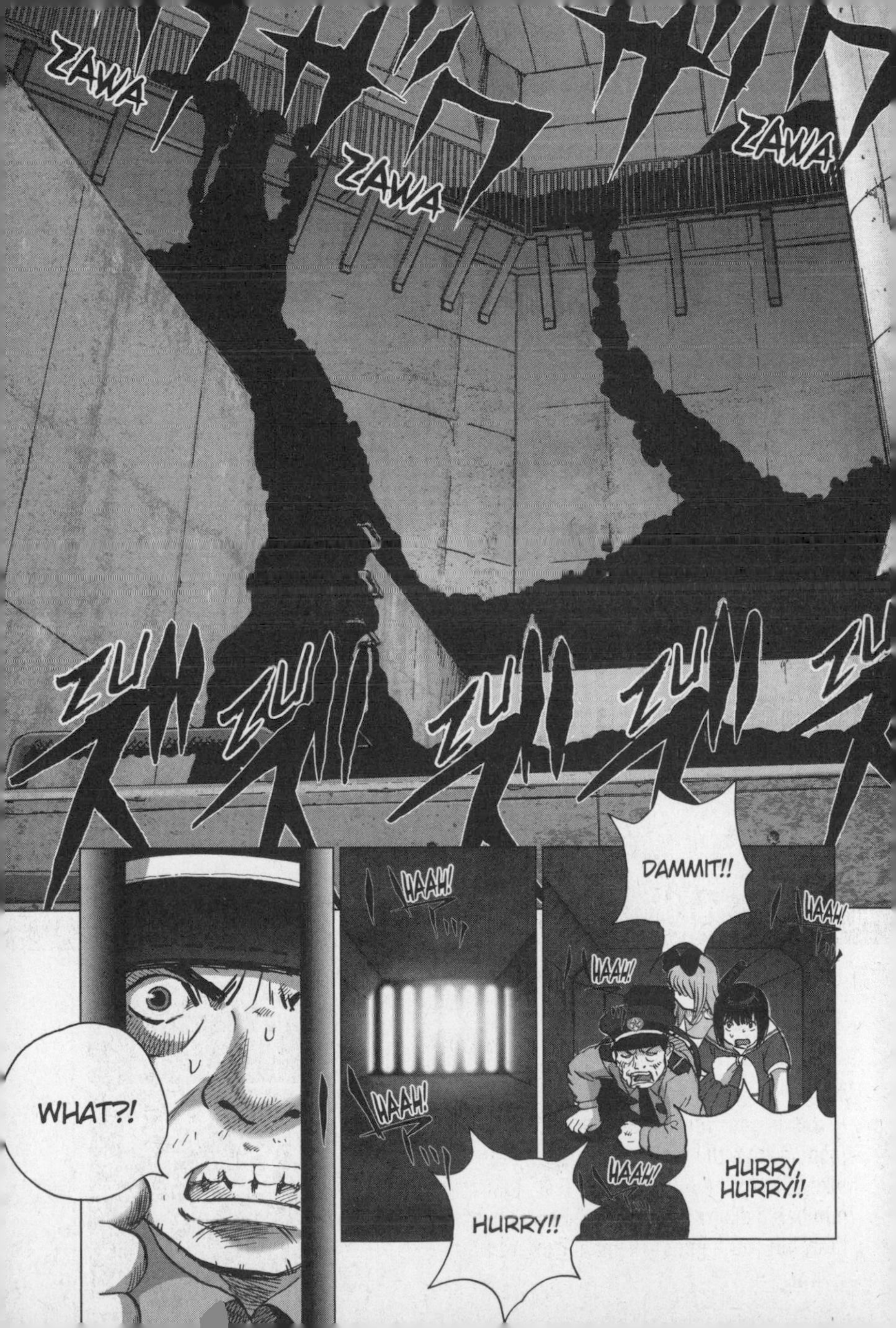
ZAWA
ZAWA
ZAWA
ZU
ZU
ZU
ZU
ZU
DAMMIT!!
HAAH!
HAAH!
HURRY, HURRY!!
HAAH!
HAAH!
HAAH!
HURRY!!
WHAT?!

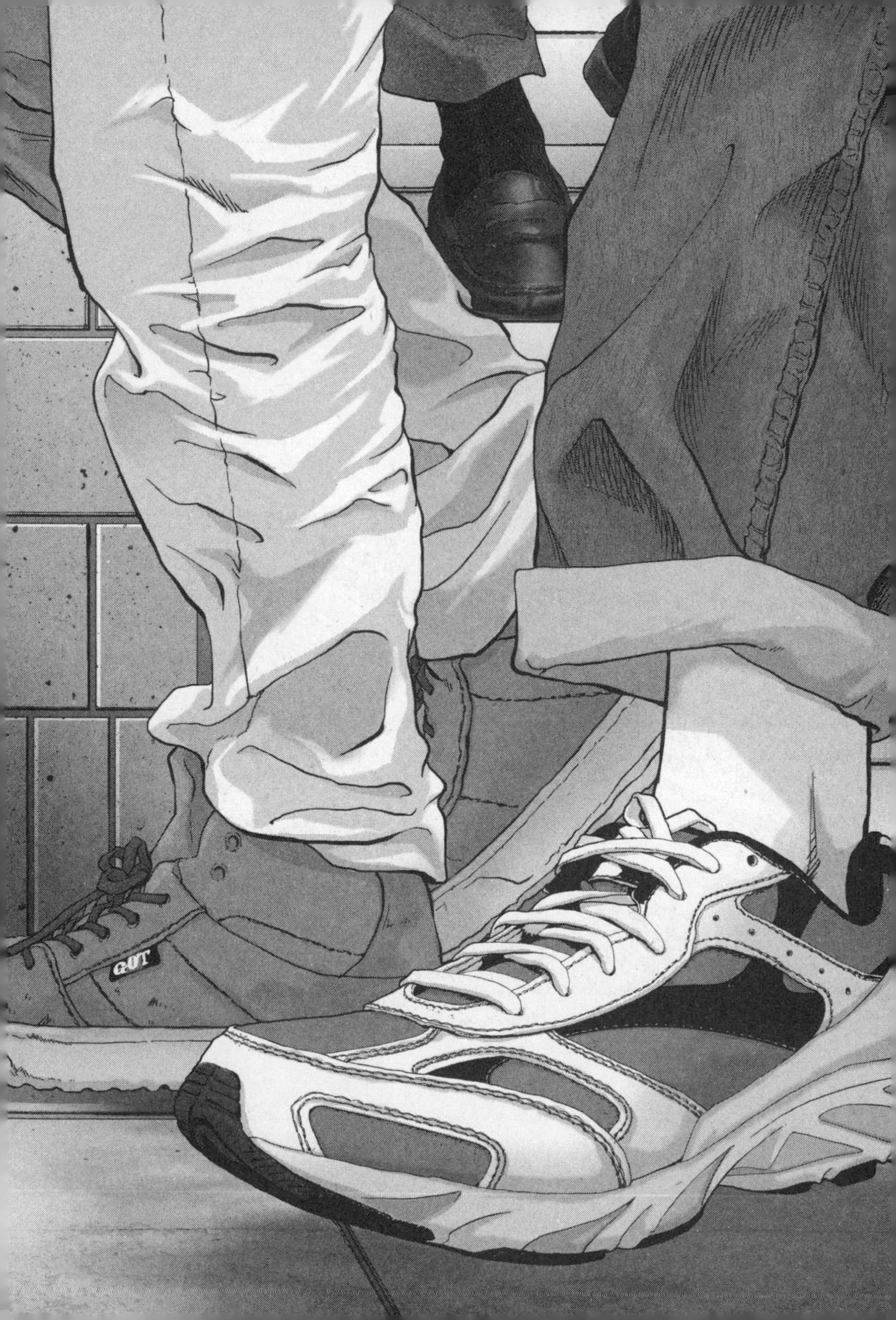

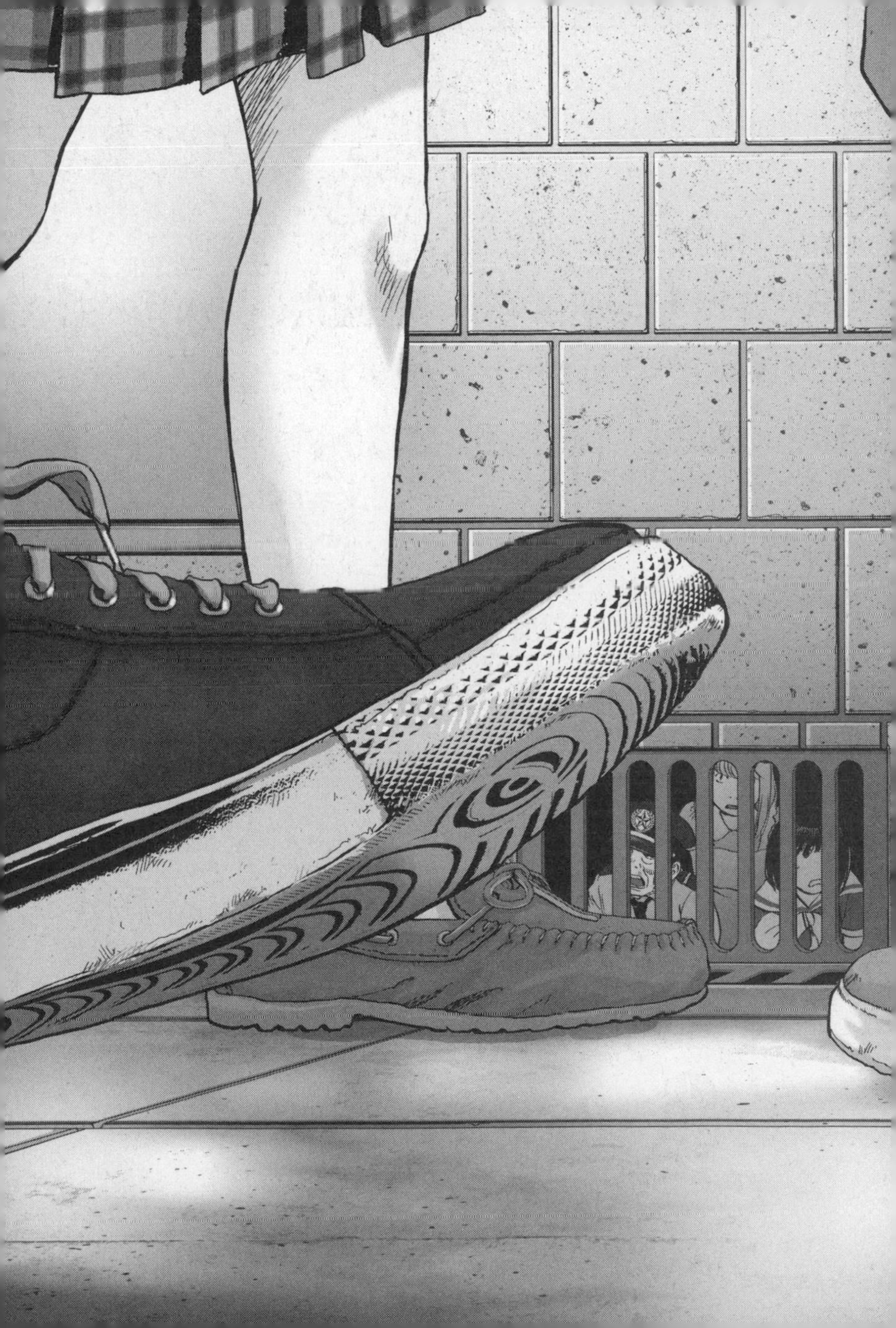

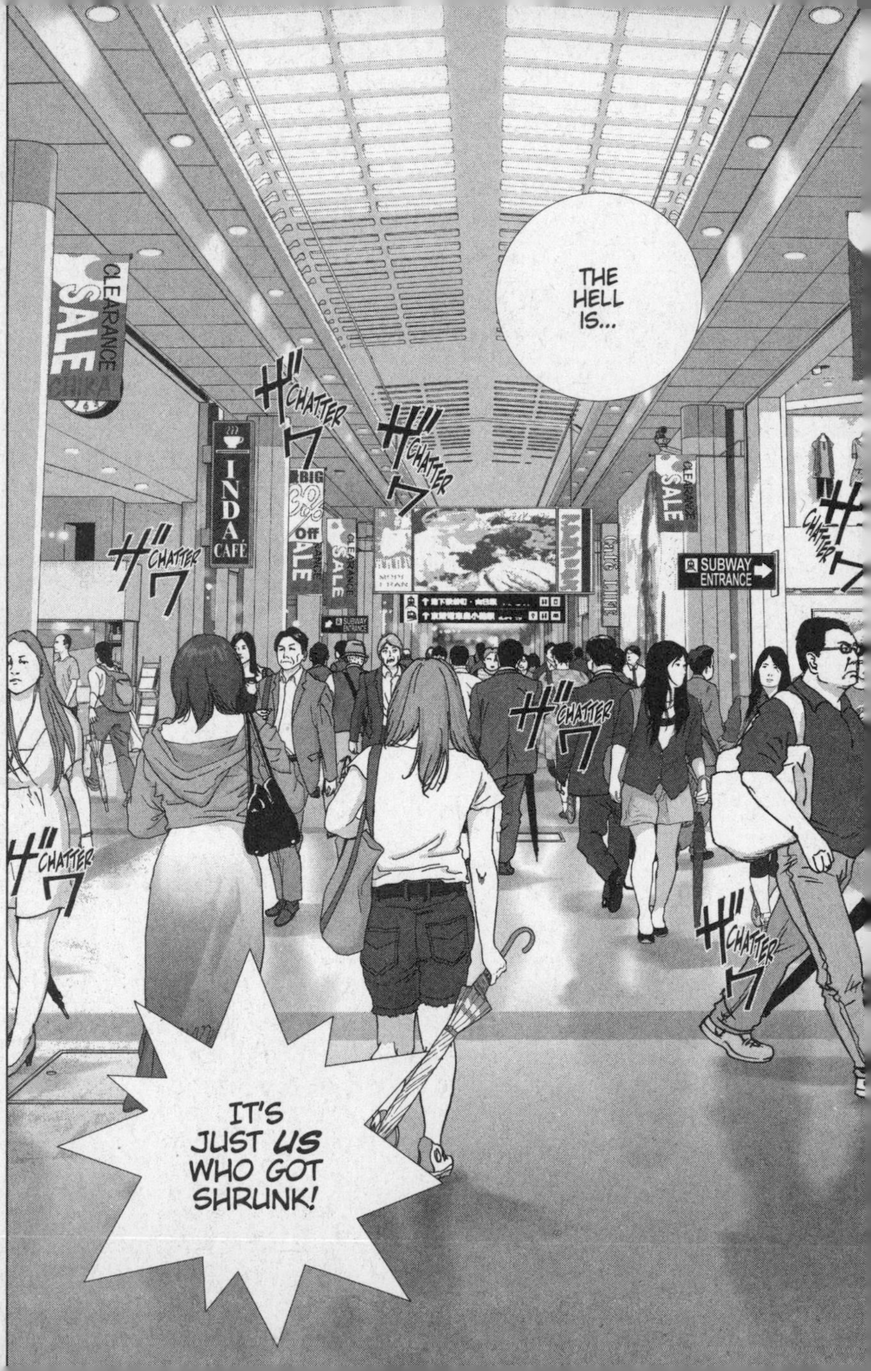
THE HELL IS...
CHATTER
SUBWAY ENTRANCE
CLEARANCE SALE
CHATTER
CHATTER
CHATTER
CLEARANCE SALE
INDA CAFÉ
CLEARANCE SALE
CHATTER
CHATTER
CHATTER
IT'S JUST *US* WHO GOT SHRUNK!

Chapter 17: The Chase

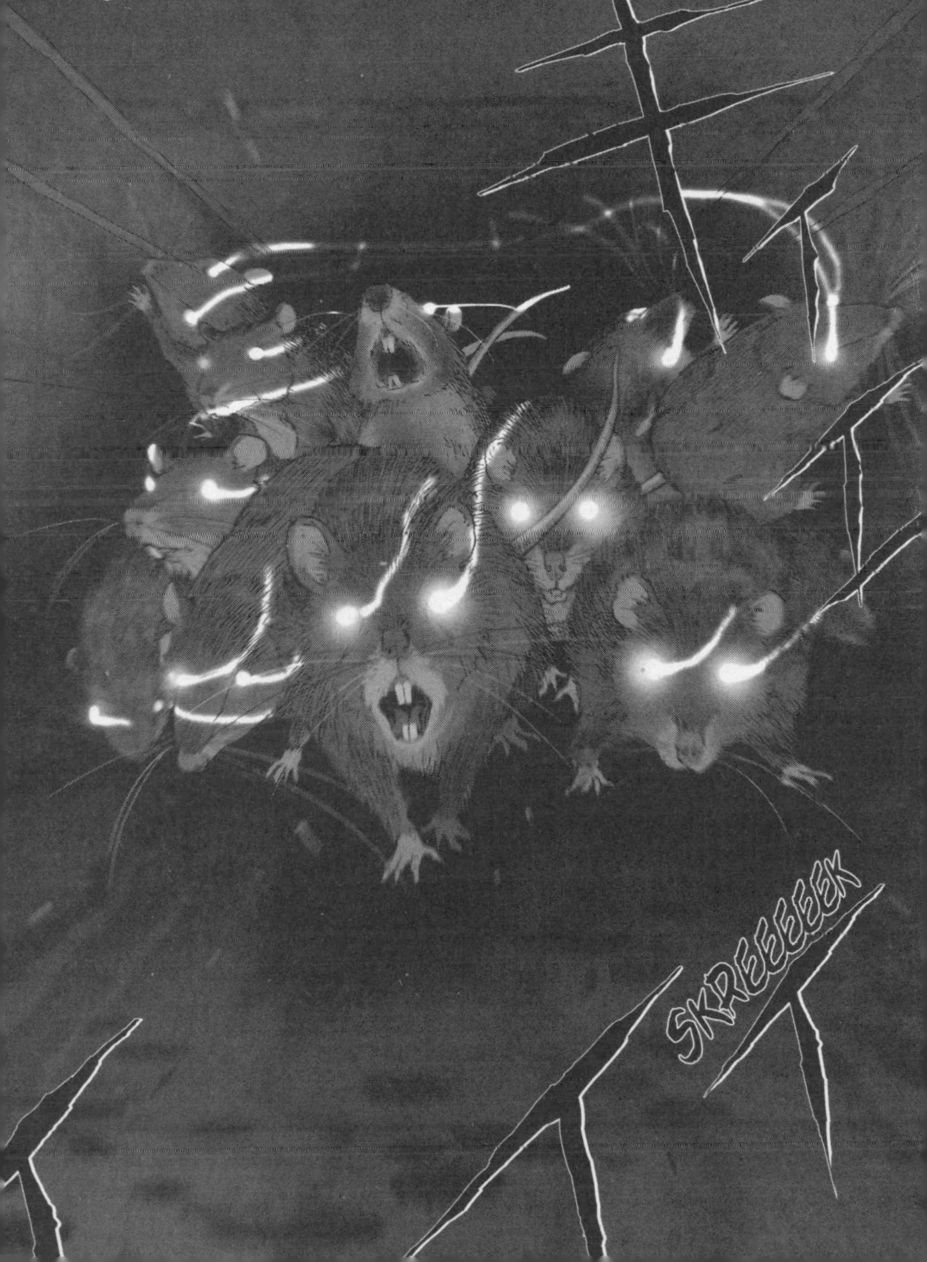
SKREEEEEK

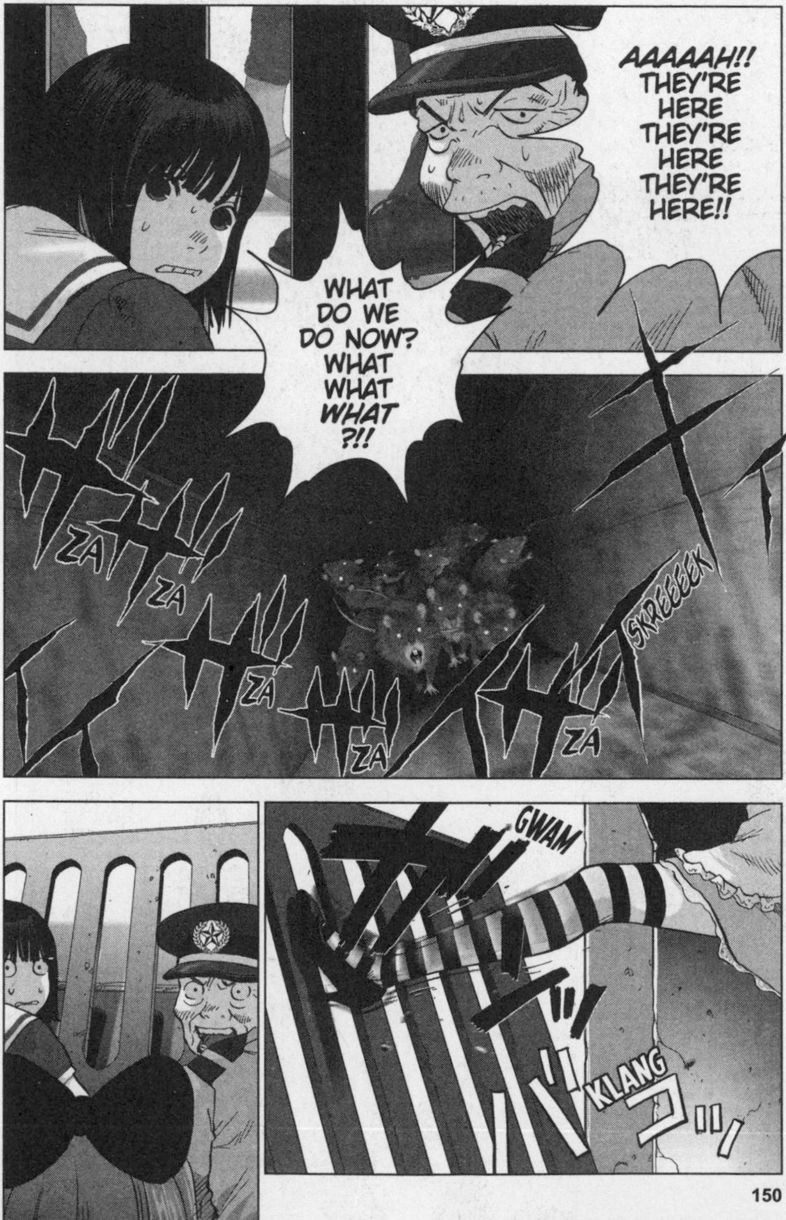
AAAAAH!! THEY'RE HERE THEY'RE HERE THEY'RE HERE!!
WHAT DO WE DO NOW? WHAT WHAT WHAT ?!!
SKREEEEK
ZA
ZA
ZA
ZA
ZA
ZA
GWAM
KLANG

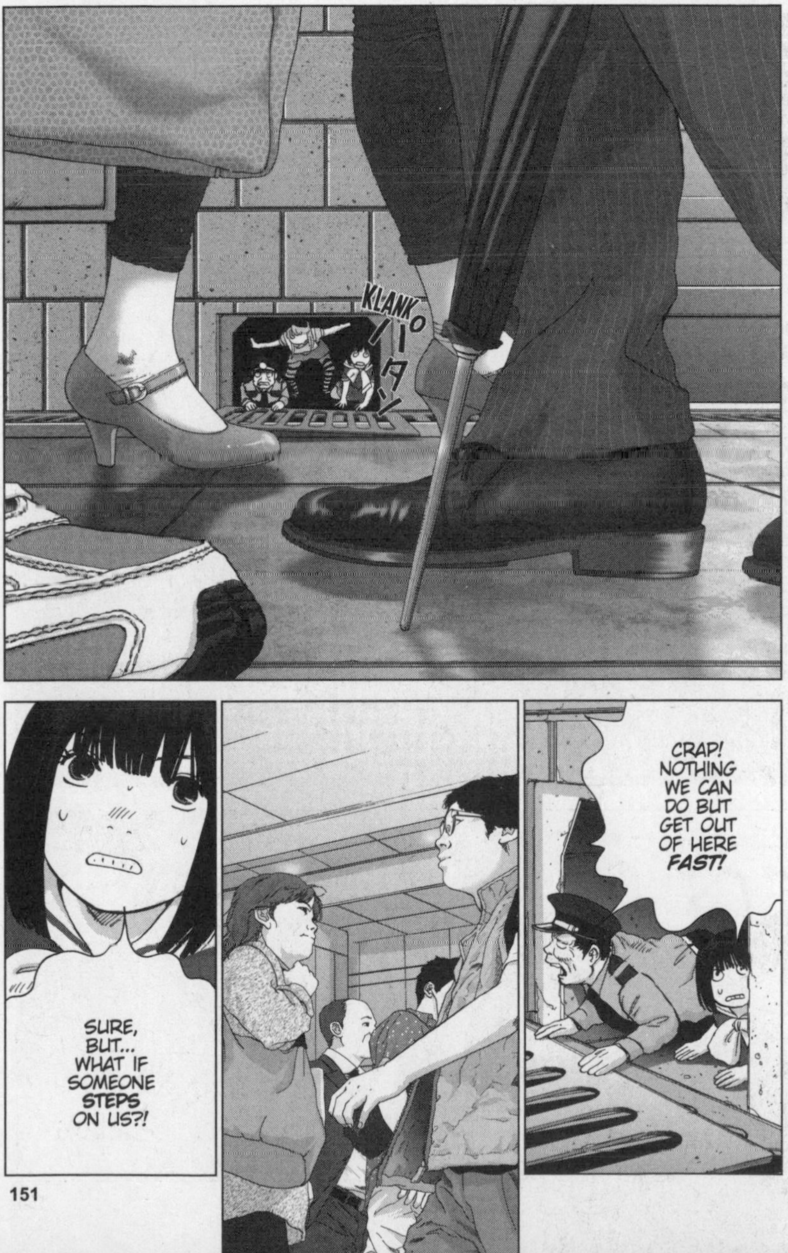
KLANK
CRAP! NOTHING WE CAN DO BUT GET OUT OF HERE FAST!
SURE, BUT... WHAT IF SOMEONE STEPS ON US?!

I DON'T WANNA GET TRAMPLED TO DEATH BY ALL THESE PEOPLE!

OR GET PULLED APART BY CROWS OR EATEN BY CATS!

I DON'T WANNA GET STEPPED ON AND GO SPLAT!

OH!
(＾◡＾)

◎☆
！

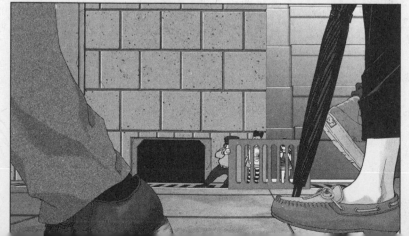

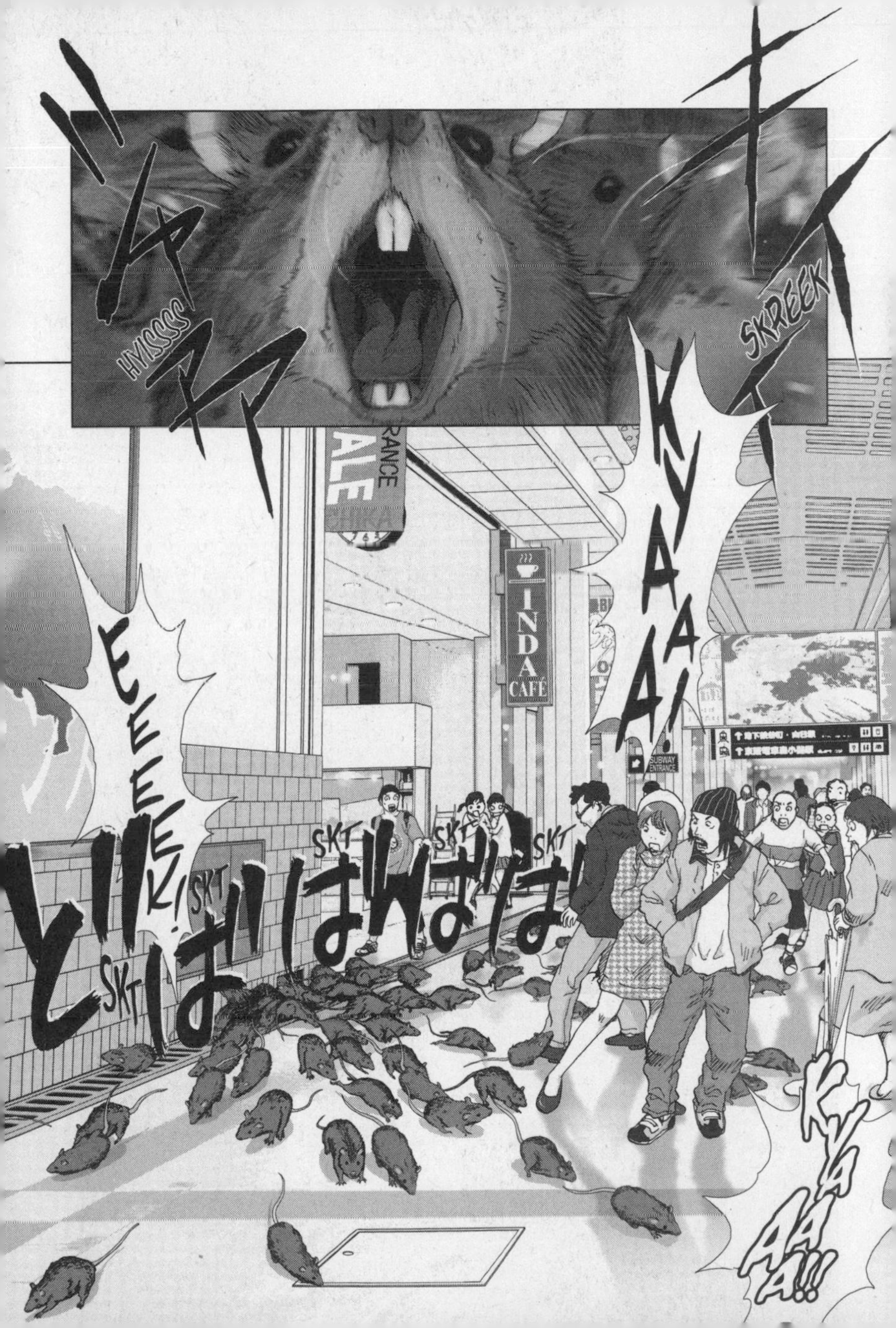
SKREEK
HYISSSS
KYAAAA!
EEEEEK!
SKT SKT SKT SKT SKT
KYAAAA!!
ALE
RANCE
INDA CAFÉ
SUBWAY ENTRANCE

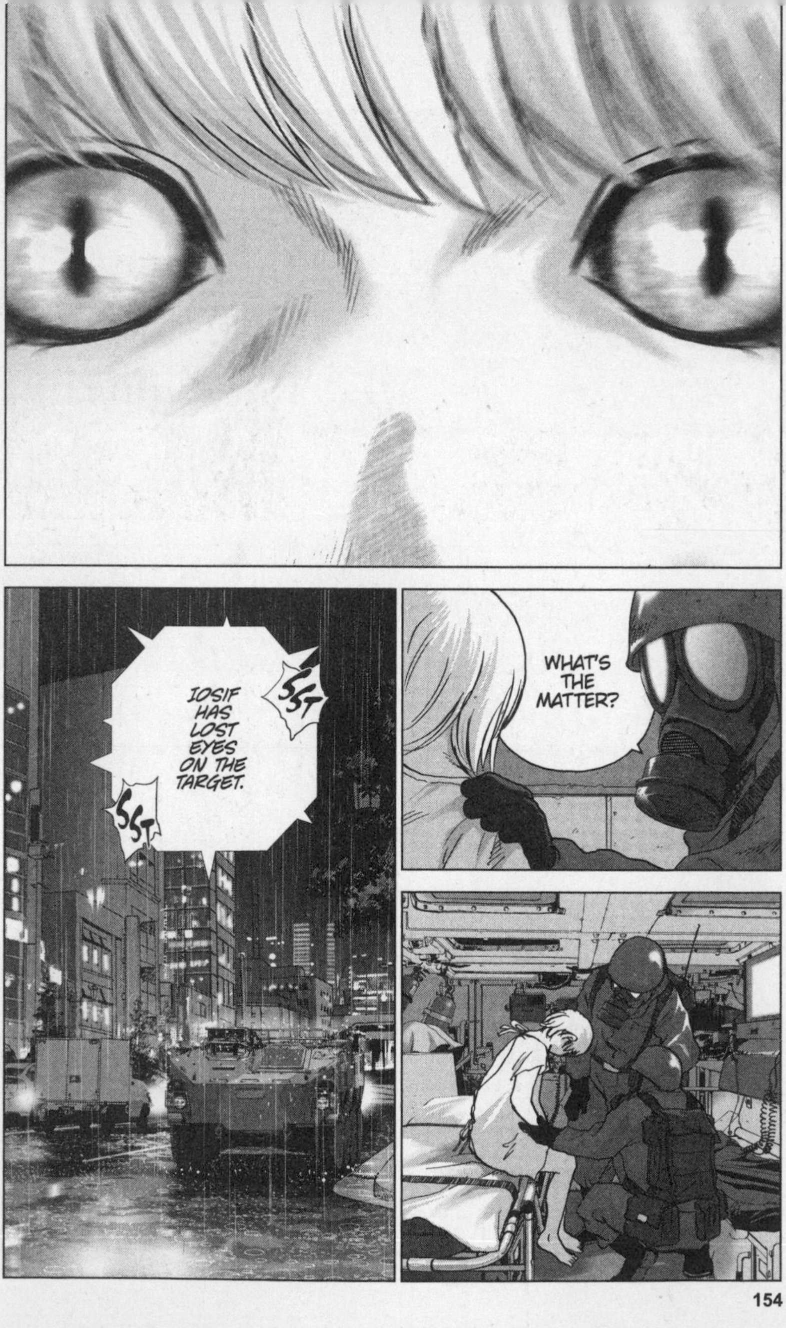
WHAT'S THE MATTER?
SST
IOSIF HAS LOST EYES ON THE TARGET.
SST

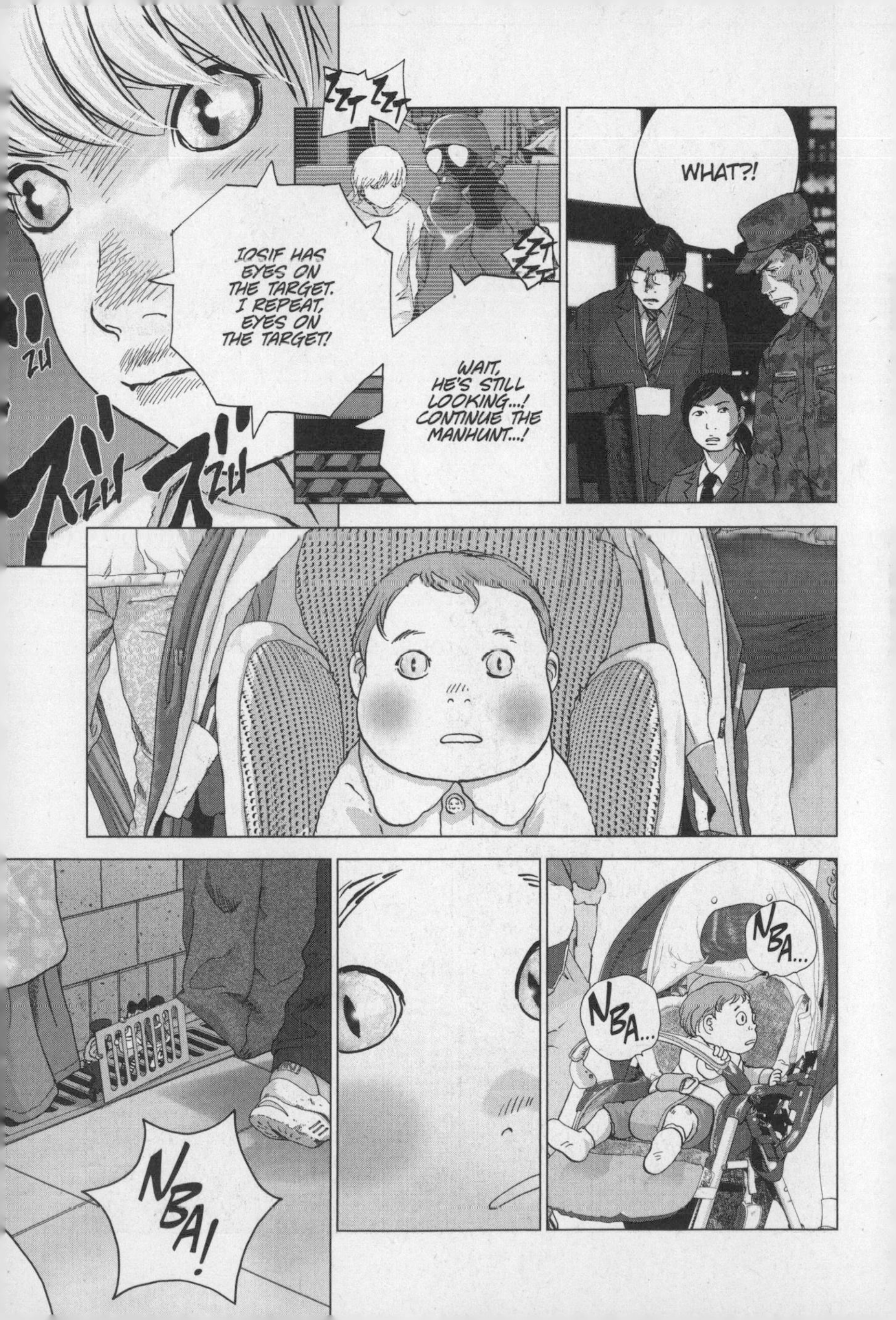
WHAT?!
ZZZT ZZZT
ZZZT ZZZT
IOSIF HAS EYES ON THE TARGET. I REPEAT, EYES ON THE TARGET!
WAIT, HE'S STILL LOOKING...! CONTINUE THE MANHUNT...!
NBA...
NBA...
NBA!

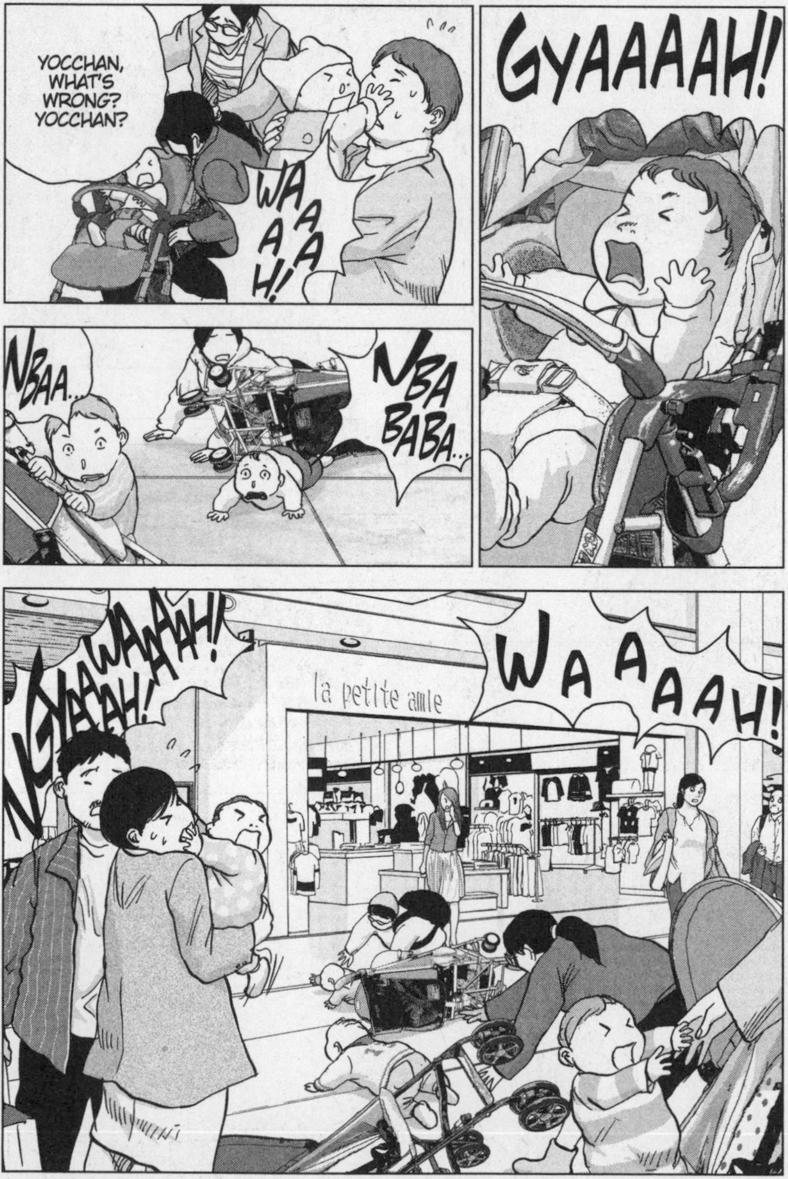
GYAAAAH!
YOCCHAN, WHAT'S WRONG? YOCCHAN?
WAAAAH!
NBABABA...
NBAA...
WAAAAAH!
WAAAAAH!
NGYAAAAH!

I DON'T KNOW WHAT'S GOIN' ON, BUT I DO KNOW THINGS ARE LOOKIN' DIRE.

LET'S JUST GET MOVING AND FIND A PLACE TO HIDE!

ERM...

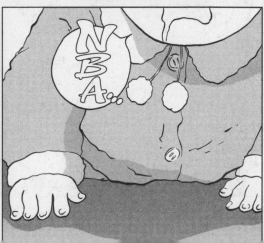

N B A...

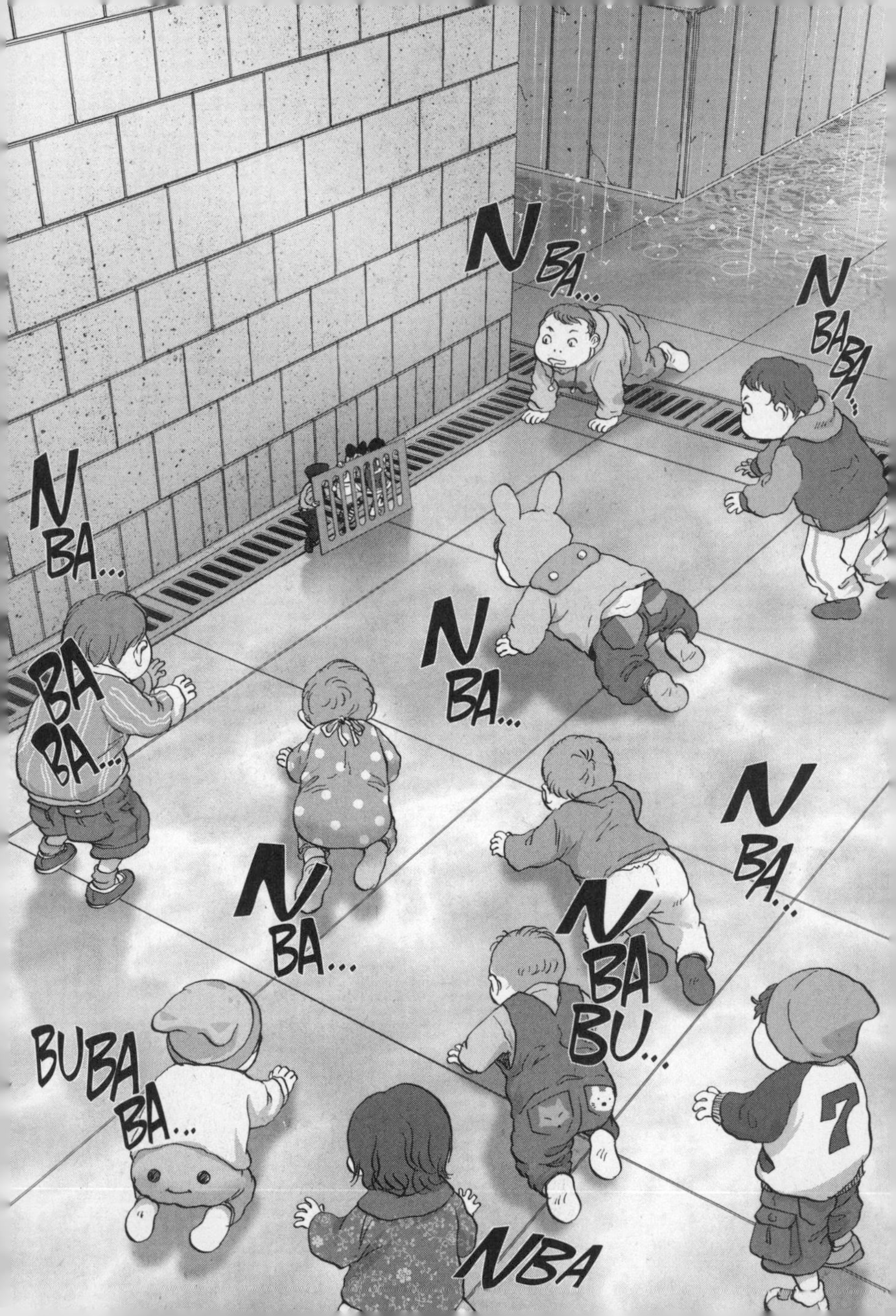
N BABA...
N BA...
N BA...
N BA...
BA BA...
N BA...
N BA...
N BABA BU...
BUBABA BA...
NBA

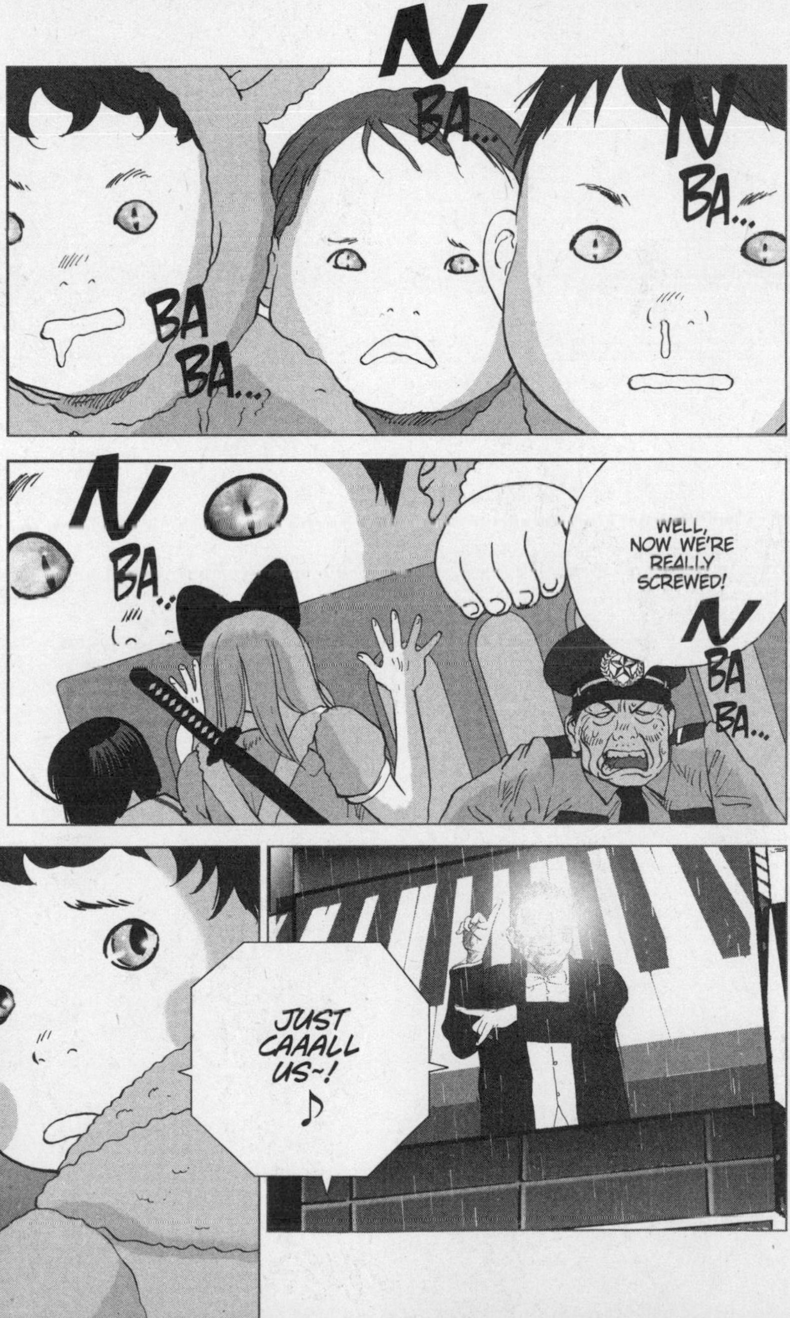
N BA...
N BA...
BA BA BA...
WELL, NOW WE'RE REALLY SCREWED!
N BA BA...
N BA...
JUST CAAALL US~! ♪

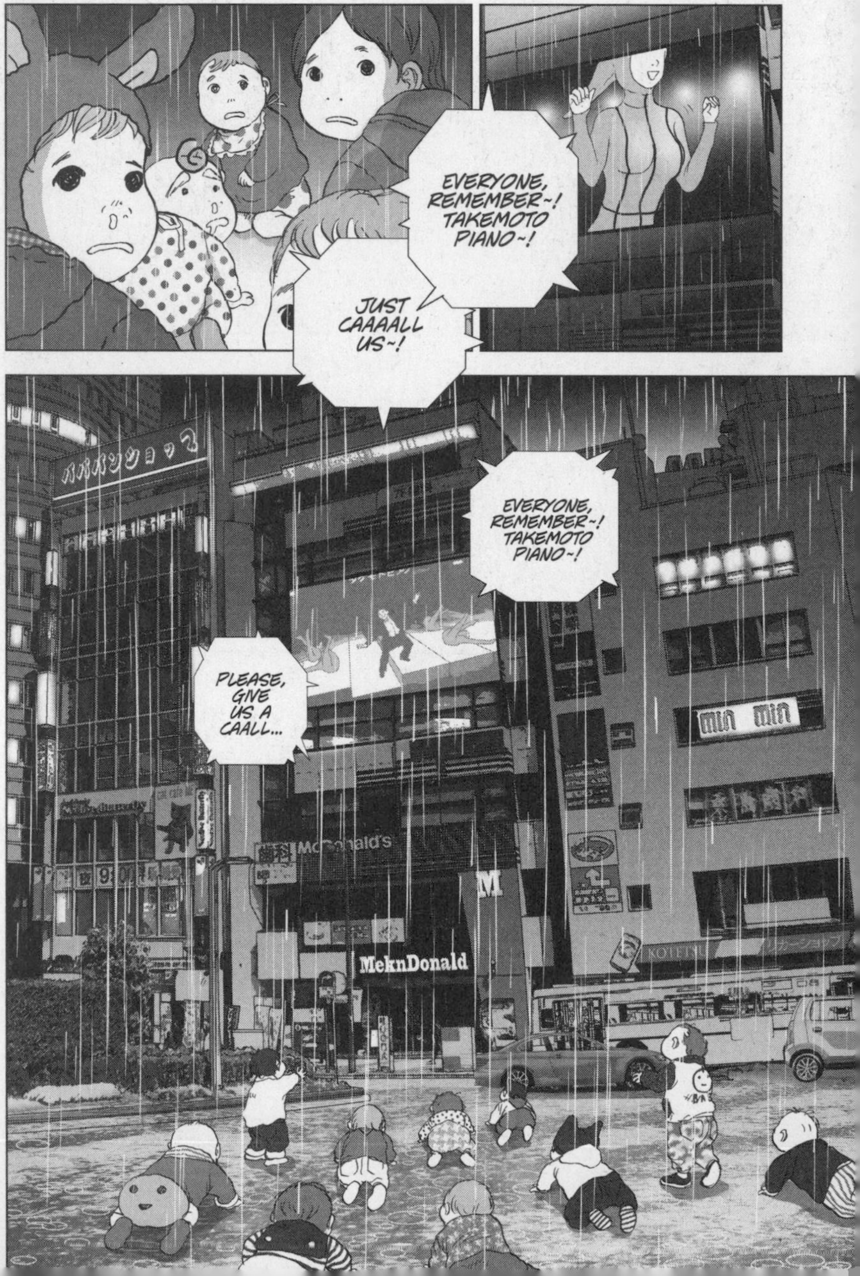
EVERYONE, REMEMBER~! TAKEMOTO PIANO~!
JUST CAAAALL US~!
EVERYONE, REMEMBER~! TAKEMOTO PIANO~!
PLEASE, GIVE US A CAALL...
min min
MeknDonald

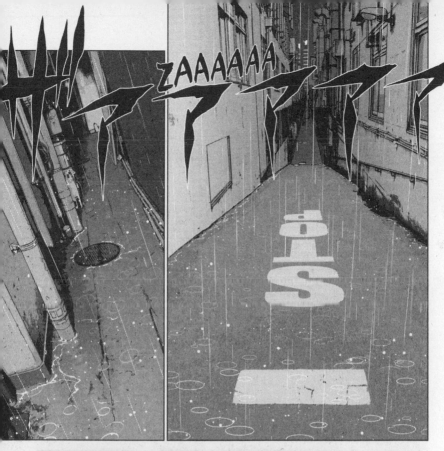

ZAAAAAA

WELL, WE MANAGED TO DODGE THE BABIES FOR NOW.

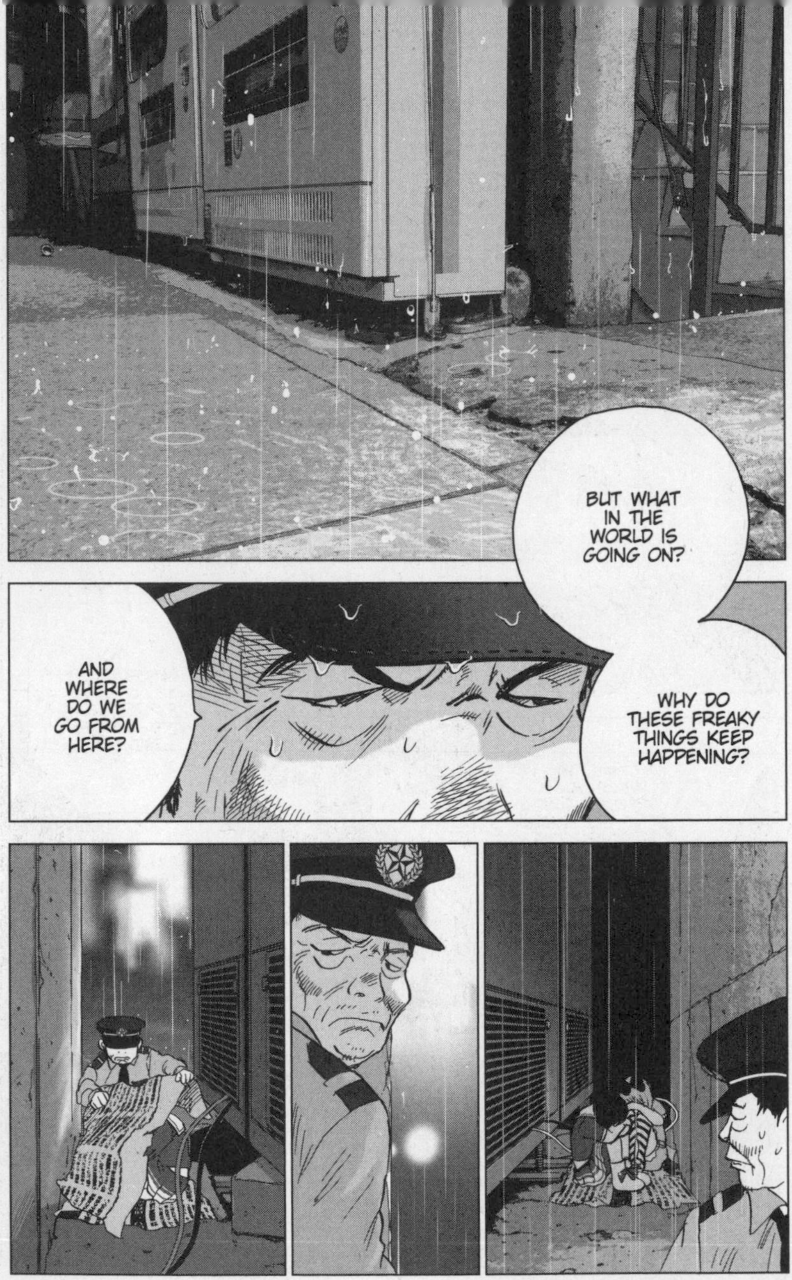
BUT WHAT IN THE WORLD IS GOING ON?
WHY DO THESE FREAKY THINGS KEEP HAPPENING?
AND WHERE DO WE GO FROM HERE?

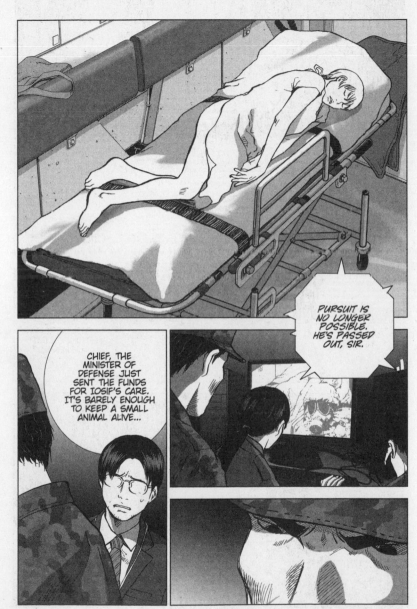

PURSUIT IS NO LONGER POSSIBLE. HE'S PASSED OUT, SIR.

CHIEF, THE MINISTER OF DEFENSE JUST SENT THE FUNDS FOR IOSIF'S CARE. IT'S BARELY ENOUGH TO KEEP A SMALL ANIMAL ALIVE...

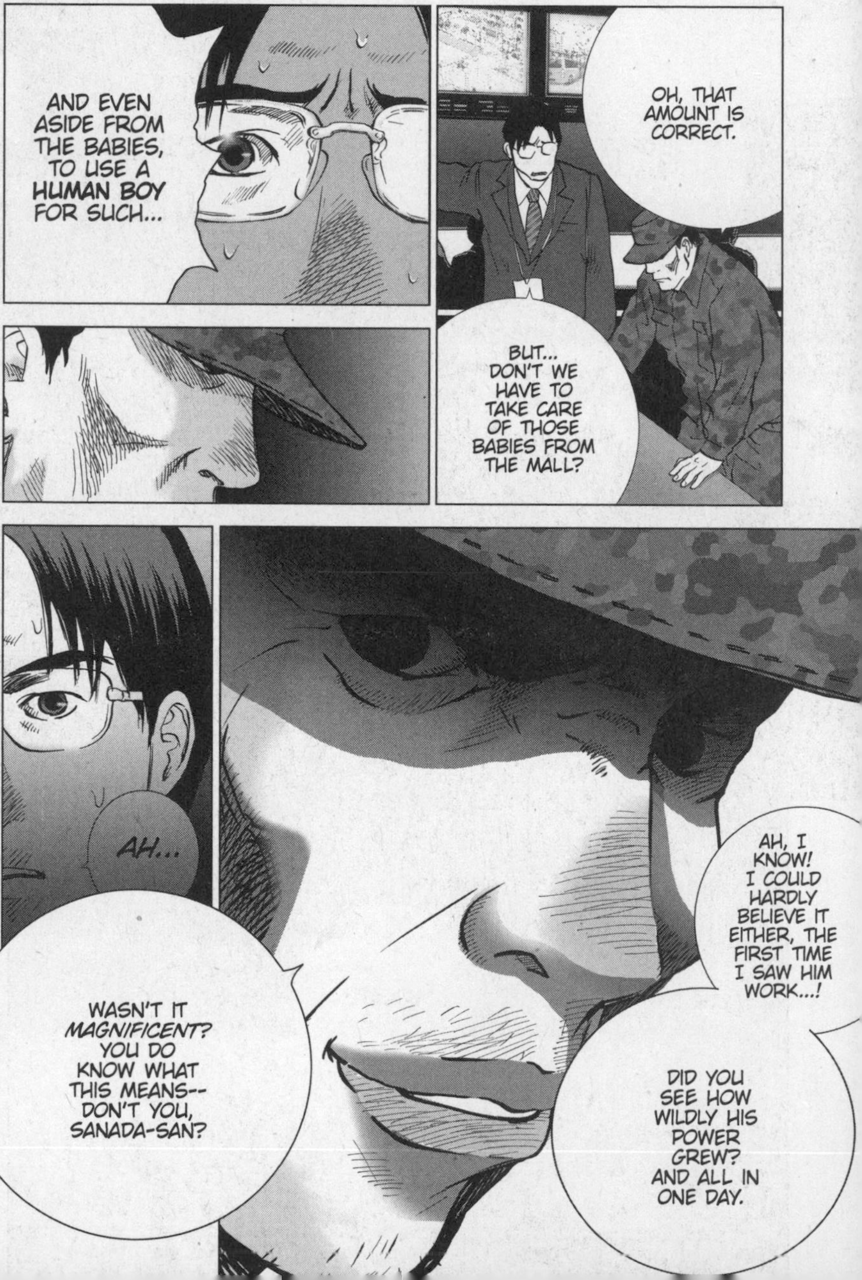

OH, THAT AMOUNT IS CORRECT.
BUT... DON'T WE HAVE TO TAKE CARE OF THOSE BABIES FROM THE MALL?
AND EVEN ASIDE FROM THE BABIES, TO USE A HUMAN BOY FOR SUCH...
AH, I KNOW! I COULD HARDLY BELIEVE IT EITHER, THE FIRST TIME I SAW HIM WORK...!
DID YOU SEE HOW WILDLY HIS POWER GREW? AND ALL IN ONE DAY.
WASN'T IT *MAGNIFICENT?* YOU DO KNOW WHAT THIS MEANS-- DON'T YOU, SANADA-SAN?
AH...

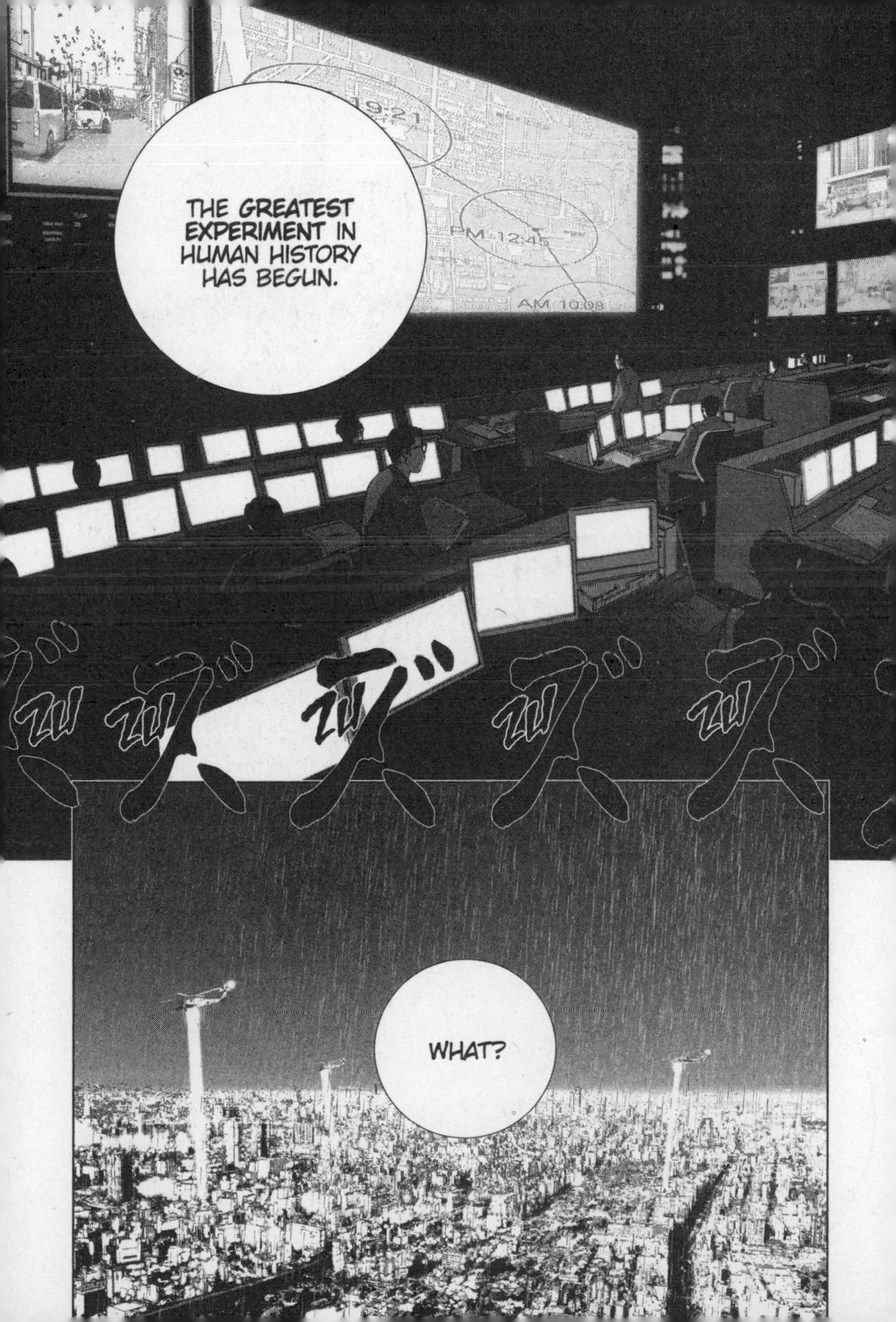
THE GREATEST EXPERIMENT IN HUMAN HISTORY HAS BEGUN.
19:21
PM 12:45
AM 10:08
ZU ZU ZU ZU ZU
WHAT?

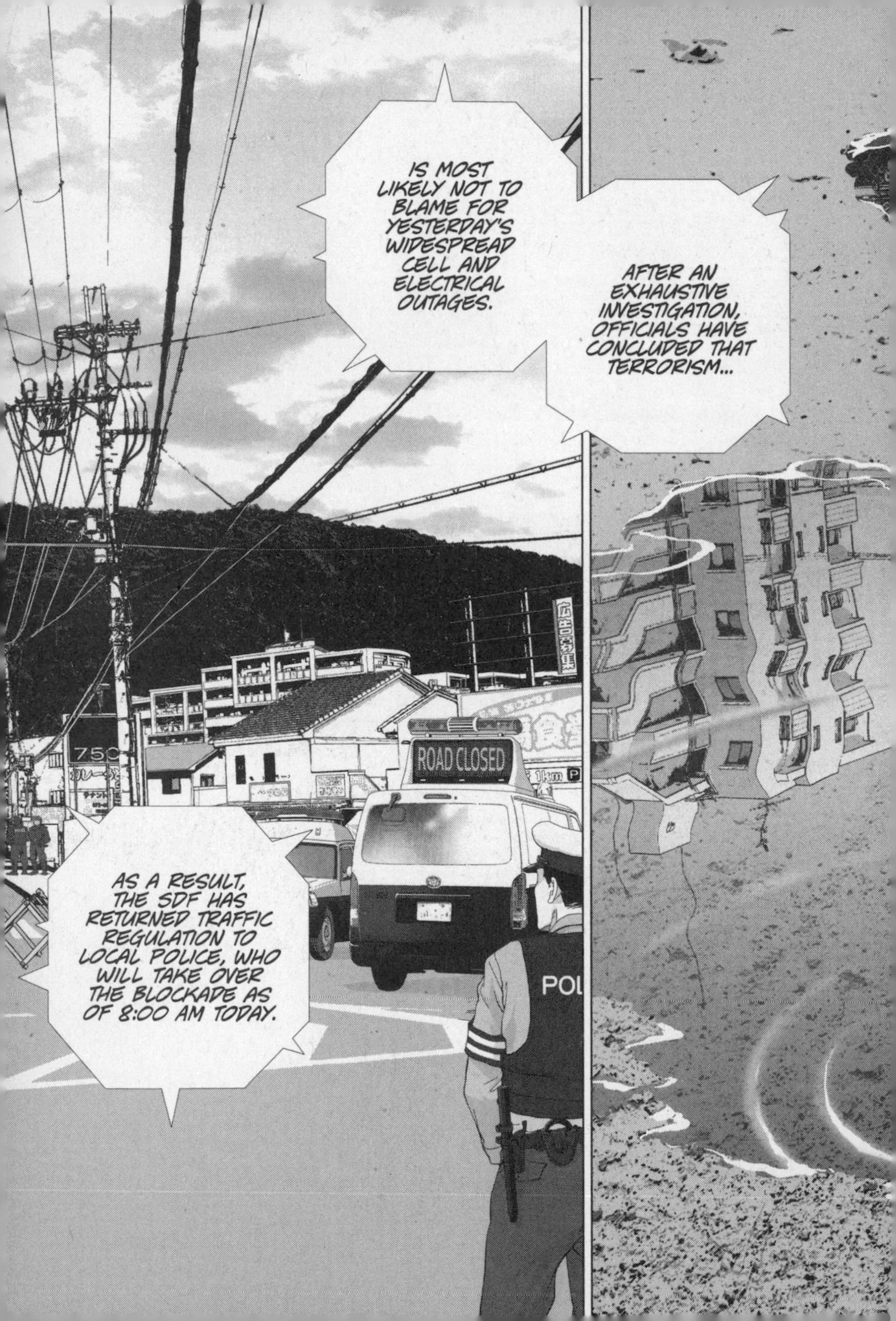
AFTER AN EXHAUSTIVE INVESTIGATION, OFFICIALS HAVE CONCLUDED THAT TERRORISM...
IS MOST LIKELY NOT TO BLAME FOR YESTERDAY'S WIDESPREAD CELL AND ELECTRICAL OUTAGES.
広告募集
750
ROAD CLOSED
1km P
AS A RESULT, THE SDF HAS RETURNED TRAFFIC REGULATION TO LOCAL POLICE, WHO WILL TAKE OVER THE BLOCKADE AS OF 8:00 AM TODAY.
POLI

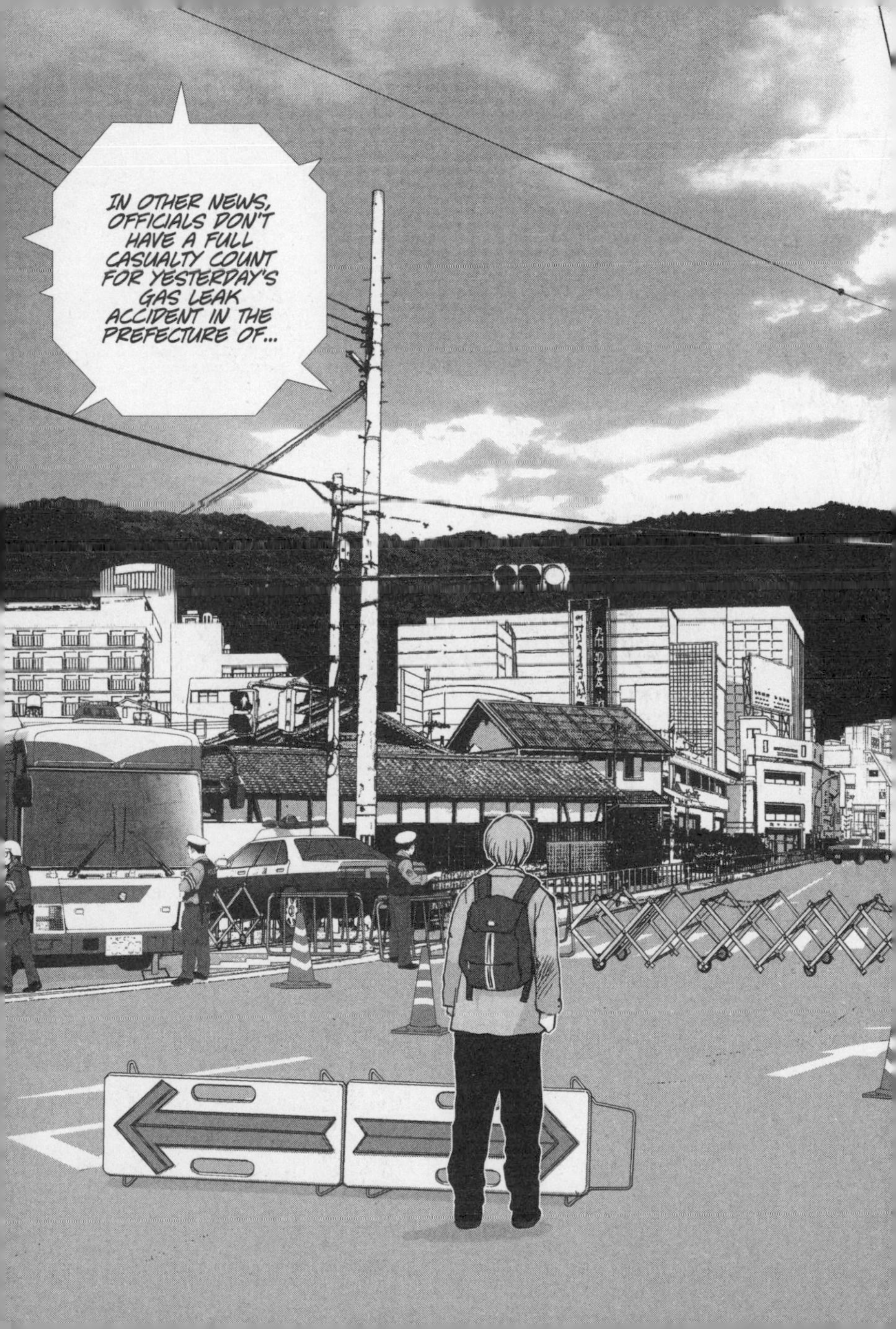
IN OTHER NEWS, OFFICIALS DON'T HAVE A FULL CASUALTY COUNT FOR YESTERDAY'S GAS LEAK ACCIDENT IN THE PREFECTURE OF...

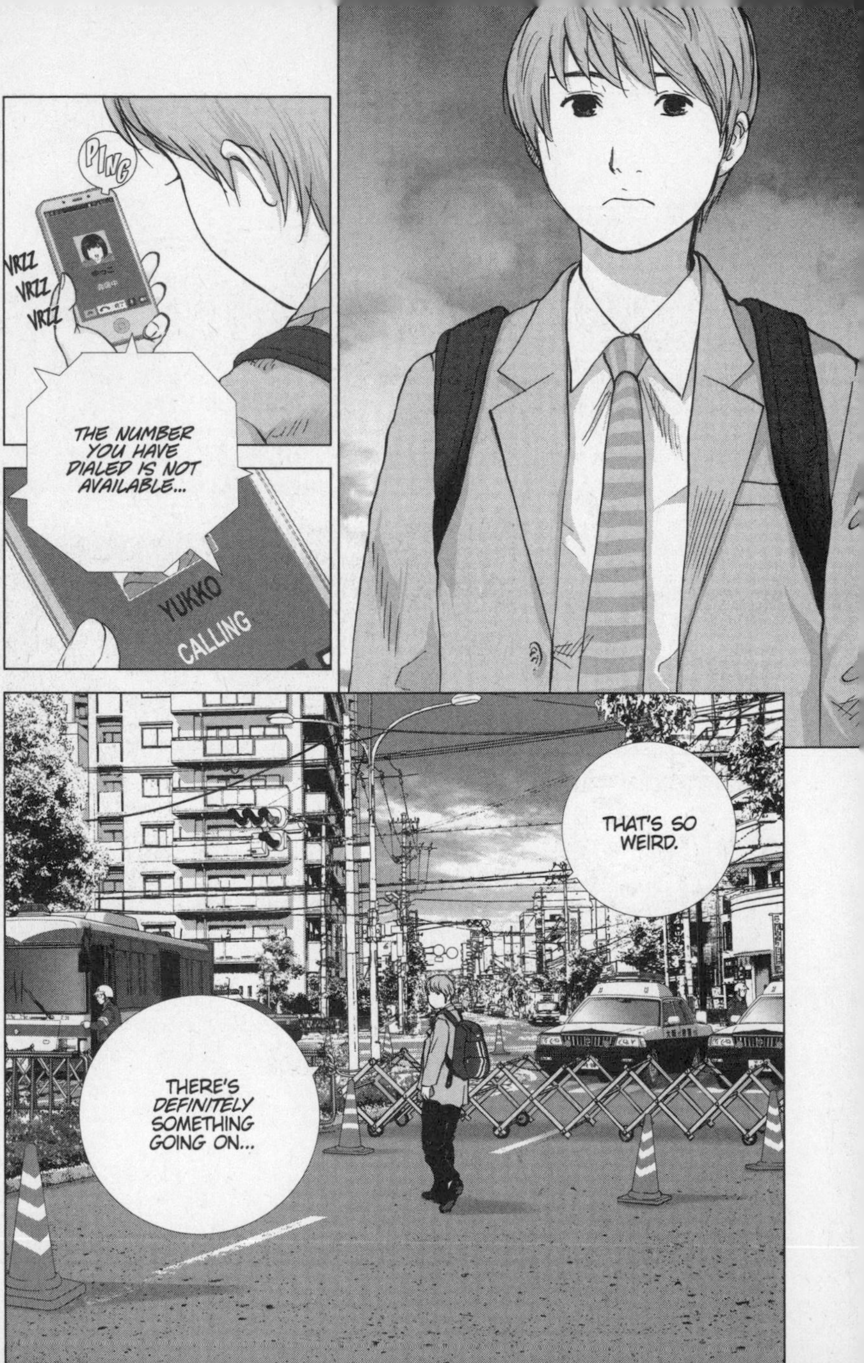
PING
VRZZ
VRZZ
VRZZ
THE NUMBER YOU HAVE DIALED IS NOT AVAILABLE...
YUKKO
CALLING
THAT'S SO WEIRD.
THERE'S DEFINITELY SOMETHING GOING ON...

Chapter 18: Mobile Phone

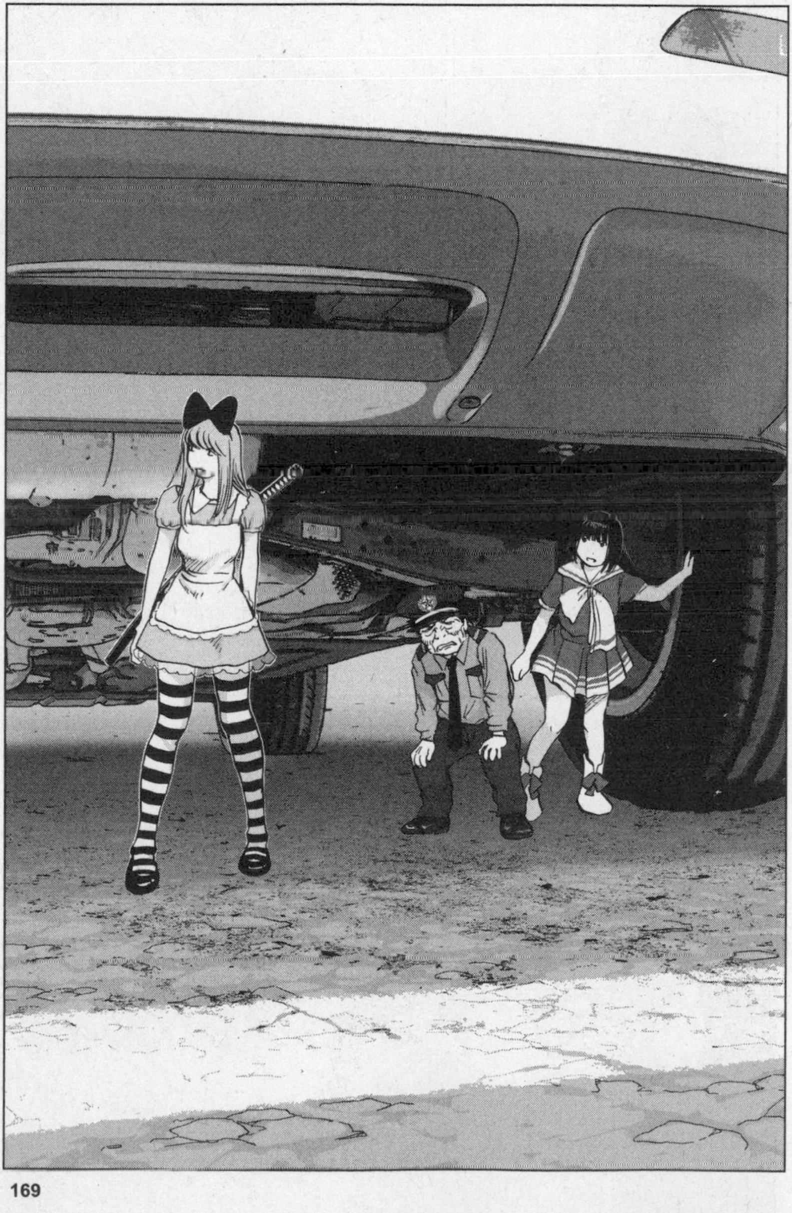

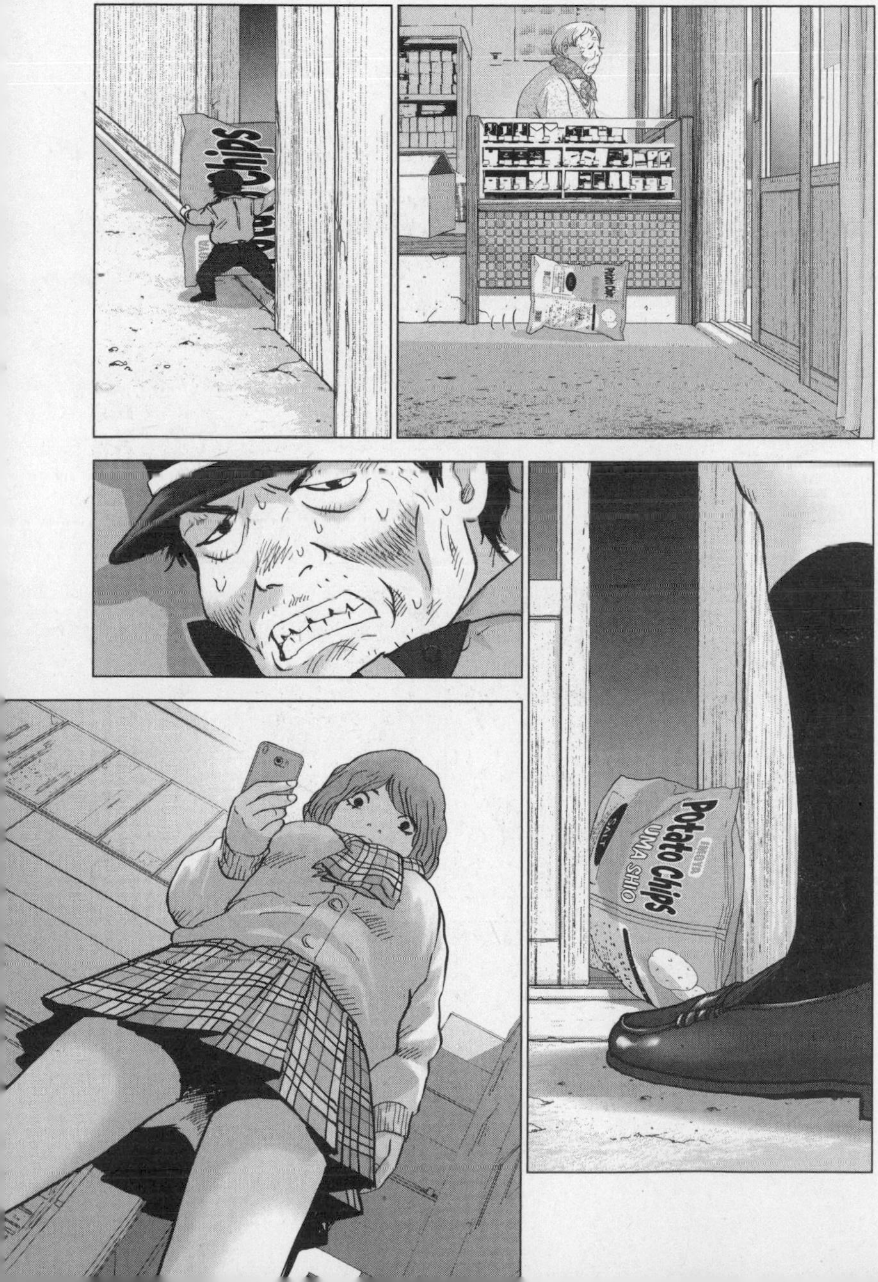
SALT
Potato Chips
UMA SHIO

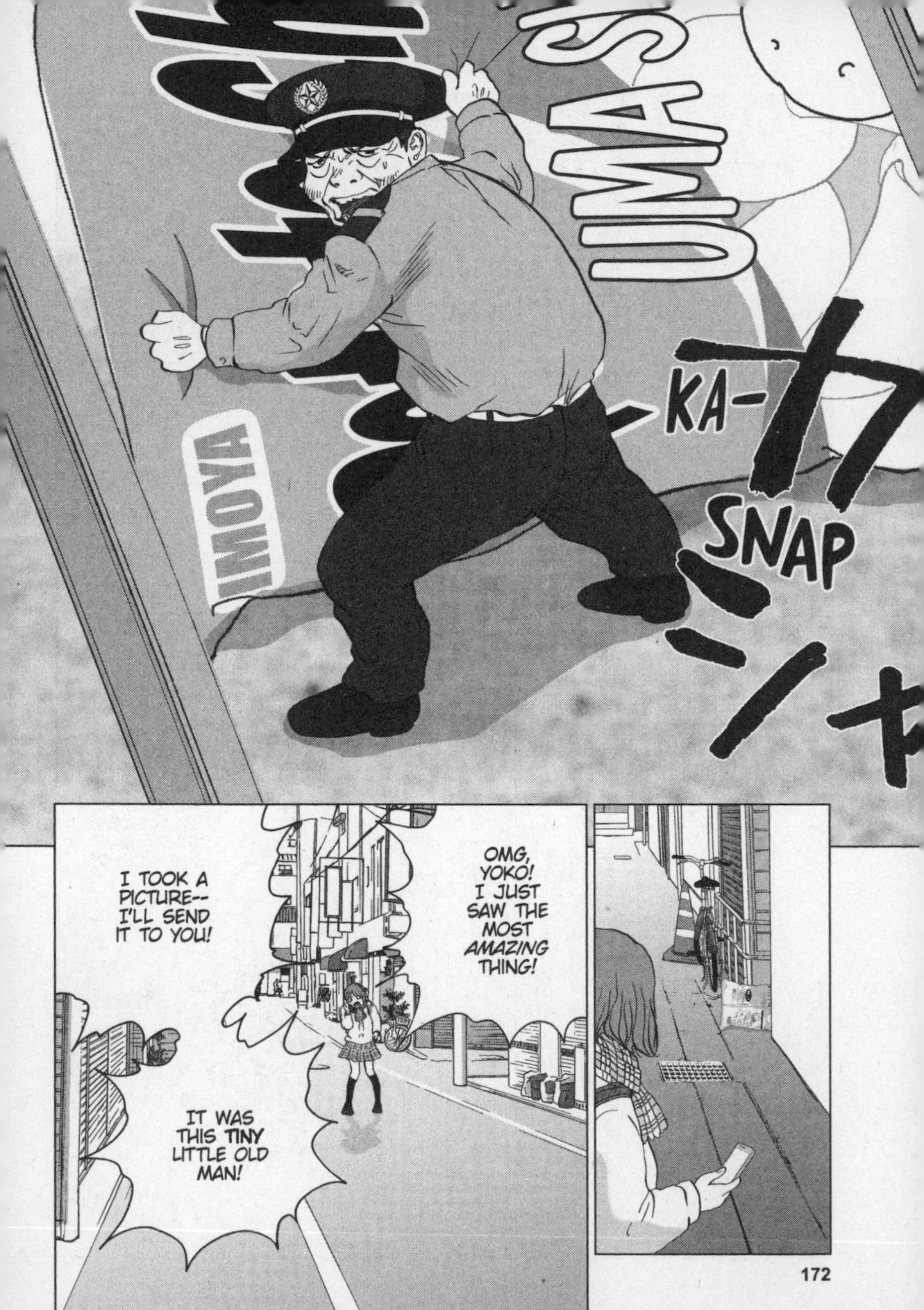
KA-
SNAP
OMG, YOKO! I JUST SAW THE MOST AMAZING THING!
I TOOK A PICTURE-- I'LL SEND IT TO YOU!
IT WAS THIS TINY LITTLE OLD MAN!

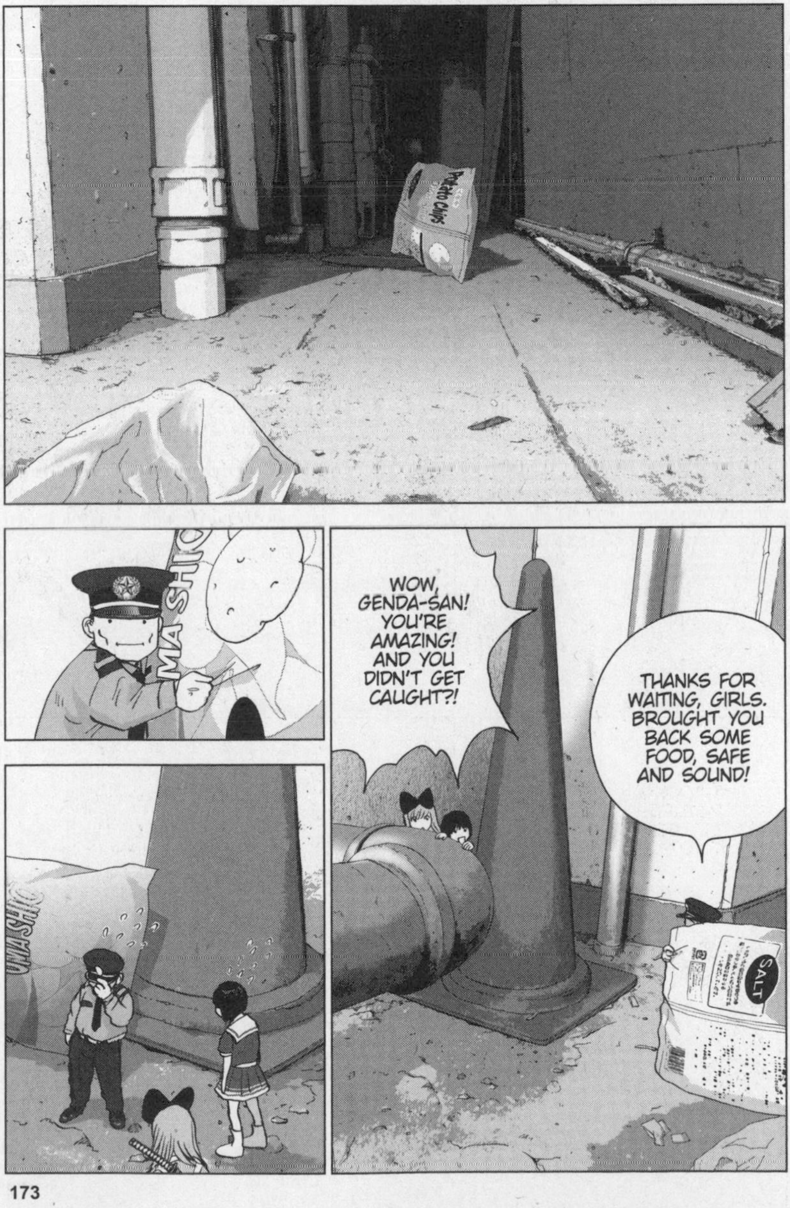
Potato Chips
THANKS FOR WAITING, GIRLS. BROUGHT YOU BACK SOME FOOD, SAFE AND SOUND!
WOW, GENDA-SAN! YOU'RE AMAZING! AND YOU DIDN'T GET CAUGHT?!
SALT

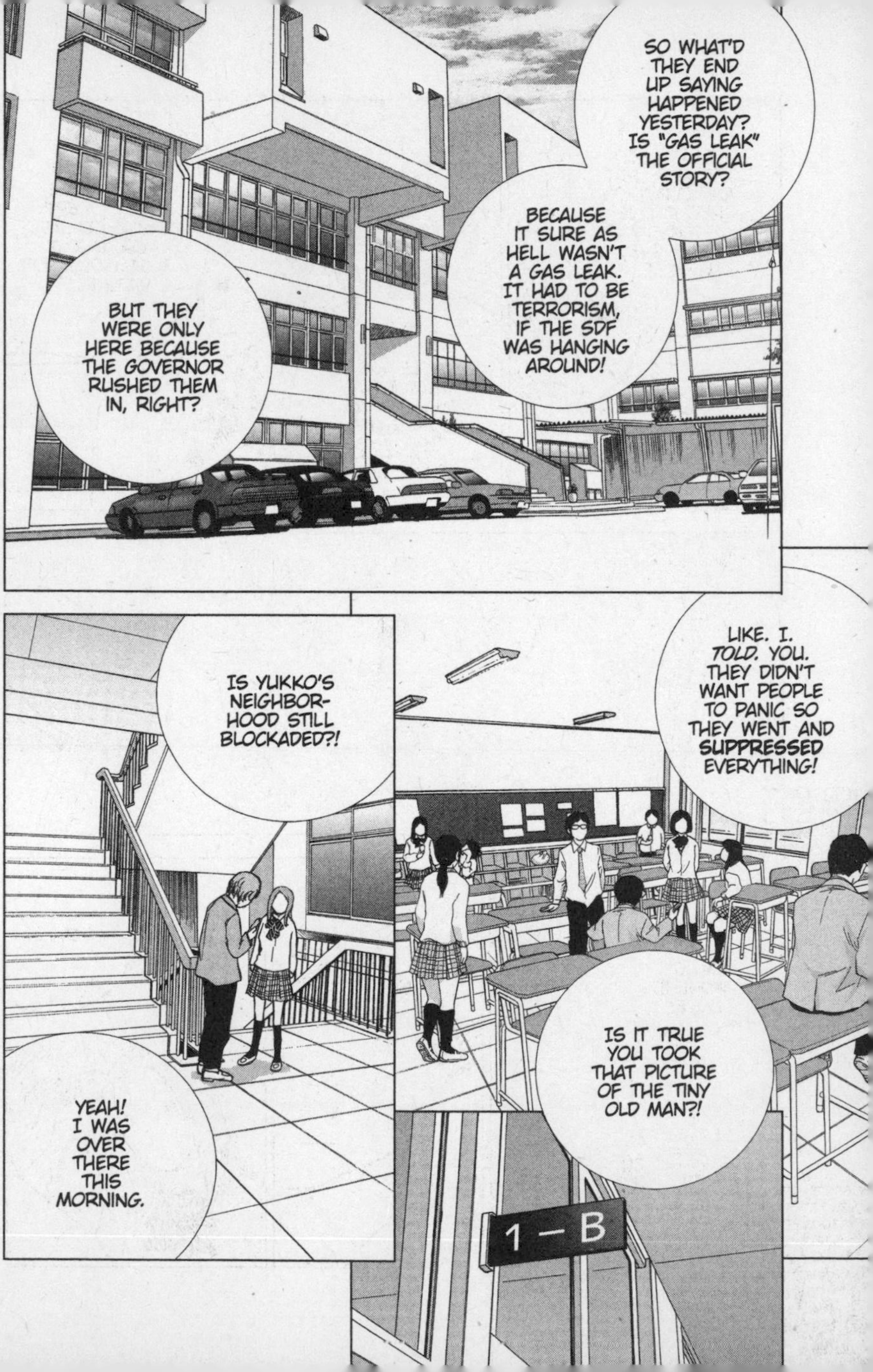
SO WHAT'D THEY END UP SAYING HAPPENED YESTERDAY? IS "GAS LEAK" THE OFFICIAL STORY?
BECAUSE IT SURE AS HELL WASN'T A GAS LEAK. IT HAD TO BE TERRORISM, IF THE SDF WAS HANGING AROUND!
BUT THEY WERE ONLY HERE BECAUSE THE GOVERNOR RUSHED THEM IN, RIGHT?
LIKE. I. *TOLD.* YOU. THEY DIDN'T WANT PEOPLE TO PANIC SO THEY WENT AND **SUPPRESSED** EVERYTHING!
IS IT TRUE YOU TOOK THAT PICTURE OF THE TINY OLD MAN?!
1 — B
IS YUKKO'S NEIGHBOR-HOOD STILL BLOCKADED?!
YEAH! I WAS OVER THERE THIS MORNING.

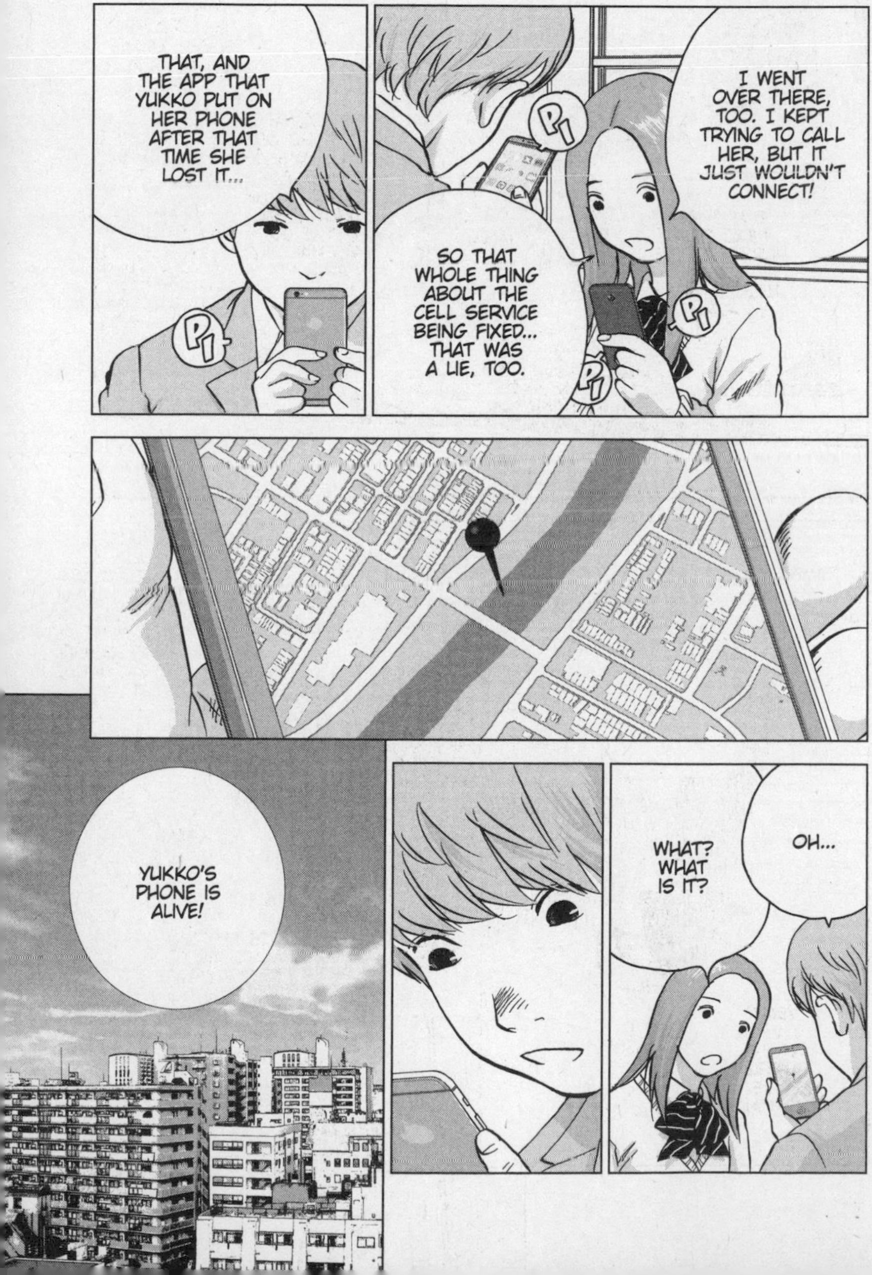
I WENT OVER THERE, TOO. I KEPT TRYING TO CALL HER, BUT IT JUST WOULDN'T CONNECT!
PI
PI
SO THAT WHOLE THING ABOUT THE CELL SERVICE BEING FIXED... THAT WAS A LIE, TOO.
PI
PI
THAT, AND THE APP THAT YUKKO PUT ON HER PHONE AFTER THAT TIME SHE LOST IT...
PI
OH...
WHAT? WHAT IS IT?
YUKKO'S PHONE IS ALIVE!

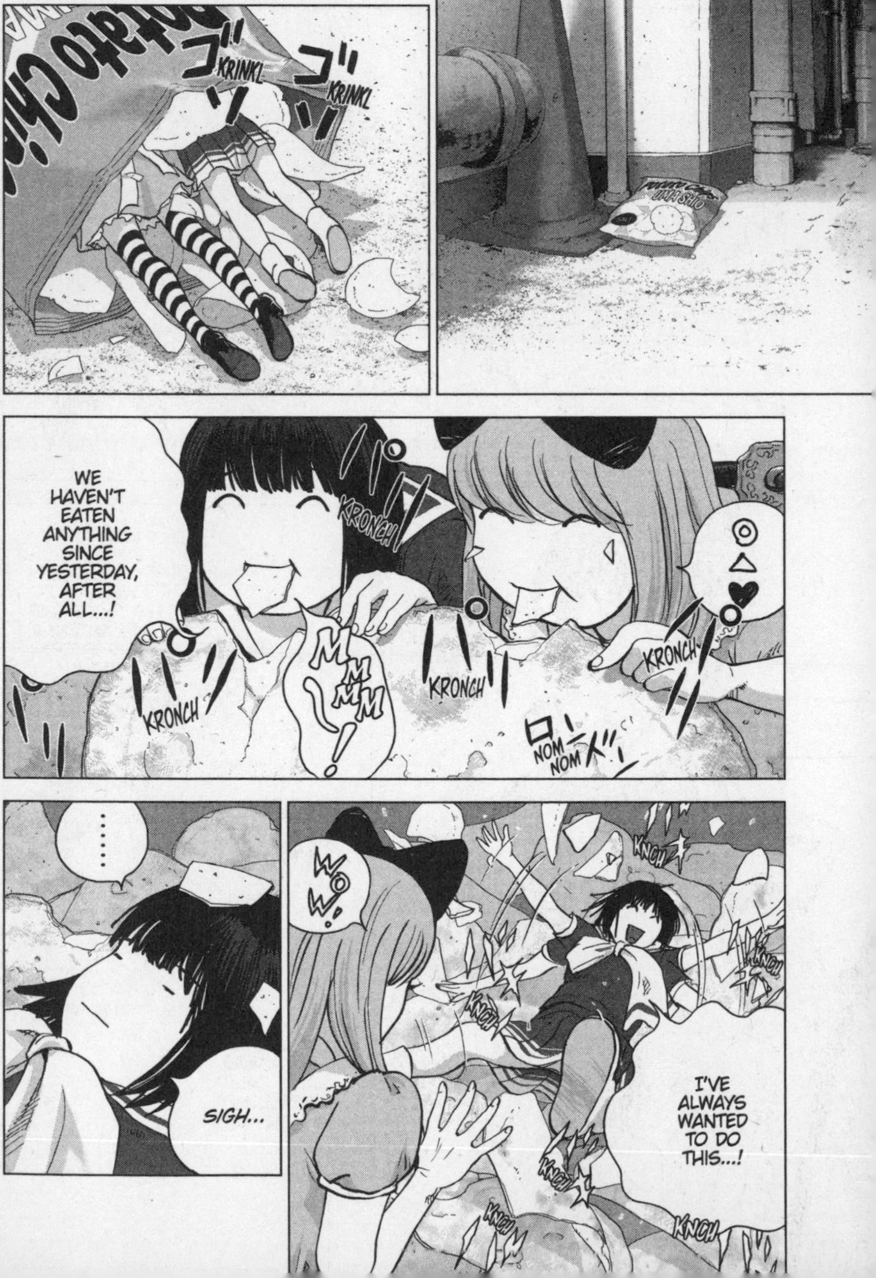

POTATO CHIPS
UMA SHIO
Potato Chip
ゴ KRINKL
ゴ KRINKL
◎ △ ♥
KRONCH
NOM NOM
KRONCH
MMMM~!
WE HAVEN'T EATEN ANYTHING SINCE YESTERDAY, AFTER ALL...!
KRONCH
パ KRONCH
WOW!
KNCH
KNCH
KNCH
I'VE ALWAYS WANTED TO DO THIS...!
KNCH
KNCH
KNCH
......
SIGH...

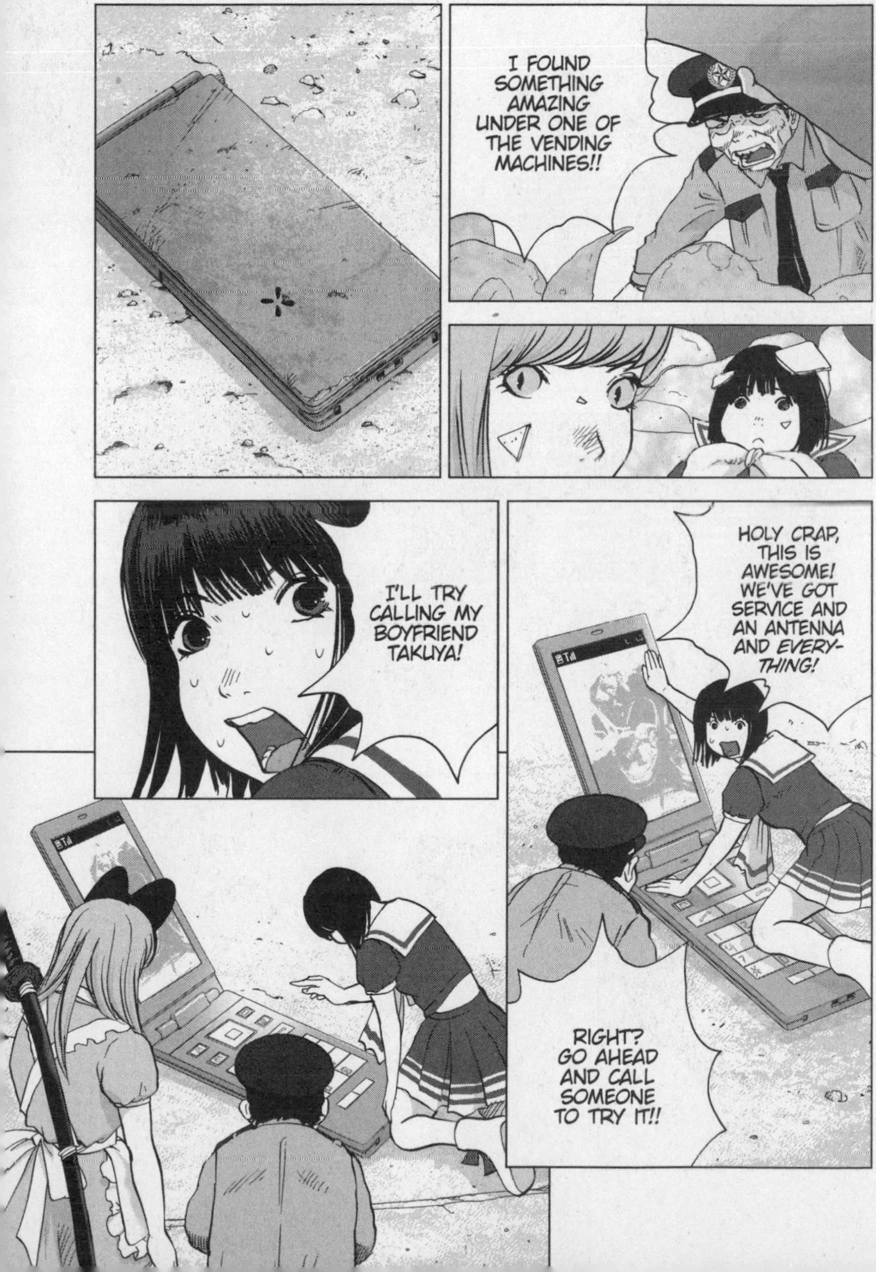
I FOUND SOMETHING AMAZING UNDER ONE OF THE VENDING MACHINES!!
HOLY CRAP, THIS IS AWESOME! WE'VE GOT SERVICE AND AN ANTENNA AND EVERY-THING!
RIGHT? GO AHEAD AND CALL SOMEONE TO TRY IT!!
I'LL TRY CALLING MY BOYFRIEND TAKUYA!

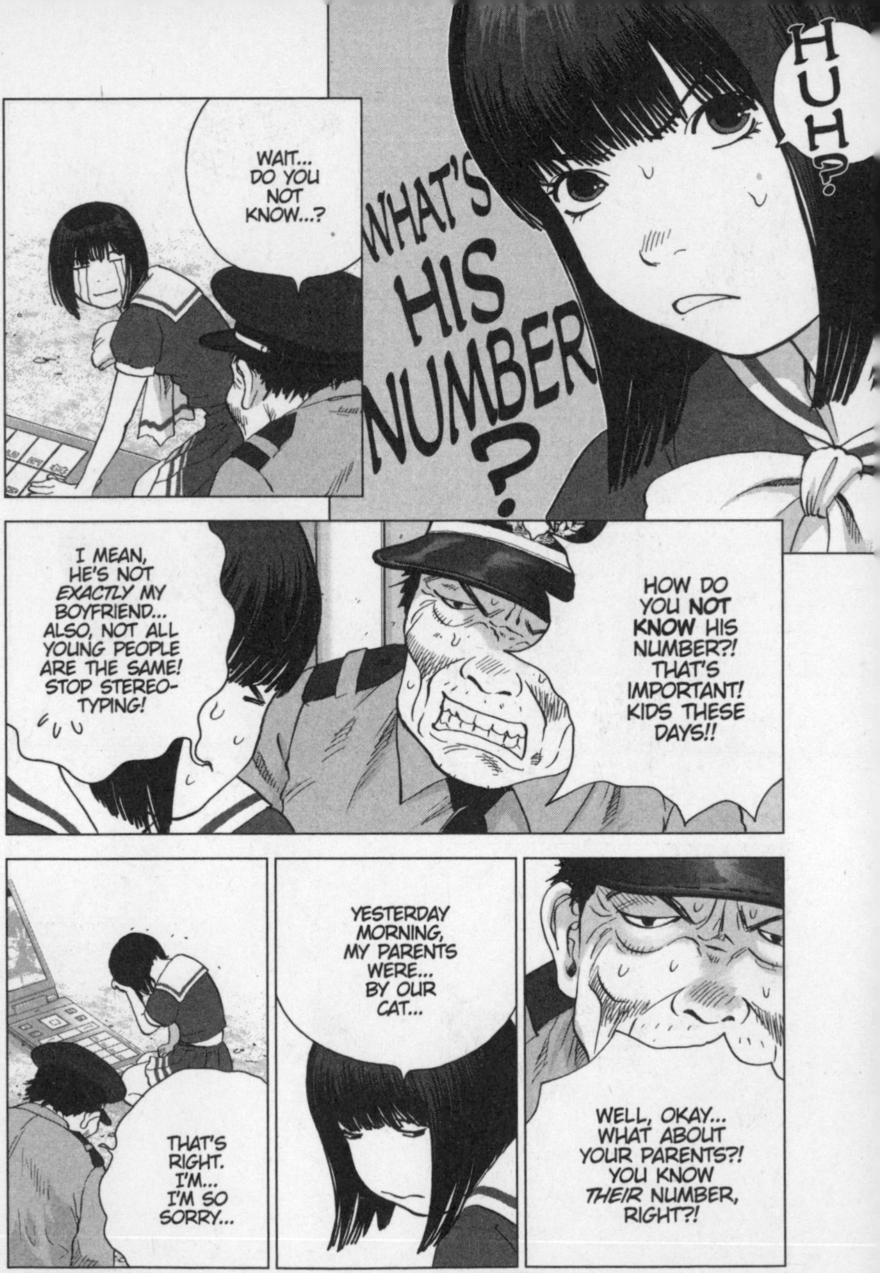
HUH?
WHAT'S HIS NUMBER?
WAIT... DO YOU NOT KNOW...?
HOW DO YOU NOT KNOW HIS NUMBER?! THAT'S IMPORTANT! KIDS THESE DAYS!!
I MEAN, HE'S NOT *EXACTLY* MY BOYFRIEND... ALSO, NOT ALL YOUNG PEOPLE ARE THE SAME! STOP STEREO-TYPING!
WELL, OKAY... WHAT ABOUT YOUR PARENTS?! YOU KNOW *THEIR* NUMBER, RIGHT?!
YESTERDAY MORNING, MY PARENTS WERE... BY OUR CAT...
THAT'S RIGHT. I'M... I'M SO SORRY...

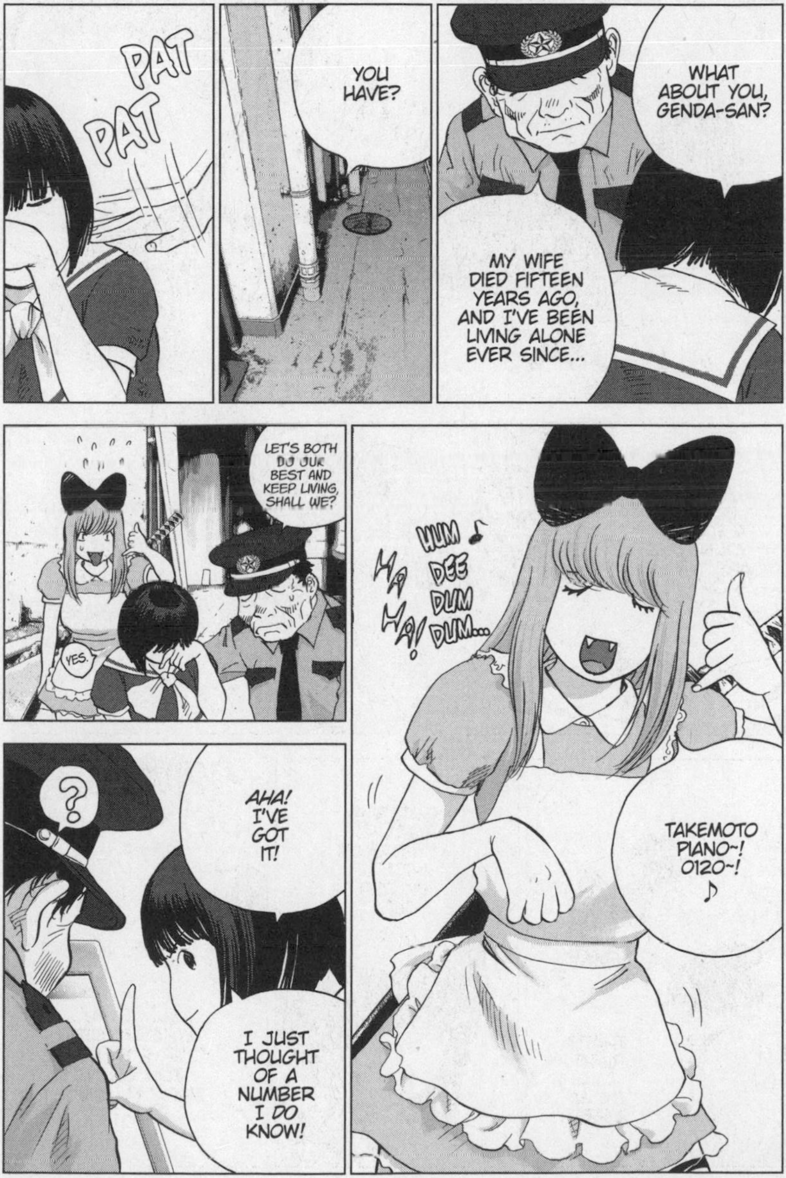
WHAT ABOUT YOU, GENDA-SAN?
MY WIFE DIED FIFTEEN YEARS AGO, AND I'VE BEEN LIVING ALONE EVER SINCE...
YOU HAVE?
PAT
PAT
HUM DEE DUM DUM...
HA HA!
TAKEMOTO PIANO~! 0120~! ♪
LET'S BOTH DO OUR BEST AND KEEP LIVING, SHALL WE?
YES.
AHA! I'VE GOT IT!
?
I JUST THOUGHT OF A NUMBER I *DO* KNOW!

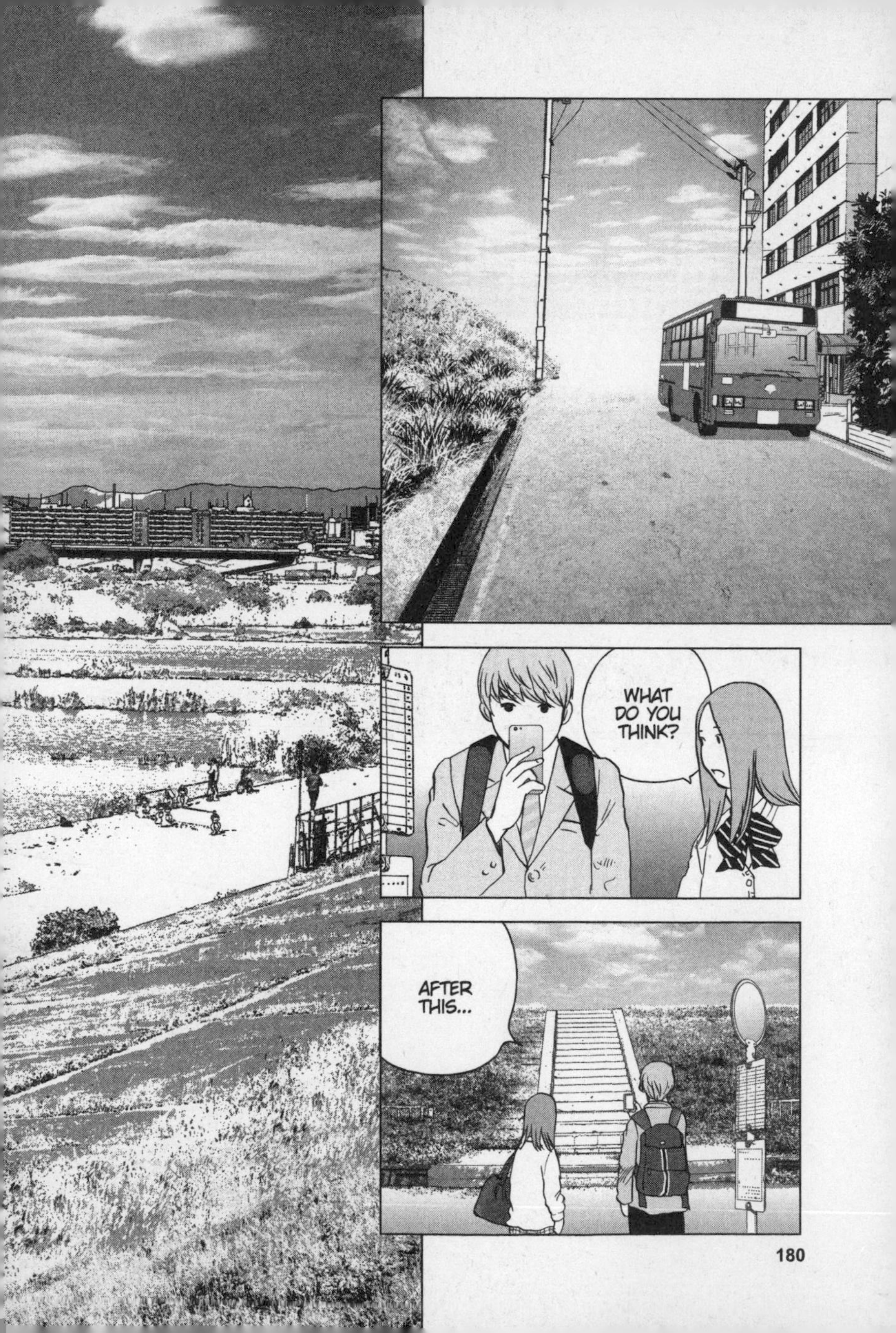
WHAT DO YOU THINK?
AFTER THIS...

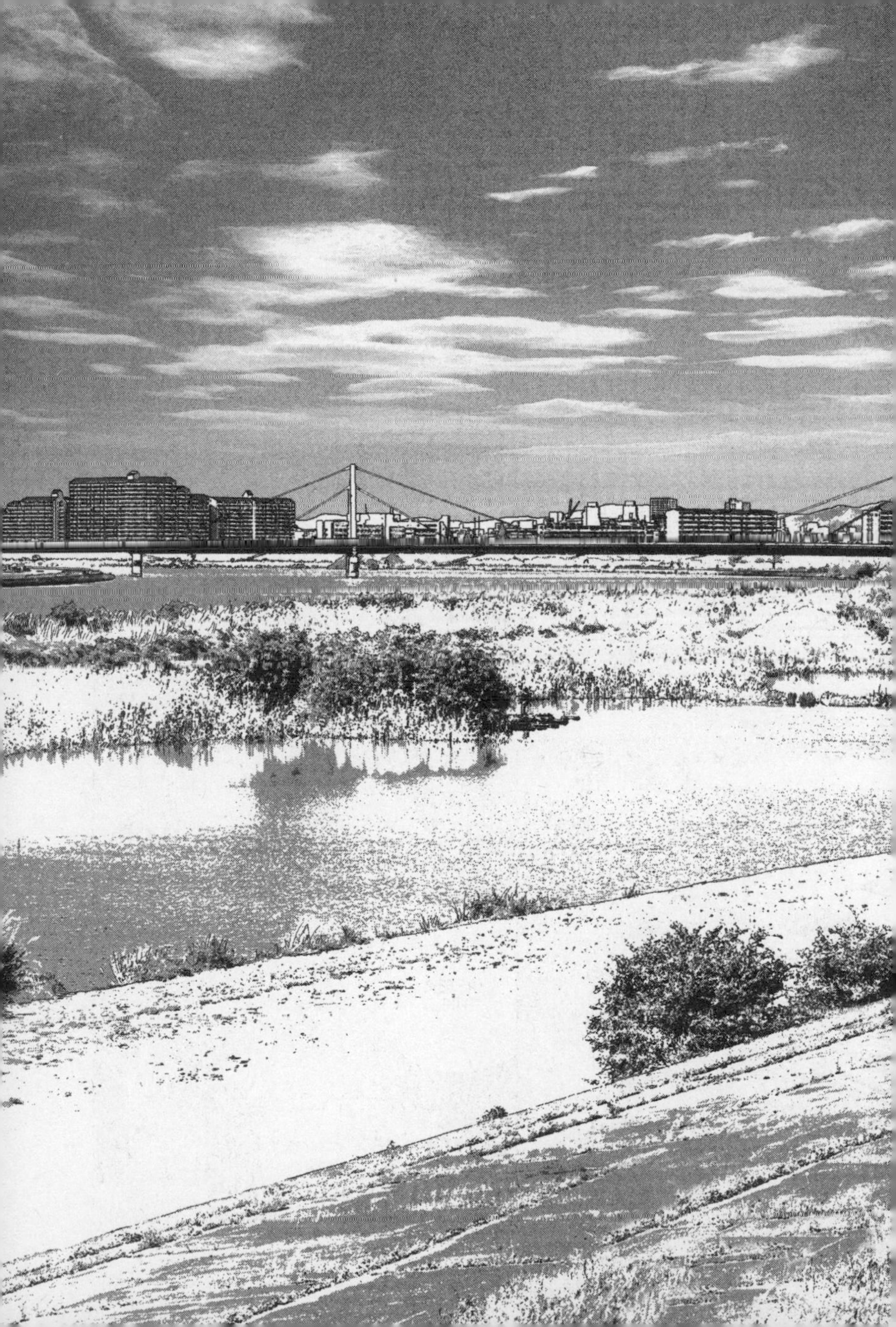

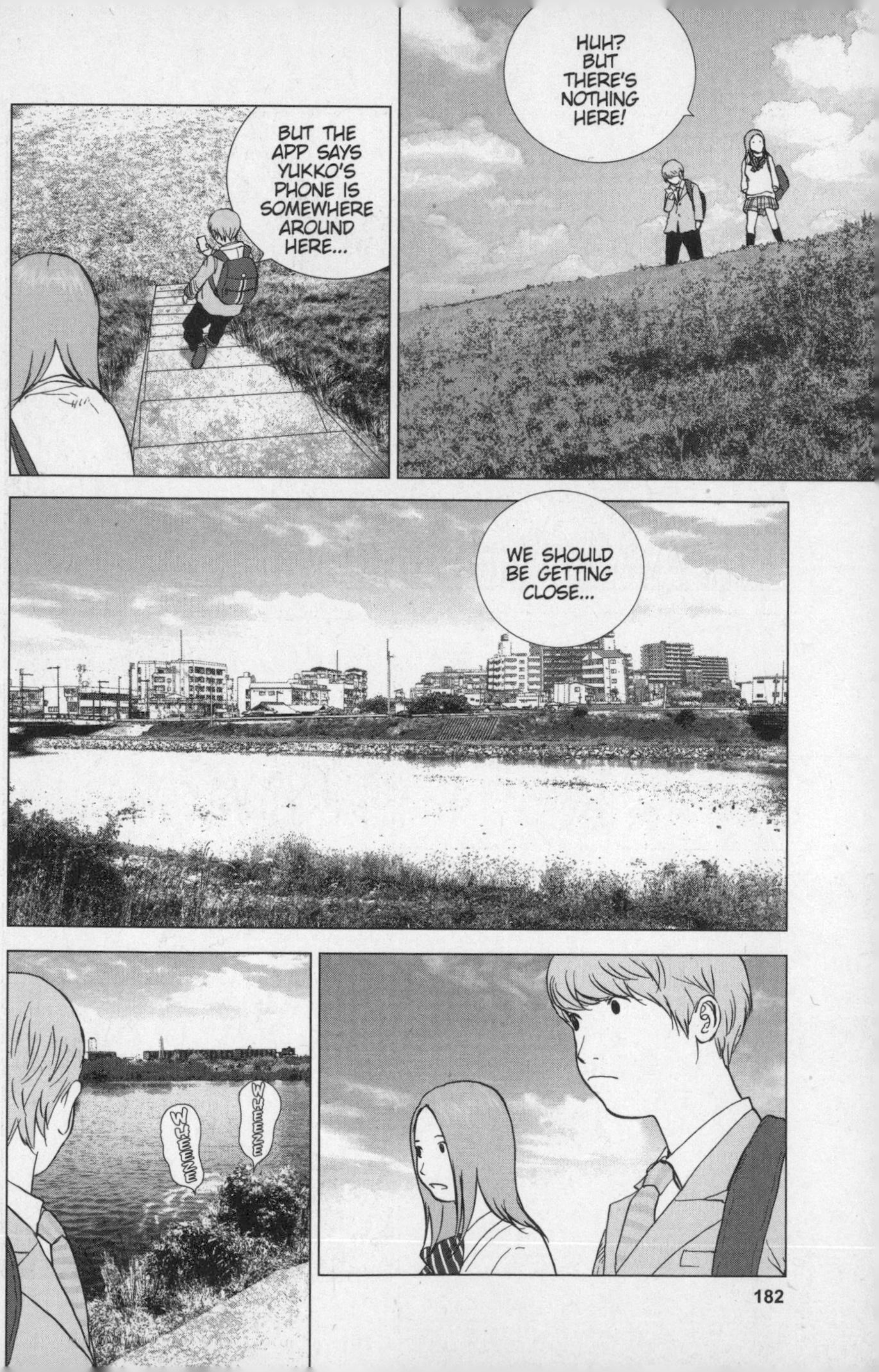
HUH? BUT THERE'S NOTHING HERE!
BUT THE APP SAYS YUKKO'S PHONE IS SOMEWHERE AROUND HERE...
WE SHOULD BE GETTING CLOSE...
WHEEZE
WHEEZE

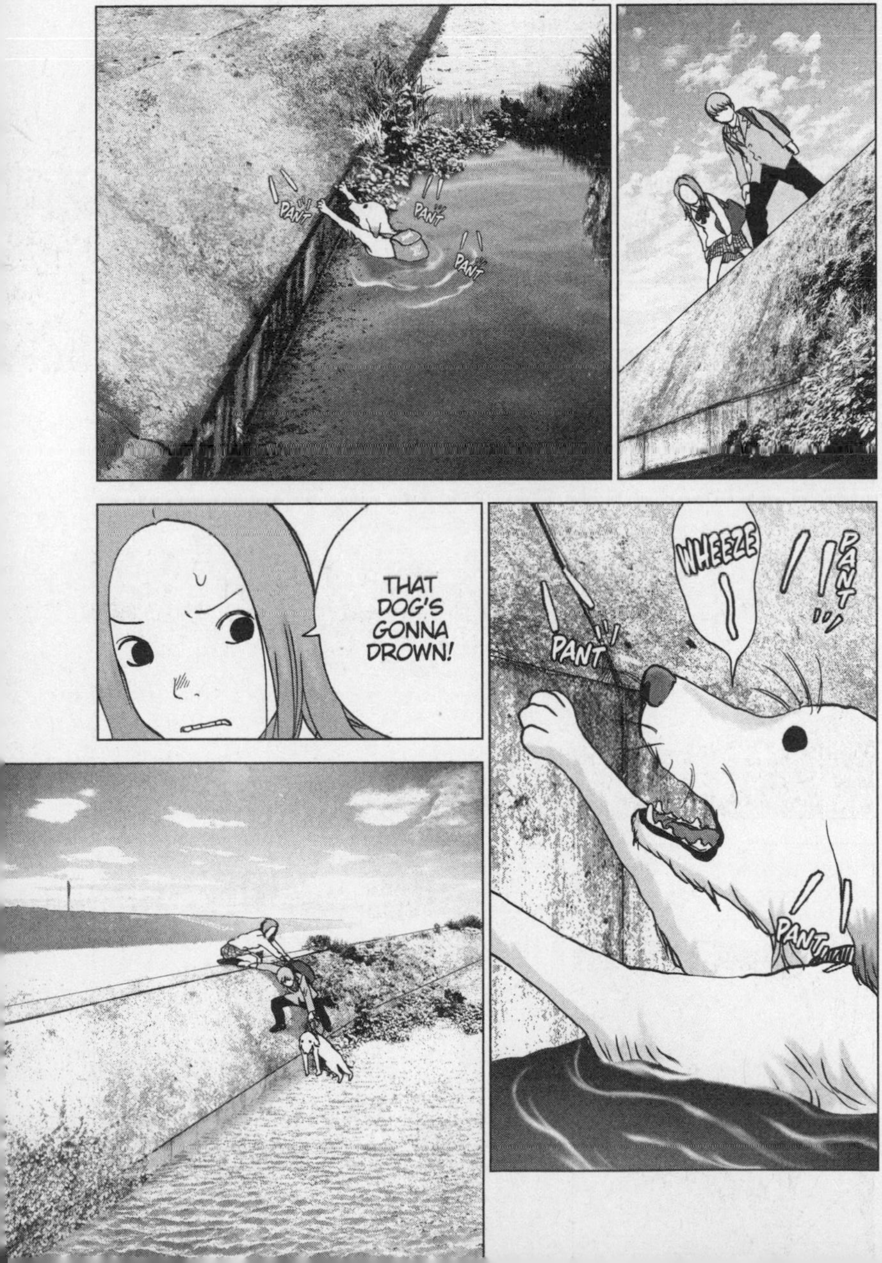
PANT
PANT
PANT
PANT
WHEEZE
PANT
PANT
THAT DOG'S GONNA DROWN!

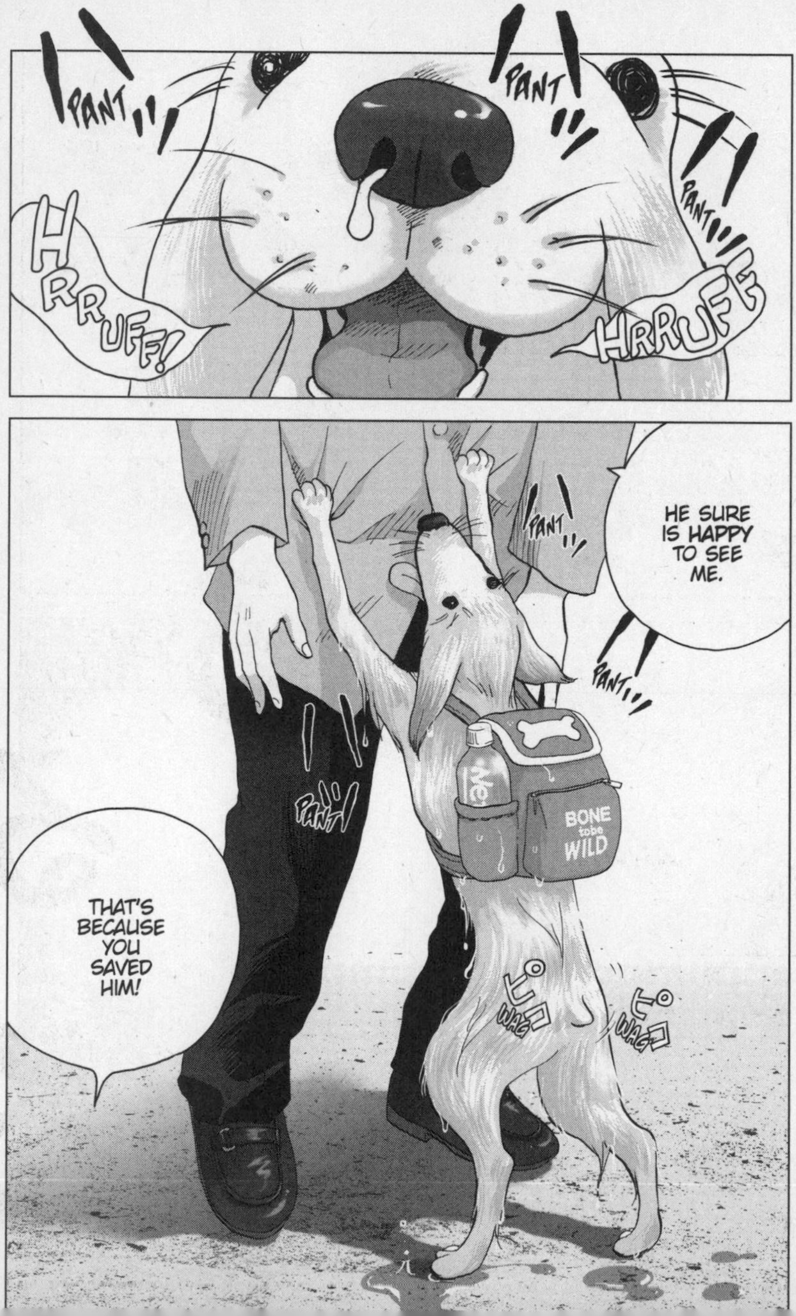
PANT
PANT
HRRUFF
PANT
HRRUFF!
HE SURE IS HAPPY TO SEE ME.
PANT
PANT
BONE to be WILD
PANT
THAT'S BECAUSE YOU SAVED HIM!
WAG
WAG

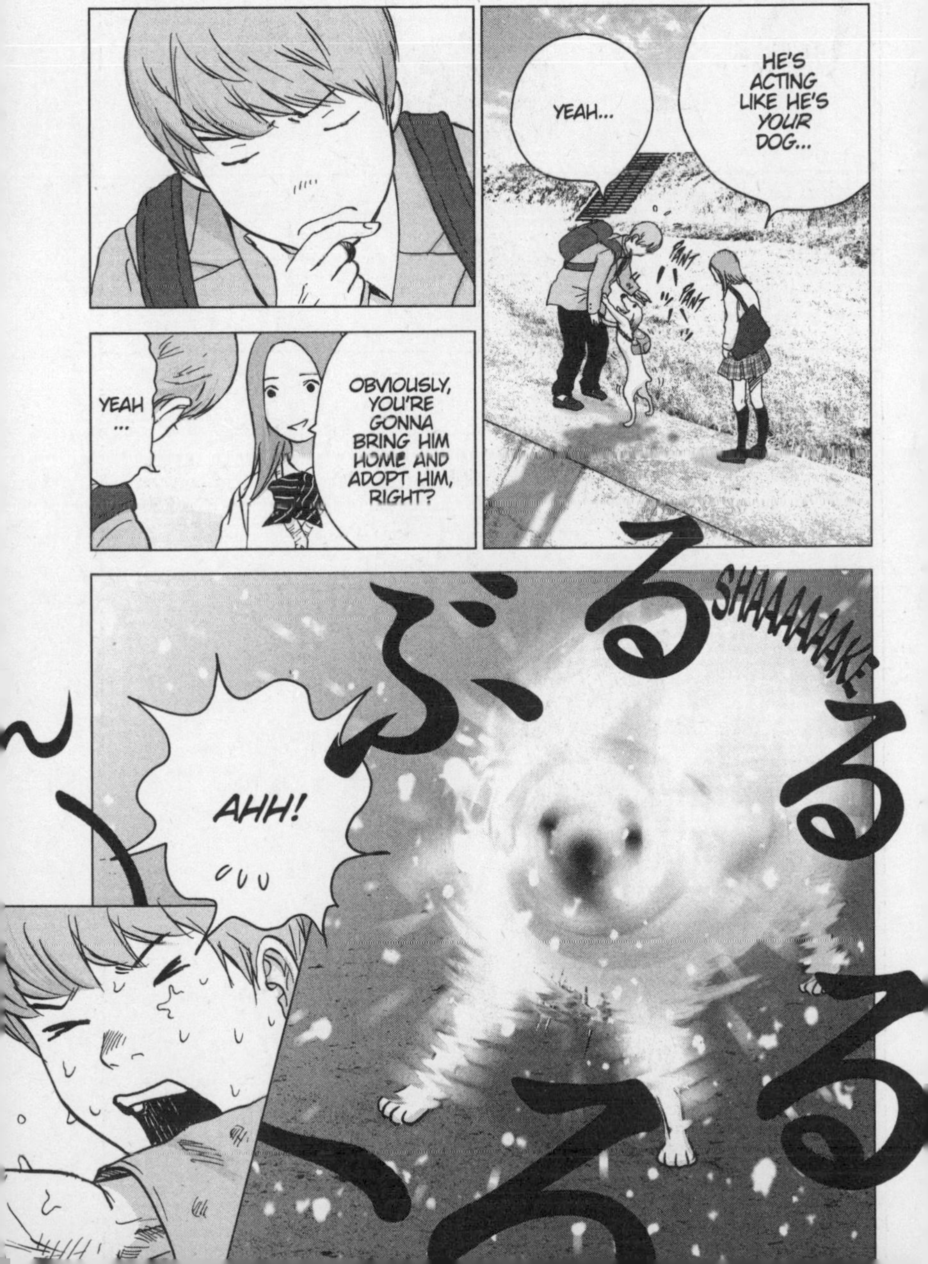
HE'S ACTING LIKE HE'S *YOUR* DOG...
YEAH...
PANT
PANT
OBVIOUSLY, YOU'RE GONNA BRING HIM HOME AND ADOPT HIM, RIGHT?
YEAH ...
SHAAAAAAKE
AHH!

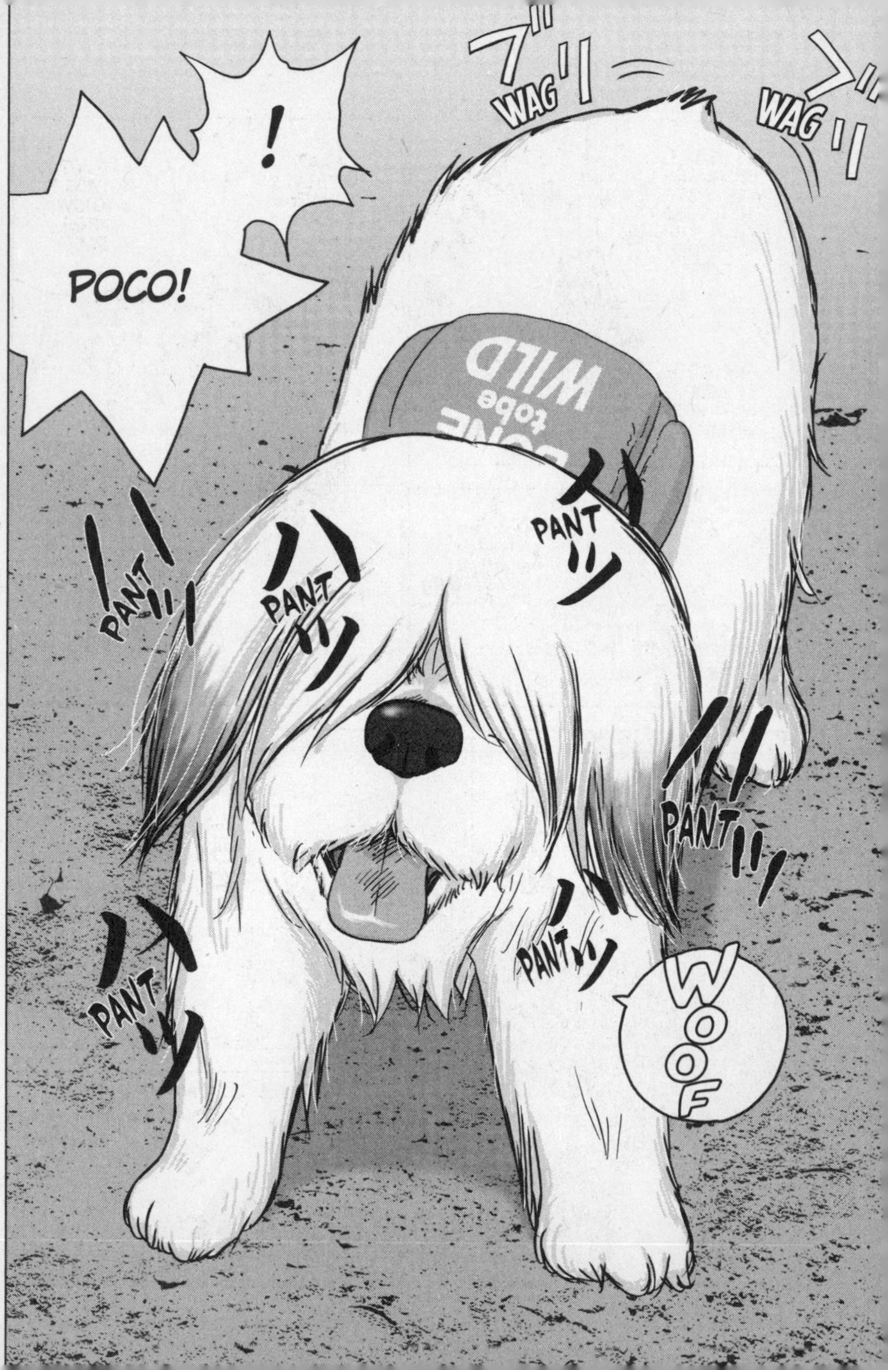
WAG
WAG
!
POCO!
PANT
PANT
PANT
PANT
PANT
PANT
WOOF

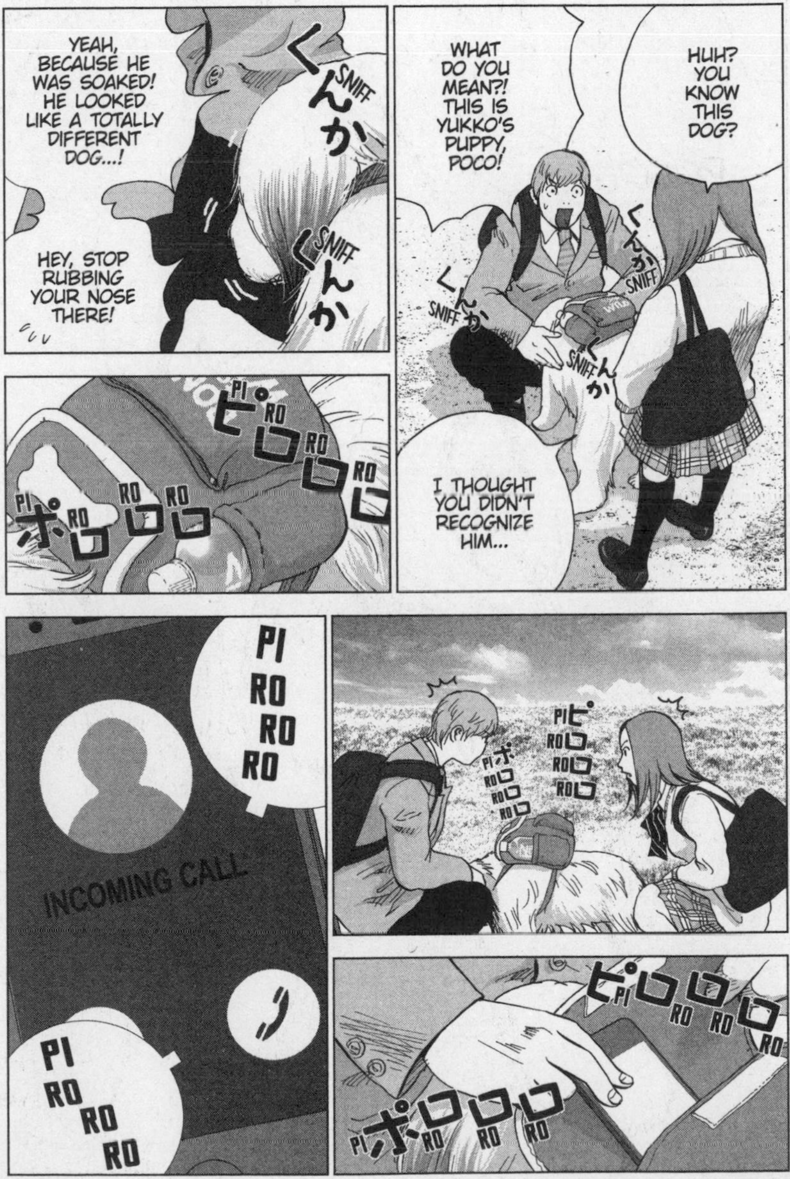
HUH? YOU KNOW THIS DOG?
WHAT DO YOU MEAN?! THIS IS YUKKO'S PUPPY, POCO!
くんか SNIFF
くんか SNIFF
くんか SNIFF
I THOUGHT YOU DIDN'T RECOGNIZE HIM...
YEAH, BECAUSE HE WAS SOAKED! HE LOOKED LIKE A TOTALLY DIFFERENT DOG...!
くんか SNIFF
くんか SNIFF
HEY, STOP RUBBING YOUR NOSE THERE!
ピロロロ PI RO RO RO
ポロロロ PI RO RO RO
ピロロロ PI RO RO RO
ポロロロ PI RO RO RO
ピロロロ PI RO RO RO
ポロロロ PI RO RO RO
PI RO RO RO
INCOMING CALL
PI RO RO RO

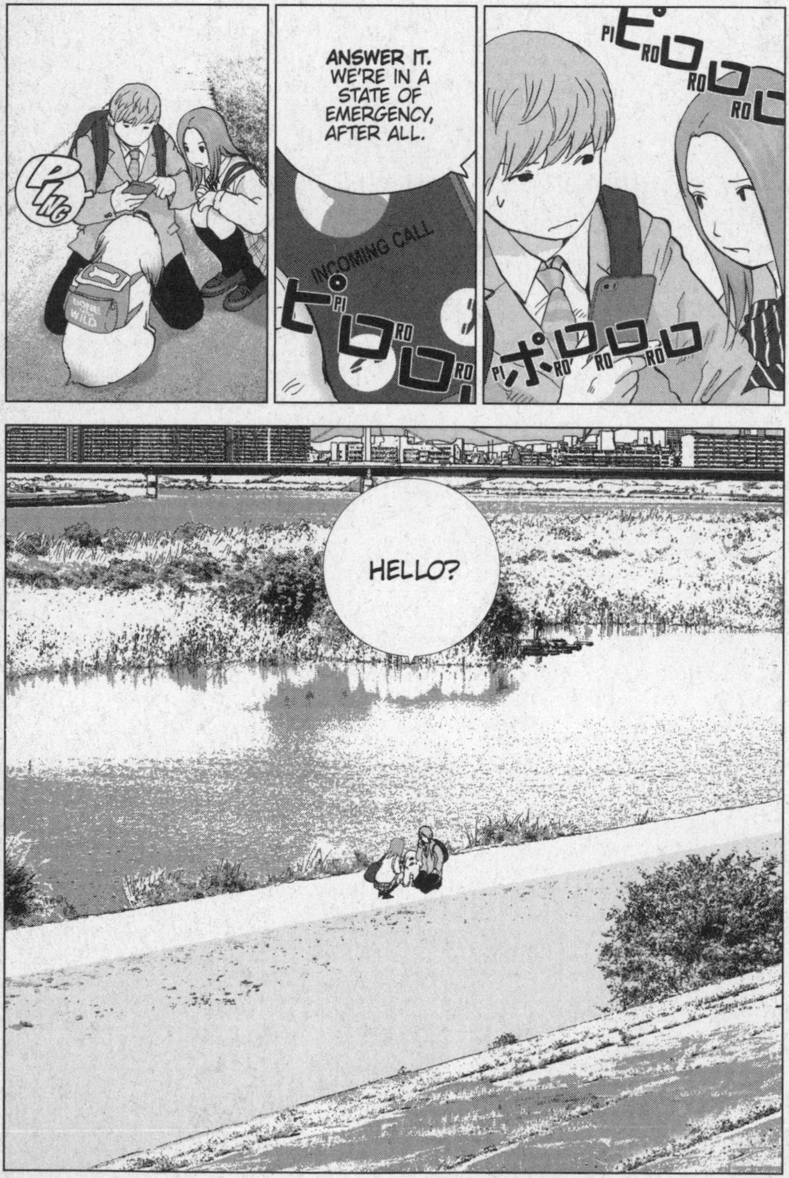
PI ピ RO ロ RO ロ RO ロ
PI ポ RO ロ RO ロ RO ロ
ANSWER IT. WE'RE IN A STATE OF EMERGENCY, AFTER ALL.
INCOMING CALL
PI ピ RO ロ RO ロ
PING
HELLO?

Wonderland

The whole world is my enemy... but surely my friend will become my ally!

Alice's powers... shrunk an entire region's worth of people...

Was Alice, the weapon... born with her powers?

Meanwhile, the SDF--who **should** be focused on protecting the people of Japan...

is hunting down Alice and her friends, all valuable test subjects thrust into this madness.

In the midst of all this, Yukko finally manages to contact Takuya!

There's no one left to trust but their friends!

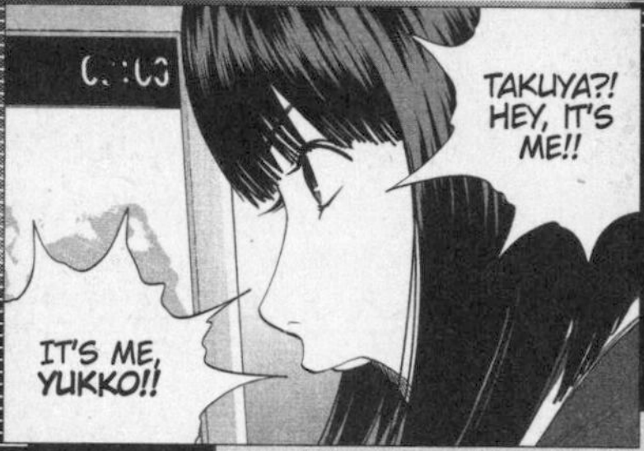
TAKUYA?! HEY, IT'S ME!!
IT'S ME, YUKKO!!

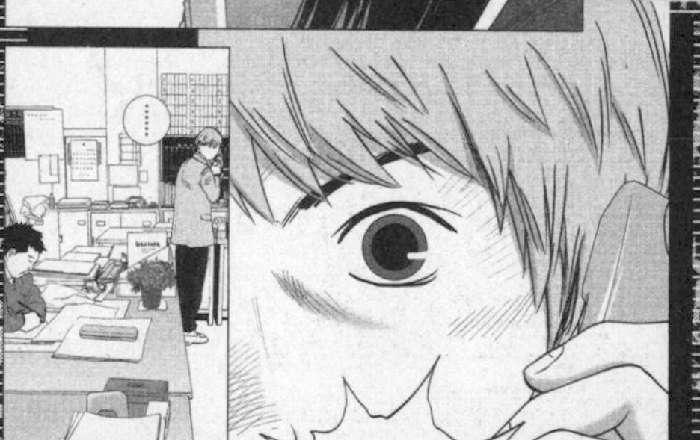
YU...!
......

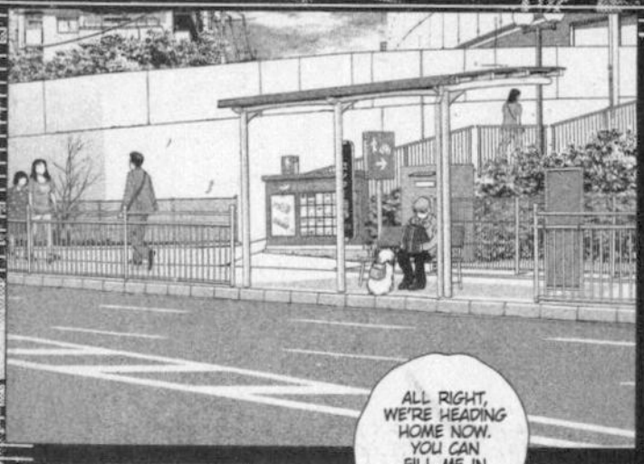

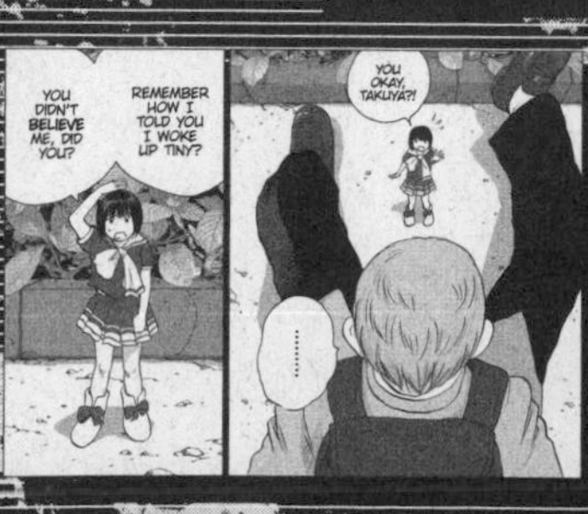
YOU OKAY, TAKUYA?!
......
REMEMBER HOW I TOLD YOU I WOKE UP TINY?
YOU DIDN'T BELIEVE ME, DID YOU?

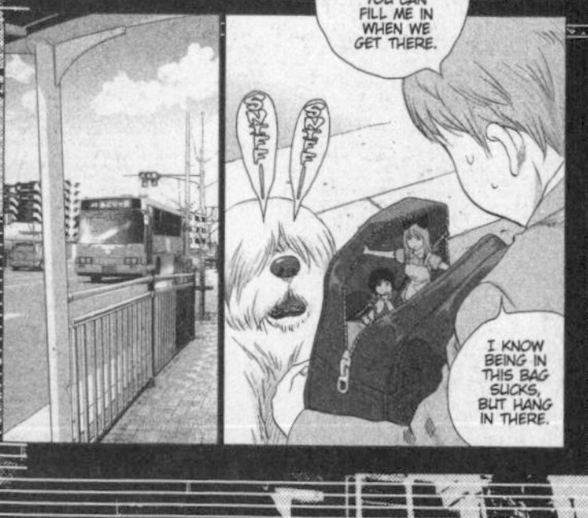
ALL RIGHT, WE'RE HEADING HOME NOW. YOU CAN FILL ME IN WHEN WE GET THERE.
I KNOW BEING IN THIS BAG SUCKS, BUT HANG IN THERE.

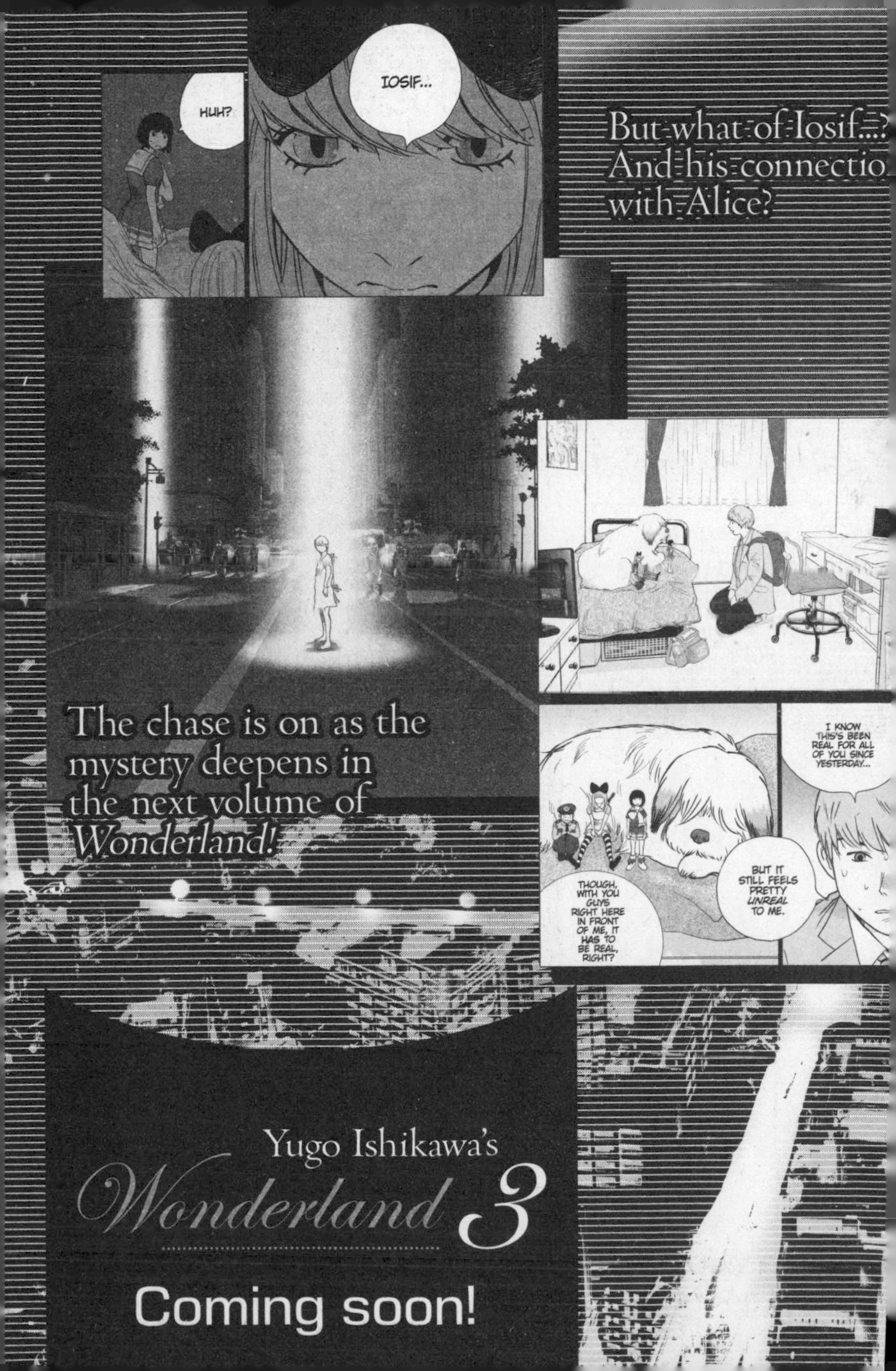
But what of Iosif...?
And his connectio
with Alice?
IOSIF...
HUH?
I KNOW THIS'S BEEN REAL FOR ALL OF YOU SINCE YESTERDAY...
BUT IT STILL FEELS PRETTY *UNREAL* TO ME.
THOUGH, WITH YOU GUYS RIGHT HERE IN FRONT OF ME, IT HAS TO BE REAL, RIGHT?
The chase is on as the mystery deepens in the next volume of *Wonderland!*
Yugo Ishikawa's
Wonderland 3
Coming soon!

SEVEN SEAS ENTERTAINMENT PRESENTS

Wonderland Vol. 2

story and art by YUGO ISHIKAWA

TRANSLATION
Molly Rabbitt

ADAPTATION
Marykate Jasper

LETTERING AND RETOUCH
James Gaubatz

ORIGINAL COVER DESIGN
kiyo Kobayashi + Bay Bridge Studio

COVER DESIGN
KC Fabellon

PROOFREADER
Kurestin Armada
B. Lana Guggenheim

EDITOR
Jenn Grunigen

PRODUCTION MANAGER
Lissa Pattillo

EDITOR-IN-CHIEF
Adam Arnold

PUBLISHER
Jason DeAngelis

Seven Seas books may be purchased in bulk for promotional, educational, or business use. Please contact your local bookseller or the Macmillan Corporate and Premium Sales Department at 1-800-221-7945, extension 5442, or by e-mail at MacmillanSpecialMarkets@macmillan.com.

ISBN: 978-1-626929-98-2

Printed in Canada

First Printing: March 2019

10 9 8 7 6 5 4 3 2 1

FOLLOW US ONLINE: ***www.sevenseasentertainment.com***

READING DIRECTIONS

This book reads from ***right to left***, Japanese style. If this is your first time reading manga, you start reading from the top right panel on each page and take it from there. If you get lost, just follow the numbered diagram here. It may seem backwards at first, but you'll get the hang of it! Have fun!!

1
2
3
4
5
6
7
8
9

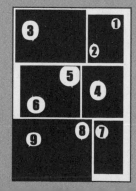